Survival of the Knitted

Survival of the Knitted

Immigrant Social Networks in a Stratified World

Vilna Francine Bashi

Stanford University Press
Stanford, California
2007

Stanford University Press
Stanford, California

©2007 by the Board of Trustees of the Leland Stanford Junior University. All rights
reserved.

Printed in the United States of America on acid-free, archival-quality paper

Library of Congress Cataloging-in-Publication Data

Bashi, Vilna.
 Survival of the knitted : immigrant social networks in a stratified world / Vilna Francine
Bashi.
  p. cm.
 Includes bibliographical references and index.
 ISBN 978-0-8047-4089-0 (cloth : alk. paper)--ISBN 978-0-8047-4090-6 (pbk. : alk. paper)
 1. West Indians--Social networks. 2. West Indians--Foreign countries. 3. Immigrants--
Social networks. 4. West Indies--Emigration and immigration. I. Title.

F1609.9.B37 2007
305.89497'0729--dc22   2006039366

Designed by Bruce Lundquist
Typeset at Stanford University Press in 10/14 Minion.

Contents

List of Figures and Tables

Figures

Table

Preface
Contradictions in International Migration

I WAS BORN IN BROOKLYN, NEW YORK, the oldest child of a marriage between two distant cousins—one in the first immigrant generation, the other
in the second (that is, born in the United States of immigrant parents). Both
my parents call themselves West Indian, and all of my grandparents came
from the same group of small islands that make up the Grenadines.

I found out I had an older brother (on my father's side) only when my
brother moved in! My mother tells me that I was three years old at the time
and he was nine. It turned out to be a great thing for me: he helped me get over
my fear of thunderstorms, and when I got my first migraine headache (which
made me think I was dying) around age eight, he comforted me by playing
Scouts in the living room with blanket tents. I remember when he first showed
up in our kitchen, straight off the boat, as they say. Although I was so young, I
had so many unspoken thoughts and mixed emotions: "He doesn't even look
like me." "So, you mean, I'm not the oldest?" "He has five other sisters on his
mother's side? Does he like them better than me and my sister?" Kelly stayed
with us until he was eighteen, and then he was gone. But he was not the first
newcomer to stay for a short while, nor would he be the last. Before him came
my father's cousin. And while my brother was still there, an aunt I had never
known about showed up too. Still later, two cousins came, and went. And then
aunts and uncles and more cousins came.

I should have been used to it by then, no? After all, I lived in a West Indian
household. Well, no, I thought, it was unusual—after all, my aunts and uncles
with whom I was close (on my mother's side) did not send for people, nor did

anyone else I knew besides my Dad. But every few years some new relatives would show up in our home, and stay for years.

I thought my family was unique in this respect—until, at the University of Wisconsin, I took my first qualitative methods course and conducted an interview to fulfill one of the assignments for the class. I interviewed a fellow graduate student who was born in Barbados. I asked about her family history and found out that her mother was very much like my father, always sending for people from back home, and was to that day still looking for new recruits. With her family also, none of the people who were sent for ever sent for anyone else. I realize that a population of two is ridiculously small, but it seemed somewhat exciting (at least to the committee at my dissertation proposal defense) that a pattern might be emerging. Because qualitative researchers start from where they are (Lofland and Lofland, 1995), I decided to study West Indian immigrants to learn how they run their networks.

Growing up in that household meant more than seeing the comings and goings of people. It also meant—because our family is so big—that there were many people living outside our home whom I had to think of as family members as well. I remember myself as a small child kissing the weathered faces of many old-timers from "back home." Seeing them again as an adult, I could hardly recall their names or faces, but I knew I had to show them the utmost respect and be on my best behavior so as not to bring shame to my family. I still remember the names of the so-called sandhogs with whom my father worked in the water tunnels of New York City; many of them I'm sure my father knew from when he was a child in the Islands. I remember seeing them at weddings and christenings, and seeing too the countless "relatives" who were somehow connected to my father and mother by blood or shared experiences. The shadowy figures that hover in the background of my life *are* my family.

This notion of family is very different from the idea of family that pervades American society. Popular culture in the United States seems to promote the idea that the family is really only nuclear, consisting of mother, father, sister, and brother. Only these people count, and if one insists, one may throw into the definition the occasional divorced or single-parent family, or a gay or lesbian one. I remember that when I was presenting the preliminary findings from my fieldwork to my professors and colleagues, there was some controversy after I announced that one of the networks in this study included family members. Only after I spoke one-on-one with individual professors did I realize that they thought I'd interviewed my nuclear family for the study. In fact, none of my immediate family members were part of the sample, and the "family" members who composed that one network were people I had not seen in twenty or more years, and many I'd never met before interviewing them. In fact, I'd gained access to their homes and their stories only because my father's name got me in the door. In a similar fashion I gained access to the other network: only my good friend and colleague's name (or her mother's name) got me in their doors. Many times I breathed easily only after I felt the respondent's own tension break when I spoke my contact's name. Sometimes I was told that if it had not been that Mister or Miss So-and-So had sent me, they would not have spoken with me at all. But then, once I'd arrived, and sometimes after the interview was over, I was offered tea, sorrel, or mauby (a drink made from boiling a kind of bark), or fed some island dish—the signal that I was welcome, and connected.

The stories of the comings and goings of new arrivals I heard while doing my fieldwork were familiar to me. In fact, I learned more about my own life than I'd known or understood before I started the research. This kind of pseudo-participant observation (where the investigator is an insider or participant in the social universe under observation) is a mixed bag. I could speak the same language they did—or so I thought—but I also felt more at risk of leading the interviewee, especially when I felt strong identification with the experiences of living in a household organized around helping others to come and go with relative ease, with little thought to the costs to the permanent household members. The process, the culture, the role to be played in these network interactions seemed all powerful as I heard these individuals recount their experiences; it often seemed that the people involved in the stories I was hearing were almost secondary.

It is for this reason that I feel the process of immigrant social networking can be modeled, as I try to show here. There actually is a process to network migration, and I argue that this process is common knowledge—accepted cultural practice, if you will—to network members, so much so that it is practically taboo to speak negatively about other network members. During the first part of the fieldwork, I thought I would never get anyone to tell me about the bad parts of sponsoring or being sponsored. But luckily I won the confidence of several people who were willing to tell more nuanced stories. I have reproduced all their perspectives here the best I can, while trying to maintain their privacy.

I must admit, however, that I feel some guilt about telling their stories. Even though I conceal the identities of the persons involved (changing the names and writing so you cannot tell who is in which family or network) it feels as if I'm airing the family's dirty laundry. But a family is the sum of both the good and the bad experiences its members share. So, this is the story of a network of people and how they arrived in the cities where they now reside, and how they helped and continue to help one another do the best they can. There's no shame in that. In fact, it makes me proud that they travailed, helped each other, and for the most part succeeded. In the end I hope I have managed to convey why these people's life stories have inspired me. Nearly all have come from desperately poor roots in the rural Third World, nearly all have achieved social and economic self-sufficiency, and most even have enough to share with others. They have succeeded on a global scale.

This book, then, is about social mobility in the broadest sense. Our normal way of thinking about social mobility is rife with stereotypes and tautological thinking. First, we think of social mobility as something that only "special" individuals achieve; moreover, we like to think that those who achieve it (that is, those who acquire secure, impressive jobs or pull down large incomes) are more deserving than others, mainly because we in the First World want to believe that the wealthy and well-off are reaping rewards merited only by their hard work. We imagine that we can tell who is a deserving soul—merely reaping what they have sown—because we want to think we can see someone's merit in their incomes and awards. The idea that modern society is a *meritocracy*—a society in which one is recognized for one's talents by being rewarded with returns like wealth, high incomes, awards, and other markers of recognition—is one we're loath to let go of. (Doing so will mean we have to make sense of meritocracy's opposite, *injustice*, and figure out how our modern world became an unfair place.)

The truth is, both in the society that resides within our respective national borders and in our global society, the achievement of individual social or economic mobility is a rare event. While we hope for it (how many play the lottery?) and believe deeply in its possibility, the rags-to-riches experience is rarely reality for most individuals. Thus, a book about the ways a formerly economically depressed group is also racially undervalued is necessarily a book about the contradictions of the society in which they live.

In international migration there's much that is contradictory. One contradiction is the way racism has shaped immigration law and the entry of those we call people of color into the Western world. On the one hand, their low status has been meant to marginalize and, for some, even exclude them. Western immigration law has considered desirable those groups who wear the mantle of a particular kind of whiteness. Those groups whose members are not the right kind are neither desired nor welcomed. Yet they are not kept out wholesale—they are incorporated, but according to the valuation of their race and color. The contradiction lies in the manner of hierarchy that race is—a top rank requires a bottom rank beneath it. Racial incorporation requires a category of people to occupy the bottom rungs, both of the job ladder (Piore, 1979) and of the racial hierarchy (Bashi, 1998). That society desires these people, even if only to maintain a hierarchical bottom, is contradictory.

In the United States, where ethnicity tends to muddle society's racial dialogue, black immigrants face another contradiction. Those immigrants who convince the racially privileged that they are ethnically different from native-born blacks may be allowed to step up a rung from the bottom, the place normally reserved for the phenotypically black. This has happened with several ethnoracial groups over the immigration history of the United States. Increased status has given West Indians in the United States a relative global advantage over the Caribbean emigrants who have chosen to go to other Western nations, for these countries have no native-born black group comparable to African Americans upon whose backs they can stand. West Indian success, where it exists, is achieved precisely because of contradictions in the varying desirability of ethnoracial groups who confront one another within the confines of a racist and classist global capitalist system.

The prevailing question in social science research on immigration is, *What defines and enables social success?* As I was writing this book, a new body of research on the second generation was being explored; some of it had already been published, but much of it had not yet. While this new generation of research makes reference to social structures that are key to the outcomes of the immigrant generation and their offspring, it still seems to focus (as decades of immigration research have) on the idea that culture makes the difference between success and failure. The unasked question seems to be, *What is the cultural legacy that the first generation of immigrants gives to the second generation?*

Race and racism are only indirectly addressed in these analyses—as if they are either less than fully relevant or remain unnamed as people work to create better lives for themselves. (Writers seem to talk only about "contexts of reception" and not about racism, not about the effects of living in a society where one is required to present oneself as black, Latino, Asian, or white—a self-identification that is the most useful predictor of what happens to striving immigrant and second-generation students and workers in the twenty-first-century United States.)

If there is a cultural legacy that immigrants leave for their American off-spring, this culture is necessarily rooted in the social structure of the new destination that the immigrant generation must navigate. Rather than writing as if immigrants bring a culture with them, we might consider immigrants as people who are inserted into a functioning culture when they move. For example, in other work I have explained that upon arrival, immigrants are inserted into localized racial structures; they are labeled by a racial category according to the hierarchy of categories in the local system and are required to contend with the socioeconomic constraints consistent with that racial category (Bashi and McDaniel, 1997; Bashi, 1998). At birth, nonimmigrants are similarly categorized, but they are instead socialized into only one such racializing system. So, this book is necessarily but unintentionally also a dedicated look at the experience of the immigrant generation as a process of systematic struggle with new experiences in ethnoracial assignment and structural segregation. (In particular, this is a study of an immigrant group that is normally inserted into the bottommost position in Western racial hierarchies.) The ethnographic nature of the research demanded that race be addressed, for it was evident that racial adaptation is an undeniable part of the immigrant experience. How well the immigrant generation struggles far from home with new structural burdens (including the encumbrance of race) is the true cultural legacy they leave for their second- and third-generation descendents. (Let me be clear here, however, that this book explores the experiences of only the immigrant generation.)

At this juncture, I wish to explain this book's title, which was chosen with deliberateness. This text presents an account of how the members of the immigrant generation have survived, with a specific reference intended to counterbalance both the new social Darwinist idea that it is the culturally superior group that survives and the Horatio Alger model that proposes that the morally right scrapper succeeds in pulling himself up from nothing because of his moral fortitude. Both of these ideas are still prevalent in scholarship about migration and ethnicity across the disciplines. I work to show that it is instead the immigrant's structured connection to others like himself or herself that helps the migrant and those in the entire migrant community to survive and thrive. While culture is not irrelevant, it comes into play as a by-product of the migrant network member's desire for community, and what drives success are the constraints on the members' networking behavior, constraints faced precisely because migrant groups confront limiting social structures as they assist one another. Because these migrants are joined together far beyond their moments of border crossing and job seeking, I chose the word *knitted* to indicate how deeply intertwined these migrants are as they live their lives in far-away destinations. The word *knitting* also gives primacy to some of the social skills associated with women; as I show, women's labor is central to the way these migrant networks operate.

Acknowledgments

THIS BOOK, LIKE MANY OTHER FIRST BOOKS of nonfiction writers, is the product of years of work that began as research for a dissertation. Here again, as in the preface to my dissertation, I would like to thank those whose efforts contributed to my graduate work, especially Arthur S. Goldberger, Chuck Manski, Hal Winsborough, Gay Seidman, Erik Olin Wright, Jane Collins, and Chas Camic. I also thank those graduate school friends who offered support, including Jim Elliott, Naima Hassan, and Andrea Nelson. I am grateful to Averil Clarke and Doug Massey for reading chapters and giving critical comments during the earliest phases of my work.

After graduate school I leaned on my Beautiful Black Women Writers group, as I call them (when I joined they were Judith Carter, Averil Clarke, Sherry Holmes, Daphne Lamothe, Kesha Moore, Stacey Sutton, and Maggie Ussery), and on a writing group of my peers at Rutgers (Paul McLean and Ann Mische); they read and commented on draft chapters of the book. I thank Leslie Fishbein for her invaluable comments that helped me strengthen the book's message. I am thankful to my mother, Vilna Joanetta Wallace Simmons Welch, who meticulously transcribed my London interviews. I am grateful also for Wendy Espeland's collegial intellectual nourishment and friendship during some very hard times, and for the smiles her husband, Bruce Carruthers, and children, Sam and Esther, gave to me. The fieldwork for this project would not have been completed without the assistance of Gloria Gadsden, Bertina and Joseph MacLawrence Hutchinson, Averil Clarke, and most especially Yvette Clarke, Odette Raphael, Judy Rein, and Eric Herschberg. These last four really went out of their way to help me find respondents or to give me room and board in New York, London, and the Caribbean as I found my way to those who educated me about their migration experiences. Neither would my work have been accomplished without financial support from the American Sociological Association's Minority Fellowship Program, the North-South Center, and the Ford Foundation Minority Postdoctoral Fellowship Program. (The latter probably saved my career—it came at a time when I so much needed the support and the break from other academic burdens.)

Some of the ideas in Chapter Two were first published in Bashi, 2004, and some of the ideas in Chapter Seven were first published in Bashi Bobb, 2001. I thank both Taylor & Francis (which publishes the journal *Ethnic and Racial Studies*, http://www.tandf.co.uk/journals/titles/01419870.asp) and Temple University Press, respectively, for permission to use this material.

I must also acknowledge the enormous gratitude I have toward the editors at Stanford University Press for their support and patience, but particularly Kate Wahl, who was the midwife for the final product. I want especially to acknowledge the emotional support I received from Averil Clarke and Daphne Lamothe, who were seemingly bottomless founts of friendship and generosity as they did all manner of things to keep me going both in my work and in my life away from the writing. Finally, I ask forgiveness from those who gave me help and support to write this book but who find their names wrongly omitted from this list.

Before I close, I would like to acknowledge the stabilizing and joy-generating force that Christian Treitler has become in my life, building with me the happiness I always knew a man and woman could conjure up if they made a real partnership. Not only did he read every word, twice, and comment, but he did me the honor of building a desk and bookcases so that I have a beautiful space in which to write. To him I say, *It's finally done: Prost! Und danke! I'm more grateful for your support and for God's gift of your presence in my life than I have words to say.*

I have dedicated this book to two groups of people. One is those wonderful Caribbean people who generously told me their life stories. The other is my husband and son, whose presence on this earth and in my life is to me as surprising as the reality of seeing this text in print. Finding this husband, carrying my son to his blessed birth, and saying in this book the things I truly wanted to say represent to me the fulfillment of daunting and at times seemingly impossible achievements, accomplished only because I, like the migrants I interviewed, never gave up my search for a better life.

Survival of the Knitted

1 Networking the Globe

PAMELA JAMES HAD A TYPICAL LIFE for a young woman of some promise living on a small Eastern Caribbean island.[1] She was living away from home, being educated to become a teacher. Her education, not available to many, would lead to one of the few available career paths for promising young men and women. By these standards she was doing well. But migration overseas might offer better opportunities and a better standard of living, so she often considered leaving her country, as did her family members and friends, who thought they could improve their lives through out-migration. In London when I interviewed her, Pamela told me the story of how she came to live there.

I was going to be a teacher. I had gone to the University of the West Indies in Trinidad. I knew that it wasn't what I'd settle for. Prospects for teaching there are slim, and you only move up with age. There's no promotion, per se. No middle management. You just reach a certain age and, *boof*, you go up [get promoted]. I was living at home and not earning enough to buy a property! And my sister and her husband were finding it hard to make ends meet. Even with a job you couldn't see yourself doing well.

My uncle came here in the 1950s. I didn't know him at all, 'cause I was so young when he left [our island]. After thirty years away he brought his family back home on holiday. He even agreed we were just living [and not getting ahead]. He said, "Oh, in London they're looking for teachers. There's a man who is looking to recruit teachers." And he told my sister about it and she got in touch with him. My uncle sent back [to my sister] a TES, that's the *Times Education Supplement* [the education newsletter that advertised the recruitment notice].

You have to know that at that time it was the Thatcherite period. Oh, it was bad, horrible. Teachers were leaving their jobs to drive cabs and such. She [Thatcher] began the process of selling off national properties to put money in the pockets of the rich. She crushed manufacturing here, and now the economy is run on services. She instituted a community tax, but people with large properties didn't pay as [in relation to what] they own. She had lots of policies to cripple the poor. She was a very heavy-handed bureaucrat. A whole generation of women followed her style—there are still plenty of them around. Anyway, a lot of people migrated to Australia. A lot of people were in retraining.

My sister contacted the man [the education director]. He said, "Right. Come right up." They had been recruiting [whites] in the U.S., in Australia and New Zealand, and other places. But not from the Caribbean. You understand, he [the education director] was a Caribbean man himself. He brought up forty [black] teachers and their families. Myself and two others were secondary teachers, the rest were primary school teachers. I did PGC, postgraduate retraining [to be certified to teach primary school]. No, I wasn't the only single person. Some people were single, but they had kids. But, you understand, I had my extended family with me.

At this point, I asked her, "Did you ever think of migrating to England before then?"

Oh no. England doesn't present the kind of prospects—I would have gone to Canada instead. You know, we [who had not migrated] had this idea of the English being crusty and behind the times. You know, relatives who returned from England do not look as shiny and spiffy as those who were coming back from the U.S. So, no, I didn't think about coming to England. But then I could live anywhere. I fit in but I brought my environment with me.

In many ways, this excerpt from Pamela's life story is typical of many immigrants, and can be considered a model for the ways sociologists and economists normally understand the migration process. It describes a woman who left her economically poor but culturally rich Caribbean island homeland and moved to a more economically stable life in an international urban metropolis in the more developed Western world.[2]

Upon hearing a story like this, many migration theorists might understand it as an *economically driven* one. They might suggest that the relative poverty (despite her educational attainment) that Pamela and her sister suffered pushed them to move away. Or they might infer instead that these migrants were pulled toward better prospects for job advancement and property ownership. Many scholars would interpret Pamela's story either in terms of the push factors that drove her away from the economic malaise of her homeland or in terms of the pull factors that drove her toward greater economic opportunity in the developed world. While such interpretations are comfortingly familiar, they fail to explain fully the complexities of Pamela's decision and that of other black Caribbean migrants who leave their native lands to migrate to more affluent nations abroad.

Ironically, while most exponents of push-pull theory would repudiate social Darwinism as an antiquated social model based on an economic worldview more appropriate to the world of fixed assets posited by Adam Smith than to current, more fluid conceptions of economic wealth, those scholars who support push-pull theory retain many elements of social Darwinian thought that my research challenges. Push-pull theory assumes that individuals act out of notions of their own future economic welfare and that out of such individual economic decision making arises social benefit. Thus most such scholars assume that it is the best and the brightest who have the energy, desire, and skills that make them the most likely to migrate; hence the migration process, like the social Darwinian struggle, becomes a means of sorting out the wheat from the chaff, enabling generally the most talented and fit to enter the migration process in the first place. My research indicates that migrants do not select themselves but rather are selected by others who facilitate the moving process on the basis of the character traits best adapted for survival in the new environment. Ironically, these character traits comport well with those demanded by the proponents of the nineteenth-century gospel of wealth (such as Horatio Alger, Andrew Carnegie, and others who lauded the characteristics of piety, diligence, future orientation, and ability to defer present gratification in pursuit of long-term goals).

In contrast to economic reasoning, theories of *migration networks* or *migration chains* focus instead on social mechanisms that facilitate movement, arguing that potential movers achieve migration by activating the connections they have to others already in their chosen destinations, that is, the people who have migrated before them. These theories model migration as a series of linked dyads, in which one migrant in a pair helps another, and the one who received assistance then helps yet another migrant, and so on.

The linked pairs form a chain of migrants who follow one another to a single destination. As new links are added to the chain, the migration stream of that particular group is perpetuated. This understanding has been widely influential in shaping the way we think about why people move, and about how they choose where to go. However, my research indicates that networks are far more complex, extensive, and long lasting in their impact on migrants' lives than this dyadic notion of immigration networks posits.

Pamela's story might alternatively be interpreted, then, as one involving a complex of immigrant social networks—social entities thought to be made up of family, fictive kin, and friends linked together by the assistance they receive from one person and give to another in the form of information and material resource transfers. In this excerpt, evidence of Pamela's involvement in networks is clear. She received help indirectly from the education director and her uncle, and directly from her sister; and each of those who helped Pamela helped many others besides Pamela.

Both push-pull and chain migration theories have had long-standing impacts on migration theory and policy development. In light of these theories, Pamela's story seems unremarkable. But one would have to ignore some basic facts in order to have her story fit the conventional migration models, for in many ways her story tells us something quite different than both theories would predict.

For one, theory suggests that migration flows are rooted in individual incentives: migrants decide to move in response to push or pull factors, or they choose to activate their connections to migration chains. But while Pamela explains that she, her sister, and her sister's family all had contemplated leaving their island home, their target destination was neither London (where they ended up) nor anywhere else in Europe. Their choice was, instead, Canada; Pamela even states a preference for the United States over England. How is it that they move transcontinentally and uproot their lives, to live, work, and perhaps die in a place they never really considered a desirable option? If (as theory explains) migration is driven by a migrant's own desires, a story like Pamela's would not make much sense. It was the good opportunity afforded to her—by someone in a place she really did not care to be, someone she really did not know but who had experience in moving a number of people like her—that made taking the chance to move to Britain something she did not want to pass up.

To understand this point, think of the difference between *choice* and *chance*. Pamela's migration story is less about the exercise of her individual choices and preferences in making economic change, and more about taking advantage of the chances for change that come about because and only when network members solicit new migrants to fill opportunities available in certain times and spaces. Here we see that the impetus for Pamela's migration began neither with her own efforts to seek work nor with a conscious choice she made to call on someone she knew. The move began with the actions of her uncle—a veteran (not potential) migrant in a destination (not sending) country. Pamela had thought about moving for a long time but did not actually move until the opportunity to do so was created and made available to her *by someone else.*

If we are mistaken in measuring migration from the vantage point of the potential immigrant who we assume initiates her or his own migration by calling on contacts in more developed nations, at what point does migration networking begin? Those at the destination (the uncle and the education director) made migration happen for Pamela, and for scores of others, when her desire to move and her acquaintance with migrants in a number of destinations were insufficient. Looked at this way (and contrary to what migration theorists predict), migration in the network context occurs not when potential migrants decide to migrate and switch on their connections to overseas others but instead when people who have already migrated actually create opportunities and then choose a newcomer to take advantage of one of these opportunities. That Pamela and the others followed this uncle (and Jocelyn, who ultimately disbursed information about the opportunities) may indicate that potential migrants have a lot less agency in choosing their destinations than we might think, and may also imply that the one who hoards opportunities to migrate actually holds the decision-making power. More important, the fact that a potential migrant knows someone overseas is not equivalent to that migrant having network connections. The "someone overseas" would have to be someone who controls access to the jobs and other information that ease the relocation and resettlement process, and indeed would have to be one who chooses to use his or her knowledge and power to enable a potential migrant's overseas move. The evidence for this is that Pamela claims she knew people in three destination options: people in Canada, where she most wanted to go; "spiffy" people in the United States who came back to visit often; and others in England whose demeanor and appearance did not induce her to migrate there. Instead of choosing Toronto or New York, Pamela and her sister moved to their least desirable choice, London, and they did so at the impetus of someone she claims she hardly knew.

A third enigma in this excerpt suggests that the chain model most commonly employed in migration studies might not accurately describe much network migration. Pamela reports that she did have help in arranging her relocation to London, but the helping network she describes is clearly more complex than a series of dyads in a chain. One woman (Pamela's sister Jocelyn) helped Pamela, but she also helped seven other teachers and their families to migrate and secure jobs. Jocelyn in turn was helped by one man—the education director—but he helped, altogether, forty teachers who brought their families. If we focus on the helper (Jocelyn or the education director) instead of on a single migrant being helped (Pamela), this story of a number of immigrants connected to a key individual invokes not the image of a dyadic chain but more the image of a wheel, in which several spokes are connected to one hub. Pamela's sister and the education director are hubs, central figures who ensure the arrival of the teachers and family members whom we can consider spokes. When hubs hoard overseas opportunities, solicit spokes to fill them, and do this repeatedly, ensuring job placement and housing success for a whole group of migrants, they create extensive networks that are dyadic only on the smallest scale. To rely on the chain model to describe migration, we would need to ignore the broader network-organizing work these individuals do.

Fourth, one can read additional significance in the fact that this uncle was someone with whom Pamela was merely acquainted and someone with whom she did not keep in contact. We expect that migrant network ties are strong, that is, they are connections between people who are intimates or who have bonds of obligation.[3] This man acted out of neither benevolence nor obligation but, if anything, out of a detached sort of altruism or activism. The uncle (and the education director) was reportedly motivated by concern that black immigrants from the Caribbean be afforded the same opportunities as the white immigrants that education officials were trying to recruit from Canada and Australia. Jocelyn (as explained later) was motivated by her own religiosity and used her knowledge of job openings to handpick those she deemed pious enough to be in her new postmigration community. Neither of these people had strong ties to the migrants they helped but instead activated weak ties. They became aware of job openings and decided they knew where to find the right people to fill them—for example, the uncle provided invaluable aid in the migration of Pamela and her sister, despite his tenuous ties to them.

Consequently—and this is the fifth and final point—theory understands network assistance as helping with border crossing and perhaps job seeking but presumes that once the emigrant has moved and begun work, the newcomer's connection to the information giver seemingly ceases to have a great deal of significance in the newcomer's life. Perhaps that is why migration theorists have for decades focused on *assimilation* and *acculturation* (whether and how well the new migrant adapts to his or her new surroundings) as the new immigrant's greatest challenge. It was not clear how the newcomer gets postmigration information. Pamela says, by surprising contrast, that she did not think twice about whether life in the new and less-than-desirable country was at all strange. Instead, she argues that she fit into the new environment just fine because "I brought my environment with me." She fit in because she joined a transplanted community of Caribbean people—some who had migrated before her and some who made the trip when she did but in any case a community organized by her hubs. Stories like Pamela's show that the one-who-helps-many also shapes the newcomer's postmigration experience for years to come by community building via networking in their mutual workplaces and neighborhoods.

We return to Pamela's and Jocelyn's migration stories in later chapters as we examine the migration experiences of many such Caribbean persons who now live in London and New York. Suffice it to say, however, that the seemingly unusual or aberrant elements in Pamela's story were echoed by the nearly one hundred immigrants and potential immigrants I interviewed while conducting the research project described in this book. As I hope is clear, existing theory about the formation and perpetuation of migration networks is scanty, at least in terms of its ability to explain these other migration factors. New theory is required because, while migration scholars have written much about networks, there is little in the available theory that explains why someone moves to a place she did not really intend to go, following someone with whom she had little contact prior to migration—a person who brings several other migrants in similar fashion—and then feels quite at home once she moves because the other migrants help to form a ready-made community at the new destination. Surely having at least tenuous connections to a network is important, but perhaps more important is the central figure who lends assistance to so many others in the network configuration. As I argue in this book, this key figure is the reason that networks are formed and maintained, because he or she enables migration and resettlement for dozens if not hundreds of international movers. Moreover, this person's actions help to secure socioeconomic mobility for the entire ethnic group he or she helps to create in the chosen destinations.

This figure is central in the sense that he or she surrounds him- or herself with a configuration of new migrants (drawn from a pool of potential migrants) with whom he or she creates strong economic and cultural ties in what may best be described as a hub-and-spoke network of immigrants. The ties among the immigrants appear and solidify as the hub works to bring the newcomers into the destination country and helps them find jobs and housing. In the best-case scenarios, when all is said and done, groups of people connected in this way transform their lives, sometimes in ways that mean escaping poverty and prospering socially and economically. This is a major feat given that most groups that come to a more economically developed country in this way are unwelcome, for whether by virtue of their nation's relative poverty or because people in destination countries understand themselves as the migrants' racial betters, newcomers like these are most often seen as undesirable additions to the populations of wealthier nations. This book describes how migration and mobility occur and explains what role the network plays in both processes. This chapter starts that discussion by outlining the theories that sociologists and economists use to explain who moves internationally and why, especially those theories that center on the immigrant social network—now understood to be an important catalyst to new migration and a key element in whether a group succeeds or fails socioeconomically.

Theorizing About International Migration

Some researchers argue that we are in a new and fourth phase of global migration, marked by an increasing rate of postindustrial international movement that began in the mid-1960s and has been dominated by outflows from the developing nations of the southern hemisphere and Asia (Castles and Miller, 1993; Massey et al., 1998).[4] The standard interpretation of history suggests that former immigrant-sending nations have of late become receiving nations, a change that has garnered a flurry of social and economic research meant to explain exactly why it has occurred and what the societal repercussions are (Massey et al., 1998). Other interpretations suggest instead that all countries have sent or received migrants, although roughly only twenty-five nations have accepted three-quarters of the world's immigrants in recent years (Zlotnik, 1999). We may pose here three questions that theorists have tried to answer with regard to the "new" migration of "people of color": *What causes migration? Who makes migration happen? Which migrants are successful?*

What Causes Migration?

Economists believe that forces at both the macro- and the microlevels (that is, at the level of the social structure and the individual level, respectively) interact with one another in ways that bring about economic equilibrium, or a steady state of economic activity that produces predictable outcomes. The idea behind economic modeling is to find out what inputs best predict those outcomes, assuming that knowing and controlling the inputs to the equilibration process would allow us to bring about desirable economic outcomes. Neoclassical economic models of migration once held sway over theoretical thinking about migration, during which time we developed both macro (focusing on inputs at the societal level) and micro (focusing on the actions of the individual actor) economic models.

One important set of macro-inputs are wages. High wages are presumably a pull factor that attracts migrants to jobs that offer more pay than other jobs. Economists have theorized that economic imbalances in factors of production (labor, capital, and raw materials) or factor prices (wages for labor, costs for capital, and commodity prices for raw materials) generated states of disequilibrium in national economies and thus in the world economy (Todaro, 1969, 1976). For example, places that have fewer laborers than jobs are assumed to have to pay workers more, while places with an abundance of unutilized labor may pay their workers less. High wages, then, are a pull factor that attracts migrants from low wage areas. For a time it was decided that the solution to the macrolevel problem was to encourage development—if we work to increase local employment and provide wage-earning opportunities at home, the incentive to leave would presumably disappear. However, research showed that economic development was actually a catalyst rather than a salve for increasing migration pressure because it severely disrupts the developing economy and society (Massey, 1990a, 1990b), at least in the short run (Commission for the Study of International Migration and Cooperative Economic Development, 1991; Vogler and Rotte, 2000). Furthermore, the real trigger to the initiation or cessation of any group's tendency toward international movement is the attainment of bearable conditions of life in the area of origin—after which people find migration not worth the effort—not the fact that the nation from which they come is still "developing" (Massey et al., 1998, p. 8).[5]

At the microlevel, migration was understood to be undertaken by economic actors who rationally and individually weighed the returns of migration. As long as, after paying for the trip, they would reap more in wages than if they stayed in their home country, rational individuals would choose to migrate (Todaro, 1976). Further research found, however, that migrants moved whether or not they actually received higher wages at the destination. Models were then modified to try to predict the likelihood of moving based on the *expectation* of wages rather than on the actual wage received (that is, the models included estimations for expected levels of unemployment as well as expected earnings), but even these and further modifications to the prevailing economic models were in the end insufficient to explain the increasing levels and growing upward trend in international migration from certain nations. Why? Well, the models could not explain why, if wage differentials are real incentives to international movement, all laborers in a poor country do not try to move away to get more money. These macromodels also failed to explain why some nations with very low wages did not send migrants in any great number while other less impoverished nations sent far greater numbers. Nor did these modified macromodels explain why the extent of global migration overall was small given that the numbers of poor and the disparities between wealthy destination countries and poor nations of origin are so great (Arango, 2000, p. 286; Massey et al., 1998, p. 7). Critiques like these emerged partly because economic models failed to predict levels of migration accurately and could not efficiently suggest effective recommendations for creating policy that would help control the flow of migration.

Who Makes Migration Happen?

Reading prevailing theory in neoclassical economics, the "new economics" of migration, and network migration theory you would learn that the impetus for migration is found in the individuals and family or community groups resident in the country of origin. To say this more succinctly, migration scholarship would have us believe that prospective migrants cause their own migration to happen.

Neoclassical economic models are based on the assumption that people make rational choices, so the decision to move out of one's country for not very high wages, or to do anything else economically "irrational," could not easily be predicted by mathematical models. Scholars in the new economics of migration suggested that problems in predicting migrants' economic behavior lay in faulty models, not irrational decision makers. They noted two problems with the way decision making was modeled. First, they suggested that nonmigrant members of the potential migrant's household are involved in making the decision to send someone away to work. According to Stark (1991) and his followers, households decide to send one of their residents overseas for all kinds of reasons that involve their need for temporary and relatively large infusions of extra (or *target*) income, to finance projects like enlarging or building a home, paying tuition, or recovering from financial crises such as the disabling of a wage earner or crop failure. Out-migration is the necessary solution for people in poorer and less developed economies who have less access to credit and insurance markets than earners in more developed economies do. Evidence supporting this family-household aid model may be found in a glance at the enormous economic volume and social value of remittances, or transfers of wealth and earnings from foreign-born individuals to others in their country of origin. Migrants in the United States are believed to have sent $70 billion overseas in 1995—a 250-fold increase over the dollar value of remittances in 1970 (Castles, 2000, p. 276)—but these figures are likely an underestimate; in 2002–2003, new calculations showed that we were grossly underestimating remittance values (Scott-Joynt, 2004). Newer estimates show that in 2005, $52 billion was sent back to Latin America and the Caribbean alone (Smith, 2005). In 1990, between 10 and 13 percent of Mexican American householders and between 15 and 25 percent of Mexican immigrant householders supported kith or kin outside of their own household (Glick, 1999, p. 758). Recent migrants and those on temporary sojourns are most likely to send remittances (Glick, 1999), and a startlingly high number of migrants report that they are migrating only temporarily (Piore, 1979). Clearly, many post-1965 migrants work for more than their own individual well-being.[6] Second, traditional models expected that absolute income levels would drive migration, as if migration results simply from Third World poverty versus First World riches. The new economics school argues that relative income disparity (relative to some marker of economic well-being for one's own reference group) and not absolute poverty drives migration. "In brief, if one is poor among poor, incentives to migrate might be lower than if one is poor among (relatively) rich" (Vogler and Rotte, 2000, p. 488). But even with modifications, these models still claim that the impetus for migration can be found among potential migrants in sending countries.

Similarly, network theories of immigration presume that when migrants are ready to move, they will. In these models, migrants move when they activate ties to persons they know in the desired destination, soliciting from them the help or information (that is, *social capital*) they need to carry out a move. The social capital available in the network presumably remains untapped and at the disposal of potential migrants until and unless the potential migrants take advantage of these network resources. Massey and colleagues (1993) explain that the costs of migration are lower for potential migrants with network connections than for those without and that simply having these connections may actually cause one to undertake an international journey:

> Once the number of network connections in an origin area reaches a critical threshold, migration becomes self-perpetuating because each act of migration itself creates the social structure needed to sustain it. Every new migrant reduces the costs of subsequent migration for a set of friends and relatives, and *some of these people are thereby induced to migrate*, which further expands the set of people with ties abroad, which, in turn, reduces costs for a new set of people, *causing some of them to migrate*, and so on. [p. 449, emphasis added]

Further, in their discussion of ways that maturing networks imply ever declining risks for potential migrants, Massey and his coauthors also tell us that the potential migrants are the decision makers in this networking process:

> When migrant networks are well-developed, they put a destination job within easy reach of most community members and make emigration a reliable and secure source of income. . . . This dynamic theory accepts the view of international migration as an individual or household decision process, but argues that acts of migration at one point in time systematically alter the context within which future migration decisions are made, greatly increasing the likelihood that *later decision makers will choose to migrate*. . . . Once begun, international migration tends to expand over time until network connections have diffused so widely in a sending region that *all people who wish to migrate can do so without difficulty*; then migration begins to decelerate. [Massey et al., 1993, pp. 449–50, emphasis added]

Portes and Bach (1985) suggest similar thinking when they explain why migrants tend to concentrate themselves spatially in ethnic clusters. Here they suggest that settlement locations and job sites are chosen according to newcomer preferences for remaining near kin:

> Overall, the entire process of immigrant settlement is "sticky" because new

arrivals tend to move to places where immigrants have become established, and later generations do not wander far off.... [The logic behind this, we argue, is that] by moving away from places where their own group is numerically strong, individuals risk losing a range of social and moral resources that make for psychological well-being as well as for economic gain. [p. 55]

In sum, neoclassical, new economics, and network migration theorists have assumed that the primary decision maker was always a person in the country of origin. While having ties to the destination is certainly crucial to the relocation process of any person who is unwilling to be a pioneer and strike out on his or her own, the existence of ties to veteran migrants is by itself an insufficient catalyst to ensure that the person's migration will take place when he or she desires it. "Studying social networks, particularly those linked to family and households, permits understanding migration as a social product—not as the sole result of individual decisions made by individual actors, not as the sole result of economic or political parameters, but rather as an outcome of all these factors in interaction" (Boyd, 1989, p. 642). To answer the question *Who makes migration happen?* one should consider that the immigrant social network itself and the interpersonal ties it represents are both important factors in international migration. However, we need to know far more about how network ties are activated, and about how information and assistance travel along these ties, if we are to explain better the migrant network experience. As Pamela's example suggests, both the existence of network connections at a destination *and* a key figure's willingness to transmit the information to help the potential migrant actually succeed in the migration and adaptation processes may be required.

Which Migrants Are Successful?

Much of the "new" research on the "new" (post-1960) immigration is focused not on new ways of understanding immigration, per se, but instead on issues of incorporation, or whether and how immigrants "succeed" after crossing the borders in destination countries. Modern vocabulary in this area questions the extent to which new arrivals ever achieve *Americanization, incorporation,* or *adaptation,* but these echo older terms—*assimilation* and *acculturation*—and as such do not invoke new ideas at all (DeWind and Kasinitz, 1997). In addition, the term *ethnicity* also has emerged as a factor by which the relative success or failure of foreign-born groups could be assessed. (While it may be a factor in how immigrants fare, as bodies neither the newer nor older sets of literature focus explicitly on the condition of race or racism for these nonwhite newcomers.)

The literature is only slightly divided on the question of migrant success. Some writers say that migrants come to wealthier destinations for target earnings, so success should be measured by whether these targets are achieved, not whether the migrants have established a new and permanent way of life. As Piore (1979) suggested and Stark (1991) later reiterated, large numbers of the new immigrants chose to migrate in order to achieve something in particular, perhaps by earning a specific amount of income, and planned to return to their homelands. These earnings would be applied toward the achievement of a target milestone that would be extraordinarily difficult to achieve in the absence of migration, such as building a new house, adding rooms to an existing house, or earning enough to fully educate one's children in societies where schooling even for young children requires tuition payments. Piore (1979) further suggested that "failed" migrants are those who stay in destination countries long after they intended to return. Even if they succeed in gaining earnings, they do not (or are unable to) return to their homelands as they expected to when they first moved. Often, target earnings and expected lifestyle improvements are never achieved, and migrants find themselves living lives quite different from what they thought they would have (Mahler, 1995; Menjívar, 2000). Policymakers and researchers have also suffered failed expectations. They had hoped that when they admitted laborers they were solving temporary labor shortages with only temporary workers, so they gave little thought to issues of migrant incorporation. To their surprise, and often disdain, they have faced a different reality. "To paraphrase a European aphorism, 'We imported labor, and we got people'" (DeWind and Kasinitz, 1997, p. 1096). The newcomers are not just workers who came to do a job, but people who have created new lives as they have stayed on and become variously interwoven into the fabric of their new societies.

In times past and now, immigration has been seen as a force potentially damaging to a nation's well-being (depending on the kind of migrant stock available), even if that nation is one with a booming economy that could put foreign labor to good use.[7] The "immigrant threat" has occupied thinkers from the nineteenth century until today, as they have worked to assess the value of each new or potential migrant group and have recommended policies to control immigration. Although the explicit racial bias in the public and political discourse lessened during the 1960s, when several nations of "non-white" persons secured their sovereignty independent of the colonial powers that had previously controlled them (Bonilla-Silva, 2000; Winant, 2002), many theorists have argued that this "threat" was based primarily on racial difference (Waters, 1990; Almaguer, 1994; Salyer, 1995; López, 1996; Paul 1997; Clifford, 1997). As discussed earlier, the search was on to figure out the mechanisms that caused migration and how we can best understand international movements in order to control them, but national governments found their controls largely ineffective at sufficiently regulating migration. Then questions about the ability of the new immigrant group to succeed economically became joined to questions about the quality of the culture that arrivals would import along with their nonwhite bodies. Studies of assimilation were launched to explain varying socioeconomic success among groups—explanations that avoided racial labels and focused on culture and ethnicity instead. These thinkers suggested that immigrant success is marked by cultural and economical assimilation (rather than by the immigrants' achievement of economic targets).

A few researchers intent on explaining differential immigration success have focused specifically on the structural reasons for segregated economic, social, and geographic outcomes among persons of foreign birth status. Some have found that Western economies are structured to require consistent inflows of immigrant labor to continually replenish bodies to hold up job ladders by filling the spaces on the bottom rungs (Piore, 1979; Sassen, 1988). Markets are sorted into primary and secondary sectors. Native-born workers are concentrated in the primary labor market, identifiable by the higher skill and capital-intensive nature of their jobs, which are known to be more stable. The secondary market, where immigrants are concentrated, has lower paid, labor-intensive, unstable, lower- or de-skilled jobs that are far less attractive; workers are subject to greater instability (firings, layoffs, downsizing, and pay cuts) and dangers, and their employers invest far less in their training (Massey et al., 1998). Race similarly sorts workers: the primary labor market is largely reserved for whites while those considered nonwhite are forced into degraded employment; such "occupational apartheid" is argued to so degrade the secondary market workers that their ethnic-racial group is similarly anointed with low racial status (Steinberg, 1991; Brodkin, 1998). Researchers who study market structures in these ways argue that advanced economies sort job seekers of different nationalities into a bifurcated or dual labor market (Bonacich,

1972), diminishing economic competition between foreign- and native-born workers. Although labor and housing markets have generally excluded immigrants and native-born persons of color from high status positions by use of discriminatory practices (Piore, 1979; Betancur, 1996; Lipsitz, 1998; Jaynes, 2000; Moss and Tilly, 2001), the majority of classic writings in this literature have questioned why these groups haven't "made it" the way Europeans immigrating in previous eras did (for example, see Glazer and Moynihan, 1970; Sowell, 1978). When immigrants have made the best of their exclusion by capitalizing on whatever income opportunities are available to them, these segregated successes have been lauded in recent studies of ethnic "enclaves," "niches," and entrepreneurship. Thus, assimilation is still the expectation, and "success" that looks like the white and native-born experience is still the standard measuring stick.

Note, however, that the immigrants in Pamela's story "made it" neither by wholly assimilating (for she noted the group's exposure to systematic racial exclusion rather than inclusion in job recruitment) nor by conscious socioeconomic self-segregation (for the jobs they finally did attain were in the regular and not the secondary labor market). These workers succeeded by hoarding jobs in a particular segment of the regular labor market and using their own recruitment channels to find migrants and get them into the country and into those jobs. They did similar kinds of networking in housing markets, and by encouraging home ownership, they secured for themselves an important source of wealth often made out-of-reach to nonwhite workers (Massey and Denton, 1993; California Newsreel, 2003). In these ways, they worked together within local and global socioeconomic structures to secure the social mobility they desired.

Immigrant Social Networks

Scholars have suggested that migration is best studied as a process rather than an event. Two important theoretical developments have helped in this effort. First, migration theorists no longer understand migration to begin with departure from one's native land and end with arrival in the new country. Instead, migration is understood as a long-term set of adaptive practices or even as a way of living, linking people and places to one another despite their apparent separation by national boundaries. Moreover, in this new way of thinking, the migrant is engulfed for a great length of time in a process that is located neither wholly in the place of origin nor in the destination, but simultaneously in both, in new social spaces that transcend and therefore complicate the idea of migration as mere geographic relocation. (See Glick-Schiller, Basch, and Blanc-Szanton, 1992; Kritz, Lim, and Zlotnik, 1992.) Catchwords in this line of thinking include such terms as *international migration systems*, *globalization*, and *transnationalism*.

Another development has occurred as scholars have changed their views on the value of a group maintaining its ethnic distinctiveness—seen no longer as wholly detrimental to socioeconomic mobility and instead argued to have certain benefits. Scholars have also learned to focus on how migrant groups accumulate group-specific or ethnically based traits that have value in capital markets and social status hierarchies. These group-specific sociocultural resources with economic value are generally described as social or cultural capital, which emerges from relationships among migrants and important socioeconomic gatekeepers and allows or prevents access to higher levels in hierarchical social systems. Catchwords in this vein of migration research include such terms as *social capital* and *immigrant social networks*.

These theoretical developments lead us to understand migration as something greater than we thought before, that is, more than a single individual's rational-economic decision to move made in a context set by the macrolevel socioeconomic structures in two nations. Migration is instead a phenomenon rooted in the decision making of networks—groups of people that may reside in several households and go beyond nuclear family households to include extended family and others who feel like family, such as fictive kin, friends, and compatriots. Migration is now seen as a process that affects and is affected by the economies and cultures at all levels of society, from neighborhoods to entire subcontinental regions, in ways that knowledge about networks may well be able to illuminate.

Networks are understood by immigration scholars to be webs of persons who share knowledge and resources that affect the collectivity, sometimes for the worse but, we presume, most often for the better. While social networks operate within many kinds of groups, not just among immigrants, immigrant social networks are given a special importance in understanding how migration, and upward social and economic mobility, actually occurs. Social networks are the connections individuals make to one another that form a web of relationships, and these relationships are valued because they hold social capital, the resources that network connections bring to network members. (While *social network analysis* is the term for the set of complex methods for studying patterns in the kinds of connections people in networks have, much of this research studies network effects in areas other than international migration. Conversely, those scholars who study migration write extensively about networks but tend not to use the analytical techniques used by methodologists of social network analysis. Instead they focus on the effects that network relationships have on the migration and acculturation experiences of international migrants.[8] Here I follow this tradition, eschewing formal network analytics both in this review of the international migration networks literature and in this book's use of qualitative methodological techniques to analyze migration networks.

Migrant networks are made up of the interpersonal ties—of kinship, friendship, and shared community of origin—that connect international migrants in the new destination. Depending on how networks are defined, they may also include former migrants now returned and nonmigrants who themselves may be considered potential migrants as long as they remain in touch with those who have emigrated to the new destination. The social network concept is valuable because it is a way to show how people's everyday lives (which are presumed to operate on a microlevel) may be influenced by larger (or more macrolevel) social structures, because individual action is embedded in those structures in ways that are most visible when one looks at network members' connections to people both inside and outside network communities (Boyd, 1989; Portes and Sensenbrenner, 1993). This connectivity is especially true for networks of international migrants.[9] In one study in Wilmington, Delaware, nearly all of the immigrants surveyed reported having been helped in their migration and resettlement to that American city, and only 13 percent could not name a source from which they had received help to arrive there (Tilly and Brown, 1967). Networks have been implicated in facilitating migrant groups' abilities to create niches in housing and labor markets, start their own businesses, financially shore up network members who need assistance, and offer co-residence to help other immigrants establish themselves right after migrating (Massey, 1986; Gilbertson and Gurak, 1992; Waters, 1999; Waldinger, 1996). Immigrant networks also offer nonmaterial social support and encouragement, reinforce cultural practices and help maintain identities, and foster children of migrants who leave their homelands to find work (Tilly and Brown, 1967; Kuo and Tsai, 1986; Ho, 1993; Levitt, 1999; Glick, 1999). Networks may be at the root of the good works of many voluntary associations whose purpose is to knit communities and help shield them from society's discriminatory blows

(Basch, 1987). They also may have influence in political arenas—encouraging immigrants to take advantage of periods of favorable immigration laws or even assisting the relocation of refugees (who are generally thought to participate in a wholly different migration process than "legal" or undocumented voluntary migrants) (Hagan, 1994: Koser, 1997).[10] Helpers seem willing to distribute resources to newcomers when there is a sufficient surplus to share with others, although such help falters or may be withheld entirely if physical and material resources are severely restricted (Mahler, 1995; Menjívar, 1997, 2000). In the sociology and demography of immigration, social networks are key mechanisms in making things happen for new and potential migrants.

The immigrant social network is a group made up of potential, new, and veteran immigrants who are connected to one another. Bigger than the household and smaller than the migration stream itself, social networks are said to play many important roles in organizing the process of international migration and perpetuating its flow. We presume that through these connections, migrant networks transfer information and other resources that make immigration and resettlement easier.

To date, research on social networks suggests that additional network migration occurs because links with veteran migrants give potential migrants a social advantage in initiating their own movement (Massey, Alarcón, Durand, and González, 1987; Massey, 1990a; Palloni et al., 2001). Once the necessary and sufficient condition for the initiation of a migration stream is established—that is, a socioeconomic link is made between sending and receiving countries—social networks among immigrants in destination cities and potential immigrants in the country of origin will perpetuate international migration between two countries in the migration system (Massey, 1988). Once the number of interconnected migrants in a destination reaches a critical threshold, the costs and risks of movement are reduced, which raises the probability that new migrants will join these veterans. As the network expands to absorb newcomers, additional resources become available to network members, which in turn encourages further network expansion, a process that may be repeated indefinitely as the expansion continues. Over time, migratory behavior spreads outward to encompass broader segments of the sending society (Massey et al., 1993). It is clear that social network migration maintains and perhaps increases the initial migration flow, despite laws intended to prevent or control its flow to individual states in the system (Massey, 1998; Donato, Durand, and Massey, 1992).

Networks are said to be important because, it is assumed, important socio-economic consequences follow from a migrant's connections to others. These benefits or detriments are known by the shorthand phrase *social capital*. Social capital is intangible, inherent in the relationships between dyads of network members, and presents itself as information or (real or potential) linkages to socioeconomically important others who have been alternatively described as sources of social control, family support, or benefits (Portes, 1998). While most writings on social capital see it as a positive thing, social capital can have negative consequences, such as excluding outsiders and restricting choice for insiders in ways that negatively affect their life chances (Portes, 1998; Portes and Rumbaut, 2001).[11]

Among networks of immigrants, social capital is evident in transferred information that assists network members in migration and resettlement, and in the obligations one accumulates being in reciprocal relationships with others in the exchange community (Massey and Espinosa, 1997; Massey, Alarcón, Durand, and González, 1987; Portes, 1998). As far back as 1890, French sociologist Pierre Guillaume Frédéric Le Play suggested that family and kinship networks both facilitate and encourage migration (Brown, 1963, cited in Tienda, 1980). Scholars who have studied the United States have found that kinship ties to persons with international migration experience significantly increase one's likelihood of migrating oneself, as does one's own experience in the United States (Palloni et al., 2001; Massey and Espinosa, 1997; Massey, 1990a). Douglas Massey (1998) has also found that these kinds of connections are the key to explaining why changes in legislation tend to be ineffective in slowing new waves of immigration. (See also Donato, Durand, and Massey, 1992.) Moreover, new efforts to control illegal or undocumented migration in sectors where the undocumented have traditionally been employed may only worsen the problem, for migration networks will work to increase their effectiveness in new locations and new occupations, and if successful, these efforts will only increase the level of undocumented immigrants overall (Djajić, 1999). Alejandro Portes (1998) explains that networks shape the new immigrant's acculturation and warns that these effects may be maladaptive as well as positive, and Roger Waldinger (1987, 1994, 1996) has shown in great detail that networks are effective mechanisms by which immigrants obtain jobs. These and other researchers have convincingly argued that networks are important in understanding all aspects of the migration process.

Network members use social capital to create ethnic niches or clusters of jobs and residential spaces of persons who share ethnic identifiers such as foreign-born status or racialized phenotype. Mostly we think of these spaces as monopolies that empower these groups, even though for some these concentrations may also result from apartheid-like exclusion (Kirschenman and Neckerman, 1991; Neckerman and Kirschenman, 1991; Steinberg, 1991). But even when migrants are stuck in isolating and unstable workplaces, such as private domestic service, such information exchanges can allow workers greater leverage in job negotiations, and networks may become even more valuable as one's career as a domestic advances (Hondagneu-Sotelo, 1994b, 2001). Networks are said to be powerful enough that members can hoard jobs for their group to such a degree that outsiders are virtually excluded from whole segments of the job market (Kasinitz and Rosenberg, 1996; Waldinger, 1994, 1996).[12]

Outside of markets as well, people in social networks benefit from social capital. Immigrant social networks are understood to join compatriots who may be separated by geography but still feel linked by a sense of shared economic and cultural destiny. Through networks, immigrants, potential immigrants, and those left behind transfer economic and social resources. Sometimes these exchanges are flows of economic resources, including barrels of goods and, more often, cash remittances, the magnitude of which can be so great that these transfers can restructure entire national economies. Sometimes what is exchanged is information (about job openings, places to stay, or the best ways to stay employed even without the proper documentation) that drives the continued flow of persons between linked origins and destinations. Sometimes these exchanges are political, for example, when migrants are allowed to vote in elections back home. And sometimes the exchanges are cultural, as when birthdays and weddings are transnational events creatively reconstructed in time and space—people sharing public viewings of wedding videos or by meeting in conference calls. Networks represent collective behavior that can accomplish much: they pool resources, which smoothes otherwise unstable flows of cash and goods to compatriots in the destination country and to those back home; provide child fosterage for young ones whose parents migrate for work or education; encourage communication of religious practices within and across denominations around the globe; and provide emotional support that stabilizes immigrant mental health (Kuo and Tsai, 1986; Kibria, 1994; Ho, 1993; Smith, 1993; Wilkinson, 2000).

Although migration scholars now agree that the social network is seen as one of the more important factors in perpetuating international migration and shaping migrants' resettlement experience, even after more than three decades of new immigrant network research, we know very little about how networks actually operate (Gurak and Caces, 1992). We know that people are more likely to move to the destination site if they know someone there (Massey, 1990a, 1998; Donato, Durand, and Massey, 1992; Massey et al., 1993; Massey and Espinosa, 1997), but we do not know how that interpersonal relationship is transformed from mere familiarity to actual migration assistance. We know that as these interpersonal relationships are transformed, the people within them become linked to one another by their network ties (Mahler, 1995; Levitt, 2001; Menjívar, 2000), but we do not know how these particular individuals (and not others with similar relationships) become members of those networks. We know that households within the network are connected, but we know neither how nor whether and under what circumstances network connections remain strong or attenuate. We are certain that, for the most part, if resources among network members are sufficiently robust and plentiful, members accrue positive benefits from being in the network (Waldinger, 1996), and sometimes negative outcomes when resources are few (Mahler, 1995; Kelly, 1995; Portes, 1995b, 1998), but we have not systematically and sufficiently examined networks to explain what the benefits are and to whom in the network they accrue. Moreover, we have for the most part left unexplored how the resources and knowledge we collectively call social capital are transferred within the social network from one household to another or from one individual to another. In other words, although we have decided that understanding network migration is crucial if we are to understand migration as an international or transnational process (Levitt, 2001), we know little about the immigrant social network itself—how it forms, functions, is maintained, and doles out benefits and sometimes trouble to its members. Absent from extant immigration network analyses are details about how one joins a network, how one triggers the mechanisms that bring about subsequent migration, what network members do for each other, how one transfers information that can help other network members accomplish tasks that foster social mobility, and what the network structure may be. As important as we say the immigrant network is, it remains a black box in migration research.

Part of the task of this book is to unlock that black box to reveal how the network is created and maintained, how it functions, and what its structure may be. Taken together, the chapters in this book dissect the structure and activities of a social network made up of immigrants who moved from their economically less developed nations to one that is more economically advanced. The argument of the book is that hub-and-spoke network members are able to achieve social and economic successes due in no small part to how their networks operate. Network experts (whom I have called hubs) emerge as they become skilled at finding jobs and housing for newcomers, and these experts increase their knowledge each time they assist someone else. Further, they become known for their ability to dole out resources, and those who wish to migrate will soon seek out their help. Hubs base their selection of new migrants to join the network on particular criteria, which vary depending on the situation at hand but almost always consist of the potential migrant having some characteristic that will enhance either the lifestyle or the reputation of the hub. That is, even though, of course, the person being helped will benefit from his or her own migration, the expert doing the selecting also benefits. Conversely, the hub will exclude those migrants who have limited ability to enhance the hub's own reputation or lifestyle. Sometimes this exclusion is a failure to assist the person's migration, but sometimes (if a migrant has benefited already from that hub's help) it means he or she will be shipped back home if the hub has the power to make that happen. (Perhaps surprisingly, this effort to return a migrant to his homeland happens with some frequency.) These hubs are easily identifiable because they are different from other migrants. They keep closer ties than other migrants to relatives and friends back home, visit their countries of origin more often, expect to retire there (while other migrants have no specific plans to return), and consider that place home. They also tend to reach positions of some power—that is, they become close enough to their employers to have their ear and gain the ability to recommend others to the employer when there is a need for more man- or womanpower in the workplace. These hubs also secure for themselves specialized knowledge that makes subsequent migration possible—they learn how to do the paperwork that will obtain legal status for newcomers and how to connect newcomers to those employers who can make legal status possible. These hubs hoard this information so that they are the people to know both back home and in the destination. This is also how they gain the power to select new migrants.

At the same time, of course, the new migrants benefit as well. They are able to come to a First World nation where they earn a significantly higher wage and (often but not always) hold a job that is higher in status than the one they could have obtained had they not migrated. In these kinds of helpful networks, working members also receive wages that allow for remittances to be sent back to support kin left behind (including, most often, the immigrant's own offspring, who are fostered and cared for by others while the immigrant works overseas). The migrants are the recipients of gifts from the hub and his or her family that are so generous that the newcomers feel they will never in their lifetime be able to repay such largess. They are often given migration assistance, which might include a coat when they arrive (for they did not own coats in the Caribbean), a comfortable bed or room of their own, a warm home to stay in, a job waiting for them, and rent-free co-residence until they establish themselves.

While newcomers are most often not expected to repay the hub for his or her generosity, they are not free of obligation. There are expectations on them that go beyond reciprocity to their benefactor and often obligate them to another person in the network or to someone sooner or later to be invited into that network. (While the hub's activities perpetuate the network, the network is also extended and reinforced when newcomer obligations are fulfilled in ways that repay the hub by having spokes give assistance to another spoke.) The unwritten rules of obligation, gift-giving, and repayment are understood by all parties and constitute what I call a *culture of reciprocity.*

When considered as a whole, these helping activities together make possible immigrant and network structural incorporation into local and global structures. The geographic and economic mobility achieved by migrating individuals, families, and networks amounts to a summary transformation of their individual and group life chances—presumably for the better. Network-connected immigrants simultaneously cross boundaries of national sovereignty and the ever-important global politicoeconomic boundary that separates the world's rich and more developed from its poor and underdeveloped, the First World from the Third World, and white from nonwhite.

As stated, one goal of this book is to show how mobility and migration are linked and what the role of networks is in both processes. Achieving this goal necessitates an explanation of the socioeconomic inequality that both makes migration desirable and makes socioeconomic mobility so difficult to achieve for someone who lives outside of the more developed regions. Relevant too is a discussion of the ways that global conceptions of race shape migration, for these ideas help determine whose admission is welcome and whose is not. The desirability of a particular migrant group is also shaped by the legal and social scientific understandings of the effects and repercussions of immigration. But

I will leave the discussion of these various forms of political and economic inequality for the next chapter while I focus here on introducing the relevance of the Caribbean case for learning about immigrant networks.

How the Knitted Survive: A Case Study

Social science scholars of migration and ethnicity too often presume that the key to an immigrant group's socioeconomic success can be found in the moral, religious, or cultural ways that distinguish them from other groups. I do not dismiss the cultural entirely but instead give primacy to the ways in which social and economic structures determine how a group's members fare postmigration, even as their interactions with those same structures ethnicize them. Where culture enters is in the crucial role hubs play in selecting among potential migrants whom hubs believe have moral, religious, and cultural traits in quantities sufficient enough to be asked to join the hubs' idealized communities. Only then do hubs offer potential migrants the assistance that makes migration possible in the first place and that enhances the likelihood of postmigration socioeconomic success.

This book looks at a particular case of network migration in order both to add to our knowledge of networks (particularly in areas defined as crucial in the beginning of this chapter) and to show how the network can serve as a tool for the upward mobility—on a globally economic, racial, and transnational basis—of the group transplanted by aid of its network connections. This is a study of immigrants to the London and New York metropolitan areas, and of friends and family they left behind in their home islands in the English-speaking Eastern Caribbean, who are connected to one another by their network ties. The information presented in these chapters was obtained by interviewing a sample of persons in two networks comprising West Indian immigrants now living in London and the New York Metropolitan Area (including Newark, New Jersey, and Long Island, New York) and their relatives back home. Given that the migration literature discusses networks as configurations of immigrants who help (more often than hurt, it is hoped) one another by providing information and resources that assist in border crossing and resettlement. I determined first that network members would be identifiable by their receipt or transmission of information and material assistance. As a result I followed a "snowball" sample of immigrants who were asked to recount their immigration experience and, in doing so, identify people who had helped them come to the United States or England. Respondents were also asked to identify people they had helped come to the United States or England. The snowball developed, then, as I followed these leads, and I considered people connected in these ways to be members of one network. I used an ethnographic method of interviewing, which meant I would let the respondents' own experiences and ways of organizing themselves inform me about the boundaries of the network.[13] In other words, while I did predefine network membership by deciding that anyone who received help from another migrant or any migrant who gave help to another migrant would be considered a network member, I learned about the bounds of network membership by asking each respondent to teach me how network members provided assistance to one another and what help was transferred.

This method then led me to a working definition of *help*. I noted three modes of assistance that immigrants in the network explained prevailed in their relationships with others. *Help* in these Caribbean networks is defined by allowing a newcomer to co-reside with the sponsoring family during the newcomer's resettlement period, using one's reputation to find a job for an immigrant in the network, providing legal assistance in complying with immigration requirements, or any combination of these three activities. Thus, if a respondent told me that his coworker was an immigrant who had helped him find a job, or if he knew of a coworker who helped other immigrants from the same set of origin countries, I would attempt to interview the coworker also. To the best of my ability, then, I followed all such leads and interviewed all immigrants who were willing to talk about their migration and resettlement experiences, as long as they were connected to others through the provision of help as the respondents had defined it.

I began my interviews in New York City with two unrelated persons from different islands (one born and raised in Saint Vincent and the Grenadines, the other in Trinidad and Tobago) in the hope that I would map out two separate Caribbean-based networks.[14] I did not limit the network sample by either time of immigration or by geographic origin or destination of the immigrants who would be considered for interviewing because I let the sampling method dictate the connections I would follow. It should be noted, then, that the respondents in the sample came from several different islands in the West Indies, settled in different parts of New York and London at different times, and are related to one another in very different ways. The oldest and youngest respondents lived in New York at the time of the interview—the oldest came to the United States in 1930, the youngest came in the 1980s. I also traveled to the Eastern Caribbean to interview family and friends of these New Yorkers—people who were connected to the network but not themselves émigrés. Using this snowball sample technique, I interviewed about ninety persons in two networks. In 1995 and 1996 I spoke with West Indian immigrants living in the New York Metropolitan Area (including Newark, New Jersey, and Long Island, New York) and their families, friends, and relatives, first on five islands back home, and later, in 1999–2000, in and around London. Although there were a small number of immigrants from elsewhere in the West Indies, about 90 percent of the sample came from two island nations, Saint Vincent and the Grenadines (an archipelago of thirty-two islands and cays, eight or nine of which house the country's population), and from the Republic of Trinidad and Tobago (a twenty-three island nation, the two main islands of which give the country its name).[15] Altogether, forty-four immigrants were interviewed in the New York area, twenty-six in and around London, and twenty in the West Indies.

Why Study the Caribbean Case?

Immigrant groups of all kinds have networks. It can be said that Polish, Irish, Jewish, Central and South American, Mexican, and Chinese migrants all form interpersonal networks of some kind (Mahler, 1995; Ignatiev, 1995; Thomas and Znaniecki, 1996; Brodkin, 1998; Menjívar, 2000; Massey, Alarcón, Durand, and González, 1987; Cornell and Hartmann, 1998). I cannot say with any certainty that there is a group that did not use networks! Surely there are elements of network formation, maintenance, and operation that are common to all these groups, even as they all have elements that make them unique. A study of any of these cases can be illustrative in teaching us how migration happens, how and why networks form and what they achieve, how migrants adapt to a new environment, and what effects migration has on those left behind. Caribbean people are a good example of a group with continued contemporary dependence on networks for their migration—in one study of immigrants from two islands now living in New York, more than 90 percent reported belonging to a network (Basch, 1987).

Caribbean network migration is also a significant case to examine because of the place of the Caribbean peoples in the unequal economic and racial systems that encompass our globe. For example, Caribbean migration may be analyzed as a prototypical case of any Third to First World flow. Caribbean migrants can serve as one of several historical examples of the movement of persons attempting to better their station—that is, to achieve

upward socioeconomic mobility—despite the constraints to mobility represented by the international economic inequality, clashes of culture or military might, and political uncertainty that exist during the group's attempt
to migrate. Moreover, their migration flow is an important example of Third
World newcomers, if not because of their volume in absolute numbers, then
proportionally. While transplants from the Caribbean island nations constitute only a small percentage of all the migrants to Canada, the United
Kingdom, and the United States, the Caribbean nations have sent great proportions of their populations to these Western destinations. For example,
it has been found that between 1955 and 1985, Haiti sent up to 9 percent and
Barbados up to 25 percent of its total population to the United States.[16]

To consider a third angle, this case, like any study of the global migration
of a group said to be "of color," is also a study of racial adaptation, a process
that now occurs upon the arrival of each group considered to be different
from the native-born population.[17] Because Caribbean people represent the
largest black migrant group in the United Kingdom, the United States, and
Canada, their case presents an important example of adaptation to the racial
regimes of Western destinations. Moreover, the study of migration of persons of color can be read as one that attempts to restore balance to the historical record by giving voice to a less well accepted version of events about
the racialized meaning of travel and global social interaction as peoples considered to be racially different meet and find assimilation and acceptance (or
lack thereof).

In this book, black migration from the Caribbean is, perhaps ambitiously,
considered from each of these angles: as a general case of a group using its
networks to strive for upward mobility, as a general case of international
movement, and as an empirical example of inter- and intranational racial adaptation and racialization. The focus here, in particular, is on the migration of
persons born in the English-speaking islands of the Eastern Caribbean (also
known as the Leeward Islands, or the Lesser Antilles) to the New York and
London metropolitan areas, under circumstances of mutual aid (also known
as network migration).

What to Expect from This Book

Human migration began when we branched out in bands from the place
where our species began on the African continent, and from there people fully
traversed and populated the globe. As we moved, settled, and created human

communities, we changed our social organization and divided ourselves. We developed nations, created geographic borders for our states, invented races by which to differentiate one people from another, and created ethnicities that we believed bound us culturally and ancestrally to one another. Generally speaking, we tend not to think of migration as a phenomenon that encompasses all corners of the globe and all facets of humanity. We tend to think of, analyze, and see the problems of international migration from a national perspective—that is, from the perspective of the nation in which we live (if we are a native-born person), or perhaps the one in which we were born (if we are an immigrant).

In nations that serve as destinations for flows of newcomers, policymakers and the news media debate the consequences of accepting new persons into one's polity. Although the desperate need for wage labor required open borders as the United States was formed, within decades the founding immigrants and children of immigrants instituted legal strictures specifying who would now be allowed to enter. Canada, the United Kingdom, and other Western nations instituted similarly restrictive policies over their nation's history. Often, conservative thinkers see immigration as a zero-sum game, where immigrants gain and native-born persons lose; their concerns emerge as to whether or not the newcomers will drain or replenish economic resources, soothe or stir intergroup relations, and strengthen or fray the social fabric.

While international migration is a global process that may play out on local stages, it has global consequences because our individual nations are linked in ways that have global effects. For example, the nations of the world are linked to one another by a worldwide system of material and cultural production. Some refer to these linkages as *globalization*—a term that has a meaning on which we do not agree but which we generally use to connote the idea that today few economies or cultures stand alone or remain untouched by others. We were always linked internationally in some fashion, whether through the human migration that populated the globe, through the progress or economic exchange that saw us move from mercantilist to capitalist trade, and through periods of imperialism, colonialism, and sovereignty for colonized peoples. Some argue, though, that our society is *newly* global because we are joined more easily by increased communication (telephone, online communication, more accessible air travel) and interdependent economic processes (such as the system of capitalist production, in which manufacturing in the Third World is assumed to be run from financial centers in global cities of the First

World; or commodity chains, in which manufactured goods are produced in piecemeal fashion by shipping them from factory to factory through various stages of completion). These connections also make us culturally interdependent, as more economically developed nations export aspects of their consumer lifestyles to other regions.

On the local level, each nation has defined its own set of laws that determine who are the legitimate members of its polity (citizens), who is allowed access to citizenship, who is allowed entry on only a temporary basis, and who will be granted no access at all. Each nation has also defined its own racial paradigm (which itself has global aspects), deciding the meaning of race and the language of racial categories, and defining a corresponding racialized social and economic hierarchy (Winant, 2002). Newcomers to these individual societies must somehow be inserted into these localized social, economic, and political systems.

To reiterate the task I outlined in the Preface of this book, my intent is to draw network migration as a multifaceted global mobility project in which immigrants of color succeed in inserting themselves into positions of greater status and wealth in global systems of hierarchy and live lives across national boundaries that are meant to exclude persons ordinarily considered outsiders. I hope to achieve this goal through this case study of network-fueled international migration among black migrants from the Caribbean. Despite a history of Western disdain for the black migrant, West Indians, like other immigrant groups, have used networks to move out of their former circumstances (marked by depressed economies and limited opportunities) toward a different future (one that they hope will be marked by economic prosperity and increased status). When migrants, with the network's help, succeed in traversing geographic, political, economic, and social boundaries to the betterment of their socioeconomic station, the mobility project is realized. The remainder of this book is organized in chapters intended to address several facets of a mobility project of this kind.

Chapter Two explains the international context in which the immigrant social networks that are examined here operate. I explain how destination nations for Caribbean persons came to be chosen, and the global political, economic, and racial reception that awaits immigrants from poorer nations such as the Caribbean islands from which my respondents come. The history of disdain for the black migrant (referred to earlier) will be outlined in some detail here.

Chapter Three begins to examine Caribbean migrant networks more closely, describing in some detail the central figure in the network who manages to bring several new immigrants into niches in the labor and housing markets and explains how they select potential migrants to join them. Here I develop and present the hub-and-spoke model of the immigrant social network, named for the two main roles I found among migrants who moved to the West using assistance from their network. One kind of migrant (the hub) is the central figure. He or she becomes an expert at getting his or her compatriots into the country (both by legal means and without the benefit of legal papers) and at finding appropriate jobs and housing for the newly relocated emigrant; he or she also identifies others for network assistance. The spoke is the beneficiary of the hub's assistance. My description of the links between hubs and spokes, and of the ways these links join to create an entire immigrant network, is based on interviews with West Indians who left their island nations and migrated to New York and London and the ex-urban areas surrounding these cities.

Hubs and spokes perpetuate the network and assist in the adaptation of new migrants to their host societies through a number of activities that are the subject of the subsequent three chapters. Chapters Four through Seven are of a piece, for they describe different aspects of the processes by which these black migrants achieve the network's mobility. Chapter Four describes ways that network members enter host countries and make arrangements to stay, thus taking their first steps, literally, toward mobility, across national borders that simultaneously indicate one's crossing over from the so-called Third World into the First World. Chapters Five and Six are devoted to summarizing the process of immigrant insertion into the destination country's labor and housing markets, and to explaining how networks help migrants navigate host economies. Market insertion is achieved by creating what the literature calls *niches* in labor markets and *ethnic neighborhoods* in housing markets. Immigrant social networks operate within market structures affected by tendencies toward racial and gendered clustering to make these concentrations of immigrants happen. Chapter Five focuses solely on the labor market, while in Chapter Six I elaborate on other economic and noneconomic forms of immigrant adaptation processes, such as home ownership and participation in savings and ethnic associations.

To understand how immigrants are actually inserted into a new society in terms of the racialized factors that shape such insertion we also must consider the influence of the local racial paradigm and the way it is formed (Winant, 2002). Racial paradigms are creations localized in historical time and geographic space, and groups are racialized by other humans, not by nature (López, 1996). Migration, then, requires a process of racial adaptation. Chapter Seven explains how these immigrants of color adapt to their new racialized surroundings, given both their racial experiences back home and the experience of their entry into Western housing and labor markets. That chapter's discovery is that the network provides a special kind of racial immunization—these black newcomers to the United States have adapted to a paradigm so different from the one they knew best that they have not readily accepted their new inferior status, even though racial inferiority is in general terms ascribed to people who resembled them phenotypically.

The book's final and eighth chapter summarizes the findings of the previous chapters, chronicling the migration outcomes for members of immigrant networks who successfully migrate to the Western world. Specifically, I catalog the assistance that black Caribbean migrants in New York and London received, and I tally the ways these networks helped or failed to help network members achieve social and economic mobility on a global scale. To be sure, I neither suggest that all networks are good and reward members with benefits (for surely there is plenty of evidence that network connections can be problematic and even detrimental to the network's members) nor argue that all of the benefits listed accrue to all members. The point of this final chapter, and implicitly of the book as a whole, is to set up the immigrant social network as an ideal type of exercise in socioeconomic mobility on a global scale. I argue here for the generalizability of the hub-and-spoke type of network and suggest that other groups in the United States may have similarly used this form of network for their own ethnic mobility projects.

Network formation and the mobility that accrues from it are certainly not unique to the Caribbean case but are common to several socioeconomically successful migrant groups. (That is why migrants form networks; most migrants who join a network—even those who appear to be givers rather than receivers of help—appear largely to benefit from their membership.) However, it bears repeating that the research project on which this book is based was designed to study these immigrant network structures only in the light cast by the oral retelling of their migration experiences. Thus (given the limitations, imposed by my research design, of the data I collected) I will be unable to estimate the proportion of black English-speaking Caribbean transplants who migrate with the aid of a hub-and-spoke network, nor will I be able to conclude without doubt that other groups use these kinds of networks. (That said, I do believe that hub-and-spoke migration is a widespread phenomenon. I explain why and present what scanty evidence is available on this subject in the chapter that concludes this book.)

To reiterate, this book details the Caribbean case so that it serves as an illustrative tool for learning about migration networks. I document the characteristics of network structure and illustrate the processes of formation and maintenance. I also try to shed some light on the reasons that immigrant networks play such an important role in the perpetuation of international migration. I argue that the network plays an important role in redistributing wealth and opportunity—from persons at the top of the supranational hierarchy of races and at the top of the hierarchy of nations that compose a world system, to persons who otherwise would remain at the bottom. Certainly if the network is the tool for equalizing benefits within these important and intersecting global hierarchies, then it can be argued, as I do in the closing chapter, that the immigrant social network is ultimately a powerful tool for upending socioeconomic inequality on a global scale. To make the case, however, I need to explain what socioeconomic inequality the network confronts. This explanation forms the core of my next chapter.

2 Globally Incorporating and Marginalizing the Black Caribbean

THE PRECEDING CHAPTER SHOWED that using a network perspective to study international migration can lead to new insights about how migration works. This chapter provides the *international* part of the context, examining theories that explain migration internationally. We should also understand theories about the ways nations are connected with one another socioeconomically. In the first part of this chapter I discuss the larger hierarchical systems of inequality, particularly race, gender, and economy, with which potential migrants (and everyone else in our global society) must contend. (Of course, each of these systems has local variations that become important in immigrants' adaptation and acculturation experiences, a topic addressed in later chapters.) In this chapter's second section I explain how the hierarchical systems described in the first section specifically shape black emigration as people depart the Caribbean and move overseas. This chapter, then, contextualizes Caribbean migration within global inequality, setting a historical context for black Caribbean migration to the more developed Western nations. I also set a context in which to show later how transformative membership in an immigrant social network can be when members use it to turn geographic mobility into socioeconomic mobility.

Reinternationalizing International Migration

Generally speaking, immigration theory (like theory on any subject) is written from the perspective of the theorist, reflecting the ideological agenda the theorist has in mind when they are writing. Works on immigration have largely focused on issues important to thinkers in the destination country. More specifically, as we saw in the last chapter, migration studies have focused on the localized aspects of the immigrant experience, looking mainly at the reasons that migrants leave their country of origin, why they enter a given country (and the best ways to stop or hinder that entry), whether they assimilate, and whether the new society and economy decline or flourish after the migrants arrive.

But migrants' lives are not lived solely within the borders of the nation in which they happen to be at the moment we study them—migrants don't simply depart one nation and then enter another in a one-way process. We miss much by focusing only on the immediate national or binational aspects of such a move. Scholarship on three aspects of internationalism are helpful in reinterpreting the significance of cross-national movement in global terms: works on the *global economy*, on *global racial hierarchy*, and on *transnationalism and migration systems*. These three areas of scholarship allow a less individualistic and domestic-policy interpretation of the migrant experience than national or binational theories. They also serve to focus our attention on migration as a phenomenon that takes shape at the international or global level of social interaction and involves socioeconomic and cultural groupings of peoples and nations. I explain what I mean by this as I examine each of these scholarship traditions in detail.

Unequal Global Economic Systems

In relocating internationally, migrants physically traverse the globe and navigate its hierarchical systems, transforming themselves into refugees, contract laborers, seasonal agricultural workers, or other categories of movers who are defined in terms of an international division of labor (Munck, 1988) that operates within an *unequal global economy*. One glance at national statistics, or often-rebroadcast television commercials about starving children, will remind us that some nations are poor and some are rich. There is much debate about the root causes of that inequality, but some scholars argue that it is systematic—that is, that there is a global system of inequality in which nations are ranked hierarchically according to their power to control international labor and capital, and that it is the more powerful nations that set prices of commodities and labor in the global economy. Probably the most well known school of thought in this tradition is that of the *world system*, which I discuss

in the next section. Suffice it to say here that theorists believe that poorer people respond to inequalities of this kind by moving, either from rural areas to
urban centers or from poorer nations to richer ones, in search of a better life.

The legacy of colonialism is one cause of the lagging economic fortunes
of the world's migrant-sending nations. In the fifteenth through twentieth
centuries, colonies were either settled by foreign administrators or subject to
foreign rule from afar. Colonization reorganized the world by marginalizing
indigenous people and taking away their control of their land, extracting native labor and other national resources, and creating an international division
of labor (designed to stimulate European industrialization in a way that forced
the decline of native industries). Together, these actions caused the colony's
underdevelopment (McMichael, 2000). It was not until the mid-twentieth century that many African and Latin American nations finally managed to overthrow colonial powers and regain decision-making control over their nation's
political and economic infrastructures. In 1960 alone, seventeen new African
nations joined the United Nations, and by 1970 there were 127 UN member nations—a 50 percent increase in the number of new nations for the decade, including many new Caribbean, African, and Mideast nations (United Nations,
n.d.). Newly won struggles for independence marked a period of optimism
about the power and promise of newfound political sovereignty and economic
independence as catalysts for economic prosperity, geographic and regional
security, and greater global equity. Even politically and economically conservative scholars and policymakers (who subscribed to theories of modernization) believed that newly independent nations could finally develop by going
through stages that other, more developed nations had gone through, until
they too reached a level of modernity in culture and economy generally understood to represent progress. For former colonies, a new era of development
was ushered in. Here development means European or Western economic aid
for economic stimulation in a context where the formerly colonized attempt
to emerge from legacies that left their own cultures permanently changed, and
where they struggle to attain political legitimacy in a world not of their making (McMichael, 2000).

Few could fail to see that the 1960s' promise of progress was not fulfilled for
most nations, despite attempts at implementing strategies for development.
Scholars who have noted that colonial ties still reverberate in current political
and economic relationships, even in this presumably postcolonial world, have
blamed failure on a new form of colonialism (neo-colonialism) (McMichael,

2000). Some scholars have blamed forces outside of the poor nation itself, arguing instead that the global economy is organized so that the growth of more powerful nations occurs at the expense of the less powerful. They have also questioned whether significant economic progress is possible for today's poor nations in this kind of regime. Using case study analyses of early 1960s Brazil, Chile, and Mexico, Andre Gunder Frank (1967) first popularized this *dependency theory*. Other early thinkers in this tradition include Argentinian Raul Prebisch, who argued that economic trade with rich nations have not benefited Latin American countries that export agricultural goods and primary products such as raw natural materials (Chirot and Hall, 1982), and Samir Amin (1973, 1977), who applied a similar analysis to African economies. In a more complex elaboration of similar themes, dependent development theorists believe that economic progress is possible for some but it will come at some cost (including rising domestic inequality, rapid urbanization, and other social and economic ills), and will not likely be achieved by governments that try to opt out of the world economy and be economically isolationist in order to avoid the downsides to participation in global capitalist markets (Evans, 1979).

Providing an even broader and longer-term view of how inequality among nations began and why it persists are theories about the modern *world system*. These theories suggest that nearly all nations are unavoidably involved in the global economy dominated by capitalism, that opting out is nearly impossible. In this capitalist world system, a core set of nations drives and therefore benefits from global capitalism at the expense of those nations that remain in the periphery. Immanuel Wallerstein (1974) and his followers believe that as the system develops, it reproduces the subordinate status of peripheral nations so that the hierarchy of nations is retained over time, even though some nations (constituting the "semi-periphery") do manage to move developmentally toward the core. (See Chase-Dunn and Grimes, 1995.)

Of course debates persist among the thinkers in these traditions. The theorists who work in the world-system tradition argue about the age, size, scope, cyclical nature, and uniqueness of the political and economic organization of the current world system and about the conditions under which nations can develop, while non-world-system theorists either question the theory's validity or altogether ignore its contributions (Chirot and Hall, 1982, p. 97). Similarly, the dependency school may have seen its heyday come and go, but its insights still represent an important corrective to naive assumptions about the ease of achieving economic development in poorer nations (Chirot and

Hall, 1982). Whether we agree or not with individual theorists or theories that proffer specific critical ways of thinking about how nations are economically and politically linked, we cannot ignore the economic and political connections among nations in our newly globalized society, or the seeming permanence of inequality among nations.[1]

To understand migration within this unequal global political economic context, we should understand migrants as laborers. The wealthier and more powerful nations of the capitalist-oriented and economically more developed First World (presumed to include the United States, Western Europe, Australia, and Japan, or the Western capitalist nations of the post–World War II era) control the international movement of capital and labor in ways that benefit them. First World employers have a great demand for the labor of Third World peoples (those of the economically poorer and politically weaker nations of Asia, Africa, and Latin America). The latter normally will work for less pay and under less desirable conditions than will First World natives. At the same time, migrants from poorer Third World nations have to contend with the strict border controls and unequal access to naturalization that hinder those who wish to enter and remain in the First World and share in the fruits of those richer economies they helped to build. Global systems with interdependent capitalist relations also create economically depressed former colonial economies, where it is difficult to gain education and to find jobs that provide wages sufficient to sustain families and secure working conditions. Where a migrants' network helps them succeed, then, is in achieving global economic mobility, for migration signals conquest over barred entry as people traverse both controlled geographic borders and economic obstacles toward stable and well-remunerated employment.

Global Racial Paradigms

Even though scholars who write and study in the area known as *political economy* are critical of the conventional ways that local and global economies are said to operate, they tend not to engage racialized critiques of that kind of domination. For example, although racializing arguments were used to justify the commodification and sale of African people as chattel, and the colonial domination of African, Native North and South American, and other sovereign peoples, the development of the world system is not generally discussed in a way that puts race as a central explanatory factor in the creation of systematic global inequality. Even those political economists who abandon the idea of the "impersonal" market and argue instead that there is a politics and ideology of market processes still presume that economics (and not race) is the engine that drives nations and the world. Economists accept two standard economic assumptions that give primacy to economic solutions to inequality. The first assumption is that the global economy can be made equitable. Conventional economists point to modernization theories and development strategies, while political economists' belief in the promise of equality in markets and economies is evident in their explanations about the poor functioning of market systems, even as they admonish that abandonment of markets is unfeasible. A second assumption is that race is exogenous to the functioning of global and local markets. Neither race nor gender has predictive value in macroeconomic analyses, seemingly, for economic models of neither the conventional nor the critical kind devote a great deal of energy to explaining why women and nonwhite peoples consistently fail to share in the economic profits that are so unequally distributed. Nor are economists preoccupied, generally, with the long-term effects of such inequality on economically disempowered and disenfranchised peoples awaiting economic corrections to the current state of political and economic affairs. The idea is that economics, done right, is the great equalizer, and that race has little predictive or corrective value because it cannot be altered or managed as other economically manipulable factors may. For these reasons, race is here given analytical treatment separate from the political economic and world-system literatures.

Less well understood as a coherent body of scholarly thought, this second tradition of scholarship focuses on a global racial system that is as hierarchical as the global economy. While local variations exist, this global racial system is organized by forces that conspire to keep phenotypically defined races in a relatively stable *global racial hierarchy*. A people's place within global and local racial hierarchies defines its freedom from economic deprivation, its ability to hoard privilege, and its cultural desirability in the polity of the nation in which it resides. For instance, those who in the United States are euphemistically labeled "people of color" are less able to determine their own socioeconomic destiny than are people labeled colorlessly "white."

Race, as a biological concept, does not exist. That is, there is no biological or genetic marker that with any degree of certainty can identify the members of a given race of people (King, 1981). Racial categories, then, are imagined configurations of mainly physical differences that are meant to classify humans into groupings. The differences among these groupings, further, are imagined to have explanatory power about such things as why some people obtain greater economic and educational outcomes, why some have what are considered superior cultural practices or hold dominant social status, and why others are considered to be lesser on these counts.[2] Although the categories themselves are relatively meaningless from a biological standpoint, the act of classification and the act of using classifications to determine the just allocation of our world's political, cultural, environmental, and economic resources is literally a matter of life and death.

Race (systems of racial classification and the categories that compose racial hierarchies) and racism (the exercise of doling out injustices according to the recipient's racial category) are key components of the political economy of the globe. The racism that was used to carry out the colonial reorganization of indigenous societies permanently transformed these societies and destroyed local cultures. But the development of race is not just a historical artifact that was prevalent in organizing societies in bygone eras that can be marked by the time a given racial category was introduced. Race and racism remain central organizing tools of modern society (Winant, 2001), capitalist accumulation (Miles, 1989, 1993), and even the building of powerful nation states (Marx, 1998). The meaning of race continues to be fought over by different factions with competing political interests (Omi and Winant, 1994; Solomos, 1993). Ultimately, national-level discourses about the repercussions of letting immigrant "others" enter is, at its root, a racial debate about European and North American national identity (Solomos and Back, 1996; Bashi, 2004).

Surely we don't have to hold onto a biological notion of race as the basis for today's form of global racism, for "the [continued] existence of racism does not require the existence of races. (You don't have to believe in witchcraft, after all, to believe that women were persecuted as witches in colonial Massachusetts)" (Appiah, 1989, p. 40). Today, race and racism have postmodern forms, and racial hierarchies are no longer articulated in the same explicitly racist ways they once were. Racial language today is less openly and officially racist, articulating instead nationalist and cultural themes that focus on difference and differentialism while presenting a presumed colorblindness to phenotype categories coupled with a perception that racial equality has been achieved (Winant, 2001; Bonilla-Silva, 2000, 2003; Williams, 1997). A more complex notion of race—but of race nonetheless—is now articulated on both sides of the racial justice scale, where race is used both to achieve domination and to formulate resistance against that domination. Still, racism survives, even in a new era that has witnessed successful struggles both to end colonialism in all its forms and to win mass mobilizations for equal rights for all races (Winant, 2001, p. 293).

Racialized peoples, particularly those who are diasporic (that is, scattered and away from their homelands), use their ethnicity to formulate an articulate racial resistance. Rather than formulate ethnicity as their way of assimilating into the structures on which a nation's racial discourse is based, they instead purposefully ethnicize themselves to shrug off racist notions of their outsider status and recreate themselves and their culture in their new homeland (Appiah, 1989; Hall, 1996; Buff, 2001; Hintzen, 2001). For example, migrants of African descent were racialized when they were labeled "black," having first been involuntarily transported as slaves and then incorporated as the only non-European settlers (albeit peons) in Europe and the United States (Winant, 2001). While seen monolithically as racially "black," they struggle to be viewed as distinct peoples: African American, black Caribbean or West Indian, North African, and so on.

Assimilation was the term used to describe the historical trajectory that is said to have marked the upward mobility experience of immigrants from Europe to the United States in the earliest decades of the twentieth century. Writings by scholars and politicians like Nathan Glazer and Daniel Patrick Moynihan (1970), and many others, proffered a version of history that described immigrant groups such as the Irish, Italians, and Jews as newcomers to U.S. soil with little resources who succeeded as an ethnic group because of their supposed determination and superior moral and cultural values. Horatio Alger's novels became famous for fictionalized immigrant stories of pulling oneself up by one's own bootstraps, the classic assimilation model assumed to have worked for the majority of European migrants to the United States. A subgroup's cultural values were assumed to explain its potential and desire for greater economic attainment. By the same token, cultural inferiority tautologically "explained" a group's economic failure (Steinberg, 1989). Cultural inferiority was cited as the factor that justified the continued economic segregation of poor immigrants and native-born people of color (Glazer and Moynihan, 1970; Sowell, 1978).

Surely, while desirable (read white northern and western European) immigrants were welcomed during the industrial era, migrants from other areas (considered nonwhite or less than white) were not (Clifford, 1997; Brodkin, 1998). Although a new cadre of scholars has reviewed the historical record and determined that the scholarly findings of assimilationist thinkers were largely mythical (Steinberg, 1989; Brodkin, 1998; Ignatiev, 1995; Clifford, 1997), those myths persist. Certain groups had economic endowments and social privileges that others did not, and the "assimilated" were racially anointed only as their group became favorably compared to the racial pariahs of their day (Steinberg, 1989; Ignatiev, 1995; Massey, 1995; Clifford, 1997; Brodkin, 1998; Plaza, 1998; Paul, 1997). A great deal of recent scholarship on immigration still reflects on the question of whether holding onto the remnants of one's separate economic space in ethnic enclaves, labor market niches, entrepreneurial endeavors, or culture is the key to success or failure.

Many writings about immigration discuss assimilation as if it became an issue only in the last third of the twentieth century, but determining the appropriate type and number of immigrants was always a concern for the more developed white-majority nations of the Western Hemisphere. As the twentieth century progressed, increased immigration was looked upon as a problem, and more controls were sought to limit the numbers and kinds of persons who were allowed to enter. Formerly unwelcome southern and eastern European immigrants were reclassified as white and given the privileges that accompany that racial classification (Lipsitz, 1998), while simultaneously gaining new status as successes rather than as scourges (Steinberg, 1989). No similar embrace was extended to the people of color who crossed the same borders in subsequent years (López, 1996).

Immigration scholarship is still being challenged to look beyond old essentialist understandings of race, traditional disciplinary boundaries, and social scientific ways of writing. Required is a more effective and overarching analysis of the racial incorporation or exclusion of immigrants, aliens, and refugees, and a critical understanding of the racial impact of migration on both the migrant group itself and on the society of which they become a part (Salyer, 1995; Fan, 1997; Glenn, 2002). How can this perspective help to analyze immigrant social networks? Networks comprise people who are linked (by blood, country, and culture) in ways that are seen as racial or ethnic or both. Furthermore, as network members use their connections to help those within their group succeed socioeconomically, they struggle for positive incorporation into the society and economy in ways that are met with prejudice and discrimination. To the extent that who they are and how they struggle to succeed are racialized, any analysis of their migration experience must also engage their struggle with and incorporation into racial systems.

Transnational Migration Systems

Migration scholars have for some time argued that we were wrong to see the migration experience as a simple and singular move from point A to point B, for migrants continue to live lives connected to relatives and friends in the country of origin. When migrants exit one (more impoverished) position in our global society and reinsert themselves into another (more lucrative) one, they still keep ties with those left behind by sending remittances, visiting and calling, and participating politically. We are also challenged to rethink our ideas about nations: they are not the stand-alone independent entities we once thought, for new interstate relationships suggest that national boundaries may be less important now than before. (As an example, think of the ways that membership in the European Union has changed the meaning of migration for European citizens.) When sociologists think about international migration as taking place within a group of historically connected states (as opposed to unidirectional travel across the well-defined boundaries of separate sovereign nations), they may use a *migration systems approach*. When they focus on relationships that individual migrants have to loved ones left behind, they are using a *transnationalist approach*.

According to the migration systems perspective, the dynamics of migration involve the entire global and international political, economic, cultural, and social context in which migration takes place, as well as the dynamics of the migration streams themselves and the feedback mechanisms they generate (Massey et al., 1998; Kritz, Lim, and Zlotnik, 1992). Migration systems "fundamentally consist of countries that exchange relatively large numbers of migrants, [and] they are also characterized by certain feedback mechanisms that connect movements of people (immigrants, students, tourists, and employees) to concomitant flows of goods, capital, ideas, and information. Economic, cultural, and political links form a network of relationships holding international migration systems together" (Massey et al., 1998, p. 60). Migration systems are configurations of countries linked to one another through political and economic relationships that continue today, although the links originated in past eras of imperialism, colonialism, or the trade in slaves and other commodified natural resources. In a way, a migration system may even be understood as a small configuration of the world economic system and world racial hierarchy. Though history has reshaped relationships—for example, the colonizer no longer rules over the colonized in the same way—political and economic ties are still in evidence today in things like shared languages, interdependent economies, and conjoined politicoeconomic systems that may designate former colonies as today's commonwealths. Nations in migration systems transfer among themselves capital and labor because the economic and cultural ghosts of these historic connections linger.

The systems approach explains why a given set of migrants chooses unique destinations at select historical moments instead of choosing among an innumerable number of towns and cities all over the world. Accordingly, historical political and economic ties and close geographic proximity explain why black Caribbeans move in large numbers to Britain but not New Zealand, and why West Indians began to move to the United States only after it began recruiting these same black workers to labor, first, in the U.S.-run Panama Canal Zone and, later (under the Bracero Program), in U.S. groves and plantations. The systems approach, then, causes us to look at political and economic history to explain migration links among particular sets of nations. But political and economic national histories are only part of the story of how migration has "gone global."

With the aid of newer technologies, such as aircraft transportation and electronic communication, migrants have not only transported shared information but have also carried on increasingly more global lives, a phenomenon that has come to be known as *transnationalism*. Transnationalism emphasizes that crossing borders is more of a process than a unique event that begins when someone departs their homeland and ends when they arrive on the opposite shore. As migrants often and regularly share the wealth they earn with those they have left behind, they socioeconomically support extended networks of family and friends to a degree that has considerable impact on a nation's balance of payments (Basch, Schiller, and Blanc, 1994, p. 278). Migrant voices are also heard transnationally through their exercise of political rights and the sharing of cultural events in ways that were not possible before (Levitt, 1999; Smith, 1993; Kasinitz, 1992).[3]

Between the systems and transnationalism approaches, then, we can be sure to know that migration is more than a one-time geographic relocation. At minimum, we must consider long-term and continuous two-way relationships among migrants, their kith, kin, community, and state.

Summary

A truly international approach to international migration will not simply focus on the ways newcomers affect the host society they enter, or on whether they succeed or fail, but instead will also take into account the ways that migrants and the societies with which they come into contact interact with larger international systems (such as those of economy, politics, and race). It is useful, then, to know the global context in which Caribbean network migration takes place before examining the specifics of Caribbean network operations. Thus, the remainder of this chapter is devoted to applying the global economic, global racial hierarchy, and transnationalist migration systems approaches to understanding Caribbean migration.

Historical Overview of Eastern Caribbean Emigration

The term *West Indies* was coined to describe the islands that Christopher Columbus found in the Caribbean Sea while he was on a mission from the King and Queen "to go by way of the West to India" to secure land and riches for Spain (Parry, Sherlock, and Maingot, 1987, p. 2).[4] (Although he had contemporaries who disputed his claim, until his death Columbus believed he had landed off the coast of Asia.) He brought these already inhabited lands to the attention of Europeans eager to transport back and forth people, plants, animals, and goods. An avid naturalist as well as explorer, he wrote letters describing his exuberance at his findings. "No where is the ambivalence of the European psyche toward the New World more evident than in Columbus' description of the innocence and generosity of the natives, which is followed by a discussion of how they could be Christianized and converted into slaves."[5] In the ensuing years of international contact the islands' population of native inhabitants (the Arawaks, Tainos, and the Caribs, or as the latter called themselves, the Calinago) were decimated by attempted enslavement and outright slaughter as well as disease; the current inhabitants who remain descend mainly from a mixture of transplants from the European and African continents (Parry, Sherlock, and Maingot, 1987; Murray, 1991; Hart, 1998). As Knight and Palmer (1989, p. 1) write, "The European intrusion abruptly interrupted the original pattern of [the] historical development [of indigenous societies of Caribbean states]. It severely altered their physical environment. It diversified their diet, complicated their epidemiological systems, produced new biological strains, and linked them inextricably to the wider world beyond the Atlantic Ocean. There they have remained."

The term *Caribbean* normally refers to "the islands from the Bahamas to Trinidad, and the continental enclaves of Belize, Guyana, Suriname, and French Guiana" (Knight and Palmer, 1989, p. 3). Africans may have first arrived on these lands bordering the Caribbean Sea in the pre-Columbian era as visiting freedmen (Van Sertima, 1976; Williams, 1984). European domination came with the Spanish during the 1500s, and later the English, Dutch, and French. In some cases, rival colonizers divided individual West Indian territories (such as Hispaniola, St. Kitts, and Guiana) between them, and in other cases colonizers succeeded one another after gaining control through war or purchase (such as in St. Croix and St. Vincent) (Knight and Palmer, 1989; Williams, 1984). Though small, these islands had astounding value both as territories in their own right and as centers for trade (Williams, 1984).

Via Columbus, the Spanish introduced the region to sugar cane and to enslavement to procure labor for both gold mines and cane fields, while in Hispaniola the English initiated the trade in slaves (Williams, 1984). The Spanish also sought white labor in a series of migration schemes that unsuccessfully first targeted convicts, white slaves, and non-Spaniards, and only later, Spaniards, whose status as colonizers made them poor laborers. Initially, "the free colored population grew relatively rapidly as compared to the (small) slave population and to the white population (though overall population growth was slow), and the free colored were generally not very distinct from white or Indian free people" (Stinchcombe, 1995, p. 12). But in the sixteenth and seventeenth centuries, with the native population decimated,[6] about 4.5 million Africans were imported as slaves into the Caribbean islands (Simmons and Guengant, 1992). Slavery was not universally applied; it did not dominate those islands that had no sugar plantations (Stinchcombe, 1995, p. 55), and in the fifty years before the end of the institution, slave conditions improved somewhat (Parry, Sherlock, and Maingot, 1987). But on sugar islands, where the region's black enslaved population could be found, slavery's practices were particularly barbarous. Whites were found in larger numbers where sugar plantations were not (Williams, 1984; Parry, Sherlock, and Maingot, 1987; Stinchcombe, 1995). Extremely high mortality rates for these involuntary migrants required tens of thousands of annual replacements. Still, slave trading was so profitable it was the cornerstone of the "triangular trade."[7] Escape from the plantation was extraordinarily difficult, although it happened with some frequency (hence the harsh punishments for those who succeeded in escaping); revolts were frequent too—and some of these were successful in establishing freedmen's communities. Unfortunately, white abolitionists in the Caribbean did not construct an Underground Railroad as they did on the colonial mainland, even though in the late 1700s a slave brought to England would be free (if only he could escape the master who had brought him there) (Williams, 1984).

The creation of races was not solely or even primarily to justify enslavement, but it became part and parcel of a larger project of political and economic domination, and the creation of inequality and protection of privilege was this domination's expressive counterpart. For example, mulattoes (persons of both black and white parentage) were free but did not enjoy rights equal to whites, and neither did freed former slaves.[8] Emancipation spread throughout the region during the 1800s, and with it came a freedom of movement that allowed former slaves to move to other Caribbean islands, a trend that quickly gained momentum (especially in the Eastern Caribbean). Former slaves knew that new labor arrangements forcing them to remain on their home islands meant working for the same masters who had once considered them chattel, at wages and under conditions too abysmal to ensure survival; and newly imposed land taxes and the outright destruction of land and trees stunted the efforts of many to establish self-sufficiency through land ownership (Williams, 1984; Simmons and Guengant, 1992; Parry, Sherlock, and Maingot, 1987). In other words, black people emigrated within and away from the Caribbean plantations as long as they were free to do so, with only relatively brief periods of lessened outflow (Marshall, 1987). To rid themselves of ties to plantation labor but retain the ability to feed their families and keep their societies afloat, first men and later women had to be ready to migrate to work wherever opportunities were open. Since the beginning of the era of free and voluntary movement and to the present day, Africa's descendants in the Caribbean have lived by a philosophy of *strategic flexibility*, a mind-set that allows and encourages one to take whatever economic mobility opportunities may become available (Carnegie, 1987).

Although many did remain and worked the lands, for much of the 1880s people moved by sea away from their homelands for opportunities on other islands. Inter-Caribbean movement to Trinidad and Tobago and British Guiana dominated the five decades beginning in 1835. Planters in these countries had active recruitment programs that represented most of the available Eastern Caribbean economic opportunities at the time, so persons from all the Eastern Caribbean islands participated. In the case of Barbados, so many people left to find work that the government enacted legislation to cease emigration, which they soon had to rescind because they determined that out-migration was the better alternative to the polity's starvation. Active encouragement of emigration has remained the region's policy since (Marshall, 1987). This was also when Asian (mainly Indian and Chinese) indentured migrants arrived in large numbers, but more West Indians left than Asians entered (Williams, 1984).

After 1885, Caribbean emigration fluctuated between high and low levels and extended to territories beyond the immediate Eastern Caribbean islands. Black movers searched for work on sugar plantations in Cuba and the Dominican Republic, on railroads and banana plantations in Central America, on dry docks in Bermuda, and in the United States. Between 1880 and 1914 West Indians sought work in Panama on the canal. Railroad construction was also available in Panama from 1850 to 1855, employing about five thousand black Caribbeans. The French ran the canal project between 1880 and 1889 during which time fifty thousand arrived. Next, the British controlled the area with a new system of racism—one that relied on an unstable system of cajolery, flattery, tokenism, and cooptation of lighter-skinned blacks and was different from the French system. Another 150,000 arrived between 1902 and 1914, during American canal construction, when racial discrimination involved segregated and differently remunerated labor markets, and a replication of the Jim Crow racism that gripped the United States at the time was instituted (Conniff, 1985). During the early years of American tenure in the Canal Zone, a small proportion of black West Indians followed opportunities in the United States. Movement to the United States from 1821 to 1831 averaged about four hundred persons per year and more than a thousand persons per year from 1831 to 1880; the numbers then increased steadily until 1921 (Simmons and Guengant, 1992). Altogether, between 1885 and 1914, about 130,000 persons left the Caribbean (the largest numbers coming from Jamaica and Barbados). When Canal building ceased in 1914 and sugar prices crashed in 1921, emigration from these islands all but ceased, and unemployment forced many to return to their islands of birth.

The United States forged important geopolitical links with much of the independent Caribbean, above and beyond its protection of the Canal Zone area. American fears of and efforts to control European influence in the Caribbean caused President Roosevelt in 1902 to issue a corollary to the Monroe Doctrine that "logically implied the intention to exercise, where necessary, a degree of supervision over the internal affairs of independent states" (Parry, Sherlock, and Maingot, 1987, p. 224). This translated into military intervention in Cuba, which resulted in concentration of "economic control of the island

more firmly in the hands of a relatively small group of New York financiers"
(Parry, Sherlock, and Maingot 1987, p. 229). Cuba, having the closest proximity to the United States of all the Caribbean islands, was seen as most strate-
gically important, while the other states that were independent at the time
(Haiti and the Dominican Republic) suffered less from drastic interventions
of this kind. When the U.S. forces finally left the Dominican Republic and
Haiti, they gave up control of politics but not of customs (Parry, Sherlock,
and Maingot, 1987, p. 233). Puerto Rico, once one of the poorest of the Spanish
colonies, was ceded to the United States by the 1898 Treaty of Paris. Its uneasy
protocolonial relationship with the United States continues. It is representative of those islands that were targets of U.S. intervention in order to turn
them into Cold War-era models of the triumph of capitalism; other islands
(such as Cuba) whose governments leaned away from capitalism were made
into negative models (Grosfoguel, 1997).

In the English-speaking Caribbean, the situation was somewhat (although
not entirely) different. Even though some islands had mineral resources (Trinidad had oil, asphalt, and natural gas; Guyana, Jamaica, and the Dominican
Republic had bauxite; Guyana had gold and emeralds; and Jamaica had gyp-
sum) and pioneer industries were set up and protected, sugar production was
still central to the region well after the days of plantation slavery had ended,
to the extent that "the price of sugar was still the barometer of West Indian
prosperity" (Parry, Sherlock, and Maingot, 1987, p. 253). Industrialization and
diversification, first prevented by colonial administrations' worship of King
Sugar, never reached levels sufficient to absorb the available labor.

The Early Unwelcome

There was always a black presence in the United States; the first blacks to arrive
in the lands that would be the U.S. nation were free, but the United States ac-
quired most of its black population through a long history of forced migration
of enslaved African persons. Moreover, black people have not made up a significant proportion of the large stream of voluntary immigrants to the United
States at any given time. Racism in U.S. immigration law began with a focus on
other groups (Asians in particular), but once immigration policymakers' eyes
were focused on race they would hardly be unable to ignore it as a condition of
entry (Lee, 2002). The first racially exclusionary law, in 1882, barred the Chinese and ushered in a long history of racial discrimination in immigration.

In this early period, black immigration was not on the radar for U.S.

officials, perhaps for two reasons. One, since slavery ended in the United States later than in the United Kingdom and Canada, those designated as racially black were more likely to leave the United States in this period (and travel to Canada, as we have seen) than they were to enter. Two, levels of West Indian migrants reached significant levels only in later periods, so U.S. legislators only later codified legal language that would specifically exclude blacks.[9]

From 1920 to 1940 the only real migration outlets for Eastern Caribbeans were to go to Venezuela to work in the oil fields (about ten thousand entered until 1929, when Venezuela restricted entry of foreign-born blacks) or to Curaçao to work in the newly built refinery (whereupon Curaçao became a migrant receiver rather than sender). The ebb and flow of migration ceased around the Great Depression: island populations increased and economic crises occurred as people were forced to remain in their home countries. Sugar producers tried to offset low prices by increasing and reorganizing production in the 1930s, but they had to negotiate with the Ministry of Food (from 1939–1952 the sole importer of sugar to the United Kingdom), which would negotiate prices and quotas each year. West Indian producers traded some measure of control for industry stability. Sugar producers (along with Jamaica's banana producers, Grenada's nutmeg growers, and growers of cotton, rice, coconut, citrus, and cane elsewhere) formed coalitions to sustain and improve production (Parry, Sherlock, and Maingot, 1987, pp. 254–55). When workers struck to demand attention, they created "the first enduring labour organisations of the British West Indies. Trade unions sprang up overnight, and some unions became political parties" (Parry, Sherlock, and Maingot, 1987, p. 258). The concerns of labor became a big part of the national and nationalist agendas of rising politicos such as Vere Cornwall Bird (Antigua), Grantley Adams (Barbados), Marcus Garvey, William Alexander Bustamante and Michael Manley (Jamaica), Robert Bradshaw (St. Kitts), and Eric Williams (Trinidad) (Parry, Sherlock, and Maingot, 1987, pp. 256–58), some of whom, along with a number of ascendant intellectuals, also addressed issues of race.

As for the Canadian populace, enslaved black people were some of its earliest entrants. In 1628 the first slave arrived in French-owned Canada, and by 1750 there were four thousand (Winks, 1971). In 1843, all slaves were manumitted in Canada, by then a British territory. Antiblack discrimination in Canadian immigration policy began in 1818, well before emancipation, with a law that disallowed black immigration (Marshall, 1987). Two antiblack themes were evident in the public and private statements of Canadian immigration policymakers, although neither applied when black labor was sought, either by enslavement or labor recruitment, to do the worst of the available work.

First, they agreed that blacks from tropical regions could not survive or succeed in cold climes and therefore should not be admitted. This argument was first promulgated in Canada in the late 1600s by the governor of New France, Denonville, but was also used throughout the 1950s (see Winks, 1971, pp. 5–6, 436). Blacks strongly protested this characterization (Winks, 1971, pp. 438–39). Although Canada viewed itself as a haven to runaway slaves in the pre-Civil War period, immigration of free blacks was never welcome—whites were always preferred immigrant stock.

When the state government of Louisiana appeared to have fallen into Negro hands in 1868, the Montreal *Gazette* asked its readers to "imagine us in Canada, as the result of war, or annexation, or anything else, ruled by blacks." Nowhere, said the editorialist, may the two races "exist together as equals"— certainly not in the new Dominion of Canada after 1867. By the end of the century most of the original fugitives who had remained in Canada had died [but many remained, and most of these were under age twenty-one.] For the first time some Canadians became aware that their country might continue to be a home for a small but highly visible black minority, and that the Negro race could well increase. Earlier postures of acceptance shown by whites could now turn to gestures of rejection, for Canada was susceptible to the same pseudo-anthropology and pseudoscience that grew between 1870 and 1930 in Western Europe, Britain, and the United States (Winks 1971, pp. 291–92).

The second theme in Canadian policymakers' arguments was the idea that admitting blacks meant the nation was just asking for problems (that is, race riots) that Britain and the United States had to bear for having black residents. To solve whatever race problems might arise, so the thinking went, it was better just not to have any more blacks in the country than necessary. In 1899 the Department of the Interior issued a report noting "it is not desired that any Negro immigrants should arrive in Western Canada" and the secretary of immigration instructed a Kansas City immigration official that Canadian immigration agents should not promote such immigration (Boyko, 1995, p. 156). In 1910 the government created "Okfuskee County, where the Negro population ran over forty percent, in order to put all Negroes in one township" (Winks, 1971, p. 302). Yet only one settlement (Amber Valley) survived beyond World War I and the Great Depression, mainly because the government did not allow immigrants to enter and replenish the community (Winks, 1971).

As a Toronto *Mail and Empire* editorial argued, "Canada wants no negro question . . . no race riots" (Winks, 1971, p. 310) while the *Globe and Mail* issued an editorial warning, "If Negroes and white people cannot live together in the South, they cannot live in accord in the North" (Boyko, 1995, p. 155). From 1911 to 1914, scandalous writings were traded in the Toronto and Canadian newspapers regarding the Canadian immigration authorities' desire to prevent Negro immigration. (In the papers, black migrants from the United States and the West Indies were referred to as "Black Demons," while the inflow of their migration was labeled the "Black Peril" (Boyko, 1995, p. 155). It is unclear whether these editorials reflected or incited similar sentiments among the Canadian populace; however, Boyko argues that constant repetition of these stereotypes made it easier to organize against black immigration, as some did. For example, "In 1910 and 1911, the Boards of Trade of nearly every prairie town, as well as the cities of Winnipeg, Calgary and Edmonton, passed resolutions demanding that Black immigration be stopped and that those already in Canada be either strictly segregated or, even better still, deported. Most claimed to be speaking on behalf of their entire community and not just the business elite" (1995, p. 155). For their part, government officials had already been taking action to stop black immigration.

The term *race* was first used as a category of exclusion in Section 38(c) of the Canadian Immigration Act of 1910, whereby those "deemed unsuitable" or "undesirable" or having a "probable inability to become readily assimilated" could be denied entry (Jakubowski, 1997, p. 16). Black immigration to Canada was banned by the Laurier Cabinet, which in May 1911 passed Order in Council 115 which was rescinded on a technicality of legislative procedure when U.S. officials voiced objections to the official blockage of the exit of U.S. blacks to Canada (Boyko, 1995, p. 155). Canada then imposed bureaucratic barriers to immigration in the form of set minimum educational and financial requirements for entry. It had become obvious that these normal barriers to entry would not keep out blacks, since those who attempted to cross the border routinely exceeded the minimum entry requirements for education and visible means of support. To further restrain black entry, officials only threatened to institute some legal means (to institute head taxes for blacks and amend the Immigration Act of 1910 to make Negro exclusion official) but successfully implemented others and, when necessary, resorted to underhanded measures, such as paying kickbacks to medical staff for each black person turned back at the border after the required medical examination (Winks,

1971), or turning back entire families because of the medical problem of one member (Boyko, 1995). It was expected that many Negroes could be turned back at the border by a strict application of standing regulations on health, literacy, and financial support,"[10] and many were. Immigration officials were aided by railroad companies, which cooperated in the ban by removing black riders while reducing or waiving fares for white migrants (Boyko, 1995).

While Canadians recruited white Americans to relocate, whatever means necessary were used to keep blacks from entering and settling. Great Northern Railway workers were informed that train tickets should not be sold to Negroes because they would not be admitted to Canada under any circumstances. All blacks from below the Mason Dixon line were understood to be unable to withstand the northern clime; this particular stereotype was applied to black West Indians even up to the 1950s.[11] In Canada, black people supposedly smelled bad; were biologically and mentally inferior, lazy and unreliable, and sexually promiscuous; and embodied other standard characteristics found in black stereotypes promulgated throughout the United States, South Africa, and Australia.

The account of Britain's early black in-migration presents similar themes. Certainly, there was a resident black population from early in Britain's history. Black slaves were brought into England in 1555. By 1600 Queen Elizabeth I determined that "the black presence in England had become a 'problem' and in January 1601, she issued a proclamation to deport 'Negroes and blackamoores'" (Ramdin, 1999, p. 14). But the transport of black slaves from the West Indies and North America continued, even long after a 1772 order declared that blacks could not be forcibly transported across the seas without their consent. Enslaved persons were recruited to fight against revolutionaries in the Americas starting in 1775 by the promise of their freedom at the war's end. Many freed in this way traveled to the West Indies and Canada, while others went to Britain. Jobless and destitute, they were provided assistance by the newly established Committee for the Relief of the Black Poor, but the relief plan evolved into a 1786 House of Commons-approved plan to expel the black poor and send them to a settlement in Sierra Leone. Some blacks did leave on a fateful voyage in 1787, where harsh conditions that were equated with transport under slavery caused death and drove some to suicide by drowning (Ramdin, 1999).

During the colonial era, British subjects were, in principle, freely able to travel to the English motherland. However, the popular image of a nation of unrestricted entry for former colonials is less than accurate. During Britain's period of colonial domination in the Caribbean, residents of the colonies in the Caribbean and elsewhere were technically British subjects. Prior to 1900 and continuing into the early twentieth century, black seamen settled in port towns (Liverpool, London, Cardiff, Bristol, and so forth), yet these men were subject to "state reinforced discriminatory practices" which attempted to severely restrict their settlement and see that they were remunerated at wages lower than white workers. The men were also subject to racist violence and "repatriation" from a country where they, on paper, belonged (Solomos, 1993). The prevailing sentiment about black settlement was captured in the *Western Mail*, distributed in Cardiff:

> Morality and cleanliness are as much matters of geography as they are dependent on circumstances. The coloured men who have come to dwell in our cities are being made to adopt a standard of civilization they cannot be expected to understand. They are not imbued with moral codes similar to our own, and they have not assimilated our conventions of life. They come into contact with white women, principally those who unfortunately are of loose moral character, with the result that a half-caste population is brought into the world.[12]

World War I, the Interwar Period, and World War II

In the period of world wars that overwhelmed Western nations and economies, policymakers struggled to balance disdain for black entry with the need for combatants and laborers. Economic and political pragmatism ushered in a period of black recruitment during the world wars and the interwar period that was to bring temporary black sojourners who, it was hoped, would leave when no longer needed.

Black soldiers and seamen migrated to and served for Britain during World War I and World War II, but these recruits were expected to return to their land of origin after their service. To ensure their return, the government fought to have them repatriated from the land where they were supposed to be citizens, and throughout their stay they suffered maltreatment and were racially segregated. Intense efforts were made to ensure that those who remained faced extreme difficulty in finding employment, as well as the threat of deportation: the government confiscated military recruits' passports, legislated strict limitations on recruits' ability to work, and in whatever ways possible actively limited their ability to stay in Britain (Paul, 1997).

A similar fate faced blacks who desired to live in Canada. From emancipation until 1930 "the Negro there found himself sliding down an inclined plane from mere neglect to active dislike" as Canadian immigration authorities struggled to ensure that blacks would not enter and live in Western Canada (Winks, 1971, p. 292). Fearing a black exodus from the Bahamas, officials re-assured themselves with the idea that "presumably, many Negroes could be turned back at the border by a strict application of standing regulations on health, literacy, and financial support" (Winks, 1971, p. 308). Until the outbreak of World War I, blacks were readily denied entry into Canada, either on an ad-hoc basis or by variously applied institutional means.

At first Canada did not search for World War I recruits among the black population and took the extra step of limiting enlistments to very few and broadly rejecting black volunteers. Only in 1916, "in Nova Scotia, contrary to regulations, they enlisted black Bermudans as officers' servants and such Negro seamen as deserted from West Indian schooners" (Winks, 1971, p. 317). During the Second World War, according to Winks (1971), West Indians were cut off from going into Britain and turned to Canada as an alternative. Canada again turned away black volunteers at the beginning of World War II, and college students from the West Indies were turned away from officer training because training program administrators interpreted "British subjects" to mean whites. But later, blacks were "accepted as equals into both the regular army and the officer corps, the majority (among whom would be the first premier of independent Barbados, Errol Barrow) receiving their training virtually without incident" (Winks 1971, p. 421). But disdain for new black immigrants continued unabated, for at the end of the Second World War, Canada had the opportunity to acquire Dominion territories, including Bermuda and British Guyana. Canadian officials declined the offer. Even the possibility of acquiring territory as part of the spoils of war did not appeal to the Canadian government if that meant acquiring the blacks who live in it.

By the end of World War II, Canadian West Indians were organizing to liberalize Canadian immigration law. They had two main concerns: first, to change the personal affront represented by the 1910 immigration law, and second, to help other West Indians come to Canada (Winks, 1971). The Immigration Branch of the Canadian government had a longstanding bias against black workers from the Caribbean. In 1952, the Prime Minister declared that "persons from tropical countries or sub-tropical countries find it more difficult to succeed in the highly competitive Canadian economy" (Avery, 1995, p. 204). Policymakers in 1958 publicly noted that although British whites were encouraged to come from their Caribbean colonies, "no encouragement is given to persons of coloured race, unless they have close relatives in Canada or their visas have exceptional merit, such as graduate nurses, qualified stenographers, etc." (Avery, 1995, p. 204). "A January, 1955, immigration policy statement also claimed that West Indian migrants did 'not assimilate readily and pretty much vegetate to a low standard of living . . . many cannot adapt themselves to our climatic conditions.'"[13]

In the United States, a national quota system was begun with emergency legislation in 1921 that was solidified in the 1924 National Origins Act. The provisions of this act remained in effect until 1965, effectively barring Asian and severely limiting Eastern European immigrants (even during the Holocaust of World War II). The "facts" in Senate Report 1515 provided much of the "research" that congressmen used to decide the law. The report's authors based their racial knowledge on Blumenbach's 1775 racial classification. Blumenbach used Linnaeus's term *Caucasian* to rank highly those he deemed to be more beautiful than other human beings in a racial classification scheme that further classified whites from different regions into even more specific subgroups (Gould, 1994; Jaffe, 1961, p. 104).[14] To ensure entry for greater numbers of whites from western and northern European countries, legislators set entry quotas for each nation at 2 percent of that nation's resident population according to base population numbers from the 1890 census (purposefully ignoring the changes to the population composition that would have been reflected in later censuses and would have given greater access to other "racial" groups) (Idea Works, 1995; Wang, 1975; Jaffe, 1961). "The conceded purpose of the Act was to preserve the racial and ethnic makeup of the United States as it had existed in 1890. There was no attempt to deny this purpose or to sugarcoat it. The day the Act became law, the *New York Times* announced it with the following headline: 'Chief aim . . . is to preserve racial type as it exists here today'" [sic] (Glasser, 1996). Even if language did not legislate specifically against black entry, in the 1920s scientific racism was used to justify the exclusion of all such "inferior races" on grounds of inferior intellect or concern for the health of the larger population (Wang, 1975; Jaffe, 1961), and scientists argued that "immigrants' poor performance [was attributable] to Negroid strains inherent in their biological character" (Wang, 1975, p. 61). While not overstating the importance of the Klan's political views in shaping public policy, it may be important to note that "the Imperial Wizard of the Ku Klux Klan proclaimed the passage of the [1924] immigration law to be one of the group's 'recent and important triumphs'" (Wang, 1975, p. 125). But the Klan's sentiments were not outside the norm, for "there is no question that the 1924 law had an exceptionally wide base of congressional support" (Wang 1975, p. 125).

However, as the front door closed to Europeans with the 1921 and 1924 acts, the Bracero Program "opened the back door" of hard agricultural labor once again to Mexicans (Calavita, 1994, p. 59). It is not well known that between 1942 and 1945 this door gave access also to black West Indians, who comprised 17 percent of the 400,000 workers entering under the program (Marshall, 1987), which ended in 1964.

Western Hemisphere nations were, on paper, exempt from the 1924 national quotas imposed by the United States, and some writers believed that the natives of the West Indies were also exempt (see, for example, Garis, 1927, p. 261). However, the islands of the British West Indies were not independent states and for most of the quota-free period they did not qualify to send migrants freely to the United States. Thus, black persons from the Caribbean desiring to travel to the United States had to apply for visas as British subjects and vie for immigration visas in the quota set aside for British citizens. Certainly there were ways to differentiate racially among those applying for admission, even in the presumably quota-free and independent Western Hemisphere; this was accomplished by discriminating on the basis of the race of the majority of applicants from a given Western Hemisphere country (Hutchinson, 1981, p. 488).[15] However, even if those measures could not be counted on to restrict black immigration, an amendment put forth by Congressman Walter Judd and accepted into the bill that became law would do the job. Adopted were both his "cleverly conceived plan simultaneously to remove and retain discrimination" and an ancestry test for admission eligibility specifically designed for "curtailing Negro immigration from the West Indies" (Jaffe, 1961, p. 69). To further curtail black immigration, Congress accepted a dependency provision, making a separate quota for black Caribbean migration from British territories. "Although these migrants were formerly chargeable to the United Kingdom, [with the new law] they were now assigned to a special annual quota of one hundred within the mother country quota" (Jaffe, 1961, p. 77). The special limits to British territories, then, were specifically intended to limit black Caribbean immigrants, for the United Kingdom had a designated quota for white admittees that it did not fill. In 1922, for example, the United States admitted 42,670 immigrants from the United Kingdom; they represented only 55 percent of the quota allocated for that year (National Industrial Conference Board, 1923, p. 69, Table 9).

Presumably, then, Caribbean people should have had free access to travel to Britain during its colonial domination in the Caribbean, as residents of the colonies were technically British subjects and legislation did not specify travel restrictions on subjects of color. But this idea is inaccurate for, as we have seen, efforts were made to restrict movement and repatriate seamen and servicemen, and these measures foretold how other black immigrants would be viewed. Black laborers were discouraged from staying or entering, despite widespread postwar labor shortages in

> agriculture, coal mining, textiles, construction, foundry work, health services, and institutional domestic service. In an attempt to meet these shortages, the [British] government quickly arranged to import an additional 180,000 prisoners of war from the United States and Canada, launched a domestic productivity drive, urged women to return to work, and in October 1947 instituted a Control of Engagement Order. [Paul, 1997, p. 67]

Still the shortages were not alleviated, and the search for labor was further expanded—but not to include blacks. The British Colonial Office recruitment drive was focused on Polish and Irish immigrants and other more assimilable types. Governors in the West Indian colonies first responded to the Colonial Office's general call for labor by encouraging black West Indian migration—to the horror of British mainland officials, who threatened outright bans on black migration (Dean, 1993). Instead of openly banning black migration, government officials issued warnings to colonial governors that they could soon issue new controls on black colonial departures. The Ministry of Labour tried to convince groups recruiting colonials that the labor shortages they'd advertised did not exist. They then set out to prove that West Indians would be unsuitable workers. In this vein, they appealed to the often-used climatic reference, this time to suggest that black immigrant women could not "stand up to the Lancashire climate for any length of time" (Paul, 1997, p. 122). Finally, British officials appealed to black potential immigrants themselves: "the information given to would-be immigrants was distinctly discouraging, stressing cold winters, unsatisfactory employment, poor accommodation prospects and even the peculiarity of English custom" (Dean, 1993, p. 58).

Postwar Period Through Caribbean National Independence

Two themes marked the postwar period of antiblackness in Western immigration. First, there was movement to restrict the influx of black persons without specifically using racial language or appearing racist. Second, Anglophone nations demonstrated codependent racial relations—Western legislators in one country monitored and reacted to racial changes in the others. (Note that evidence of codependency in policy existed in earlier periods. Before the postwar period, legislators noted they didn't want to inherit the race problems of other countries, and to do this they avoided accepting black immigrants.) Legislators in this period were more explicit about how the actions of one nation's leaders affected policy in another.

In the United States in 1952, the passage of the Walter-McCarran Immigration Act finally imposed national quotas on formerly exempt Western Hemisphere nations. As before, they resorted to the use of an earlier census (this time, 1920), which would provide a basis for quotas that was more favorable to whites (this time using a broader definition of who was white) (Jaffe, 1961). Quotas for all of Asia were 2,990, compared to Europe's 149,667; but the African continent had a quota of only 1,400 visas (Keely, 1979, p. 54). This immigration act slowed the renewed postwar migration of Caribbean migrants to the United States to a trickle, causing black migrants to again seek out English shores instead. The NAACP publicly expressed their

> disapproval of the new law, particularly those provisions with racist implications which damaged America's "image." Negro leaders also attacked the 1920 census basis, the failure to provide for pooling [of the unused quota admission slots], failure to provide adequate review machinery, unfair procedures, and the distinctions between native-born and naturalized citizens. But Negro opinion was forthcoming only well after the critical stages in the struggle [against this legislation] were over. [Jaffe, 1961, p. 207]

Along with the NAACP, the Congress of Industrial Organizations publicly condemned the act, the *New York Times* printed critical editorials for the first seven months of 1952,[16] and the Catholic Church issued a statement of their objection (Jaffe, 1961).

It is thought that the flow of West Indians to Britain became significant in size only after the Walter-McCarran Act came into effect. The Act was passed

> over the strenuous objections and veto of President Truman, who considered the act discriminatory and unnecessarily restrictionist. Known also as the McCarran-Walter Act (after its sponsors in the Senate and House), the INA

[Immigration and Nationality Act of 1952] allotted each country an annual quota of immigrants, based on the proportion of people from that country present in the United States in 1920. It thus perpetuated the so-called national origins system that President Truman and others found offensive. In addition, it put a ceiling of 150,000 individuals on immigration from the Eastern Hemisphere but set no such limit for Western Hemisphere countries. Finally, it established the preference system for immigrant workers and close relatives of U.S. citizens and residents, the basic structure of which remains intact today. In brief, the preference system placed priority on family unification, giving first preference to the immediate family of citizens and legal residents, but still keeping the door open to skilled and unskilled workers in certain occupational categories. [Calavita, 1984, p. 62]

Thus, the United States solved its racial dilemma by using the language of "family reunification" to assure that the white-dominated immigrant population would continue to bring other whites. This caused problems for Britain, for it narrowed an important outlet for potential Caribbean migrants. In this period, the transnationalization of antiblackness in immigration became quite clear.

In December 1954 . . . the [U.K.] Cabinet [instructed] the home and Colonial Secretaries—the principal advocates of [immigration] control—to prepare an immigration control bill. The Cabinet's decision was partly influenced by the tide of colonial migration, which, according to Gwylim Lloyd George, had risen from two thousand in 1953 to ten thousand for 1954. In response to this significant increase, and convinced that "these large parties do not just happen," U.K. officials searched for those responsible. They need not have looked far. Throughout the nineteenth and early twentieth centuries, the vast majority of West Indian migrants had remained within the Caribbean or traveled to the United States, where entry was fairly easy for those who could pass basic literacy and medical tests since the Caribbean was included within the generous British visa quota. In 1952, however, responding to domestic pressures to reduce black immigration, the U.S. government through the McCarran-Walter Act separated the West Indies from the United Kingdom and gave all the islands a much-reduced single visa quota of eight hundred. This dramatic curtailment of opportunity forced potential emigrants to find an alternative destination. [Paul, 1997, pp. 141–42]

In 1965, U.S. policymakers changed the Immigration Act's terms for formerly exempt Western nations. The intent was to keep immigration levels similar to those of the 1960s (Keely, 1979, p. 57). Besides instituting a new cap of 120,000 on immigrants from the Western Hemisphere (to begin after a four-year transition period intended to cushion the blow Western Hemisphere quotas were expected to be to diplomatic relations in the region), policymakers established labor certification requirements for all entrants not being admitted under family reunification. Then, too, colonies were given their own admission ceilings, again with the intent of limiting black entry.[17]

Moreover, former nonquota immigrants were replaced by two new immigrant classes, *immediate relatives* of citizens and *special immigrants*. These classes were broken down into five categories. One such category includes natives of independent countries of the Western Hemisphere (which now included Jamaica, Trinidad-Tobago, Guyana, and Barbados, formerly charged to the British subquotas), and their spouses and children (whether accompanying the migrant or following him or her later). Beginning July 1, 1968, admissibility of the category of "special immigrant" was limited to 120,000 annually (exclusive of those within the category who were also "immediate relatives" and entering as such) (Sloan, 1987, p. 12). Thus these black nations became subject to quotas, which they shared with nations sending the more desirable white immigrant. Between 1955 and 1959, 20,000 to 33,000 migrants per year moved to the United Kingdom. Thus, the 1952 McCarran-Walter Act had successfully redirected the Caribbean outflow back to England—at least until 1962, when the U.K. Conservative government finally successfully instituted new restrictions that made the United States once again the target destination for black migration.

But the postwar migration of skilled and semiskilled black workers to Britain actually began earlier, in response to the already-mentioned reports of labor shortages. The large-scale flow of black migration from the Caribbean is said to have begun with the arrival of 492 Jamaican immigrants aboard the *Empire Windrush*, which docked in June 1948, but 108 persons of color had arrived on the ship *Ormonde* the year before. Paul (1997) argues that the arrival of the *Windrush* is significant, not because of its false but legendary role in initiating a flow of black immigrants, but rather because of the government's response to these newcomers—a "policy that would hold steady for the next seventeen years . . . [whereby] both government [officials] and administration [civil servants] did all in their power to prevent further arrivals" (p. 111). These civilian British subjects did not fall under the jurisdiction of the Colonial Office, and their migration could not be as easily controlled as the migration of military recruits who entered Britain in the earlier period. "What seems to have alarmed officials," is not merely that these immigrants were black, but that they came under their own volition, which seemed to officials "a premonition of a limitless, uncontrollable invasion" (Paul, 1997, p. 121). The 492 on the *Windrush* were met by government officials and housed under conditions that might be better described as internment. Migrants of color on subsequent ships were treated even more poorly than the *Windrush* arrivals who came before them, and considerably worse than white postwar immigrants who continued to arrive by sea (Paul, 1997).

The British resisted race- and geographic-specific language in 1950s-era legislation because of postwar negotiations with the Commonwealth colonies from which it had begun trying to extract itself (Dean, 1993). Explicit declarations that black immigration to Britain from the Commonwealth was unwelcome would only aggravate independence negotiations, particularly after years of seemingly open and unrestricted entry. Thus, instituting restrictions in the late 1950s and early 1960s required a balancing act, for care had to be taken not to alienate those politicos of color with whom British government officials were negotiating. Indeed, in February 1961, Eric Williams warned Prime Minister Macmillan, "if [Britain] were to withdraw her support and stop West Indian immigration, there would be a social revolution and a Cuban situation in the West Indies" (Dean, 1993, p. 60). Macmillan's political rival, Home Secretary Richard A. Butler, spent quite some time and effort to avoid answering questions from West Indian governments wanting to know the British government's position on immigration. The British government also "agonised about public opinion," trying to keep their seats in power, which meant responding to public opinion calling on them to restrict unwanted nonwhite immigration (Dean, 1993, p. 61). The result? "Faced with [both] electoral and Commonwealth [colonial] considerations, most ministers [of Parliament] clung to the indirect approach, which, of itself, implied that immigration was a matter to be dealt with outside the glare of publicity" (Dean, 1993, p. 63). Meanwhile, Butler worked to have U.S. President John F. Kennedy ease restrictions on West Indians going to the United States, because the Colonial Office believed that these restrictions contributed to the rising numbers of West Indians going to Britain at the time.

The British government finally settled on labor vouchers as the solution to the country's labor shortage dilemma. Dean quotes directly from Butler, who in justifying this policy said:

> The great merit of this [labour vouchers] scheme is that it can be presented as making no distinction on grounds of race and colour. We must recognize that, although the scheme purports to relate solely to employment and to be non-discriminatory, its aim is primarily social and its restrictive effect is intended to and would operate on coloured people almost exclusively. . . . It was hoped to disarm those critics who were prepared to attack any legislation on the grounds that it was discriminatory. The approach satisfied senior mandarins [civil servants] in Whitehall [the seat of government administration]. Norman Brook, the Cabinet secretary, informed Macmillan, "But at least there is no element of racial discrimination in the Bill itself, and the emphasis of the scheme is upon the limitation and not the elimination of coloured immigration." [Dean, 1993, p. 68]

Race-based immigration controls drove the British immigration policy of the 1960s. The 1961 Commonwealth Immigration Act, which finally restricted colored immigration to the United Kingdom, was to be expected, given the long-standing climate against black newcomers. By 1964, the Labour Party was openly expressing "the need of control over Commonwealth immigrants entering this country"—for there were no longer pressing political considerations that required hiding these sentiments. Policymakers were instead concerned that they needed to control the influx of black labor before Britain pushed for admission into the European Economic Community (Dean, 1993, 73). Moreover, as legislators debated and discussed their fears about blacks on English soil, they kept one eye on the events taking place in the 1960s United States, for the U.S. black-led civil rights movement affected public life and politics in Britain, most notably by instilling the fear in white politicians that admitting blacks invites social unrest.

> [Home Secretary] Butler made these anxieties clear to his colleagues when he declared [in May 1961]: "It was now accepted by government supporters generally that some form of [immigration] control was unanswerable if there was not to be a colour problem in this country on a similar scale to that of the USA." Increasingly, [the] Notting Hill and Nottingham [riots of 1958] fitted a wider world context. They were precursors of troubles as resources became more stretched, authority broke down and leisure for larger sections

of the population grew. Britain was supposed to have escaped some of these tensions because of its previous homogeneity. Politicians now feared that such harmony and stability were becoming more fragile. In this light, new communities and new faces were regarded, at best, with suspicion and often with outright hostility. [Dean, 1993, p. 67]

The fear of black immigration in Canada was in the 1950s joined by the greater fear of Asian immigration. Legislators considered removing discriminatory language from immigration legislation and issuing an acknowledgement that Canada needed immigrants, but there was a fear that hordes of Asians and some blacks would rush to enter and that their presence would depress wages (Winks, 1971, pp. 436–7). Contradiction prevailed: the idea was to eliminate undesirables while preserving the notion that "Canada [was] a democratic, humanitarian nation willing to help the distressed" (Winks 1971, p. 437).

Accordingly, the provisions of the act of 1952 gave the minister the power to prohibit the entry of an immigrant because of "nationality, citizenship, ethnic group, occupation, class or geographical area of origin," because of "peculiar customs, habits, modes of life or methods of holding property," and in addition to other provisos, because of "unsuitability having regard to the climatic, economic, social, industrial, educational, labour, health, or other conditions, or requirements existing [in Canada], temporarily or otherwise." . . . Thus, Pickersgill admitted Hungarians without an extensive canvass of public opinion, while Harris, also without resort to polls, rejected West Indians. Blacks protested in particular against the application of a "climatic" criterion to their suitability as immigrants. [Winks, 1971, pp. 435, 437–8]

In the mid-1950s, however, employer recruitment of black workers brought a small group of Caribbean workers to Canada, and recruited Caribbean domestic workers were in high demand in Canada throughout the 1950s and 1960s. At first, domestic workers were imported from Britain, but these workers quickly left their jobs in domestic service and the demand for their replacement was high. Schemes of varying success were tried with Italian and Greek migrant women, but the search for a stable flow of incoming labor caused officials to look toward the Caribbean. In 1955, one hundred domestics were admitted from the West Indies under strict criteria (workers must be unmarried and between the ages of eighteen and thirty-five); by 1960 that number was three hundred. The antiblack anti-immigrant racism that operated in Canadian society and government was equally evident in the domestic worker scheme. Avery writes:

> In the short term, the scheme was regarded as a success since a high proportion of the [Caribbean] immigrants remained in domestic service, not necessarily because they liked the work but because racism excluded them
> 960, Department of Citizenship and Immigration officials
> ng the program despite the generally good performance of West Indian domestics. The reasons for this decision were set forth in a May, 1960, memorandum from the director of immigration, who noted, with some concern, that "these girls, as soon as they are established, are free to apply for the admission of their relatives and fiancés . . . [who] are likely to be unskilled workers." He also claimed, without a shred of evidence, that most of these Caribbean fiancés were frauds since illegitimacy was "a fact of life . . . [and] it is not uncommon for a single girl to have children by 2, 3, or 4 different men." These ethnocentric and biased attitudes, combined with the department's new emphasis on recruiting highly educated workers, meant a curtailment of the program in 1966. When the movement was reinstated in 1973 it was quite different. Caribbean domestics now entered under the temporary employment authorization program, which meant they could only remain in the country if they kept their positions—changing occupation or employers could result in deportation. [Avery, 1995, p. 209]

Beyond the 1960s

Migration remains a viable choice for household and individual economic solvency for many people because Caribbean economies are still far from sufficient to support the polity. Parry, Sherlock, and Maingot (1987, p. 260) note that some island states, smaller territories especially, could not support themselves under conditions of complete independence because the natural resources of the region were limited, agriculture was declining, and industrialization was a small proportion of even the most advanced island economy. In this period, to increase political and economic strength, the region's leaders made a three-year attempt at creating an often-discussed federation. The effort ended in May 1962: once Jamaica quit the federation, the United Kingdom dissolved it, although the causes for its failure are deeper than that (see Parry, Sherlock, and Maingot, 1987, pp. 260–64). For one, the larger states (especially Jamaica and Trinidad) resented having to carry the smaller states, which they saw as properly London's economic burden. Their suspicions of England's motives solidified only when England first passed the Commonwealth Immigrants Act intended to limit Caribbean immigration, and then made immediate efforts to join the European Common Market. In the end, "the larger countries decided to press forward to independence separately, and the smaller countries were left to make the best arrangements they could with Britain" (Parry, Sherlock, and Maingot, 1987, p. 263). Both Jamaica and Trinidad and Tobago achieved independence in August 1962, Barbados in November 1966, Guyana in 1968. Antigua, Barbuda and Redonda, St. Kitts-Nevis-Anguilla, Dominica, Grenada, St. Lucia, and St. Vincent were the first to become Associated States, which allowed for self-government, with military protection and foreign affairs arranged by Britain. The smaller islands gained their independence some years later: Grenada in 1974, Dominica in 1978, St. Lucia in 1979, Saint Vincent and the Grenadines in 1980, Antigua and Barbuda in 1981, and Saint Kitts and Nevis in 1983.

Diplomatic relations with states struggling for or just having newly won independence required a change from indirect racial restriction in the United States, United Kingdom, and Canada to a more explicit language of equality and rights, but policymakers' liberal speech actually served as a mask for continued illiberal immigration policy. Policy in this period also marked a site of continued ambivalence about the merits of admitting the black labor that anchored the racial and economic system even as antiblack racial sentiment would suggest that blacks were altogether undesirable as residents. Thus, the racism in law was couched within a set of contract labor schemes (begun, for the most part, in the 1950s) that attempted to force black workers to be temporary sojourners with neither equal opportunity nor rights.

Even though much of the published immigration literature on Canada suggests that the Canadian government in 1962 removed the most discriminatory provisions from their books, Canadian policymakers continued antiblack sentiments in this period as well.[18] Some argue that this newly perceived antidiscrimination stance must have been right, because "as a result, 75 percent of the immigrants admitted to Canada directly from the West Indies entered after 1962: 149,741 between 1962 and 1976" (Marshall, 1987). To be specific, until 1967, Canada used the family reunification policy to ensure a white immigration pool by operating under the assumption that the Europeans admitted in the past would bring their family members in the future. In 1967 they abandoned this project to emphasize occupational restrictions, at that time declaring family reunification policies to be racist, and implementing a points system emphasizing occupation and education as the criteria required for entry. Black West Indians subsequently arrived in far greater numbers. More than 70 percent of black immigration into Canada at this time was from the Caribbean (Winks, 1971, p. 444). But the application of the new law brought back ad hoc means of discrimination, particularly through the act of requiring potential immigrants to present bonds to prove they had enough money to support themselves. No whites had such a burden (Boyko, 1995). Undeniably, although the racist letter of the law may have changed in the early 1960s, politicians' antipathy toward the black immigrant did not. A longstanding "White Canada policy [was] officially abandoned only in 1962" (Jakubowski, 1997, p. 11) and "indeed the whole lengthy episode of White Canada is often downplayed, or clothed in discreet silence or simply not extrapolated from its historical context."[19]

In January 1966, for example, Tom Kent, the newly appointed deputy minister, was informed about "the long range wisdom" of preventing "a substantial increase in negro immigration to Canada," particularly given the current "racial problems of Britain and the United States." Another brief warned that Canadians, who "in normal circumstances would not have any prejudice in respect to race, colour, or creed, have shown concern that through rapid increases in the intake of under-educated and un-skilled immigrants, especially if multi-racial, we could end up with situations [race riots] similar to those in the United Kingdom" (Avery, 1995, p. 204).

It was agreed that Caribbean workers might be brought in as seasonal contract labor to relieve shortages in the agricultural sector, because as temporary workers they "would not have the privilege of sponsoring innumerable close relatives"—a quote from a letter to the deputy minister from the assistant deputy minister at the time.[20] Canada also began to recruit West Indian migrants by contracting for the entry of one hundred domestic workers in 1955. In the domestic worker scheme Canada instituted in the 1970s, permits were issued to women to work as domestics for two years. At first, women recruited under these schemes were not allowed to apply for citizenship or government benefits, but the government responded to the many complaints by changing the scheme to allow application for citizenship after three years (Henry, 1987). Conversely, few restrictions were imposed against whites who desired to immigrate to Canada. As was the case in the United States, prior to 1966 Canada's immigration pool was composed mainly of unskilled or semiskilled whites from Europe. "Despite some unsatisfactory behavioural traits ascribed to certain ethnic and national groups from Europe, Anglo-Canadian immigration boosters claimed that these traits were primarily based on their past cultural and environmental background. Time and Anglo-Canadian institutions, it was held, would ultimately erase these differences and facilitate the absorption of all-white immigrants into the Anglo-Canadian community" (Avery, 1995, p. 12). In the later years, except for those black Caribbean immigrants entering under the farmworker or domestic recruitment schemes, most immigrants were selected on the basis of skill, that is, they were white-collar professional workers.

The United States, in a 1965 act, significantly changed the racial language and, supposedly, the spirit of its immigration policy, just as Canada had done years before. By one researcher's reasoning, this occurred because "Lyndon Johnson [was] in the presidency and a liberal Congress [was] focused on expanding civil rights" (Calavita, 1984, p. 62). However, as is well known, the impetus behind many of the changes instituted with the 1965 act was the interest in retaining the racial and ethnic immigration structure of the national-origins system, even as they were abolishing the overt mechanisms of that system (that is, the quotas themselves) (Briggs, 1984, pp. 68–69; Borjas, 1990, pp. 30–33). Just as had been done in 1924, in 1952 legislators sought ways to racially discriminate among immigrants, but they sought not to project an obvious racial bias in the law.[21] Occupational preferences were reduced to 20 percent of the available visas and were given downgraded levels of priority, while a new family reunification preference group (for brothers and sisters of citizens) was added and allocated 24 percent of all available visas. In addition, a 1968 amendment to the 1965 act imposed a ceiling of 120,000 immigrants admitted from the Western Hemisphere. This ceiling created a huge backlog of applications for visas, which by 1976 "translated into a waiting period of more than two and a half years for many new applicants" (Briggs, 1984, p. 67).

Prior to 1965, President John F. Kennedy and his administrators decided that language specifically excluding black immigrants was not deemed necessary because blacks were not coming in large numbers to the United States. Of course, in the 1960s that changed and black immigration unexpectedly increased. Three developments may have prompted the changes to U.S. immigration law that were made in 1965. First, when Britain closed its doors with new legislation in 1962, it successfully reversed the flows of black Caribbean people, redirecting them once again to the United States. Second, the American civil rights movement was at hand and glaring racism in immigration law proved an obvious target for protest. Both the United States and Canada made changes to their immigration laws at that time, supposedly to erase discriminatory legislation. The United States removed the national quota system and instituted a policy of family reunification on the assumption that the white Europeans who dominated the inflows to date would continue to bring their relatives. In this way, U.S. legislators could avoid language directly legislating against the entry of nonwhites. Interestingly, at that time Canada's government chose to eliminate family reunification, and its justification was that reunification policies were racially discriminatory. It replaced reunification laws with targeted admittance based on occupation, a move that would take the United States another fifteen years to make. Third, with the new independence of Caribbean nations in the mid-1960s, Caribbean nationals would now qualify for Western Hemisphere exemptions. Because there were not many Caribbean nationals in the United States in the 1960s, replacing the open-door policy for the Western Hemisphere with family reunification rules could seem a less obvious way to exclude the relatively free entry of blacks from the Caribbean Basin.

Thus, the impetus behind many of the changes instituted with the 1965 U.S. Immigration Act was the interest in retaining the racial and ethnic immigration structure of the national-origins system even as the overt mechanisms of that system were being abolished (Briggs, 1984, pp. 68–69; Borjas, 1990, pp. 30–33). Those who did not have relatives already in the United States were forced either to compete for the few visas available under the occupational preference categories or to resort to illegal immigration, unless they qualified for refugee status. By eliminating the hemispheric quota, competition among potential immigrants of different nationalities was equalized, although white collar professionals were given preference. Given the structure of global (and local) inequalities in education and skill levels, white-collar preferences surely have a racial caste. In 1976, the Immigration Act established a limit of 20,000 per country, while retaining the 120,000 limit for the Western Hemisphere (Keely, 1979, p. 59). Certainly, by 1978, when an amendment to the 1965 act eliminated hemispheric quotas and made all individuals equal in the competition for visas, immigrants of color had dominated the flow of persons to the United States, and white immigrants were the minority.

Even with renewed restrictions on blacks desiring to enter the United Kingdom and the United States, recruitment of labor under contract conditions was the order of the day. These contract agreements staffed New York City and London hospitals with black women and ran the operations of British Rail and London Transport (London's unified bus, coach, trolley, and rail service) with black men. For example, of the nearly forty thousand workers (including supervisors) in the employ of London Transport in 1975, seven thousand were "coloured" immigrants, nearly all black workers from the Caribbean islands, and likely from Barbados, Jamaica, Trinidad, and Tobago, where London Transport had active recruitment programs (Brooks, 1975). The ambivalence over inviting black labor persisted, for black workers faced job discrimination and found that their coworkers held a general antipathy against immigrants, while a more vehement brand of animosity was reserved for black immigrants in particular. In Britain, the image of black women workers was particularly unfavorable (Brooks, 1975).

Finally, in this period in the United Kingdom, West Indians' "undesirable" status was solidified by the 1981 Nationality Act, which made aliens of the former black colonial subjects by removing their rights of citizenship. This law, introduced by Prime Minister Thatcher, made explicit the assumption that Britain was threatened by outsiders of a different color, and Home Secretary William Whitelaw supported it, saying that it was necessary because some "holders of the present citizenship may not unnaturally be encouraged to believe, despite the immigration laws to the contrary, that they have a right of entry to the United Kingdom."[22] This act seems to suggest that Britain was moving away from a territorial understanding of who is British, and moving toward a familial understanding. In the words of William Whitelaw, this move would "dispose of the lingering notion that Britain is somehow a haven for all those whose countries we used to rule."[23]

Conclusion

More than two-thirds of émigrés from the Caribbean moved to the United States after the close of the Second World War (Simmons and Guengant, 1992, p. 97). From 1956 to 1998, nearly 1.5 million non-Hispanic Caribbean nationals (1,412,004) left the Caribbean to move to the United States; from 1954–1992, 253,900 persons emigrated from the Caribbean to the United Kingdom, and from 1956 to 1976, 159,711 moved to Canada. Increasing numbers have left their island homes for destinations in the lands of their former colonizers, as well as to go to other places to which their countries were historically and politically linked.[24] Figure 2.1 shows the trends in Caribbean migration to these destinations. The joint causes of continuing large numbers are political and economic fragmentation of Caribbean islands, and dependence on

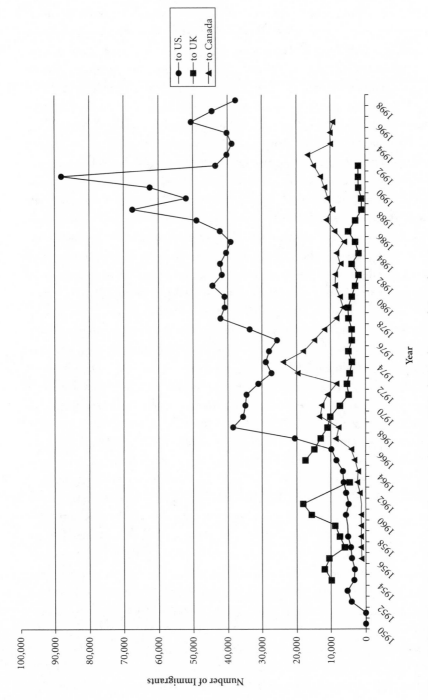

Figure 2.1 Caribbean Immigrants to the United States, United Kingdom, and Canada

metropoles for economic aid, market protections, and "emigration outlets for their surplus labour" (Williams, 1984, p. 500). Figure 2.2 shows how the migration stream was distributed among these three Western destinations. While the United Kingdom dominated as a destination choice in the early 1950s, the options to go to Canada and the United States became more popular in later periods. Still, the United States turned out to be the preferred destination throughout the latter half of the twentieth century.

Caribbean migrants' uneasy hosts (Canada, the United Kingdom, and the United States) gave contradictory responses to black migrants, being neither welcoming nor exclusionary in total and absolute fashion. On the one hand, a desire was evident to exclude Caribbean migrants intentionally because they were considered racially black; however, full exclusion was neither acceptable nor possible. While Caribbean islands were not as strategic to the new post-Cold War global economy as they once were (Grosfoguel, 1997), one of their most valuable resources—black labor—has shown itself to be critical to the development of Western power. As workers, black Caribbean men and women fit the bill for cheap and controllable laborers, and the demand for such labor was simply too great—hence, the resort to occasional recruitment of labor from this region. Still, each host nation's government made clear the wish that black persons who did gain entry in order to provide military service or to labor at less-desired tasks and wages would not remain; they voiced their policy-influential opinions that black immigrants were wholly undesired as potential citizens in these participatory polities. In this respect, the Caribbean migration system reflects the racialized world system of which it is a part. The same processes that separate nations into north/south blocs and make that dichotomy synonymous with developed/less developed or rich/impoverished also racialize these nations' peoples, redefining European peoples as native-born relative to the non-European international migrant. Black migrants not only confront their status as citizens on the poor end of an unequal global economy, but also receive a racializing reception when confronting those who control the borders of the First World nations.

Several themes are evident in the portrait I paint here of transnational antiblack culture in immigration policy in the United States, United Kingdom, and Canada. First, one should note an early reliance on *cultural and biological arguments* in official statements arguing for the unsuitability of Caribbean blacks to the climate and demands of regular employment. A second theme common to all three nations is the use of *contract labor agreements and other*

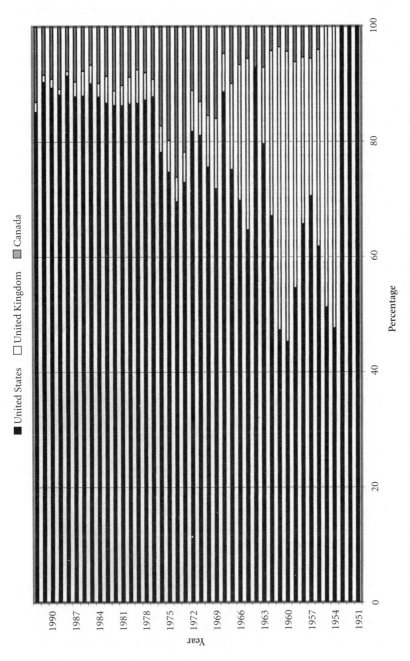

Figure 2.2 Caribbean Immigrants to the United States, United Kingdom, and Canada as Percentage of Total Immigration

forms of recruitment to ensure that black labor was available to fight Western wars and perform certain kinds of service and agricultural work. The reliance on temporary arrangements was often intended to ensure that after black workers and warriors fulfilled immediate demands for labor, soldiers, and seamen they would return from whence they came—an expectation based on the certainty that black persons were inassimilable. Third, because of the contradictory nature of public policy that both has great disdain for black immigration and makes available opportunities to recruit black labor, we can also establish that there is an *ambivalence* around blacks in immigration policy. This ambivalence, however, is tempered by a fear of a black inflow—a fear partially fueled by the racial climate each nation sees in the other nations, and also by the extent to which other nations excluded blacks (or failed to do so). That is (and this is the fourth theme), *governments monitored one another's handling of the "black (immigration) question."* Fifth and last, it is clear that, over time, racially segregated access to immigration has become *less racially overt and specifically racist in language*, for Western nations now employ nonracial language to achieve similar racialized (and specifically antiblack) ends. In practice, though, one can note a reflexive relationship between immigration laws and the demography of migration flows. Just as governments shape the law to respond to changes in the composition and size of various migration streams at a given time, migrants also respond to the law and shape their migration streams accordingly, with the goal of reaching their target migration and economic remuneration goals. But how did migrants respond and what factors enabled them to do so effectively? How did potential migrants find out about opportunities that were available in economies and labor markets larger and more developed than their own? Among the options they could consider worthwhile, how did they decide where to go and how to get there? How were potential migrants able to overcome barriers and enter places in Western economies, labor markets, neighborhoods, and schools in order to achieve their goals? Finally, how exactly did black migration and adaptation occur in such an unwelcoming context? The next four chapters sift the empirical evidence from approximately ninety migration histories in order to answer these questions, focusing on the ways in which the immigration network helps to make the migration and adaptation processes possible, and successful. Key are the ways networks enable the migration stream to be flexible, and even responsive, taking advantage of loopholes in immigration law and opportunities for both legal and undocumented employment, helping migrants to achieve the economic and educational successes for which they left their home countries. In the end, I argue that it is network membership that allows the migrants in that stream to go beyond the unequal positions with which they are left to contend in economic, racial, and social systems in the various host societies to which they are linked. In these ways, networks may be seen as fighting global inequality and the legal systems meant to reinforce that inequality.

3

Hubs, Spokes, and
a Culture of Reciprocity

BLACK PERSONS FROM THE CARIBBEAN have been able to migrate to the
West despite facing forbidding global geopolitical, economic, and racial obstacles. While they have arrived in numbers far smaller than those coming
from other nations, their numbers have been quite large relative to the population of their home islands. How have they been able to achieve such a force-
ful stream of migrants to Western cities? The answer is found in their networking stories. As network members help others they trigger a process that
enables newcomers to escape limited economic opportunities in depressed
island economies, circumvent active discouragement or barring of their entry
via legal means of migration, cross geographic barriers (more often than not)
meant to keep them out, find jobs in which black foreigners were likely to
be hired, find places to live, and adapt to a racial regime that disdains them.
Chapters Four through Seven explain the way these separate steps in the network migration process have occurred for migrants in two networks operating between the Caribbean, London, and New York. This chapter focuses
most specifically on the network's structure, which I argue plays a crucial role
in shaping the socioeconomic outcomes described in subsequent chapters.

Who are network members? In this book, I am using a rather narrow definition: members of an immigrant social network are those immigrants who
have either assisted other migrants to enter and adapt to their new destination, or who have themselves been helped by another immigrant. This definition excludes from the network many nonmigrants who are connected to
immigrants in other ways. Friends and relatives left behind, for example, are

connected to networks but are not network members themselves. Neither are potential migrants network members by this definition.

Black Caribbean migrants to New York and London have organized their networks in very specific ways. Evidence from their migration histories suggests that there is a Weberian ideal type of migrant who becomes an expert central figure. This *hub* is a veteran migrant who collects information on how to immigrate and uses it to help newcomers get into the country, find them jobs, assist them in gaining legal status or, if they are illegal, eluding detection by authorities, and other things that help them get resettled. The new migrants whom the hub assists I call *spokes*. My research and own participant observation experience suggest that the networks I studied are made up of only these two positions: the hub is the person who can be identified by his or her activities in providing assistance, while the spoke is largely a receiver of assistance. (See Figure 3.1.)

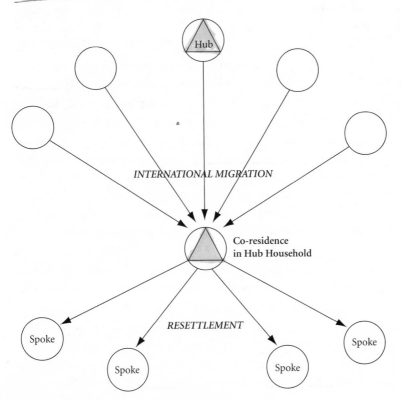

Figure 3.1 A Single Immigrant Hub-and-Spoke Module

The hub and spoke positions are not simply tropes meant to represent extreme ends of a continuum of gift and receipt. Hubs are unique people who have organized their lives around what looks like extreme altruism in helping new migrants, while spokes rarely became hubs. Their relationship is governed by the network's *culture of reciprocity,* a code that defines the resources to be exchanged among network members and the circumstances in which the exchanges should take place.

The Hubs

Dawn, a nurse from Grenada, is a good example of the kind of immigrant I call a hub. When, in my interview with Dawn, I asked whether she's helped other West Indians come to the United States, she first said, "No one." Immediately, her sister, Marjorie, interrupted our conversation. Marjorie, who was visiting Dawn the day I interviewed her, recited for me a long list of people whom Dawn had forgotten she's had come from the West Indies to live with her or was too modest to tell me about right away: Dawn's mother-in-law, father-in-law, and sister-in-law, "tons of cousins," and a friend, Tina, who had since become a sister-in-law. Dawn and Marjorie told me the stories of many of these people. Soon, Dawn interrupted herself to say, "Well, if one is on top, then you help the others." She continued the stories, speaking of people who had lived with her for periods ranging from several months to several years. Marjorie then informed me that, outside of all this, Dawn must have helped about three hundred people get jobs in hospitals and clinics in New York City.

Dawn neither objected to nor corrected Marjorie's account of Dawn's history of helping others. So, I have no reason to doubt that Marjorie was correct in her assertions, despite Dawn's initial response. To be sure, I've heard similar stories from other hubs. For example, some explain that their friends tell them they help so many people they should open their own employment or travel agencies! And more than once I have met again a hub whom I had already interviewed and they have said, "In the days after we spoke, I remembered so many other people I helped that I could have told you about, but I just never thought of it that way until I talked to you." Common to hubs are three related traits: a tradition of helping others, a pattern of forgetting who one had helped, and a tendency to forget how much help one has provided. If you speak with a hub, he or she leaves you with the impression that helping others to migrate is a "second nature" activity they neither keep account of nor easily cease. The altruistic basis for their migration-assisting activities is notable.

For the newcomers they assist, a hub coordinates job contacts, makes travel arrangements, finds people to do the immigration paperwork (or does it himself), finds a place for the new immigrants to stay (usually with the hub in the period immediately following arrival), provides support in social adaptation (that is, shows the immigrant the "ropes" of socioeconomic life in the new community), and provides housing assistance when the new immigrant is ready to move out on his own. The hub consolidates in the social network the resources required to complete these tasks, and uses these resources to find jobs and housing for new migrants as they arrive in the destination. That is, the hub manages the social capital stored in the network. As the person who amasses and controls resources, the hub is the one to whom potential immigrants and the immigrants' intermediaries appeal for assistance with the migration process.

Hubs consolidate not only extra-household resources but also those resources available within their own homes as they organize their homes and families into "hub households." The hub household is organized around its support of new immigrants, a support that more often than not involves co-resident relationships between the newcomer and the members of the hub's household. Hub household members join together to accommodate the newcomer, making space in the house and at the table for the person they will sponsor for some time, until the resettlement process is complete. (Often the other household members feel they have little choice in the matter. Often the hub will make arrangements to send for someone without getting the consent and full compliance of others in the household—including their own spouses!).

While most household-related support activities are directly arranged or coordinated by a single individual who lives in the hub household (most often the hub), the other members of the household also provide support. (Sometimes things like arranging for co-residence are left to the hub's spouse, especially if that spouse is the one who coordinates most of the household maintenance in the household members' day-to-day living.) Although the hub controls social capital in the immigrant network, and by implication also controls the capital and household resources applied to helping the co-resident newcomer, this is not the same as running the household (as a traditional homemaker might be expected to do), nor is it the same as being "in charge" (as one might think of the decision-making power of the traditional breadwinner). Thus, the hub's role in the immigration and resettlement process and in the hub household should not be confused with the role of the head of household.

It follows, then, that the hub's role is not gender specific. Both female and male hubs were found in both the New York and London networks studied here. Sex determined neither whether someone would or could become a hub, nor how much support work a spouse did to sustain hub activities and nurture newcomers. Just as female spouses did for male hubs, male spouses of female hubs did much household work to support the migration sponsorship activities that hubs had committed to doing. In one case, for example, the male spouse of a female hub did all the cooking and laundry for the household. Also, in cases where the hub was a woman, there was no indication that spouses objected to hub decisions about whom to bring from the West Indies, or under what circumstances newcomers would be welcome. Generally, the spouse of the hub—regardless of gender—behaved as if he or she had no choice in the decision to help others (whether or not that was the case). Both husbands and wives of hubs professed an inability to control their spouse's commitment of time and the household's resources toward these activities, once that spouse had decided to organize his or her life around being a hub to a network.

Hubs live by a certain ethos that makes them different from other immigrants, and they live out their migration years differently as well. I illustrate here the hub ethos with a retelling of two different sponsorship experiences.

Jocelyn

As we learned in Chapter One, Jocelyn was still living in Trinidad when she learned from her visiting London-based uncle about a program to recruit teachers, mainly from Australia and Canada, to London schools. She decided that she would seek out one of these jobs and take her immediate nuclear family to London. At the same time, she decided that she would like to take some other West Indians with her, but also that she couldn't or wouldn't take just anyone who wanted to go. From other respondents in London I learned that while she was still in Trinidad, Jocelyn personally interviewed a set of potential teacher recruits, testing each for their level of Christian religiosity. If she decided that they were sufficiently pious, Jocelyn would tell them about the recruitment program and help them to apply. Her goal was to create for herself and her fellow sojourners a community of Christian fellowship once she relocated to London. In this she was successful in the extreme: as noted,

hubs take community with them.

she recruited seven new teachers and their family members. While I did not interview all of these teachers, those with whom I did meet in London were still very active both in their church and in the school district.

Taran

Taran, originally from Tobago, emigrated to New York as a nurse when she was recruited from her Trinidadian nursing school to a first job at a hospital in Brooklyn. After arriving in New York, she wrote often to a childhood friend, Amsie, back in Trinidad. Amsie bore her first child at age fourteen; Taran had helped deliver the baby. With this birth, Amsie had a bad postpartum hemorrhage and was told not to have any more children. From New York Taran wrote to Amsie several times, but she soon stopped receiving responses to her letters. Years later, on a visit to Trinidad, Taran stopped by to see her friend. Amsie would not let her into the house and would speak to her only at the gate. Taran soon enough managed to get into the house, only to find that Amsie had borne ten children by then, with the tenth older than Taran's first child. Eight of the ten still lived at home, two lived with their grandparents. Taran saw that her friend suffered from her poverty and that the children were not doing well. She asked her friend if she wanted to come to the United States.

When Taran returned from her trip, she asked a doctor in the hospital where she worked if he needed a maid because she knew someone who was looking for a job. (Amsie was not in the States at the time.) He said he didn't but knew another doctor who did, and he agreed to turn over to the other doctor the immigration papers Taran had for him. The job was soon arranged and Amsie arrived not long afterward. Thus, Taran *created* a job that did not formerly exist to be filled by a person who was not in the country. Then she arranged for the paperwork to make her friend's stay legal. As a live-in maid, Amsie lived with the doctor's family during the week and with Taran's family on the weekends. Amsie was only one of several migrants Taran directly helped to migrate, not to mention those who were helped indirectly—in the ensuing years, all of Amsie's children were able to come to the United States.

Hub Characteristics

Clearly, hubs choose among potential migrants and, in so doing, create new communities of persons they handpick for their network-building process. They have the immigrant live with them, opening their home and committing the resources to be sure that the new immigrant is properly resettled.

After migration occurs, hubs keep ties with those they have helped, making sure that the network remains a community long after the initial migration experience. Hubs take on the role of the sponsor, a role that requires much effort and commitment and that is costly in time and money, and even in one's spouse's goodwill! Thus, hubs are a particular sort of immigrant. I have found that unique to the immigrant who becomes the hub is the willingness to apply unusual effort to accomplish five things.

First, *the hub makes great efforts to keep or renew ties back home.* Hubs call and visit often—some yearly or twice a year, others, just as frequently as they can afford to, but far more frequently than network spokes. They are sure to return for pre-Lenten Carnival; to ship a barrel filled with gifts of new or used clothing at Christmastime, or items that the friend or relative who receives them can sell to supplement their income; to give donations to the Church in the village from which they came; to buy school uniforms for village children or materials for the local school; and to do other such deeds that help to maintain connections with the home community. Most immigrants who are not hubs visit far less frequently; they may see their community as already with them in the destination.

Second, *hubs make sacrifices,* both for the larger community and for the newcomers they sponsor. One such sacrifice is to sponsor the immigrant through co-residence, which is just one way the hub makes other household members party to the sacrifices initially taken on by the hub. These sacrifices are designed not just to make the newcomer comfortable; they are done so as to help the newcomer get on his or her feet as solidly and as quickly as possible. In many cases, hubs will not charge rent to their co-resident spokes, although they will often expect the newcomer to contribute in some way to household maintenance (such as through the occasional buying of groceries or by contributing to paying for utilities). Hubs will often request that new immigrants save the money they earn so they may quickly move on to make their own households, or they may ask them to save for remittances they know the newcomer's family members need so badly. As Maryanne explained, "I send money to five generations of cousins, but they never remember that. I have to put a lid on that now because I have been here as a nurse thirty-five years and I can retire, but I'm in no financial position to do so because I have been helping so many others. You help some of them, and go home and see that they are living better than you." Still, she says, for three years in a row she has been collecting, first, toys, and now also clothing to send to Grenada for the holidays, to be given to those she describes as "the poorest of the poor."

Third, *hubs buy into the network's culture of reciprocity,* or the culturally based norms and mores by which network exchanges are made. It is well known, by hubs and other immigrants alike, that people can take advantage of a hub's generosity. Despite this awareness, it seems to be extremely important that hubs (and others in the network) know and agree that it is proper and nearly a moral responsibility that network members help one another. That is, any spoke may be willing to make some sacrifices, but not necessarily to let someone move in or to put their career on the line to help another. But hubs characterize themselves as selfless, giving people who knew that sponsoring others is the right thing to do. The hubs I spoke with were extremely modest in discussing how much of a difference their assistance made in people's lives, and those who were hub-sponsored said things that showed they were extremely grateful to be helped. Everyone, the hub and those who were sponsored alike, told me how wonderful it was to be in a hub household. Only after I had been in the field for some time did I garner enough trust of network members to hear some of the bad things about living in a hub household. Nonetheless, hubs were consistent in portraying themselves as not having done very much as a sponsor, and at characterizing their efforts as not very taxing, or even as easy to do. This was not necessarily a false characterization: as we already know, many of the hubs I spoke with were generous to the extent that they could not remember the number or all the names of the people who had lived in their homes or whom they had helped find work. And even if they did speak of negative experiences with the hub or other household members, the newcomers almost always characterized hubs as extremely generous.

Fourth, *hubs use their position in the labor market to help others.* As hubs work in their own jobs, they gain a reputation for being good workers, and then for bringing in good workers. In the networks I studied, those who sponsored others were often (but certainly not always) nursing administrators, construction foremen, or other higher-ups in the organizations where they worked, and they used their job status to influence the hiring of new immigrants. While it may help, hubs do not necessarily have to be in high-status jobs to provide recommendations that would secure jobs for newcomers. For example, a domestic worker in one network became a hub, getting jobs for other women through the contacts she made in the New York City market for household services. Regardless of the hub's job status or rank, over time hubs are given more responsibility and trust at work when it comes to hiring new workers to the extent that employer trust is almost part of the hub's job description. For example, note what Dawn and Marjorie said as they listed some of the people for whom Dawn had found jobs in the hospital in which she works:

> Dawn: My sister Sheron—my son is an orderly—he worked there since high school; my brother-in-law's girlfriend, June; my cousin Clinton is there; my best friend Hagar; Enid, my sister-in-law—

> Marjorie interrupts: And when I finish school, I know I'll get a job there too.

> Dawn continues: And in the methadone clinic I got all of the nurses jobs there—they just have to ask me, I'll get them a job. [At work] they say, "As long as they're your friends, Dawn. I know you won't bring me any riffraff."

The fifth and last characteristic is this: _hubs have control in the selection of new immigrants_ while spokes are marked by the absence of such control. This control operates on two levels: hubs choose the individuals they will help to emigrate (_select_) and hubs control the inputs to the immigration process—such as access to jobs, the means to cross borders, food and shelter—doling these out to the spokes they assist (_sponsor_).

Selection

I heard more than one immigrant say that it is impossible to help all those who would want to emigrate because "everyone I know wants to come." So, hubs pick and choose the particular newcomers they will assist. Sometimes a person is chosen because he or she fills particular household needs. For example, in the interview sample there were several instances of young women being brought to the United States for the express purpose of taking care of children in the hub household. In some instances, the person was brought to the United States because the hub decided the person deserved a better chance to improve him- or herself (as in the case of Amsie). Similarly, some young network members were sent for at a very young age; they had done well in school in the Caribbean and the hub thought they would benefit from the better opportunities for mobility that would be available to them in the United States, even as a young person (such as free education through twelfth grade).

The hub takes quite seriously his or her role in selecting newcomers who will succeed. Such success is broadly defined, although the conditions are not vague. Following are some examples from the interview data:

- She is likely to be a good worker and not to ruin the hub's reputation on the job.

- He will make a good husband for a relative.

- He is a youth who is good in school and is not likely to see many opportunities back home, so it is best to bring him now, while he is young.

- She is the right age and sex (for example, perhaps a preteen or teenage female) to be a live-in child care provider and to become a friend to the children.

Hubs must be careful about who they choose. Life can be made that much more difficult for everyone involved if a poor choice of emigrant is made, especially when the hub puts his or her reputation on the job on the line or the immigrant lives with the hub's family. I heard complaints from spokes that there was no way they would be hubs because people "could move into your house and not even help pay the electric [bill]." That a newcomer might not know or respect the limits of the hub household's generosity was shocking to these nonsponsoring West Indian immigrants. It was the main reason they gave for why they chose not to become hubs.

Just as hubs choose new immigrants and do the work to facilitate their smooth integration into the new society, hubs also watch carefully to see whether they have made a poor choice and may even take steps to correct their mistakes, which sometimes means sending persons back from whence they came. I learned of at least two instances in one network in which young women were, or were going to be, sent back because there was "trouble." One young woman was sent for in order to be a nanny for a female hub's second child. When things did not work out, the hub sent the young woman back to her island. At the birth of the third child, the returnee's younger sister, Jacinthia, was sent for in order to be the new nanny. When "boy trouble" started, Jacinthia knew the next step would be to send her back home, so she packed her bags and ran away, finding shelter elsewhere in New York to avoid being returned to the West Indies. In a separate incident, Jonita found work as a domestic in New York City through her sister (also her hub) and left behind her children in the West Indies. The husband of the couple who employed her soon began making sexual advances toward her. Her attempts to leave the job were problematic for two reasons. First, the employer was sponsoring her application for legalization, and second, if she quit she would be jobless as well as undocumented. To solve the issue, the hub had already decided to send her sister back to the West Indies. Jonita did not become discouraged; her brother-in-law (the hub's husband) secretly told her, "Don't worry, you'll make it. You don't have to go back because you can make it." That encouragement caused her to search for a new job, which she found without help from her hub, and that saved her from being sent home.

Of course, from the spokes' point of view, this all looks quite different. They see themselves only as helped or not helped. Potential migrants who desire to leave their countries of origin but do not have willing sponsors within the network may not be able to leave easily. This is not due entirely to the constraints imposed by immigration laws. While the constraints of immigration law might suggest that one did not migrate because legislation allows for family reunification only of siblings, parents, or children of residents or citizens, there were many cases in the data where veteran migrants in the network sent for people who by no means fit the guidelines for family reunification. (Both Taran's and Dawn's stories, presented earlier, provide examples.)

As I have shown, people have sponsored friends and distant relatives using network ties and influence on the job to enable legal and illegal entry and to secure employment for those for whom they wish to send. In London and New York the networks of black Caribbean people worked similarly. Note that Jocelyn did not widely advertise the open teacher positions and notify all who may have wanted to go or all who had the right professional qualifications. Neither did she choose relatives to whom she might otherwise have felt obligated. Instead, she hand-picked her future black coworkers for that London relocation experience. Other researchers have reported similar findings, where hub equivalents in other networks act as "bridgeheads and gatekeepers" who are often unwilling to help friends and family back home fulfill their wishes to emigrate (Böcker, 1994; Thomas and Znaniecki 1996). Thus, not everyone who stays back home chooses to do so.

Significantly, where family reunification is designed to work, many veteran migrants choose *not* to send for relatives eligible under reunification who could and want to migrate. Thus, although one may desire to emigrate to the United States and may even be connected to networks there, simply having these connections may not be enough to ensure that migration will actually take place. For example, James explained to me that he is still angry with his sister (who now lives in Canada) for not sending for him years ago when she lived in New York. His wife, Heddy, said that—even though he's been in the United States since 1975—he still "holds it against her for not sending for him. He says so every time we meet [her]: 'If you had sent for us, we would be way ahead in this country.'" While it is evident that in some cases the hub figure considered the input of others in making a decision to send for someone, and although it was clear that spokes whose emigration was blocked by some hubs worked to find alternative means to get into the destination country, emigration among these networked immigrants rarely occurred without a hub's support.[1]

Sponsoring

The other level of hub control has to do with the actual process of sending for someone, a control that pertains throughout the immigration and integration period. Hubs may be willing to help particular individuals, but not unconditionally. Help is given only under circumstances that the hub determines are acceptable or sufficient. An example may be helpful here. Valencia's phone rang in the middle of my interview with her. On the phone was a woman in Canada who asked Valencia to help her find her way to New York. The woman on the phone feared for her safety, saying she had fled from her island home to Canada with a couple who had brought her there "to do baby sitting" (that is, to be a nanny) for them. Valencia had known that the woman wanted to come to the United States and was sure that her urgency to get to New York and her reason for hastily going first to Canada had all to do with her fear from having been the only witness to a crime that had occurred in the West Indies. They talked on the phone for a while and Valencia told her that, in order to better receive Valencia's help, she should go back home to the West Indies. Valencia said to her over and over again, "You got to do it the right way. I think this is wrong. You got to come the right way." Later, after hanging up with the woman, Valencia told me the whole story. Surprisingly, she then explained that it would be very easy to get the woman into New York. I asked how. She said, "She would have been here already. Even now, I could have just take her with me to Barbados and [because I'm old] say, 'She [is the one who] take care of me, and she got to come back [to New York] with me.' It would be very easy." She told me too that the woman has the same last name as Valencia's ex-husband. "Her name is Simon and my husband's name is Simon and her birth paper says Simon. I could get my husband to write a letter for her because her name is Simon." This letter would be a request for family reunification consideration, despite the fact that Valencia made it clear in the interview that the woman seeking help was not a close relative.

Three important points emerge from this story. The first is that Valencia had the ability to bring this woman to New York and she knew there was more than one way to do it. She could indicate to the proper authorities that the woman was her caretaker, or alternatively, even though Valencia had been divorced for years, she could call on her ex-husband to support her hub activities. Second, this story shows that the potential migrant does have access to persons in social networks who have the knowledge it takes to achieve migration and resettlement, and the potential migrant feels free to call on them. But again, merely having ties is insufficient social capital if one desires to migrate to a particular destination on a particular timeline. While this spoke knew personally a hub experienced at getting people into the network and into the country, and needed only to share a last name with her contact, she could not get help to get to New York City unless she was willing to do it the hub's way, even if her life was at stake. The third point is that help would be forthcoming only if the hub found sponsorship conditions to be agreeable and agreed to provide that help. This is the kind of evidence that supports my assertion that the network's hub controls the social capital that is only latently available to potential newcomers.

One hub in the sample, Dawn, did seem to be less discriminating than others in offering hub services. I was told that her husband, James, once told a caller from the West Indies who was seeking help when Dawn was not at home that she should not worry because, "If I know my wife, she will help you and you'll be here in no time." The data from this sample suggest that although it is important for the hub to be perceived as exceedingly helpful, and for the hub to perceive him- or herself that way, most hubs are not so indiscriminate, particularly because they must go to great lengths to sponsor any person they have decided deserves their help.

That veteran immigrants may largely control the network migration process is an idea that has not emerged in the existing migration literature. One reason may be that few studies of the immigrant social network are done from the perspective of those who are already here. Much of the research in this area tries to predict who in the developing world will come, and researchers, to find the answers, somewhat understandably study the people who have not yet arrived. Another reason that the true locus of control in a network is not visible is that hub household members do not easily speak of their power and control over the migration of others, nor of their ability to be selective. They instead portray themselves as generous and willing to help, and undiscriminating in doing so. To speak of themselves otherwise is to sound selfish and arrogant. Obviously all who choose to move do so because they believe they will have a better life—and many do achieve it. Hubs may find it difficult to admit that their own achievements, which may seem like great successes compared to the lives of those left behind, are precisely what enable them to pick and choose those who should follow. It makes sense that a "share-the-wealth" philosophy is commonly espoused among those who leave hardship behind to live a relatively prosperous life—even if one cannot and will not share the wealth with everyone who wants part of it.

To summarize, five characteristics describe people who become hubs in the West Indian social network:

1. Hubs make great efforts to keep or renew ties back home.

2. Hubs are willing to make great sacrifices, both for the community and for the newcomers they sponsor.

3. Hubs buy into the culture of reciprocity, which defines the extent of altruism they are to offer and the conditions of sponsorship—conditions that spokes have found to be excessive.

4. Hubs tend to have positions in the labor market that allow them easily to find jobs for newcomers—a job characteristic that does not necessarily derive from high rank.

5. On two levels hubs have great control in the selection of new immigrants. They both choose the individuals they will help to emigrate and control sponsorship—the spoke's entire immigration process—sometimes to the degree that a hub might send an undesirable immigrant back to the home country.

Figure 3.2 and the accompanying key in Figure 3.3 illustrate the types of help that were exchanged among New York City network participants, and Figures 3.4 and 3.5 map actual network relationships among some of the metropolitan New York City residents.

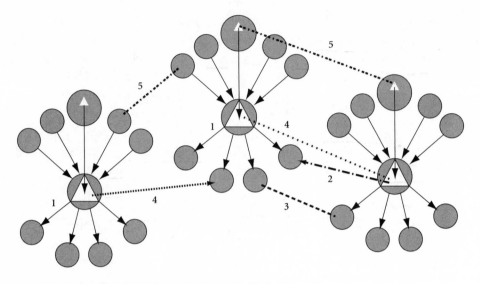

Figure 3.2 Model of the Immigrant Social Network

Persons and Households

 Hub household

Spoke household

Network Lineages

Note: The direction of the arrow indicates the direction of network assistance.

1 ──────────▶ Current /former co-resident links

2 ─·─·─·─·─▶ Non-co-resident housing assistance

3 ─────────▶ Legal assiatance with immigration papers

4 ··············▶ Former or current workplace connections

5 ─·─··─··─··▶ Premigration linkages

Figure 3.3 Key to Network Diagrams

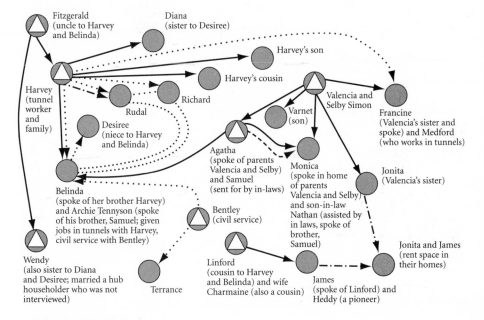

Figure 3.4 Network A

NOTE: Not all links are illlustrated. Hubs are named first among household members.

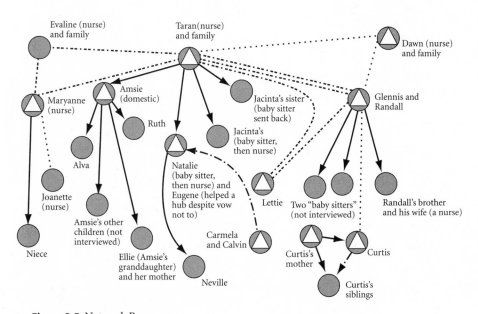

Figure 3.5 Network B

NOTE: Not all links are illlustrated. Hubs are named first among household members.

Spokes

Spokes differ from hubs in many ways. By definition, all spokes come to the United States with assistance from a social network, while some hubs enter as pioneers. Almost all of the spokes I talked with chose not to form hub households and many gave voice in particular to their unwillingness to enter into the co-resident relationships that the West Indian migration pattern seems to call for. They often reported that either "everyone I know is already in the United States," or that they had few remaining links to the islands from which they had come (perhaps, for example, because of the deaths of significant elders). As a result, they reported visiting home less frequently than hubs did. They also seemed to have fewer, more attenuated ties to the home community than hubs did. Their orientation toward their new lives in the destination country explains their unwillingness to perpetuate the network in the destination country; that is, they are focused more on bonding and building a life with the people who surround them postmigration than on the community of persons they have left behind. It is the latter group that contains the people who desire to migrate and with whom spokes have fewer ties.

Despite their reticence about becoming hubs, some spokes provide support to newcomers in the network. This is not unexpected, given that spokes do not sever their ties to the social network once they move out of their hub household. They continue to participate in network activities and remain well integrated in the West Indian immigrant community, even as they integrate themselves into American, Canadian, or British society at large. Spokes will help people when asked to by their hub or the hub's representative, or when they are aware that someone new is being sent for by that hub (that is, they take pains to accommodate another newcomer soon to arrive). While not offering assistance to the extent that they become hubs themselves, spokes make "deposits" to the network store of resources, as happens when they show the ropes to a newcomer on the job or help to arrange the legal papers for someone else, as had been done for them. Again, often enough these efforts come at the request of the hub who sponsored them. But just as they make deposits to network stores, they may also continue to make withdrawals over the migration experience (such as by asking their hub to help them find places to stay in the West Indies on their visits back home or new jobs for their friends in the United States, and so on). Thus, throughout the life course, the immigrant social network serves as a resource base for many of its members, and does so for individuals, couples, and families. Its relevance is not just to the border-crossing moment.

Who Are the Spokes?

Spokes are family members with blood ties, fictive kin, and friends who have particular ties to hubs. They can be young children, adolescents, adult siblings, old friends—basically there is no one who is automatically exempt from spoke status. How are spokes chosen? It is difficult to ascertain whether it is the circumstance of migration (the existence or lack of job openings, the ease or difficulty of securing legal papers, the household needs of the hub) or the individual hub him- or herself that determines which potential immigrants will become spokes. In this I am limited by my data and can list here only the circumstances that the data reveal are important in spoke selection.

Hubs tailor the timing and selection of newcomers to correspond with what is allowable by immigration law or, alternatively, with the parts of the law that are most easily circumvented. For example, during the period in which the social networks studied here operated, the law stated that children of immigrants had to be sponsored by their parents before they reached age twenty-one. Thus Amsie (as did others) timed the sending for her children to coincide with their age distribution and her own budget. This strategy allowed for the arrival of children according to birth order, leaving the maximum amount of time between the current ages of children left behind and their twenty-first birthdays. The strategy also allowed the older ones to be put to work soon after arrival, and greater sums of money could be pooled so that the group could be more quickly reunited. In this case, the spoke (Amsie) became a hub herself in order to be reunited with her children in the destination. But this kind of reunion did not always happen: in Ingrid's case, she went on to New York and lived in a hub household without any of her children by her side. At the same time, she sent two of her children to live with her brother Harvey, who by then had moved from New York to Florida. Thus Harvey was her children's hub. Yet another of Ingrid's daughters was sent elsewhere in New York, to live with Ingrid's Uncle Steele. At no time did Ingrid ever set up a hub household to get her children Stateside.

Sometimes West Indian children are brought to New York specifically to be educated in the United States. Some of the smaller islands of the West Indies do not have high schools, and where high schools exist they have only a certain number of entry slots, a situation that guarantees that some youth cannot attend. If network members determine that there is a promising young student who is sure to find success if brought to the States, where both the schooling and employment opportunities are greater than in their native country, arrangements will be made for the children to come. This migration of children can occur before or after and with or without the parents. Sometimes, in fact, children are sent abroad without the full consent of their parents, if more influential family members deem this is the thing to do. More than once I heard about some bright young woman being sent for so that she could have greater opportunities for educational and economic mobility and also provide child care for the hub household's children in return for network sponsorship. These reciprocal arrangements suggest that gender specificity is important (albeit sometimes only implicit) in spoke selection.

Sometimes children are sent for in order to benefit both the child and the hub's household. Hubs may look for a young person (usually but not always a girl) in the family network of the West Indies who seems likely to become a good friend to the householder's own children and to perform child care duties adequately in the after-school hours, while the adults of the hub household are still at work. This arrangement benefits the young person as well, of course, because his or her chances for success are increased by coming to the States for education or job training. In at least two of the hubs in the networks I studied, a different young woman was sent for with each successive birth to the hub. The woman brought in to do child care did not need to stay in that job for very long. The hub then allowed for and, in some cases, encouraged the spoke's social mobility, even if the spoke was originally brought to the United States specifically to benefit the hub's household. It is the culture of reciprocity—social rules under which help is given and received—in these networks that deems that spoke social mobility takes primacy over the fulfillment of the hub household's short-term needs.

Sometimes hubs make plans to bring particular individuals in the family, strategizing with other network members on how this should be done. It is difficult to ascertain the exact reasons why one individual may be chosen over another. Moreover, sometimes the needs of the potential migrant and the needs of the hub or the hub's household overlap. For example, MacClaine was invited to fill a job opening under a West Indian foreman at a job site of the New York water tunnel construction union (the sandhogs) and at the same time he was sent for so that he and the foreman's sister and spoke, Belinda, could marry.

Declining to Build the Network

The network is extended when a migrant decides to send for one of his or her fellow island countrymen, and only a few choose to do this, for it takes expert knowledge and the dedication of considerable material and emotional resources to make someone else's migration experience a success. Most spokes choose not to become hubs. Some cannot afford to sponsor others, but hubs are not necessarily wealthier or more established. Many hubs are at the earliest stages of their own work trajectories when they send for their first spoke. For many spokes, lack of wealth is not the obstacle; some say that no circumstance would have them act as hubs do. As Eugene told me, "My wife and I made a pact when we got married: no one can come in here. They can come for a visit, but no way are they staying. I've seen people come in and break up a marriage! No way." Others were more benign in understanding the difficulties of becoming hubs. As Belinda explains, "Now that I have my family I realize how hard it is to have someone living there. It puts a strain on a relationship." Spokes are not as willing as hubs to tolerate the co-resident relationships that seem to be expected in the West Indian migration pattern. Many of those I interviewed recounted stories of how spokes have broken up hub marriages, did not (or at least did not offer to) contribute financially to household maintenance, and otherwise wreaked unwanted havoc on the hub's household. The difficulties caused by these relationships—or at least the horror stories about them—were the main reasons given as to why some spokes chose not to become hubs. In sum, the spoke differs from the hub in his reticence toward having a new immigrant in the household.

Keeping Fewer Ties

The spoke also differs from the hub in his relationship to the home community. Spokes explained to me their lives in the United States in two ways, one really the flip side of the other. One explanation they gave was, "Everyone I know is here." They claimed, then, to have no reason to send for others or to keep ties back home. As one respondent explained, "Everyone I want to be around is here. It's as if we all took a trip together. Even my girlfriend at the time [I emigrated] ended up in New York one month after I came. So it's as if I never left home." Spokes made a second type of statement that revealed the attenuating of ties back home when they explained, "There's no connection anymore" with the home community. Here's what Belinda, a spoke who did not become a hub, said to me when I asked if she went back to visit regularly:

> My mom died six years ago, on my anniversary. It was very—I haven't gone back. I used to go every year or every two years when my mom was alive. But now there's nobody there, there's no family there anymore. My mom was all I needed. She was my anchor to say, "This is home." She died in [19]86, I went back in [19]87 and put a headstone. And I felt I didn't belong. If you go back [to visit] you won't recognize it. And it's hard to go by yourself. I grew up there. But you need somebody there that you can—to do—I don't know where I'm going to stay, and that is frightening. There's no connection, and it's scary. We're just going to land on this place. You know there was always somebody to greet you and say "I'm glad you're here!" and [now] there's no one.

To be sure, Belinda's brother, who served as her hub, felt differently. He returned to the West Indian island where they are from several times a year. We might contrast Belinda's spoke philosophy with the following statement from a female hub. She responded to a question about what it was like to go back home for visits now that she lived in the United States:

> It's improved a lot from the time I was there. It's nice. It's small. Tobago is small, and the village where I really come from is very small but the people are very friendly. And when you go back there you don't want for anything, because this or that person will bring it all for you, whether it's a mango or an orange or a breadfruit. They treat you very nice when you go home. You get your fish, your coconut water. They talk about the sea baths that you can get, you know, and there's places you can go and visit. It's small, but it's nice.

This sentiment is not uncommon among hubs. In fact, this feeling (that is, the feeling of connection to the home community) is probably what moves hubs to create hub households. Pioneers may be particularly inspired to become hubs; because pioneers arrive without network connections, they may be sufficiently nostalgic to, on a smaller scale, recreate in new destinations the community they had back home, if they have the resources. Spokes seem not to have similar home community connections; they describe the destination community as the one to which they are oriented. Thus, those who arrive with network assistance rarely became hubs after leaving the home of the hub who sponsored them. In fact, although I cannot with any accuracy predict the numbers of spokes who go on to make hub households, most spokes in the two networks studied in this research project did not become hubs, nor after co-residence ended did they create households where they or their spouses sponsored new immigrants.

The Culture of Reciprocity

The immigrant groups using the hub-and-spoke network structure developed their own culture of reciprocity about proper comportment and behaviors among network members, and about rules of exchange for migration assistance.[2] These rules delineate expectations about the kinds of help that should be exchanged, the degree of assistance to be given (the quantity or value of the material and the duration of the helping relationship), and the set of obligations with which the spoke is yoked upon acceptance of that assistance. Further, the way the culture of reciprocity operates dictates the hub's ability or inability to gain power and control over the social capital in the network.

This culture of reciprocity is not a wholly new invention of newcomers to a destination. Instead, transplants adopt and adapt practices from the home country, and in the new community they develop a new culture of reciprocity. Here Elaine describes growing up watching her mother's own hublike activities back on her island.

> Even though I was living with a single parent, because my father had died early, my mother continued in the same nature of extended kindness to people, some of them strangers, some of them people from Union Island, and some from other Grenadine Islands. One in particular, I remember we called her Aunt Nora. I [did not know] she was not my blood relative for many years, but she lived with us for periods of six months each year, and she became part of the family. In fact, up 'til now she is one of the greatest [influences] in my life, for the respect, you know. She is like an aunt that grew us up. So it's just that my mother was very kind; she extended whatever resources she had to visitors, friends, family, just the same. At first it might have started like a vacation, but after a time she just lived there with us. She would do all the things we were doing. She would work in the garden. There was never a charge; we washed and eat together and then she would just pack up and say "I'm going over back to Canouan" and then a couple of months again and she'd be there. And then we had another lady, Betty, she was no relative, no blood relative either, but she lived most of her years with my mother, and eventually her children [too], some of them lived with Mom.

Together, the mores about how assistance should be transferred and about how the spoke should behave in return make up the group's culture of reciprocity. The hubs in these networks help their spokes in three key ways: by finding them jobs, by offering co-residence until someone gets on their feet, and by keeping ties back home.

Finding Jobs

Most often, the impetus to move adults is related to finding them a job. (The main exceptions are youths sent to perform child care for hubs in exchange for a U.S. education.) Finding a job or creating an opportunity for an education in the United States, England, or Canada creates a state of indebtedness and gratitude for someone who comes from a Third World economy who may not have the chance to obtain either easily. If that job comes as a result of a recommendation made by the hub at his workplace on behalf of the spoke, the spoke is obligated to perform well on the job site so as not to disappoint the hub, who has made obvious and inordinate sacrifices on the newcomer's behalf as well as possibly put his own workplace reputation at risk. Similarly, a youth is expected to perform well in school and to behave in an upstanding manner.

Fulfilling one's obligation to the hub by being a hardworking employee makes the employer grateful to the hub—bringing benefit to the hub but benefiting the employer also. The spoke's hard work, in turn, increases the employer's likelihood of accepting future recommendations from the hub. Thus the hub's influence at the workplace is increased, as is the likelihood that the hub will use that influence to send for another potential migrant.

Co-Residence

Normally—unless the terms of employment include residential arrangements, as is often the case for domestics—a hub does not arrange separate housing for the spoke he or she sponsors. The hub most often brings the spoke to live with the hub's family until such time as the spoke "gets on his feet." As one hub, James, said about the decision to help others,

> I will not go hungry if I let this person live with me. I would not go [hungry] because I work for a living, I work for a salary, and I make do with what I work for all right. I buy a home, and there's extra room in the house, and somebody needs a place to stay, I let them stay.

Normally this period continues until alternative housing and the means for the spoke to pay for it are secured, and most often the hub does not charge any kind of rent during the co-residence period. Living for free in another's home for an indefinite period of time certainly encourages the beneficiary to see him- or herself as indebted to the benefactor in a way that can never be repaid. The experience of sharing a residence with one's benefactor as he or she sets you up in a new country is one that immigrants regard as especially altruistic, one for which the hub earns long-term (and perhaps a lifetime of) gratitude.

The co-resident but (usually) rent-free arrangement is designed to help the beneficiary get on his feet in the fastest way possible. This arrangement has several implications. First, it means the spoke will be able to save what earnings he is able to secure either to pay rent on his own place sooner or to be able to send remittances back home. As the spoke begins sending remittances and telling others of his good fortune in finding work and earning and saving income, the reputation of the hub is again elevated among those still in the home country. For example, although remittances from a spoke to his family back home are not earned by the hub directly, those remittances may be interpreted as having been made possible by the hub. Finally, if the spoke, because of his ability to save, moves out sooner than expected, it becomes all the easier for the hub to move on and assist the next person. High turnover in the hub's household will also increase the hub's reputation for helping others.

As stated, some expectations are made of persons who live without charge in their migration sponsor's home. Most often, migrants explained to me that they were expected to "make a contribution" to the household, in the form of paying the electric bill or contributing to other utilities. While spokes were not expected to pay what would normally be considered their share of all the expenses to run a home, it was considered rude if one failed to share some of the rewards earned in the marketplace. Minimally, one is supposed to offer to help sustain the hub's household, that is, to offer to pay rent or some of one's earnings to those who are sponsoring one's immigration. Many times that offer is turned down.

There is also a code of conduct for spokes. For example, there is little expectation that a spoke will have a significant social life outside of the hub's household, especially if the spoke is female. If the hub's household members are churchgoers, for example, the spoke often is expected to attend services. Similarly, dating is proscribed or controlled for young women, especially if they are brought over at an age when they are expected to be primary child-minders for the hub's own children. As Glennis explained,

> Many [domestics] stay with us on the weekends and go to work [that is, live at their employer's home] during the week. Right now I have someone in my house. [Laughs.] See, I always have somebody. One of my cousin's daughters and her mother came in from Trinidad not too long ago, and the mother went back but she is at my house now. Some other body got a job for her, so she goes to work on the weekends and she's there now. There's somebody at my house right now. No problem, I like company. I'm an only child. I don't have my children in my house; there's just one girl in my house and she's going to move out shortly. But I always want company, isn't that funny? People don't usually like company and a lot of people . . . don't want anybody in their house. But like I told her, I said I don't like people who tell lies and I like people who I can trust. I don't like people who steal and stuff like that. As long as you understand me you can stay here forever. Those are the ground rules. [Laughs.]

Of course not all spokes are co-resident with the hub who sponsors them. Not often, but sometimes, a hub might send for someone and request that a former spoke put the newcomer up in their own home. So, not all hubs do it all; some hubs specialize in finding jobs while others become "legal experts" who help with documentation. Still others are jacks-of-all-trades who help fewer people but offer them a broader array of services that only begin with co-residence. To date, my father (the first hub of whom I became aware) has had a half-dozen persons be co-resident, but he's helped many dozens more find jobs. Similarly, Dawn has helped many hundreds of persons find jobs; she cannot remember how many people have come to live with her, but it has certainly been fewer than these hundreds. While these tales may seem strange to the average American-born person, they are not so unusual among West Indian immigrants.[3]

Keeping Ties Back Home

Since hubs keep ties with nonmigrants and returnees who live in the home country, it is nearly guaranteed that people will hear of the hub's generosity to those who migrated with the hub's help. Even in the absence of bragging behavior, all a hub or spoke has to do to increase the hub's reputation is visit and explain the hub's activities in the past year. (The co-residence of the latest newcomer is unlikely to be a secret; even if that information is not volunteered, knowledge of the new spoke's whereabouts is likely to be spread by the spoke's family, who likely live in the same town or village from which the hub originates. Thus the hub's altruism in New York or London earns him or her goodwill back in the Islands.)

Keeping ties back home helps the hub gain a reputation for being the person to seek out when one is desperate to move to the West. Status accrues to the hub in cyclical fashion. Potential migrants still in the home country endow the hub with an increasingly good reputation as the person to know if one needs help getting overseas. The employer endows the hub with an increasingly good reputation for bringing in good workers, and seeks her out when additional labor is required. Finally, with each newcomer successfully resettled, the hub herself gains more expertise, and therefore finds it easier to send for additional newcomers.

Obligations in the Years Beyond Co-Residence

Migration networks do more than provide information for border crossing and job searches—they are important resources for the entire period of resettlement and social adaptation. Spokes remain tied to the network as they become integrated into their new environment, and keep connections with the hub's household that sponsored them. Rather than going on to integrate into the destination society and leaving their transplanted West Indian extended family members and neighbors behind, the West Indians I studied joined ethnic associations, participated in ethnically concentrated labor markets, were involved in churches with sizeable West Indian congregations, and had friends drawn from the West Indian immigrant population. Transplanted and networked immigrants together helped form the community that encourages spokes to say they feel at home in their new environment.

The rules of reciprocity apply throughout the years of newcomer socioeconomic integration. From what I witnessed, there is no point at which the spoke is no longer obligated to the hub. The obligation is not structured as a financial debt to be repaid to the hub; as noted, the spoke is not expected to pay money to the hub for the expenditures the hub or the hub's household incurred during the spoke's co-resident period of sponsorship. Rather, the obligation seems to be expressed in two socially significant ways.

First, the spoke is *beholden* to the hub—for life, it seems. After all, the hub is the person who has made the migration experience possible for the spoke. It must be said that, for the most part, most hubs I interviewed were quite humble about their altruistic behavior. They did not talk about their help as something they valued highly or that they would label "sacrifice." They tended to downplay their efforts and sacrifice to an extraordinary degree—so much so that days after the interview they remembered many things about sponsoring others that they could not remember while I was questioning them, because they hadn't previously thought about what they did in the ways in which my interview made them think. But the spoke's indebtedness is evident: if the spoke is asked to do a favor for the hub (usually this means doing a service for another spoke or for a hub's family member), the spoke finds it nearly impossible to turn the hub down. One spoke explained that while she was co-resident she had to go on family outings involving early rising for day-long car trips to picnic areas every time her brother (the hub) wanted to, even if she'd rather spend her time in other ways. In another case, a spoke was given the benefit of migration for a specific circumstance. A hub had sired a son in the West Indies before migrating to New York and marrying his current wife. As it was thought best to educate the boy in New York, the hub arranged with the boy's mother, who by then had several other children with someone else, for the boy's release. The spoke was asked to bring the boy to the States. The spoke's own migration would be his reward for accompanying the child. But the spoke showed up at John F. Kennedy Airport alone, without the boy; it was one of the severest violations of the culture of reciprocity I'd heard about. It has been decades since this occurred, and although that spoke was not sent back home, he was certainly ostracized by some of the network members I interviewed. Still, in almost every case, spokes talked very fondly of those who'd helped them, even if they reported that their immigration experience was not a good one. Their gratitude toward the hub for getting them into the Western global city where they found work was marked.

What Do Hubs Gain?

Clearly spokes gain the opportunity to secure social and economic mobility, and remittances that bring increased economic well-being and security to those left behind. What is the hub's gain in this reciprocal migration culture? One outcome is that hubs accrue gains to their reputations when they help others, and these gains increase with the number of persons aided. Nothing in my interviews suggests that hubs are consciously proffering help in order to reap gains.[4] Their altruism seems to derive directly from the experience of being a successful Third World migrant—an experience that likely differs for hubs and spokes because their relationships to their national and ethnic peers are significantly different from each other.

One hypothesis about how hubs' and spokes' experiences differ derives from my speculation that many who become hubs started their own immigrant lives as pioneers—that is, persons who arrive without the help of a network. Randall's comments suggest that this is true:

Yeah, we helped a lot of people while we were here—you have this connectivity—people know they have a relative in the States, even [to] say they come on vacation or something like that. But in my days, when we came up here, as I said, when my wife came I think she went straight to the hospital that sponsored her. They didn't have a relative or anything like that. But today it's entirely different. My wife is up here thirty-six years and I'm here thirty-four years, 'cause there were two years—so by then, maybe you have enough roots so those who are coming today could enjoy, you know, the idea of having somebody able.

There is much about pioneer status that would motivate a migrant to become a hub. He is the first to try something new: to take a job in a new sector of a Western economy, try a new route out of the West Indies, enter a new country or city where he doesn't know anyone who has gone before him. After he arrives, there are two possibilities: he can succeed or he can fail. When moving from a Third World country, securing a steady job with enough pay to have some left over for savings is often all the success one needs.

If a pioneer is successful in securing work and housing, two things immediately become clear. First, there is no one with him in the destination with whom he can share his success, because by definition pioneers arrive alone; it is the spoke who has relatives and friends in the destination. Also, the pioneer's success comes at a very high price—very long work hours, little pay, and therefore few avenues of recreation. Down time, however little of it there is, is a lonely time when one is alone in a foreign country. Thus, pioneers immediately orient themselves toward the home community. They have to—there's no one yet at the destination who can be interpreted as central to their ethnic community.

The other thing that is immediately apparent is that the pioneer becomes better off relative to those he has left behind. This is obvious to a pioneer on his first visit back home or the first time he sends a remittance of a substantial size, if such relative wealth is not evident sooner. Someone experiencing success is happy to share it with those less fortunate, especially if the less fortunate person is a beloved friend or dear relative. Sending for a peer who is equally committed to success is a way of sharing one's own good fortune.[5]

VB: How did it happen that [all the people you helped] came to the United States? Did you invite them, or did they ask you to come?

Randall: Well, they're invited. I mean the point is, as I said before, when I came here and I was so fascinated, and I could see the opportunities that—and I figure, back in the West Indies so many of us are really endowed with some good talent but there is no scope, there is no place to realize it. And I felt that this place, you know, affords the opportunity to help yourself if you are willing to do that. So, you encourage people to come. I encouraged my brother to come, my wife's uncle, other friends. And as a matter of fact one of the friends who stayed with me on vacation, when he went back home he started—he didn't want to come here, but the people whom he worked with for a little while—they called me and ask me how I could get in touch with him. I phoned in Trinidad and let him know that the people wanted him back. And he came back and he was able to bring up his family and everything, brought up his wife and kids, brought up some of his brothers and sisters, and this is the way we all help each other—

VB: It must be hard, though, sometimes, to have people in your house, no?

Randall: No, we never look at it that way. Listen, I grew up in a house where shelter and food was something my parents are also willing to extend. This is one of the things that I found here that [troubles me]: parents are making the children pay rent—save money—back on the island we never [did those things.] It's kind of an extended family.

It makes sense that few spokes become hubs. Spokes arrive with help. Spokes have a ready community with which they can identify in the destination. They are not alone in the destination, and therefore not as likely to experience the loneliness a pioneer might. With their destination orientation, they share with their new community members the experience of adapting to the new environment. They likely feel part of the new community. Because spokes are more destination oriented, they are probably confronted less often with the cognitive sense of relative wealth (compared to those left back home) that might motivate hubs to help others who have not yet migrated. In sum, one's relative position in one's community depends on whether one's cognitive home is in the destination or in the West Indies.

Another factor that keeps spokes from becoming hubs is that hubs raise the cost of becoming a hub to a prohibitive level. On the basis of the data presented here we may assume that hubs in West Indian immigrant social networks promote co-resident sponsorship, are knowledgeable in both labor and housing markets, have sufficient market power to make confident referrals that will become actual jobs and domiciles for those referred, and are committed enough to the culture of reciprocity to sustain post-co-resident sponsorship that is indefinite in duration. In doing all this, hubs substantially raise the price of entry into the hub role, discouraging spokes from following suit and becoming hubs themselves. Moreover, because entry into the hub role is restricted, existing hubs retain and enhance their exclusive expert status. The fewer hubs there are, the more the existing and potential network members (the latter being those who have not yet migrated) have to rely on the knowledge and resources of the few hubs in the network. Thus, exclusive hub status reinforces itself while discouraging entry into the hub positions in the network, thereby establishing and maintaining the hierarchy of network positions.

What does the hub get out of sponsorship and sacrifice? Both power and status accrue to the expert sponsor—and this occurs both back home and in the destination. Hubs tend to return to the West Indies for visits more often than spokes, and when they travel they bring along gifts—visual and tangible representations of their successes—which simultaneously broadcast their ability to help others. Even if they do not speak about their sponsorship activities on these return trips, the visits of those few successful spokes who do infrequently return will speak volumes for the hubs' reputations. Too, those spokes who are already resident in the destination continue to rely on the hub for information, whether on new jobs or promotions, on housing when someone is ready to move from an apartment to a house, or on assistance in sending for the next network candidate. Furthermore, hubs participate in the local communities both in the destination and on the islands, and the money and time they invest in mobility projects speak for themselves. Such notoriety will accrue whether the contribution is on the small scale of a given individual's mobility or on a larger scale as the hub helps a village school or makes contributions of infrastructure through a U.S.- or England-based ethnic organization. Such contributions and remittances continue over the entire period that the migrant is away, as long as he intends to return home (Thomas-Hope, 1986), as hubs tend to do.

Moreover, the hub gains the compliance of the other members of the household as they proceed with immigration schemes to assist newcomers. Few spouses of hubs I interviewed expressed objections to their partner's altruism, and many suggested that there was little they could do about it in any case. How does a hub negotiate the various family and household members' compliance with the hub household scheme, particularly as it involves having one's family agree to applying the household's collective resources to the hub's project? For one, the hub may in fact coerce household members' compliance with the hub household project. To cite examples presented earlier, recall that Taran sent for young women to do child care—something about which her husband could scarcely object, for the need for child care solutions would be obvious to him. But sponsorship often occurs even at the cost of what might have otherwise been placid household relations. (Note that Taran's hub experience included sending one spoke back to the West Indies, and that spoke's young replacement ran away from the hub household in response to what she considered unfair treatment.) Alternatively, embarrassment can be a strong motivator for household members' compliance. Assume, for example, that one householder commits resources to the family or friend left behind. The spouse and the other household members can hardly speak up and refuse to offer help without losing face in the home community or seeming petty and selfish to others in the destination-based network. Another scenario is possible also: household members may enjoy sharing in the reputation that the hub brings with his or her sponsorship activities, even if they may not agree at first or would not themselves consider taking on the hub role. For example, even though Dawn's husband was no hub himself, he clearly enjoyed telling people, "If I know my wife . . . you'll be here in no time."

Conversely, neither hubs themselves, other hub household members, nor spokes freely discussed with me the power and control that hubs wield within their network relationships. Nonetheless this power and control exists. I am not suggesting that the generosity and selflessness of the sponsors is false. On the contrary, hubs and hub household members make great sacrifices to bring newcomers into the networks. As Londoners Jocelyn and her husband told me, "God put this responsibility in our hands"—that is, it was their responsibility to be good hubs and therefore to organize the group they brought to the West so that they presented the best face they could of the various subgroups they represented. (In Jocelyn's case, she thought the transplanted migrants were called on to be good representatives and standard-bearers for Christians,

Trinidadians, and blacks.) Furthermore, the spokes I interviewed openly recognized their hubs' generosity, even many years after the initial sponsorship period had ended. It was with great difficulty that people discussed the unequal power relationship that hubs and spokes have with each other.

Hubs appear to enjoy being the go-to person in both the destination and the home country; even if they do not speak in ways that betray these feelings, they do not dislike being admired and looked up to. Hubs certainly gain a transnational reputation for their altruistic efforts within both the destination and the origin community, and they enjoy the shine from their reputation-enhancing actions. I give precedence to hub-spoke differences in ego motivations, and this is quite intentional. No quantifiable economic or human resource characteristics distinguish hubs from migrants who do not extend their networks. For example, in this sample there were both uneducated hubs and well-skilled ones. Many hubs are in high-ranking positions or (if retired) ended their careers in high-ranking positions but they each began hub activities when they were not in strong labor-market positions. Some became hubs when they owned their first home; however, plenty of Caribbean homeowners do not open up their homes to anyone outside of their immediate nuclear family. Hubs are both men and women; some are quite old and some are fairly young (although no one I spoke with was an unmarried young person in their twenties, for example). Among the hubs who participated in this sample there was no indication of anything other than the psychological motivations described in this section to explain why they displayed such seemingly altruistic behavior toward their co-ethnics.

Social Structure and the Boundedness of Reciprocity

Even when willing to provide immigration and resettlement assistance, and even when in full agreement with the unwritten and unspoken tenets of the culture of reciprocity, network members are limited in their ability to act on their altruism by the social, economic, and political structures in which immigration and resettlement takes place. No one hub will have all the information necessary to be all things to all spokes or potential migrants with whom they may have contact. This implies, then, that hub-and-spoke configurations are constrained by the amount of social capital that can possibly be generated by the members within that configuration.

The network's social embeddedness becomes structurally important, as many network and migration researchers have made clear (Granovetter, 1995;

Kelly, 1995; Portes and Sensenbrenner, 1993; Waldinger, 1996). The structural context in which migration takes place makes available or limits the resources through which network members help one another, thereby determining the methods and means for actualizing international movement. As opportunities for migration become available, potential movers and those who help them must (1) decide how money and other resources needed in migration and resettlement will be collected and spent, (2) consider whether to comply or circumvent the laws surrounding emigration and immigration, and (3) make other decisions about how to actualize an international move. The availability of these opportunities is the catalyst that makes the network machinery operate. These forces shape the network to the extent that they define who is able to emigrate and who must stay behind, and they tend to influence the size of the migration stream and the speed at which it flows. (For example, a deteriorating political climate and poor economic health of the sending society or anticipated changes in immigration law at the destination will likely change the size and speed of the migration flow.)

Providing assistance to others within the network is made even more difficult by the limitations imposed on network resources by the structural context in which networks operate. Because these networks find jobs and housing within the larger socioeconomy (and not in ethnic enclaves), these immigrants face constraints to their ability to provide assistance to one another: scarcity of jobs and housing, racial and ethnic discrimination, and so forth (Waters, 1999). The boundedness of reciprocity exists, then, even if all network members are in agreement about the tenets of social exchange, and even if the nature of network participation brings about no discord among its members.

Conclusion

Researchers have given much weight to the importance of the immigrant social network in explaining migration flows, but they have not specified what the network is, shown how it works, or accounted for how it is structured and maintained. This chapter has reevaluated and extended the social network as an analytical concept in international migration. I have presented a Weberian ideal type of the immigrant social network that I have named the hub-and-spoke network. My research, based on the experiences of West Indian immigrants, shows that all network members are not equal, that certain immigrants (whom I have labeled hubs) are much more likely to send for additional immigrants. Other immigrants (labeled spokes) may use the assistance of the network as they themselves migrate but are much less likely to send for others. Hubs have five characteristics different from others in the network: they make greater effort to keep very strong ties to the home community, make sacrifices for both the home community and the newcomers they sponsor, have great control in the selection of new immigrants, agree to a system of reciprocity in the giving of the network's social capital, and have labor market connections that facilitate their role as hubs. Spokes differ from hubs in two important ways: they have more tenuous ties to the home community and they are less willing (or perhaps less able) to accept the sacrifices required of the hub that are defined by the network's culture of reciprocity. These sacrifices include assistance getting into the country, co-residency while the spoke is getting on his or her feet, assistance in finding work, and assistance in finding housing after co-residence ends.

The culture of these networks is constructed in such a way as to give the hub quite a bit of control in deciding who comes to the United States or England and when. Hubs can do this because they hold the knowledge that allows for a smoother migration, documentation, and resettlement process and are therefore able to control the transfer of social capital. But hubs are also governed by the norms and mores that shape exchanges among individuals and households in the network, and by the social structures in which the network is embedded, so hubs' power to control resources and people in the network is not absolute.

Two important implications of this new understanding of network migration for immigration research and policy emerge from the findings in this chapter. One implication challenges our understanding of social capital. Migration research to date has led us to assume that potential immigrants still in the home country are able to marshal social capital toward their own ends when they are ready to move. The research presented here, however, suggests instead that hubs, or veteran immigrants, are the keepers and controllers of the social capital in the immigrant social network. This finding leads to a second implication: if we are aware that the probabilities of sending for others are unequal across types of immigrants, perhaps we should develop new ways of studying the processes of and estimating the probabilities for subsequent chain migration. Most migration models see all migrants as potential links in a chain that leads to future migration (Massey and Espinosa, 1997; Jasso and Rosenzweig, 1989). Perhaps we should instead question the assumptions of previous models and perhaps adjust them to differentiate among immigrants already in destinations, knowing that some immigrants seem more likely to send for newcomers than others. We may also wish to question previous ideas about selectivity: contrary to the idea (pervasive in the migration literature) that migrants are self-selecting, new migrants in the West Indian networks seem to some degree to be chosen by those veteran immigrants who control the resources of the network. Potential immigrants may request help from network members, but that help is not necessarily forthcoming.

An empirical question remains: do other immigrant groups conduct their network migration this way? This question is addressed in the chapter that concludes this book. Suffice it to say here that there is anecdotal evidence from research on other foreign-born groups that suggests that their networks operate similarly: their hublike figures are instrumental in sending for others and in influencing important outcomes in their resettlement process (Hagan, 1994; Tilly, 1998); potential immigrants such as family members still in the country of origin implore immigrants in the United States to follow cultural mores about assisting those left behind (Thomas and Znaniecki, 1996); and network power does not always work to the benefit of all who agree to participate in immigrant networks (Mahler, 1995).

4 Getting Smart About Getting In

FOR CARIBBEAN ISLAND PEOPLES, migration is their history, and it is now as normal to move as it is to stay. At least since the time black slaves were manumitted, black Eastern Caribbean socioeconomic mobility has been coupled with geographic mobility—as paid work has been made available to migrants under contract labor and other labor recruitment arrangements, movers have gone to increasingly distant geographic locations seeking jobs. As international migration researchers are well aware by now, where labor recruitment links are made, network migration begins and soon takes hold. These arrangements—especially those that contract for imported labor—can hardly be made without government sanction; thus policy begins a process that allows labor recruitment links between destination and origin sites. Legislators of the past could not, of course, converse with those of the future who many times tried to constrict or reverse the flows the former began with labor contracts meant to alleviate what they perhaps believed to be only temporarily high labor demands. But wherever network migration takes hold, legislation becomes increasingly ineffective at reversing the flows, particularly with a group like the West Indians, who are flexible in choosing destinations and at living out their lives so they can be ready to take on whatever opportunities become available (Carnegie, 1987, p. 200).

Networked immigrants use their knowledge of immigration regulations well enough to be creative and flexible in their strategies for sending for family members and friends, whether they use legal or illegal avenues to achieve their ends (Garrison and Weiss, 1979). Once the decision is made to send for someone, network members begin to arrange and apply the mechanisms by which international movement can occur. Sometimes this means coming up with a scheme by which the person can get into the country—either legally or, at first, illegally, to become legal later—and meet their targeted goal. These schemes often involve hubs who know how to file immigration papers in New York and in the Caribbean to obtain legal status for the newcomer, or who use employers to obtain legal sponsorship for new network members. Networked migrants also make informal arrangements to secure work, fix their undocumented status, send children back and forth to improve their welfare, and arrange or prevent marriages. Here, as with other aspects of networked migration, the hub is the go-to person for getting help entering the country.

Network Immigration Schemes

Overstaying Visas

Many U.S.-bound migrants come on visitor or student visas and extend their stays; as the preceding chapter notes, entering and overstaying often (but not exclusively) happen at the behest of a hub. Randall, a hub quoted in the previous chapter, confirmed that extended visitor stays are precisely the way many of his hub-spoke relationships began:

> VB: How did it happen [that all the people you helped] came? Did you invite them or did they ask you to come?

> Randall: Well, they're invited. I mean the point is, as I said before, when I came here and I was so fascinated, and I could see the opportunities—well, listen, people would come on vacation and, as I said before—you just have to think about it. If people see an opportunity where they think they can make a better life for themselves, obviously they want to stay, and this is all what you think about today in this country. You see the big hoopla on immigration policy today. I mean this country also had a type of open immigration policy, especially to Europeans—not so much the nonwhite—but all the other countries, most of them, were placed on quotas, only X amount of people were allowed to come in. And it's my opinion, again, as I said, you have a relative or a friend and the friend came here on vacation and the friend says that they would like to stay and there is a possibility that they can stay and they may only want temporary shelter until they can fend for themselves, you know—you extend it to them. We try to help each other, you know—

> I mean today it's entirely different, it's not like when I grew up as a young

person, but extending, you know, an invitation for someone, I mean this place could be very expensive, you think about it. If someone comes on vacation here and have to stay in a hotel or some kind of thing like that, they can't afford it, so this is one of the ways that probably you can help them. You give them shelter, no big deal to give them a little morsel of food, because they're not here permanently, they're on vacation and they enjoy some of the life and they say they really like it, you know, and they like the States, and if they get the opportunity to stay, why not?[1]

Glennis had a similar experience to tell:

Glennis: [I've helped] many people. Many of our friends ask us to send letters to them so they can come for a visit, and we did that.

VB: Did any of them ever come to stay?

Glennis: They all stayed. [Laughs.] They all stayed and they brought up their husbands, their wives.

I do not know whether more spokes enter legally than enter without documents—although this has much to do with what jobs they do and whether employers provide documentation along with a job, as they do for some domestics—but on this topic Briggs (1984, p. 153) writes, "Most illegal immigrants from the Caribbean are 'visa abusers.' This means they are often admitted as students, tourists, or businessmen" who convince immigration officials that they plan to return to the Caribbean. Underlying the process is normally a long period after the spoke first arrives on a visitor or student visa and finds work illegally, through a hub. In the meantime, papers for permanent residency often are filed. When the legal entry of the spoke—who is already in the country—is approved, the spoke returns to the home country and completes the proper paperwork, and shortly thereafter reenters the United States. Within the provisions for the Labor Certification Program of the 1965 Immigration Act, employers were allowed to file applications for labor certification on behalf of would-be immigrants. These provisions were fought for by labor unions; the result was that occupations allowed under the program have to be certified by the Labor Secretary as hard-to-fill because of a scarcity of native labor—either their skill levels were too high or the jobs were undesirable and native-born persons were loath to take them.

Thus the labor certification system since 1965 has actually encouraged illegal immigration: some persons enter the United States without proper documents or violate the terms of visitor visas, obtain job offers, and then use these offers as levers in applying for the labor certifications that will qualify them to become immigrants (Fogel, 1978). If the job certifications are granted, these persons succeed; but even if the requests are denied, because the visa violators are already in the country, they are likely to remain as illegal immigrants. Indeed, it was estimated in 1978 that 45 percent of all labor certifications "simply legalize the presence of workers already here illegally" (Briggs, 1984, pp. 70–71).

The 1986 Immigration Reform and Control Act (IRCA) instituted sanctions for those U.S. employers who hire illegal entrants, but these sanctions may not have the desired effect on the presence and employment of undocumented migrants if we measure that effect by rates of overstay. The 1988 rates of overstay of immigrants from many countries seemed to return to pre-IRCA levels, and nonimmigrants from the Caribbean showed a mixed IRCA-response record. Rates of overstay increased among nonstudent visitors from Trinidad, Tobago, and Bermuda, while those from Haiti, Grenada, and Barbados stayed at roughly the same rates pre- and post-IRCA. (Warren, 1990, estimates that, in addition to student visa overstayers, 16 percent of Haitians and 8.4 percent of Trinidadians who had arrived in the United States at least nine months prior to his inquiries had overstayed their visas.) Only the numbers of overstayers from Jamaica, Dominica, and the Bahamas seemed to decrease two years after the IRCA's passage. Hubs who are able to arrange for visitors to come and obtain jobs—even without proper legal status—have a great deal of power to select spokes for migration, even in a climate of employer sanctions against hiring the undocumented.

Thus, visa overstayers begin their long-term residence without proper documentation and find ways to fix their papers later. If one's papers are invalid, incomplete, or altogether missing, one has great difficulty traveling back and forth on one's own timetable. However, traveling back and forth is precisely what is required when it is time to get papers straight (that is, to legalize one's status through proper documentation) after a period of undocumented time in the States.

Several respondents in the New York City area told me that after some time in New York they had to go to Barbados when their papers came through. These trips to Barbados are required of most migrants who remain in New York illegally but want to fix their papers, because this is where the immigration office for the West Indies is located. Migrants have to pose as if they are still living in the West Indies at the time of filing, and thus have to rush to

Barbados when the papers finally come through. When the application for legal status is finally approved, migrants go back to their country of origin— presumably to make it look as if they'd never left and were waiting for the immigration paperwork all along.

> Yeah, he was from Union Island. He took me [to the job]; he introduced me to the same guy that he was working with and I worked for him. But I only worked, let's see, with him for, I think it was just about six months. By then my papers came through and I went down back to Union Island. I got my papers fixed and I came back and I went to work earnestly.

Once obtained, papers are kept up to date, even in cases where visitors or students return home, just in case they want to come back for intermittent periods of work, or in case they change their minds and want to live in the United States again. For those who hold proper documents but want to live elsewhere and keep their options open, frequent travel back and forth between the United States and their current residence is required to keep the papers up-to-date. Several respondents living in the Caribbean and in England similarly explained that they held onto valid U.S. documents so they could leave open the option to return at some other time, and they too had to travel regularly in order to obscure their residence outside the United States. One person who lives in the Caribbean but still holds a green card for U.S. residency explained that he travels just so he can keep the green card active. Presumably because his travel history (that is, his proof that he is not actually living in the United States) is evident from the documents he must show officials at the border, he has had trouble at the border on the infrequent trips he has made to keep his status up-to-date. He explained, "Sometimes, they stamp you, saying 'This person has been warned.' Then people change their passports." If the documents look bad, the solution is to get rid of them and get clean replacements.

Some of my respondents worked in the United States illegally for decades until the amnesty under the 1986 IRCA opened the doors for their legal stay. James was one who admitted that he came on a student visa and didn't change his status for many years. The 1986 amnesty enabled him finally to "get his papers straight."

> I'm forty years old [and have been here ten years]. I went to my boss and I said, "I'd like for you to sponsor me." So he asked, "What do you mean, sponsor you? Sponsor you to go where?" I said, "To become a citizen of this country,

of the United States." He said, "What do you mean 'become a citizen of the United States'? You are a citizen of the United States." I said, "No, I'm not. I'm an illegal alien." He said, "What? You mean all these years that I've known you you're illegal and I never knew that?" I used to take the immigration department into the company to inspect people when they used to make raids, and they never knew, 'cause I was a manager at the time.

His boss found him an immigration lawyer and he had documents in about sixteen months, and he sponsored his wife (who also was already living in the United States with him but who he said "was too chicken to ask her company to sponsor her").

Overstayers on visitor's visas are by definition connected to the people they came to visit. They can then, by definition, be said to be participants in immigrant social networks. Those who come on student visas and overstay may or may not be connected to networked immigrants in the same ways as overstaying visitors, but evidence from the testimonies in this study suggests that there are many such students who migrate on their network connections, which also seem to be of the hub-and-spoke variety. Whether students or visitors, visa overstayers must have places to live and work in order to ensure their livelihood during their fragile undocumented existence, and being connected to a network increases the likelihood that the newcomer can survive this undocumented state for some time. Overstayers, whether visitors or students, are likely connected to immigrant networks because often it is the help of a network that enables them to stay. James, who himself became a hub, had learned before arriving what it took to get into the country and find work, after failing to get help from his sister who was already in the United States and had attended Howard University. Here he explains how he finally got to New York. Although he wasn't able to become a spoke in the way he wanted to, and although at first glance it seems he crossed the border on his own, he clearly had help from his network, and clearly his goal was more than just to secure an education, for he started working immediately upon arrival.

> So, um, we did apply to this college and I got accepted. The next thing was to have enough money to pay for my semester and to travel, and to show that I have enough money in the bank and all this kind of [thing], you know, like a bank statement. I have to show this to the immigration department. So I borrowed money from my brother, my father, and two of my cousins, [all of them still] back home [as I was]. A total of $9,000 I borrowed and, you know, put it in the

bank, got a bank statement, and then I took it back out, gave them back the money, and I also had to travel with a certain amount of cash, you know. As evidence that I have, in the event that things didn't work out here, you know, in any way or form I could afford to take care of myself until I'm ready to go back. And once I got here I returned whatever monies I borrowed the next year. I came here Sunday; I went to the bank and I brought money out and I send it back to them along with a letter thanking them, you know, for the support and help. That was the Monday, and Tuesday I went out looking for jobs.

Creating and Maintaining Niche Employment Sectors

Adult immigrants need jobs when they arrive. The ability of hubs to send for spokes is influenced by prevailing labor market conditions, the flexibility of laws by which to bring immigrant workers, and the job niches in which veteran immigrants have some influence. Hubs decide they want to send for friends or relatives, and find or, in some cases, create jobs for them. This works best with women, for whom domestic jobs (such as maid, nanny, and home care worker) can more easily be secured. These jobs also are the kind that allow the employer to sponsor the new immigrant through the legal documentation process. Green cards can be obtained for new immigrants by finding families who need domestic help, recommending to the employer the woman in the West Indies, and once arrangements are made, sending for them to come and get the job, as was the case for Amsie (see Chapter Three) and others in these networks.

Employers and immigrants together have managed to carve out some areas of the labor market and monopolize them for jobs for the foreign born. These niches have changed over time and with the arrival of new generations of immigrants. Many of the immigrants I spoke with recalled, for example, that their parents came as sailors (men) and domestics (women). Colen's work supports the idea that network members develop niche employment where it can assist them in securing legal status:

> Although spouses or certain close relatives with permanent resident status or U.S. citizenship and some employers (such as hospitals that recruit registered nurses) sponsor West Indian women, for many, employer sponsorship in domestic and child-care work is one of the few paths to legal status. Many without green cards know before migrating that their first step will be domestic work. As Dawn Adams remembers from St. Vincent, "When you're at home, you hear that you do babysitting in order to get sponsored." [Colen, 1989, p. 173]

Subsequent generations of immigrants—including most of the people in this sample—are water and sewer tunnel workers (men) and nurses or domestics (women) in New York. The most recent adult immigrant niches for these networked men now include pockets of jobs in the New York City Civil Service, and a few of the women had moved into banking. In London, relevant current niches exist for nurses, transport workers, and teachers.

Recruiting Individual Employers

Veteran immigrants are well aware that they can use employers to gain legal status for the new immigrants they bring into the country. The key to the success of this kind of plan is to gain an employer's agreement to hire the new immigrant. Employers do not always know that they are being used to help someone already targeted for selection by a hub. In this scheme, the network's hub brings the newcomer into the country and the employer is expected to take care of the immigration paperwork. Taran helped Amsie get a job as a maid in exactly this way (as explained in Chapter Three). Taran was also instrumental in helping at least one of Glennis's spokes. Glennis's statement on this topic, quoted earlier, continues in this way:

> Glennis: As a matter of fact, there was a woman who came on a vacation and she was my babysitter; she lived with us and took care of the children. She came up on a vacation and a friend introduced her to me 'cause she knew that I wanted somebody to help me with the children.
>
> VB: So this was a friend you know from nursing school?
>
> Glennis: Taran introduced this girl to me—she lived with us, she took care of the kids.
>
> VB: And she was from Trinidad as well?
>
> Glennis: Um huh.
>
> VB: How long did she stay with you?
>
> Glennis: She stayed with me for about, um, five years.
>
> VB: What were the circumstances under which she left?
>
> Glennis: Oh well, she had to get her permanent visa, and I sent her on to somebody who could have helped her.
>
> VB: How did the person help her?
>
> Glennis: Jewish people were able to help her get her papers.

VB: So she left to stay with them? Was she their domestic?

Glennis: Yeah, um huh.

VB: Are you still in touch with her?

Glennis: Um huh.

VB: What is she doing now?

Glennis: She just retired as a nurse's aide. She just retired last year. She worked at St. John's Hospital for twenty-five years.

VB: Oh. Do you know how she became a nurse's aide?

Glennis: Um, I don't know. She took the course after she had gotten [her papers] straightened out. I know they sponsored her; she got her visa and whatnot and she took the nurse's aide courses.

The following statement from Evaline, another nurse in Taran and Amsie's network, supports my argument that sending for someone in this way is a widespread practice:

I did try to sponsor someone—a friend's daughter—through a domestic scheme. A domestic scheme is just like the farmworker scheme. Women come and work with a family. The family sponsors the maid and after some time they become permanent residents. These families have money, so it's easier [for them to do it]. Many immigrants come as domestics, although they have never done any domestic work before in their country or in their life.

Often the job comes first and the sponsorship later; thus hubs and the spokes together put their reputations on the line well before the paperwork is discussed. As explained in the preceding chapter, Taran helped Amsie in this way. Glennis, herself a nurse-administrator, explained how another spoke, her husband's friend, found work and legal status after he moved to this country:

Glennis: My husband took him down to an agency and he got a job in a Jewish school in Borough Park. They liked him so much they decided to sponsor him.

VB: What does it mean that they sponsored him?

Glennis: They helped him to get his green card so he can stay in this country.

VB: So they helped to get the paperwork while he lived with you all?

Glennis: And then, um, he was able to bring up his family.

If veteran immigrants use their reputations to get jobs for those they want to have follow them in the immigration process, and if these newcomers meet or exceed the employer's expectations, the employer often sponsors the employees in securing their immigration papers. Bentley, a civil service manager, explains:

> I can also get jobs for people in the factory, different types of factories, like sweatshops you know, and like machinist work, and making toys, and dressmaking, and things like that. I knew a lot of people who did not have permanent residence, so there were places they could not have gone [looking for work], but because I was a[n armed services] veteran, I could go and make contacts for them, you know. Same thing in mechanics work. You see, a lot of West Indian guys came up here. A lot of them came through the back door, but they have a lot of skill, but they just need a foot in the door. They just want to get a break, an opportunity, and some of them cannot get it unless they say they have a green card or they're permanent status, and these guys don't have it. Being as the guy knew me, my word was bond, and they take my word for it, and it was kept quiet, you know. In some cases the guys were so good that the employer sponsored him to keep him.

Because a domestic can use her employer to secure legal status, the job can be used as a refuge for a woman without immigrant documentation, and many women in the New York City networks chose to do domestic work precisely because it was the easiest way to overstay a visitor's visa and secure subsequent legal sponsorship. The interview data contain important examples of how women have used domestic work as a strategy for negotiating legal status. In one case, Charmaine, who emigrated to the United States as a young girl to do child care work for her aunt, was being trained as a nurse. She married Linford, who was also in the United States completing his training as a medical doctor. Neither had their papers straight, even though Charmaine had been here for so many years.

> We got married in September 1977, and I had [given birth to my daughter] Lynn in November of that year. I was trying to go to school and he was going to school, and I got pregnant [again]. My son was born at six months, maybe seven, but a premature birth. At that time we still didn't have our green card. Well, we had two choices. I think we had one choice, basically: for someone to sponsor us so that we can get our green card. In order for that to be done, I had to go and do domestic work and have someone sponsor me.

Charmaine and Linford decided together that Charmaine would leave nursing and begin work as a live-in domestic, because that was their fastest route to a green card. Then, when Charmaine was "straight," Linford would use his access to a wife with legal status to straighten out his own status. She already had a home, but she moved in with the employing family in order to obtain the legal status that came with that kind of domestic service. Thus Charmaine, who at the time had nearly completed her nurse's training, began living with a family for whom she cooked and cleaned during the week, and came home only on weekends, until she obtained the green card. Once it was in hand, she sponsored her husband, who was already in the United States as well. Charmaine is not the only example of a migrant who used employers to obtain papers in this way. Dawn too was a domestic when she first arrived. A practicing nurse in London, she had not been able to work after moving to New York because the paperwork certifying her qualification to practice nursing did not arrive for quite some time. She told me it was very hard on her husband when she began working as a domestic, because men in the West Indies were accustomed to being the breadwinner. After explaining the trouble she had—first from her mother, who thought that domestic work was degrading for her daughter, who had been a nurse; and then from her husband, himself dejected because he was unable to find work—she said this of her own domestic scheme: "For men it's hard, but a woman can do anything to feed her family."

The domestic workers and nurse's aides in the group I interviewed generally used informal (ad hoc) recruitment practices of their networks to find the employers who would hire and eventually sponsor them. Waldinger and Lichter (2003) explain that methods for securing jobs include knowing about employees who plan to leave their jobs before the employers themselves know, so that network members might know about job openings even before the employer posts the job as available. In the sample of immigrants studied for this research, nurses and domestics (women) were predominantly the ones brought to the United States through use of such informal labor recruitment schemes.[2]

Manipulating Formal Labor Recruitment Channels

Presumably, the operations of *formal* labor recruitment programs would neither rely on reputations or referrals nor involve networks or hubs. But even when migrants are brought in through formal programs designed to recruit foreign labor, social networking for immigration and resettlement of the hub-and-spoke kind operates to make migration happen. What I am calling labor recruitment schemes are those programs in which a particular class of workers is sought on a large scale, either by one employer or by a set of employers who rely on a middleman to act as an immigration clearinghouse. The employer (who is based in the destination country) sends out representatives to hire foreign nationals directly to work for him or her. In this case, the job itself is the catalyst that makes the migration happen—or so it would seem to the employer and to the government that allows and sanctions such recruitment. This method of employer recruitment differs slightly from that described in the previous section, which was more of an ad-hoc method of finding employers willing to sponsor a new immigrant and provide documentation of his or her legal immigration status.

Networking respondents both in Britain and in the United States explained to me that veteran network members already in the United States or United Kingdom used employer recruitment programs to ensure postimmigration reunion of selected potential network members. Respondents' discussions of labor recruitment programs focused on industrial sectors that targeted men and women separately. For Caribbean men, recruitment began with the search for workers to build the railroads in Panama in the 1850s, and continued when the United States became involved in building the Panama Canal in 1904 (Conniff, 1985). One migrant in my study reported having a canal worker as an ancestor. A subsequent stage in the link to male labor was recruitment for contract laborers to work in the fields of Florida. Farmwork in that state is still a draw for workers from the Caribbean, who make up nearly 35 percent of those who toil at growing and harvesting agricultural goods (U.S. Dept. of Housing and Urban Development, 2004). Women recruited from the Caribbean (along with those from Hong Kong, Mauritius, Malaysia, and Ireland) filled jobs as nurses for the British Health Service—to the extent that the number of these women increased threefold in the decade between 1959 and 1970. In the New York sample, nurses and domestics (women) were brought to the United States through labor recruitment; and in London, teachers (both men and women) were brought with their families through a recruitment program. Network members in London relied on formal recruitment programs more often than U.S. respondents did.

One example of the ways network members used formal labor recruitment was explained by a respondent in New York who described her involvement in the recruitment of nurses to work in New York City hospitals: "Kuczinsky, the lawyer, came to the island to recruit nurses. I was recruited for Bethel Hospital, which [later] became Brookdale [Hospital]. The salaries sounded fantastic compared to what we were getting [in Trinidad]: $58 per month. Kuczinsky said we'd get $300 a month." Another respondent, Maryanne, who is also a nurse, told me, "Taran told me about the lawyer who recruited her, and he brought me." Yet another nurse explained, "Many nurses came that way, through the recruitment circles. As one found out they would tell their friends. All were eager to come to the U.S." And finally another nurse told me,

> I know a lot of nurses from the Caribbean. As a matter of fact, up to two or three years ago they were recruiting nurses to come up and work up here in various hospitals. They put them up and they have to work for the hospital for a certain amount of time and during that time they file for their papers. I think most of the people—especially from the Caribbean—go in[to] [that field] because I think it's one of the places that they can [get jobs].

There were also formal recruitment programs in the United States and Canada for domestic workers from the Caribbean. Medford's mother was recruited as a domestic worker through a program that fed labor to the U.S. domestic service industry. He told me, "I got my green card in 1971. My mother is a permanent resident there, and she applied for us. She went up in the 1960s on a domestic help program. It was advertised that they would sponsor you. You have to work a period of time to be sponsored." Also, recall from Chapter One that forty families were recruited by the education director in the London school district who used the recruitment program first initiated to recruit Australians and Canadians for his own people in the Caribbean. When I asked one teacher how she managed to legalize her status in England, she explained:

> The Borough did it all. The education director sorted it all out. When we first came, we got a two-year renewable work permit. They told us that if there's still a need after two years they would renew our permits, and they assured us that there will still be need. At one year and nine months they sorted it out, and the Borough got a four-year extension for us. After being here for five years you can apply for citizenship. So after the fifth year I applied. I applied [for citizenship] because I was fed up with going all the time for visas for [my sons'] school trips, like for [my oldest] to go to China.

That networked migrants used formal recruitment channels to bring in family and friends is significant because the thinking that predominates in migration literature presumes that labor recruitment is a phenomenon of the past and that current migration is characterized by spontaneity in lieu of deliberate recruitment (Piore, 1979; Portes and Rumbaut, 1990; Portes, 1995b). As an example of this kind of thinking, I quote Portes, who writes,

> Migrant recruitment through deliberate inducements, identified by Piore as a key factor in producing labor flows from peripheral countries, represents the midpoint in the evolution of labor migration in the core-periphery structure. Deliberate migrant recruitment was responsible for the onset of Irish labor migration to the northeast of the United States in the mid-nineteenth century; for rural Italian migration to the same region as well as to Brazil and Argentina later in the century; and for the start of labor migration from the interior of Mexico to the southwestern and midwestern United States in the same period.
>
> Spontaneous migration, when people move without any coercion or without inducement by their future employers, is mostly a twentieth century phenomenon. [Portes, 1995b, p. 21]

Portes and Rumbaut (1990, p. 13) similarly report that "back in the nineteenth century, the United States was a growing industrializing country that needed labor; but because its life standards were not a global model and its economic opportunities were not well known, it had to resort to deliberate recruitment." Although the literature does not suggest that labor recruitment no longer occurs, it does leave the reader with the sense that labor recruitment has a role in starting new migration streams, and not in the continuity of those streams, especially in a global economy where information exchanges predominate.

The respondents' experiences suggest, though, that we might modify the way we think about labor recruitment and its relationship to network migration. Instead of presuming a fairly clear dividing line between eras when network migration supposedly predominated and periods when migration was presumed to be dominated by labor recruitment, we can surmise that some networks actually *incorporate* labor recruitment channels into their strategies for recruiting friends and family in the new country. Instead of thinking that the ease of information exchange in a global economy makes recruiting obsolete, we should interrogate how information is controlled even in the so-called information age. Finally, instead of presuming that labor recruitment occurs only in cases of labor shortages and not when labor is being abundantly supplied (for example, where networks operate), we might question whether the labor supply is being controlled by an outside entity (such as hubs, who bring in their immigrant followers at their own speed). We also might question whether labor shortages drive migration in all cases, for factors such as the level of labor control or skill might also be relevant. For example, one nurse told me it was their level of skill and not labor shortages in the destination that caused graduates of the nursing school in Trinidad to be recruited. "The indigenous situation in the West Indies [is one of scarcity]. A [graduating] nurse shone [in the United States, and migrated] because she knew her country could not afford all those professionals. The West Indian nurse got the opportunity to be trained to do what [the United States] had its interns and residents learning to do." It paid to recruit from the Trinidad school of nursing because the recruiting employer could hire the skills of a resident at a nurse's wage.

The immigrant network is one of the most important institutions that help newcomers find jobs even when formal recruitment programs are operating. Many nurses and domestics in the New York area networks, and the teachers and Transport Workers in networks in London, reported being formally recruited into their jobs. Recruited nurses passed on information about opportunities and about what to expect to women who were to be recruited after them. There seems to be a time-specificity to these practices, however; domestics now seem to use more conventional networking practices (word of mouth) rather than formal recruitment channels to find jobs for one another, because recruitment in this occupation now seems to be much less important to filling domestic service jobs. Teachers in London also reported that the avenues by which they came to work in the school district are now closed to black Caribbeans.

Choosing a Country of Destination or Departure

In migration systems theory, countries of the so-called Third World or at the world system's periphery are linked with at least one country in the Western core, usually the poor nation's former colonizer or imperial power. History has linked the Lesser Antilles to more than one core destination country via histories of conquest, colonization, or geopolitics. Prospective migrants from these islands have during different historical periods chosen to travel to these linked destinations, and the timing of this travel has depended in part on the relative ease of entry given by the immigration laws. Partly too, the choice of destination is a function of the operation of the network itself—that is, people already in the destination are linked to potential migrants still in the country of origin. These linkages encourage new migrants to follow those to whom they are already tied; thus new migrants travel to places where particular kinds of network ties have preceded them. Spokes move to places where their network ties are strongest—where it is easiest to get into the country and where the most help in migration and resettlement is available (Espinosa, 1997). Sometimes hubs facilitate movement of spokes, and at other times they block such movement. A spoke can potentially choose among destinations if they have willing hubs at all the places they most desire to go. Many respondents explained to me that they had relatives in Canada, New York, and London who could, *in theory*, help them move, but each spoke went to destinations where hubs, in practice, actually made movement possible.

Choosing among destinations (an activity undertaken mostly by hubs but also by spokes to the degree that spokes have a choice about where they go) is one aspect of immigration in which the transnationalism of the various interrelated immigrant networks is most evident. People have to the opportunity to leave the islands when that opportunity comes, and often this opportunity is related to two elements: where it's easiest to find employment and where it's easiest to get into the country. Destinations, then, are largely determined by one's timing—if you have the opportunity (that is, the help) you take it. One respondent explained how her relative ended up in London:

> She went to England—see, at that time the Caribbean people—America wasn't a big thing to come to, England was the big thing to go to, so everybody was moving to England—trying to do nursing, trying to build themselves through a career path—and England was the so-called place to go, so she moved there hoping to better herself.

Migrants also choose among points of departure in order to make their emigration from the Caribbean successful. One informant explained that although he was living in Trinidad for a time, he chose to return to St. Vincent in order to get into the United States, because "Trinidadians have got a bad reputation in New York now, so it's better to leave from St. Vincent—it's easier to travel from St. Vincent to the States [rather than from Trinidad]. Trinidadians have made a bad name for themselves in New York. So it's easier to get a visa [from St. Vincent]. Also, St. Vincent is smaller. Thousands want to leave Trinidad, with a smaller number wanting to leave St. Vincent." Dominicans, who come from the largest source country of Caribbean immigrants, enter mostly through Puerto Rico, an American territory they enter by passing themselves off as Puerto Ricans, who are citizens of the United States. One person I interviewed used the Puerto Rico entry point to bring his wife's three children from the West Indies.[3]

Another respondent reported that in the early 1980s it was easier to go through Toronto to get into the United States. One of her spokes—who first was a domestic and then had a U.S. employer sponsor her—had come from the West Indies via Toronto because she was not required to have a visa. James, though, had a different perspective on the Canadian route. He is the person who was cited in the last chapter as still being angry that his sister hadn't sponsored him while she was in the United States and had then moved to Canada; he waited years in the Caribbean for his next opportunity to migrate. He says his sister also had a valid green card even while she was in Canada.

> She could have done it. She had legal status in this country, she could have easily become a citizen and the laws were much [more] lenient then to allow your mom, your dad, your brothers, and sisters, whoever wanted to come to this country, but she decided to move to Canada [because] quote, unquote, it's cleaner over there. Well, she never chose to become a citizen, but she didn't have to become a citizen to sponsor anybody. She was a legal alien in this country, you know, what do you call, green card; she had a green card. And at that time, yes, [she could have sponsored me.] She tried—she tried to get me into school in Canada but, you know, things are much different over there. For one thing, you have to be able to show, I mean, all sorts of proof that you can support this person, including paying their way through college. Even though you have to do it here, everybody knows when you come here you got to survive on your own. The key is to get here; when you get here the second step is to use your intelligence and not to forget why you came here. So, in the event that you have to return, you will return with what you came for, which is basically an education—that's why most people come to this country.

Thus, in this last migration scheme, networked migrants are flexible in using varying points of entry or departure to make border crossing happen.

Network Members as Legal Experts

At least one hub and several spokes (who performed some hub functions, such as filing papers, without actually sending for others themselves) explained to me that they were quite skilled at getting the papers that meant legal status for a newcomer. If a spoke's legal status was not taken care of by their attachment to a job, some hubs either did the immigration paperwork themselves or referred the newcomer to a legal expert in some part of the network. One man explained "my father did all the papers for the relatives. So [when I married] I said to my wife 'you better just bring your family, because my father brought all mine.'" He explained that "as a child, I saw my parents trying to help; I saw that and thought I had an obligation to help others." So extensive was the assistance some hubs gave that many of these veterans joked they had thought about setting up their own businesses to deal with issues about the legality of immigration status; as knowledge of their skill spread, more people in the network would come to them for help. Bentley (who, I was told, is known to exaggerate), told me,

> Honestly, I used to get green cards for people. I would get [driver's] licenses for people, social security for people. But those [avenues] are locked up [now]. After the [19]80s you cannot. It's very hard to get in any more.
>
> VB: How did you do it before?
>
> Bentley: I used to get it from contacts. I know people on the inside, somebody in motor vehicles. I'm talking way back in the [19]60s and [19]70s when I came out—it was easy to do. It's a paper. No picture was involved on a driver's license, you know. [They were] a dime a dozen, no problem.

That people embedded in networks use these network strategies knowledgeably to navigate the legal system is not new to the sociology of migration. Indeed, migration scholars believe that new immigration laws become less effective over time precisely because network members assist newcomers. But specific network members take on the task of keeping abreast of the immigration laws or means for getting someone into the country, and of applying them when those means are needed. Colvin explained:

> Yes [I helped people in ways other than having them live with me], because of my overall knowledge, right, being an auditor, accountant, I do a lot, because of the job, you know. I'm aware of the system—the legal system and the immigration system—so I help all my relatives and all my—they bring their friends and I file the immigration papers for them to get their sons and daughters up here. I just do it. I enjoy doing it, so I just do it. Any person with a Caribbean background who needs help, rather than pay a lawyer $2,000 or $3,000, I do it for nothing.

Winston has a similar story. He remembers, after first sponsoring his sister's move from England (she became a live-in domestic), that he later brought his sister's family from England all at one time:

> "Yeah, her husband and the kids, they all came, yes. They all came at that time, at the same time, really, because I was instrumental in helping. As a matter of fact, I filed the papers; I did the papers myself because by that time, after doing so many, I know what papers to file. Because at the time, to do papers, it was very expensive, so I paid [a lawyer], then, after, I look and see what the guy did, so I just said I'll do it myself next time, so I did all those papers."

There may have been several other ways in which navigating the legal system was made easier by one's hub, but even when I asked very direct questions of hubs, most respondents were not clear about how they handled legal processes. While it could be the case that they didn't want to divulge the details of their machinations to help the undocumented enter and stay, I had the sense that respondents did not think it was important enough to talk about, even when I probed. It was almost as if when someone got a job that allowed their legal status to be taken care of (as most domestics and recruited nurses did), hub householders hardly gave it another thought. Similarly, whenever an employer hired a spoke illegally, the problem of legal status was solved— at least for some time. So, perhaps they thought these things, just like the issue of how many people they'd helped over their overseas lifetime, weren't real issues.

Additionally and conversely, many of the spokes who did benefit from a hub's legal assistance did not at all know the details of what that assistance entailed. They knew only that whatever assistance they got at the time worked for them. Here is an excerpt from my interview with Audrey in London, who explained that although she has always lived in London since she left her island home, she held a U.S. green card for many years.

VB: How did you get the green card?

Audrey: It was through my mother. She's a citizen.

VB: But how did that come about? I don't know how it works.

Audrey: I don't know how it works either. All three of us children, me, my sister, and my brother, and also my father, have our green cards. One brother, he live in Florida, one brother gave up his green card, and Daddy give up his too.

VB: You used to visit the U.S. to keep up your green card, right?

Audrey: Yes, but after I got married it was too expensive to keep up. It's funny, because before I got married [in 1978] I did it. But I gave it up about four or five years after marriage.

Audrey and her immediate family members all held green cards despite the fact that only one of them lived in the United States. They all kept the cards active by returning frequently to the United States, until they decided that arranging these trips to secure a legal status of which they might not ever make good use wasn't worth the trouble.

Expanding the Network: Motivations and Techniques

In almost all cases, the primary idea behind a hub's sponsoring or sending for someone was to give a loved one or deserving other a chance at a better life. But many people in the Third World have need of increased income and a better life, so the relative poverty of the potential spoke is likely not the hub's primary motivating factor. Other than the desire to alleviate financial need on the part of the potential migrants, and apart from the need to choose a person whose character would enhance the hub's own reputation, what social or economic circumstances would motivate a hub to move someone overseas or, instead, leave them behind?

Child Migrants and Child Fosterage

Child fosterage is a practice of African descendants both in the Americas and in Africa whereby they submit their offspring for long-term but not necessarily permanent care in the homes of others in arrangements that resemble informal adoption. Caribbean migrants and nonmigrants on both sides of the Caribbean Sea reported widespread use of the practice in conjunction with migration to allow black Caribbean persons young and not-so-young to take advantage of work and educational opportunities from which they might otherwise be barred. With the exception of one fourteen-year-old, children were not interviewed for this study. However, children's migration has turned out to be an important part of these networks' stories. Many of the migrants reported that their own migration experiences began when they themselves were fostered. Those who were from the smaller islands of the Grenadines reported this most often, because schooling in higher grades on those islands was difficult to come by and, as children, they would have to move to continue their schooling. Iona's grandmother coerced Iona's mother into sending Iona away to be educated.

> I was at the point where I was just about to start computer school when I came here from Union Island, because the secondary school system was very different. I don't know if you know the system but I'll describe it briefly. You went up a class only if you pass the end of year exam. So you could be six [years old] in the class with somebody that's fifteen. It's that six-year-old you know who was bright, okay? So I was considered bright, like, you know, I was getting tops in my class. It was between me and another girl. We were like real rivals. (Laughs.) So, I think part of the thrust to get me out of Union [Island] was because they wanted me to be able to progress. It was my grandmother [with whom I was living in Union] who felt to give me the invitation [to go to London and join my mother]. [She saw] that something in me was special enough for me to improve my life, so she was like—she was on to my mother to get me out.

Adult migrants who wish to take advantage of the opportunities of employment overseas often have offspring they must leave behind. In such instances, the children of these migrants are left in the home country in the care of persons other than their parents for extended periods. This fosterage arrangement facilitates the migration of one or both parents, and also allows for the children to be nurtured in the home culture. There is a downside, for some children are abandoned, left in the hands of people incapable of caring for them, or sexually molested by caregivers (Henke, 2001, p. 116).[4] This practice occurs all over the world (Bashi, McDaniel, and Zulu, 1995) and seemingly more children benefit from it than not. Fosterage seems to be a normal practice even among nonemigrant black Caribbean persons; it has been, not surprisingly, adapted to the migration context, where hubs and spokes have used the strategy specifically to enhance the migration to the West of the various members of the network. Potential migrants in the Caribbean resort to fosterage while they seek work in New York, London, and Toronto so that they can leave their children behind, at least until they get on their feet, as the expression goes. In these cases, parents have requested that caretakers release their children after a period, when the parents are sufficiently resettled in the new destination. When both parents migrate for work, kids must be fostered to ensure their care. As Varnet has explained, "Well, my mother, she immigrated to the United States; my father had been here maybe a couple of years and he sent for her. So we, myself and my two sisters, we ended up staying with my aunt [in Trinidad]. We all stayed there approximately three or four years." Still, it is not always the case that children are expected to rejoin their overseas parents; many times the fosterage arrangement is expected to be permanent, or at least extremely long lasting. As Iona explains,

> I should go back a spell. I started off living with my great aunt. When I was about ten months, ten and a half months old, I went to live with my great aunt Daisy. She was the only one that—well, she had a child that died earlier, near birth, so she was the only one without children. And my mother, having had this child, [me], very young—she adopted me because she would be able to give me the opportunity that my mother obviously was not in a position [to], and also that freed my mother up in order for her to continue and do whatever she wanted to do [including migrate] . . . . [It also was partly done to irritate my paternal grandmother, who was in a rivalry with my maternal grandmother and her sisters.] But the sisters decided they would show her that their niece or daughter [that is, my mother] didn't need her [my grandmother, or her money, or her son's money] (laughs). So they sent me to Trinidad to live with my great aunt, who adopted me and, really, I didn't realize she wasn't my mother until I was much, much older. As far as I know, she was my mother until I was about eight. . . . After [she] died, I went to live with my grandmother. I must have been about nine, nine and a half.

Among my respondents, fosterage occurred under various circumstances. Sometimes this arrangement is made, then, for the mutual financial benefit of the migrants and the childminder—for the new migrants get to work overseas and earn more than they would have had they remained in their home country, and they also send back remittances to the person taking care of their children. In some of these cases, it seems, foster arrangements occur without full consent on the part of the parents or the children. Varnet said he had no choice, and that he was given no explanation for why his parents were leaving.

> Being abandoned early, I tell you, my mother worked in the garden and left us home, and then she left. And it's like I couldn't stand my aunt [who fostered me]. I mean—maybe then I couldn't verbalize what I felt, but I probably felt abandoned. And nobody really took time to explain anything. That's the way I kind of grew up, you know, me against the world. If you have a child, you

[should] sit down [and say], "Well, I'm going to the United States" and it's like "You're going to live with your aunt." I guess for them they did their best for us, but things like that, they aren't aware that, you know, a child could be affected by you leaving.

On this count, one woman had similar sentiments: "One of my great aunts who had no children adopted me and sent for me. I didn't want to go. I was enjoying my life in Union Island. But here you have no opinion." Another respondent, originally from Tobago, explains,

My mother went to Venezuela, so I went to Trinidad. In those days, people had to migrate to different countries to work. When she went away she did accounting. Before that she was a teacher in Tobago. [So I was left with her sister in Trinidad.] I was excited at the beginning. Then I didn't like it. I remained there until I was seventeen. [But] I felt within myself that my Uncle loved me more, and I had a cousin that my Mom adopted. So I ran away [to my Uncle's home] and I didn't look back. He had no kids and he was glad to have me.

At least for persons from the smallest of islands, it seems that children migrated for schooling as often as parents migrated for work.

I lived with my parents up until age eleven. At age eleven we were sent away to school in St. Vincent. [That's] because in Union Island where I was born there were no major high schools; therefore you had to take a common entrance [exam] at the age of nine or ten, and that determines if you're eligible to go to one of the major high school on the mainland, which is St. Vincent.

One family reported that they all migrated together to St. Vincent strictly for that purpose, that is, "to educate everyone." The parents gave up their former lives and became entrepreneurs in St. Vincent in order to finance the scheme. Another family strategized to send all the children together to live on a larger island in a rented home along with a childminder and the childminder's own daughter (who was of similar age). In this way they ensured that all the children in both families could be educated together. That particular childminder had worked in the family home since the birth of the respondent who told me her tale. She also explained that her caretaker remained with her throughout her childhood. She "was there with us and her daughter until we graduated high school." In this case, the parents sent remittances to the childminder in the form of rent for their children's home and for school uniforms and such. Another respondent explained that she tried to put together a similar arrangement but it did not work out for her so well. (Instead she in the end divorced her husband and moved to New York.) Children are sent overseas to be educated as well. The English-speaking Caribbean's restrictive British-style education system—which promotes children to subsequent levels only after passing exams that purposely eliminate numbers of students from higher grades—makes migrating to the United States beneficial to children, because education up until the university level is both compulsory and free. This is especially beneficial to older children, who can gain their education and in return care for younger children in the household.

Respondents also reported other reasons for encouraging child fosterage arrangements, including hiding family secrets, forging emotional bonds, and reinforcing folk wisdom. A few told stories about young pregnant girls who were sent away to carry and deliver their babies in secret; thus fosterage was used to hide the relationship between a biological young mother and her illegitimate child. Others shared examples in which elders fell in love with the child of someone who either had too many children or who was beholden enough to the elder that they had little choice but to give up the tot to the smitten one. As one migrant explained, she gave up her own child to a sibling: "From the time she was a baby my sister wanted her [my daughter], so that's how she was with my sister from small [a very young age]." And another respondent explained:

> Well, my aunt didn't have any children and my mother was having a lot of kids at the time. I don't know the real reason [my sister was sent away] but I know my aunt had fallen in love with [my sister] and was spending time there, and it developed into [fosterage] because my parents used to be living in Trinidad and used to come backwards and forwards from Union Island to Trinidad. I don't know the . . . root reason but I know my aunt was terribly in love with [my sister] and [my sister] stayed with her.

Two respondents specifically explained that they had participated in a fosterage arrangement designed to jump-start the foster parent's own fecundity. As Pearl, a London transplant, told me, her parents had eight girls and three boys, and the parents sent Pearl's sister Emily to live with the mother's sister. The children's aunt had no children of her own. "In those days, my aunt had been married and was taking a long time to get any children. And everybody was waiting for the two of them to get children. In those days you lent a child in the hopes that would encourage them to procreate themselves. [It worked] because my aunt went on to have two children." (But much later, the aunt had grown too attached to the girl to release her. "My aunt was reluctant to let her go. The purpose being achieve [sic], my mother wanted back her daughter.")

Adult respondents in New York and London also reported using fosterage in reverse, that is, they sent their children back home to be cared for by family members. Circumstances under which this happened included when children were behaving badly and their parents and elders believed the children needed "straightening out" in the home country environment. Reverse fosterage also occurred when working arrangements for parents changed and child care in New York or London was too difficult or expensive to arrange, or when parents set new target earnings (such as saving enough to buy a home in New York or London) and needed to work longer hours and save more.

Fosterage, then, is a device that hubs and spokes in the West Indies employ in order to enable parents to migrate north (to the United States, Canada, and Britain) for work, and reverse fosterage is a device that helps them stay there. Fosterage seems to have been adopted as a practice that began as the migration stream itself may have; that is, it expanded from a practice first used when parents migrated between islands looking for work to one that grew as migration over time encompassed a larger set of destinations. Fosterage may also have been undertaken in order to achieve what Hondagneu-Sotelo (1994a) has called "family stage migration," in which an adult family member comes to New York, London, or another Western destination first, and only later arranges to bring the others after them, in stages.[5]

Finally, fosterage has sometimes been used as an immigration scheme to send a young person overseas without their parents so that they might gain a high school or higher education, in order to use them as a childminder for younger children in the hub's household, or both. In these cases, child migration seems to link migration for education directly with babysitting. In this exchange, older children migrate north and gain educations they might not otherwise have had, but in return they are expected to look after the younger children in the hub's household. (Normally, but not always, adolescent girls are called upon to fill this role.) In that sense, and others, it is possible that the babysitting option is itself an extension of the child fosterage practice. It has been noted that many respondents who were born on smaller islands had to move to larger ones to continue their education. In these babysitting instances, a young person is fostered overseas. When these youths reach adulthood, however, they are not expected to return to the Caribbean. Those being fostered as babysitters for younger children in the co-resident household are spokes in reality, for just as any other spoke would be, these young people are given the promise of achieving goals associated with long-term migration (such as education and social mobility), even if (unlike other spokes) they are expected to repay that promise with their own household labor.

Babysitting

Taran is the person I think of as most successfully using the babysitting practice to extend her network and have her children taken care of while she worked. As a nurse and then nurse administrator, Taran had to work many a night shift and would have needed a live-in to ensure round-the-clock child care. It made sense for her to bring into the United States someone from the Caribbean to do this for her, just as she'd brought others. I say that Taran is the most successful, but not just because she brought in persons to do the job; she is the most successful because she also sent back those who did not work out—even though (or maybe precisely because) they were relatives. Altogether she brought in sequence four women to do babysitting in her own home. Two she sent back in succession, but the two young women who came last stayed in the United States. The first babysitter arrived soon after Taran's first child was born and she was sent back after some problems ("boy trouble") emerged. The next babysitter to arrive was the same age as the oldest of Taran's children. She first came in through Canada and was brought into the United States on the birth certificate of Taran's oldest child. But because she would not go to school, she was deemed not enough of a self-starter and was also sent back. Jonelle was the third of the four women brought in to babysit in Taran's home; she was younger sister to the first babysitter. Jonelle told me that her spoke experience took a downturn when she "discovered boys" and ran away from home rather than agree to comply with house rules; because she was quite aware that the fate of the previous two babysitters had involved a return ticket to the West Indies, she must have seen her only choice to be hiding out in the northeastern United States, so she ran away. The fourth babysitter was Natalie, who was sent for before Jonelle's flight so that the two young women could share the burden of watching over Taran's youngsters. This makes sense because the culture of reciprocity would suggest that over-burdening the young women would not be the thing to do. A hub who seeks to enhance his or her reputation in the network surely wants the spokes to succeed. (Muriel, another hub, also tried to lighten her babysitter's load. She had an "old lady" who lived on a floor above come and sleep in her home at night so that her own babysitter wouldn't be overburdened. "[Debbie] did babysitting, but she didn't do all the child care. The old lady would come downstairs and go to sleep here. It was easy for me because I didn't have to take the kids out. I didn't want to put it all on [Debbie].")

Babysitters sent for in these ways are often, but not always, adolescents, and more often than not they are female. Sending for a young adolescent makes sense; the years that their guardians are most likely to allow them to be sent for are the years when seats for schooling are scarcest and most expensive, that is, nearing entry to secondary school. Since education in the United States and England is both compulsory and free, the adolescent benefits by receiving an education they otherwise would not have, and a headstart in a labor market that is expected to bring them upward mobility they otherwise would not experience.

Education

The education system of most of the homelands of the respondents I interviewed is modeled after the British system. That means there is in place a tier of examinations that cull children from the group of students who can expect to continue on to higher levels of education. Students begin with kindergarten, then go on to primary school, which continues to about age eleven. At that point, students take the Eleven-Plus educational tests, which determine the next level available to them. Students who fail go to secondary school (where the curriculum concentrates on what Americans call the "three Rs": reading, 'riting, and 'rithmetic). Those who pass go on to grammar school, where the offerings are geared toward streaming students into universities. At age sixteen, students sit for their O (or Ordinary) levels, examinations in ten, eleven, or twelve subjects that they presumably have been studying throughout their childhood. A student needs to pass a minimum of eight exams to go to university, but it is expected that someone who passes only eight will not do very well at university. Students remain in grammar school, specializing in a number of subjects in which they presumably have done well on the O-level examinations. At around age seventeen or eighteen, students take their A (or Advanced) levels in preparation for entry into university. Secondary school students may also take O levels; if they pass them with good grades they may transfer into grammar school for two years and then take A levels also. A student would apply to university in summer, for example, explaining that they plan to take A levels in July of the following summer, and asking for entry into the university in September immediately following that second summer. The university might offer the student a conditional acceptance, agreeing that if the student gets 2 A's and 1 B in the A levels, they would be offered a place in the entering class. Students who do not pass at least eight O levels—and those who do are "streamed" into secondary school—would be expected to begin working in the labor market, unless they plan to attempt again to enter university. Normally this would require grammar school students to go to community college in the evening to improve their knowledge of the subjects in which they failed or did poorly, or they would stay back in grammar school for an extra year. Entering university is normally not considered an option for the average secondary school student.

In a system like this one operating in the Third World, where the number of grammar and secondary schools is limited, seats within the schools are limited, and where school fees are required, grammar and secondary school are not options even for the student with average performance, let alone for those who are exceptional but not at the top. This system requires taking only the very top students to fill the small number of seats at the next levels—and on many smaller islands, that kind of success will require a move across the sea to a larger island. Here, then, even if most students are top scorers, only those who are good enough to gain access to a seat will have the opportunity to complete their education.

Thus, nearly all respondents talked about the importance of education to the migrants and to the young migrants with whom they are associated. Those migrants who moved to England moved into a system that was similar to the one with which they were already familiar. They understood racism to be a big factor that holds back young people, and many respondents were involved in community groups that organized to ensure the educational success of the young. One especially institutionalized and successful endeavor was the Saturday School run by the Claudia Jones Organisation. So committed are the organizers to their students' success that they agreed to let me interview them only if I in turn agreed to teach a class at the upcoming Saturday School session. I think they would normally have agreed to an interview, but they used their leverage because they thought it terribly important that the young people in the school meet and talk face-to-face with a black university professor. I did teach a session on immigration to about five adolescents and preadolescents.

Persons in New York talked mainly about migrating for education themselves. In New York, education is free and compulsory through high school, and people are eighteen years of age when they graduate. Free education for all is a great draw, especially when access to college is relatively unrestricted. In the 1970s, when many of the respondents I spoke with came to New York, the City College of New York (CCNY) had instituted a policy that made admission open to all who had graduated from high school. Until 1975 its classes were offered tuition free, and remediation was extended to those who needed it. Thus, with one move to the five boroughs of New York City, migrants could finish prebaccalaureate education, gain admission to college, and attend college (at no charge if one chose to matriculate at CCNY). Easier access to education, which many believed was the key to social and economic mobility, was a real pull factor for many who moved to that area.

Matchmaking and Matchbreaking

In a few cases, networks were extended as members made plans to unite intended lovers, or in some cases, to rejoin lovers who had been separated by migration. To be sure, I do not mean here that hubs are helping reunite spouses; rather, I am speaking of matchmaking in the commonsense use of the word, that is, meddling in the romantic lives of singles who may or may not be in love with another person. Most of the cases aimed to make matches for young women who had migrated previously but were pining for men who had been left behind. If the hubs in charge of these young women's migration experience approved of the young woman's choice, the migration of the young man was arranged through the network. But perhaps because of the West Indian custom of co-resident sponsorship in migration, the migration of potential partners normally occurred via arrangement with a hub other than the one who had sponsored the young woman. Presumably many people would be involved in sending for the future marriage partner, because it would be improper for unmarried people to co-reside together in the hub's household, and employment for the man also had to be found. And because hubs tend to know of jobs for newcomers of their own sex, they may need to enlist the help of other, opposite-sex hubs to find jobs for spokes of the opposite sex. This was Colvin's case, for he met his future wife while she was on a brief vacation in the Caribbean. Clearly she fell head over heels for him:

> I met Myrna, my wife, [when she was on vacation] in the Caribbean. At the same time [on this same visit], while wavering, she encouraged me to come

here [to New York]. And through her assistance and her mother and my brother, between the three of them, you know, they worked and they found a school for me—even her husband [my father-in-law, now divorced from my wife's mother] assist me [sic]. Like, you know, to show I was working, to show the kind of person I was, you know, what they call a recommendation, whatever they call it, to give the immigration. It's something they [used to] say, "This person is for real in terms of his goals for education and I've known him all my life and he is ambitious" . . . and he helped me, along with Myrna, her mother, and my brother. They went to the school and everything. Then I applied for the visa, and come up here.

Matchmaking isn't the only kind of meddling that hubs do, for they also work to keep apart those inclined toward disapproved-of romances or to separate persons in decidedly bad marriages. In one case, network members conspired to get a woman out of a bad relationship by moving her to London.[6] In another case, Belinda was sent for as a young woman by her older brother, who was enlisted by other family members to spirit her away from her childhood sweetheart before she "got in trouble." She refused to take on any of the suitors her hub presented to her in her early years in New York. Eventually the sweetheart himself, MacClaine, was sent for and worked with the young woman's hub in the water tunnels. The couple was married soon afterward.

Affect

If you recall her story from the preceding chapter, Taran helped Amsie come to the United States because she felt that Amsie and her children needed the financial assistance that a job in the New York City area would provide. Eventually Amsie sent for all the children still alive, and they are all doing well. During her interview, Taran listed all the occupations and recited the migration stories of Amsie's children; she knew this information because she was instrumental in getting the family into the country. Eventually Amsie's sister was brought in for health reasons. She came first to have her cataracts treated, and it was found that she also needed to have dialysis treatments and a mastectomy. She wanted to go home, but Amsie and Taran knew she would just, literally, die there, so they kept her in the States. At one point the two sisters had a falling out and were no longer speaking, and Taran intervened to keep the sister in the United States. The sister never went back, and after nine years she was buried in the United States.

The point is that while Amsie might be seen by migration scholars as a person who would come to the United States for economic reasons (although she did not want to come to the United States at all), Taran was motivated to send for her because of her continued emotional connection to her friend. Taran was not a relative to Amsie, so could not be sent for under family re-unification. Taran also could not employ her directly as a babysitter; when Asmie came, Taran had still not had children and she likely did not yet know how to send for a babysitter herself. So Taran had to find another scheme to get her friend into a well-paying job in New York City. Valencia described similar motivations; she told me she sent for her sister, and when I asked how she decided which one to send for, she explained, "You send for the one you like best."

When Hubs Have Little Influence

When I interviewed people living in the West Indies who were still connected by birth or friendship to immigrants in the two New York City networks, I asked them why they did not go to New York as their relatives and friends had.[7] Their inability to exploit network connections was sometimes cited as the reason why they did not move; most often, it seems, the decision of whether, when, and where to move was not in their hands. Idelle, a school administrator in Barbados, spoke of her regret in being left behind. She couldn't get her network connections to work for her, even though she had relatives in New York (a cousin, Eugene) and in Boston.

> At this age, I'm saying to myself, "I should have gone." It was easier for Hendricks to go because his mother was there. She was only my aunt—it would be more difficult for me because I'm not a sister to those group, like Eugene [that is, I'm not a close enough relative to merit the help that other closer family members might receive]. There's another group in Boston [too]. You know, one came in, and then sister sent for sister. [But] I'm [only] a cousin.

That said, some did not consider leaving the islands, even when they had skills, work experience, and relatives in New York, London, and Toronto who could help them resettle. This happened when persons living in the Caribbean had what they considered to be good jobs. The following quote encapsulates in one person's words what I learned from a number of people interviewed in the West Indies. These sentiments were shared both by those who were content with remaining in the West Indies and by returnees. The quote is from a woman in London who, when asked whether she'd helped anyone migrate, explained,

> We've tried sending for my uncle's children, but they did not [come]—even my mom, before we came up, she tried sending for them, because we thought she would give them a start. But at the time they did not want to come. She went through the procedure for applying for them to come, but I think when she spoke to them—and I think they didn't want to, because they were girls and have their mom and dad at home [so] I don't think they wanted to leave home [and leave their parents]. My sister, she heard of somebody who was able to get people up and she spoke to me about it once, and yes, you know, we tried, but by this time they're young people, you know? And I suppose they're set in their ways and they have their jobs and their, you know, their homes and their parents around them, their sisters around them, so. . . .

When one is able to secure employment sufficient to garner a certain lifestyle (normally that means to be able to provide for property ownership, because the rental housing market is severely constrained) and is surrounded by a sufficient number of family and friends who also did not migrate (that is, one has community in the place of origin), one has little reason to leave. Overall, though, those who wish they could leave to work in the more developed economies of North America and Europe far outnumber those who wish to stay, and generally they need a hub to make that dream of migration happen.

Conclusion

The first step in the migration process is to get the new migrant into the country of destination. This step is made easier when network members use whatever resources are at their disposal to achieve the goal of getting people in. For those persons in and connected to these hub-and-spoke networks, two prerequisites seem to be necessary before a move is attempted. First, the move should be expected to better the life of the mover (for even when opportunities to move are available, many choose not to move if life in the country of origin is good enough). Second, there must be means to accomplish the move. For pioneers, that would mean a ready job or a recruitment program, and for most others it would mean a hub that is ready and willing to assist with knowledge, resources, and co-residence. This chapter has focused primarily on the strategies and reasoning used to decide who to tap to add to the network, and on the schemes used to get the person safely across national boundaries under circumstances that would allow them to stay under reasonable conditions, even if those conditions do not mean full legal status.

For the networked persons whose experiences are studied here, there was much fluidity between legal and undocumented statuses. Many people came on student and visitor visas and chose to work instead. Some stayed illegally until their partners gained legal status and fixed their papers later, while others chose to remain illegally until the 1986 amnesty. Among the former group, women most often fixed the papers for their men, for it was easier for women (especially domestics) to gain the right papers and then send for their husbands (who indeed might already be in the destination country). Many other spokes fixed their papers by applying for documents and making return trips to their island country when the appropriate papers were finally ready, so they could reenter with the proper documentation. Some of those properly documented choose to return home or live in England with U.S. documents, making periodic returns to the United States to keep their papers active.

When adults were involved, the particulars of sending for someone generally involved interfaces with the labor market. Hubs used their reputations to get employers to commit to filling out and submitting the paperwork to make someone legal, and because the spoke fulfilled the job requirements so well, employers often were happy and eager to be the go-between for the spoke and legal institutions. Many hubs became legal experts themselves, after starting out by paying lawyers to help their charges get their papers "straight." For children and adults alike, transnational migrants chose among countries of departure and destination to transport the spoke to the desired destination.

But the process of getting someone in is not just a cut-and-dry matter, because emotional matters are considered as well. Parents who migrate must leave children behind and figure out arrangements for their care and well-being. Child migration seems to stem from a long tradition of fosterage and communal care. But many of those so fostered complained about the deafening silence that came from their elders, for Caribbean folks, it seems, have a reputation for leaving children in the dark about the whole process. Children were sometimes not even told that their parents were leaving, or were told only at the last possible moment, and they certainly were not asked about their preferences. Neither are children told much about the timing and method by which they have been sent for when they themselves become overseas migrants. They must simply move to live with whomever they're told to, whenever they're told to do so. But again, intentions are usually good: children are moved to expand their opportunities for education; to help hide their illegitimate status, thereby saving them (and their mothers) from stigma; to cure infertility suffered by their elders; and simply because they caused an adult other than their parent to love them so much that the proposed foster parent seemingly cannot live without them. Love for their children also causes migrant Caribbean parents in the North to choose to ship their migrant children back home so that they can be raised with the "right" values and not "forget who they are," or rather, so that they can learn who they are supposed to be, which means a non-Westernized person with a particular carriage. Network members also scheme to put couples together, or to break apart those couples considered to be wrongly matched.

For the most part, however, people are moved with the help of a hub who uses his or her connections to employers in the destination. These connections lead spokes either to formal recruitment programs that arrange jobs and housing for the weekdays (for domestics) or full week (for nurses), or to jobs arranged by the hub in their efforts to recruit an employer to hire the spoke. Sometimes, but not always, the employer is the hub's own, but in any event, hubs generally place their own reputation on the line to get the spoke a job. Regardless, the idea of sending for someone is to help networked persons secure a geographic mobility that could be translated into upward socioeconomic mobility.

5   Working and Networking

THERE'S A LARGE LITERATURE that focuses on migrant and immigrant labor, on the effects of that labor on the destination economy and on both foreign and native-born workers, and on the ways that labor market experiences affect workers' possibilities for future upward mobility. I don't review all of that work here, but I do highlight differences between the literature's findings, and what my conversations and experiences with immigrant networks indicate. One difference is that I make a broader study of the labor market, whereas other migration scholars have had to explore singular segments of the labor market where network immigrants are operative. The oral history, ethnographic interviewing, and snowball sampling method of data collection I employed allows me to capture all the network members' experiences over their working lifetimes (up to the time of their interview) and to link these experiences across the network, which gives a more complete picture of how networks reach into various parts of the labor market and shows how networks can be more or less effective in particular employment situations or with job placements for particular individuals.

One significant finding is that networks span jobs in both the niche and non-niche sectors of the labor market. Individually, workers use these two segments of the job market to follow upwardly mobile job trajectories, climbing to more remunerative and perhaps higher status positions over their working lives. For example, one may start off in low-paying unskilled work and hop to increasingly skilled work, or jump in or out of niche jobs to increase one's income and experience levels, entering and moving about the labor market with the help of the network. Niche and non-niche linkages allow network members to create mobility opportunities for people at all stages of the migration process—newcomers and veteran migrants, skilled and unskilled, are all able to find jobs relatively easily in the various segments of the market where migrants have influence over hiring. Moreover, people whose trajectories take them to new positions (new to the immigrant network, that is) may be able to create even newer niches for networked migrants to monopolize.

Significant too is that both the niche and non-niche positions for these Caribbean networks reside in the primary labor market, not in secondary markets or in enclaves or in the ethnically based entrepreneurial sectors that are often credited with making immigrant upward mobility possible. This means that network members' job trajectories, like those of native-born workers, are in the mainstream labor market. Where co-resident hubs have gaps in knowledge about the areas of the labor market that might best help their spokes, network members make use of employment agencies to ensure that spokes get employment footholds. And when they can, network members manipulate gender relations and working conditions to the benefit of their co-ethnics.

I begin the next section by relating the example of one man's postmigration employment experience, both to explain what it is like to try to find work in a new country and to introduce the idea of the migrant employment trajectory. MacClaine's story illustrates the ways in which migrants put their strategies into play to fulfill desires for a better life as they move between jobs. I then relate MacClaine's experience to the work experiences and occupational choices of other men and women in these networks.

One Man's Job Trajectory

MacClaine's story was introduced in Chapter Three in the section on matchmaking: he was sent to New York to marry his childhood sweetheart, Belinda, who was also sister to Harvey, her hub and a worker on the city's water and sewer tunnel construction crew (also known as the sandhogs). Belinda refused to take on any of the suitors Harvey tried to introduce to her in New York, insisting on MacClaine. To help arrange the marriage, Harvey, the first to invite MacClaine to the United States, explained to MacClaine that there were jobs available in the tunnel and that the pay was good. MacClaine made some inquiries before agreeing to come, mainly asking the advice of his brothers who were already in Brooklyn, who discouraged him from taking a job in the tunnel because the work was too dangerous. MacClaine finally did come to New York, but when he did he lived with his brothers and not with Harvey. Harvey offered his services only as an employment hub and not as a co-resident one. (It would have been inappropriate for MacClaine to be co-resident with Harvey, because Harvey had already sent for his still unmarried sister. As single persons with a love interest, the two newcomers could not have lived in the same house—not if Harvey was to be seen as properly taking care of his sister's well-being.)

After spending some time unemployed, MacClaine first worked in a commercial laundry. He was brought to the laundry by a West Indian woman who lived next door to the brother with whom he was staying. She was also the brother's friend. On her recommendation, MacClaine was hired on the spot. He was put on the presses, where he pressed new jeans sent by the manufacturer to be laundered, pressed, labeled, and shipped to the stores where they would be sold. He said that he lost twenty pounds in the three months he worked there, on account of the heat. Although he hated the work, he needed it, so he stayed on. After some time, he moved upstairs to do extraction (extracting the water from the fabrics after the garments were washed)—an extremely dangerous job because "the tops of the old extractors would fly right off while the clothes were still spinning inside." The plant soon closed because the owners were unable to overcome financial trouble and eventual bankruptcy, and MacClaine was unemployed again.

Not very long afterward, Harvey (who by then was MacClaine's brother-in-law) took him down to the tunnel construction site. Again, MacClaine was given a job that same day. Here he explains the capriciousness of the supervising staff:

> My brother-in-law brought me there often, and the [Irish] foreman liked me and put me on the job pretty regularly. After I worked seven straight days, my brother-in-law told me that since I worked the week it was time to ask the foreman about getting me into the union. I did ask, and all of a sudden the foreman would not call on me to work anymore. It was my punishment for knowing that I was able to apply for union membership.
>
> There was very little supervision of the foremen on the site. They were free to do whatever they wanted to without following the regulations on who should do what kind of work, on union membership, or how many people should do the work. They could choose not to hire, even if they were understaffed, and could just make up names and write them down, to seem like they had men on the job. Sometimes I would get hired because after payday the regular men would

not show up. There were lots of jobs open, but they would tell me that they were not hiring and that the union was temporarily closed to new members. After a while, an old West Indian sandhog approached me—the man had been there for years and wanted to retire in the West Indies with his girlfriend. He said he knew of a way to get me into the union. He went into the union and told them that I was his son. Then they let me in and I got my union book.

Soon afterward, short staffing caused MacClaine to be brought in to work on the drilling team; with no experience he did a good job. After that day, the Irish foreman called on him for work just as frequently as he had when Mac-Claine was "shaping up" (that is, working irregularly before securing union membership eligibility). But the poor economy of 1970s New York, coupled with poor geological conditions (soft rock) and a dispute between the city and the construction conglomerate, forced the crew to slow down the work and eventually shut down the job site altogether.

Securing an education was MacClaine's next step after gaining union membership, although he said he found some opposition to the idea among the sandhogs, who earned so much money (compared to other West Indians, I presume) that they weren't as interested in gaining educational credentials.

I started attending Bronx Community College, which was right across the highway from Highbridge [the tunnel job site]. I would go to school on Saturdays. The shifts were days, evenings, and nights, and I would go directly to the campus from work if I was on the night shift, fighting to stay awake in class. After the layoffs I went to school full-time.

He soon earned an associate's degree, despite having to both work and go to school full-time when workers were called back on the job before his last semester's end. Later he went back to school for his bachelor's degree. Still, at one point the stress of taking on schooling and tunnel work simultaneously was too much for him and he had to quit both because the overload was adversely and seriously affecting his health. He got back into the swing of things by first volunteering in a day care center and then getting a hack's license and driving a cab. He went back to work in the tunnels after some time and became a foreman. When layoffs next plagued the job site, he again turned to education, but this time he studied for civil service exams—he took five altogether. During one layoff round, MacClaine found he was chosen to interview for a traffic maintenance worker position—and he was hired. Two to three months after taking that job he received a letter saying that he'd been invited to interview for a sewage worker position—a job that would earn him $5,000 more per year. Ambivalent at first because he had just taken the traffic maintenance position, in the end he took the higher-paying job on the recommendation of a co-ethnic coworker (a former tenant of MacClaine's who'd later become assistant plant manager in the civil service), who suggested that the new job was easy to do and offered promotions there were easier to get. MacClaine eventually made supervisor.

•   •   •

I chose MacClaine's story to illustrate several points that I touch on here but will reemphasize later. First, notice that he jumped from unskilled to skilled work and back again in response to life crises and the availability of or choice to rely upon connections that can make an employment change possible. Job shifts like this are reflected in so many other immigrants' histories as well; they too have made moves where necessary, depending on what their employment needs or connections were at the time. Second, MacClaine switched not only between skilled and nonskilled work but also from niche to non-niche employment and back again. That is, neither time he had to do unskilled work was MacClaine stuck doing it permanently—for he went back to the tunnel when he was in better health, but in time he was able to move to a second niche, the government of New York City, as a civil service worker. Third, MacClaine used experience, educational attainment, and credentialing to make moves up the ladder of economic security. His experience gained him job security and union membership in the tunnels, he secured a hack's license, he passed civil service examinations, and he gained college degrees, all of which qualified him for upward moves. Still, he needed the extra pushes from network connections to make these moves happen, because his own efforts did not always suffice to trigger meritocratic rewards. In these three ways, MacClaine's experiences reflect the occupational and labor market experiences of other Caribbean immigrants in these networks.

Networked Caribbean Immigrant Occupations

Table 5.1 compiles a list of the occupations that the networked immigrants I interviewed mentioned when I questioned them about the jobs they had held since the time of their arrival in the destination country. The occupations are listed in alphabetical order, but the list is divided by gender and by the metropolitan location of the network segment. (To be clear, the occupations listed are jobs they held at some point since their arrival. It is not a list of the jobs they now hold.) Each occupation is listed only once, even if more than one person told me they had done or still do that kind of work. However, when many workers were found in a particular occupation, I considered this occupation to be *niche* employment. These niche occupations are listed in bold type.[1]

This very simple table reveals quite a lot. What may be noticed first is that the list of male occupations is much longer than the list of occupations in which women have worked. This fact increases in significance when it is understood that many more women than men were interviewed—for example, nearly twice the number of women (twenty-six) than men (fourteen) made the sample in New York. That the men's list of occupations is so much longer than the women's indicates that women tend to be highly concentrated in a small segment of occupational and industrial sectors, while men work in a more diverse set of jobs. As MacClaine's example suggests, Caribbean people are not eager to move around in the job market and instead are reluctant to give up jobs, even difficult and dangerous ones, especially if the jobs pay well enough or employers are unconcerned about the immigrant's ability to document the legality of their presence in the country. Thus, rather than interpreting the men's occupation list as merely reflecting lots of job turnover (although turnover is clearly evident here), we might also see that the men took these "odd jobs" because the network is less effective in getting work for men in labor market sectors where West Indians predominate. The table shows that in their career trajectories the men worked at more jobs of different kinds than the women did. Said another way, the male immigrant has a more difficult time being placed in positions where other network-affiliated men are employed. The men's jobs indicate that they had little monopoly influence over the job sectors to which network members are exposed. Conversely, the women's relative concentration in fewer job sectors shows that women in these networks do have sufficient monopoly power over these occupations to be able to place large numbers of women in them.

Another reason for the male-female differential could be that some occupations are linked to legal status. Rather than thinking that the job an immigrant secures is determined by his or her status, consider that the causal relationship might go the other way. Where a sector provides legal status for its employees and an ethnic group has access to jobs in that sector, it makes sense for that group to seek monopoly power—it will help ensure the perpetuation

Table 5.1 Networked Immigrants' Occupations by Gender and City (in alphabetical order; **bold type** indicates employment niches)

	Males	Females
New York	Air conditioning repair/maintenance Armed forces Auto mechanic Bank teller Cab driver Carpenter **Civil service: accountant, auditing, sanitation, other** Clerical worker Commercial laundry Construction/small-scale contracting Corrections officer Court library research/legal research Day care center Drafting Factory: button making, brake pad manufacturing, envelope factory, necktie factory Farm worker Finisher Hot dog vendor Janitor/cleaning agency/maintenance Jewelry manufacturing Machinist Maintenance worker Military service Orderly Physician Police officer Radiologist/X-ray technician Real estate Security guard Spray painting Stock clerk Therapy aide Transit authority **Water and Sewer Tunnel construction (Sandhogs)**	**Banking** Child care Clerical **Dietician/dietary aide** **Domestic service: housekeeping, babysitting, nanny** **Medical service: home health attendant, nurse (RN/LPN), nurses' aide, nursing assistant** Retail sales Social work Teacher's aide
London	Entrepreneur **London Transport: bus driver** **Teacher**	Factory work: garment industry/ button factory **London Transport: canteen** **Nursing** **Teacher**

(handwritten annotation) ① women have more niches — service industry

of the network because veterans can bring greater numbers of newcomers into the country for permanent or long-term stays during which the newcomers would be both legal and employed. As described in the preceding chapter, domestic service and health and hospital employers (especially in nursing under conditions of labor recruitment) make provisions for arranging legal papers for many of the women who do these jobs. Caribbean-born black female domestics and nurses have networks that help other women get jobs in these sectors. Women's ease in finding work via these networks helps encourage family stage migration (Hondagneu-Sotelo, 1994a, 1994b, 2001), in which women migrate first, leaving their spouses behind, and then send for the men while fostering their children until they can safely be brought over.

In sum, women have made themselves legal by monopolizing jobs that bring legal papers along with a paycheck, while men who are illegally overstaying visas have few such opportunities and instead do the urban jobs they can obtain without documentation. Because men do not have access to job sectors where the perks of legality are attached, they have to do more of the jobs that are less stable and do not provide for ways to gain legal status. Similarly, few men are able to get into jobs where men's occupations are clustered—such as civil service work in local government, and water and sewer tunnel construction in New York City. These jobs bring with them no legal status and, moreover, men can secure jobs here only when conditions are optimal, that is, when foremen open doors to new hires or civil service exams are passed with marks high enough to earn one of the limited number of openings for a given job title. When men can enter these occupations, they settle into stable employment; these two niche sectors are also the ones where MacClaine's longest term employment was found. For the sake of comparison, consider that in Britain also women seem to have freedom to move about the labor market, whereas males are less able to do so (Ramdin, 1999, p. 175). In the 1990s, two-thirds of black Caribbean workers in Britain were manual workers, with Caribbean men more likely to do shift work (Ramdin, 1999, p. 315). Caribbean women in Britain, by contrast, were more likely to be in the public sector (Ramdin, 1999, p. 317), and among the Londoners studied here, women had one more niche sector than the men did.

Moving in: Niches and Agencies

Networked immigrants used niche and non-niche sectors to help newcomers enter the labor market. If a hub had access to jobs in niche sectors, the ease of finding employment for the spoke was increased. When the limits of the network were reached—that is, when hubs did not know enough about available jobs to help a particular spoke—they sought out employment agencies or other hubs to help them find employment opportunities. In a way, the use of employment agencies and niches is emblematic of the extremes of network monopoly power in the labor market. Below I describe in detail the niche sectors where Caribbean networked immigrants found jobs, and later, the cases where spokes must seek out other means for finding work in the new destination.

The Tunnels, New York

There's an old saying: If it's deeper than a grave, the sandhogs dug it. Starting with their first job in 1872, the Brooklyn Bridge, the hogs have built a large part of the city of New York—the subways and sewers, water tunnels 1 and 2, and the Lincoln, Holland, Queens-Midtown, and Brooklyn-Battery tunnels, to name a few, as well as the foundations for most of the bridges and many of the skyscrapers in the city. Because their work is done mostly below street level, in an unseen world of rock, sand, and earth, recognition of their achievements has been limited.

The hogs are a lively bunch. They are diverse in backgrounds, interests, and personalities, but unified in their dedication, perseverance, and camaraderie. John Roche described his fellow Hogs: "We're like an underground fraternity, a family." Sandhogging is a tradition and is passed down through generations of families. Especially because mining projects span decades, it is not uncommon to find multigenerations of families working together on the same job.[2]

Tunnel work was traditionally an Irish-only and then an Irish and West Indian niche. Before joining the union, a worker is "shaping up" or just "shapin'," as the men call it; steady work is neither guaranteed nor fully available. During this stage, a worker shows up at the job site and, if the foreman wants him, he is chosen for a job that day. Foremen use this ability to control which shapers work on a given day and which ones don't, to control entry into the union; they carefully fail to choose someone they don't want. After working for seven consecutive days, a worker is entitled to fill out the appropriate paperwork that initiates consideration for union membership (known as getting the "union book"). But sometimes, even if a worker can prove that he has been working steadily, getting into the union proves difficult. When a black man who has been a hub also becames a foreman, he tries to help others join the union as well as secure consecutive days of work.

Nursing, New York

Occupations in the nursing field have mainly been jobs as nurse's aides or nurses; women in these networks have secured these jobs either through formal recruitment channels or through informal networking. Glennis explained how she accomplished her labor market activities as a hub for the nursing sector. She emphasized how much harder it was for networked men than for women; she could find jobs for her friends, but her husband had to take his own charges to an employment agency.

> Glennis: It was tough for my husband, easier for us [nurses]. There were lots of jobs. The Jews had hospitals on every corner. You could work one shift at this hospital, go to another and work another shift—or work two shifts at the same hospital. It was easy: if you wanted to work, you could just work.
>
> VB: Why was it tough for him?
>
> Glennis: Because he didn't have a skill or a trade. The trade people did very well. He eventually, he got his master's in engineering, within which time I went to school also and got a bachelor's in community health. . . . [We brought up a friend of my husband's once.] He [lived with us] for about two or three years. My husband took him down to an agency and he got a job in a Jewish school in Borough Park. They liked him so much they decided to sponsor him. Helped him to get his green card so that he can stay in this country. And then he was able to bring up his family. [They didn't stay with us because by then he had gotten an apartment. He moved out] when his family came up. [His wife] came up to go to school. You know [omitted] Hospital? Jewish hospital? She went to work there as a nurse's aide. Then she went into nursing. We sent her there—at that time it wasn't as difficult as now. It wasn't difficult at all. They needed help in every area. By the way, I had two of my colleagues who came up to me. [I sponsored them also.] When they came up, I was working at a Jewish hospital—you know [omitted]? It used to be Brooklyn Jewish [omitted] Hospital at that time—I was working there then, and my two friends, they came up. I picked them up at the airport. And after a couple of days I took them where I work, and they got jobs there.
>
> VB: And what kind of jobs did they get?
>
> Glennis: They were nurses also.

VB: And they lived with you while they were working there too?

Glennis: Mmm hmm. [Yes.]

VB: How long did they stay [with you]?

Glennis: About two years.

Glennis's life story also has an example of her involvement with formal recruitment. She was recruited as a nurse, a choice she made when she decided to get away from having to use the hub who had already sent for her sisters and who had agreed to send for Glennis next. I asked Glennis to explain how job placement through a formal recruiter works for this sector. She said that the lawyer had several hospitals lined up and would promise the hospitals nurses. The hospital is supposed to issue the immigrant a temporary license when she arrives. Then she takes the state boards to get permanently licensed. The forms necessary for permanent licensing are the ones they'd withhold from the nurses in order to exploit them. The immigrant pays the lawyer one-half when she gets a job and one-half later. There was not a set fee for what the lawyers charged. Some charged $300, some $1,000. Glennis said that "their secretaries started getting into that business too." The way she said this I took it to mean getting into the recruiting business, not simply the charging of fees. The hospitals later stipulated in the contract that the nurse had to stay six months minimum; Glennis left as soon as she could. The last thing she said in the interview was, "I was paid $162 and change for one month's work." Feeling cheated of her due, Glennis quit. She wondered if the woman who had exploited her was still alive, noting, "I never forgave that woman." Perhaps Glennis became a hub because she decided to help other nurses directly so they could avoid the exploitation she faced when being recruited in a formal program.

The ease by which young black persons from the Caribbean could find work in the health and hospitals sector in the 1960s and 1970s meant that hubs in that field would happily encourage others to follow in their labor market footsteps. However, hubs are not always successful at getting their spokes to do the work they are able to secure for them. One woman, aunt to Terrence, got her nephew to become a therapy aide at the hospital where she worked as a nurse. I asked Terrence how he got the job in the hospital.

Well, they have an exam that's coming up, so she told me to go and take the exam. She thought I used to teach and I'd like to be with people and she said, give this a shot. As a matter of fact, she'd like us to do nursing; she encouraged every one of us, sisters and nephews and nieces to be nurses, but none of us [ever did]—not even her kids. She's the only nurse.

Still—another example of the Caribbean worker long-tenured in his job—he stayed at the job ten years before moving on to civil service. Altogether, four men in the sample worked in medical settings in their work lifetimes, but none of these were nurses. Nonetheless, three of them (the orderly, therapy aide, and X-ray technician; see Table 5.1) secured their jobs through women in the network who were in nursing occupations. As one man explained,

> My wife's cousin, Francine, got me a job in a nursing home as an orderly. . . . She was working there as a nurse's aide, so I went and worked as an orderly, you know. She taught me what to do, to take the temperature, the blood pressure, you know, pulse, make beds, dress wounds. She give me a crash course [laughs]. When I went for the interview and they question me I knew what to say there, so they give me the job."

Nurses were able to find jobs in medical settings for people at all levels of skill—those with formal nursing education and those with little or no training at all.

Civil Service, New York

New York City's civil service system might seem an odd place for an immigrant group to find a niche, because job openings are filled according to the rank ordering of all exam-takers' performance on citywide examinations. But Waldinger (1994) showed some time ago that immigrant niches flourish there because of advantages that accrue to employees and employers alike when immigrant networks operate to fulfill these city government jobs. Among the respondents who interviewed for this research project were male civil service employees, many of whom had formerly worked in the tunnels. Bentley, a civil servant, describes how he finds jobs for other West Indians where he works as a manager:

> Well, you see, the job that MacClaine is doing here in the Department of [omitted] is a kind of hush-hush job. It's heard [about] through the grapevine. So, if I figure any of my buddies meet the qualification, I think they have the ability to do it, I will notify them and get certain books—and help them to get

in. Once they pass the exam I make certain calls. I talk to certain personnel and am able to quietly pull them in.

This testimony parallels Waldinger's findings about the creation of niches in New York City's civil service by other immigrant groups. Their monopoly power is such that there was a time when legal status was not even an issue—undocumented immigrants would be sponsored by the city because their manpower was so highly desired by the civil service (Waldinger, 1994, p. 12). Although these jobs are presumed to be available to the qualified general public, Waldinger (1994, pp. 19–25) found strong evidence that newcomers, through their networks, found out about exams and job openings that were not well advertised in the public arena.

Domestic Service, New York
The domestic service labor market niche is discussed in great detail in Chapter Four, but a brief review may be useful here. There are three ways that domestic service is used by the network as a way to bring in new immigrants: formal recruitment programs, individual employment with well-off North American householders, and more informal arrangements finagled to send for child caretakers (mainly female, mainly adolescent) to work in the hub's own home. Hubs use employer recruitment, network referrals, and their own scheming to get women into jobs as domestics. When formal recruitment was mentioned in their interviews, most respondents were referring to women in earlier generations—describing the ways that mothers and aunts had gone to the United States up until the 1950s.

Many women's first paid job in the United States was as a domestic. These women were most often "sleep-ins," who lived in their employers' homes during the week and stayed with the hub household members (or with their own families if the co-resident period had ended) on the weekends. The advantage of these arrangements was that employers would do the required paperwork for the spoke to be able to stay legally. Thus this niche, as did nursing, gave the benefit of accrued income but also doubled as an important strategy for border crossing as well as establishing legal status.

Babysitting was the term used to describe housekeeping and nanny positions as well as informal childminding for the hub household. Where adolescent immigrants were babysitters, a Western education was one of the rewards provided to the spoke in exchange for after-school care of the hub's own children.

Many older women who did work for their hub did this work only temporarily, it seems, overstaying visas while searching for other employment.

> One of the ladies that we sponsored they were—we sponsored them on the basis of babysitting. They came up on a vacation and, just like everybody else, [they ask you] to give them a little job to take care of your kids while you work and eventually they wanted to stay and they ask you to sponsor them, so you sponsor them. It was very easy in those days, you know, to sponsor.

The woman quoted here had sponsored women in this position several times. (In the preceding chapter, I used Taran's case to describe the model use of the co-resident spoke, because she too sponsored several women this way—but all of Taran's babysitters were adolescents.)

Military Service, New York
Some men interviewed in New York reported that they were drafted into military service in the 1960s.[3] They noted that when they were being considered for entry into the country they were given chest X-rays, physical examinations, and a military classification. Classification as 1–A meant that one was physically fit for military obligation.

> When I came, I came here April [19]66. I got a draft classification. I went down to Whitehall Street and I was drafted in July 1966 in the United States Army. So I was here April, the 20th of April—so May, June, July. After three months I was drafted, [just] like that I was overseas. I went through basic training; I went overseas and I came back. I saw six years of military but you're only required to serve two years active and four years in reserve for your tour of duty, that was it. After six I came out and then I had reserve for four years [in New York].

I was reluctant to classify military service as a niche (and decided in the end that it was not one, really) because no immigrant I interviewed had made a career of it and none had chosen it voluntarily. Anyone in my sample who served did so because he was drafted. Still, I thought it important to explain the men's participation in the U.S. Armed Forces.

Teaching, London
I began sampling in London with a teacher who was recruited by Jocelyn (the hub first described in Chapter One), and all but one of the teachers I interviewed had come to London in that recruited group. Jocelyn was an unusual hub in that she hadn't yet secured her own position overseas before deciding

that she should select the others who would gain jobs in this sector. Her motivation, however, was probably not all that different from the motivation of any other labor market hub—that is, she wanted all those from the Caribbean who would take jobs in the school district where she worked to adhere to behavioral and work-ethical standards that would make them a model in their home and workplace communities. For Jocelyn, this meant they would have to be Christian in their religious belief and demonstrate their commitment to that belief in their everyday life. She also thought that the newcomers and would-be teachers should be models for the black race and for Caribbean people.

Altogether, fourteen families moved from the Eastern Caribbean to London as the result of Jocelyn's work to fill these openings. As far as the data allow me to speculate, these families remain a joint work and religious community in London. Immigration laws were changed soon after their arrival in such a way that would prevent future waves of Caribbean teachers to enter the country as these families had. At least one person interviewed believes that this change was deliberate, to keep black Caribbean people from getting into the country and accessing jobs as stable and lucrative as these.

London Transport, London

London Transport, the institution that operates the mass transit network that includes both aboveground and underground public transportation systems in that city, actively recruited black immigrants from the Caribbean to run transit vehicles. Recruitment began when the organization sent a team to Barbados to convince black Caribbeans to become vehicle operators in London (after the company's attempts to recruit among Italians and then the Irish were less than successful). These black recruits began in the lowest grades after two days' training. "Two years later, some had become bus-drivers, train-guards and booking office clerks and, in a few cases, station foremen. Those in junior supervisory posts were in charge of both white and black workers, but they were only a token few" (Ramdin, 1999, p. 174).

It is not the case that these workers had been unskilled, for many had worked in sought-after occupations back home. Dennis Brooks's (1975) interview studies with London Transport recruits showed that such skilled workers' most frequently cited reason for moving to Britain was to "see the world" or "see the 'mother' country," or gain experience or adventure. West Indians in New York and London both reported to me that there was a time when people moved to Britain because it was "the thing to do" and "everyone" was going. (They did not say the same things about moving to New York. Once Britain closed her doors to immigration, migration to New York did increase, but the emotional fervor associated with moving to London did not transfer to the numbers of migrants now going to New York.)

Those who'd agreed to be set up in these London Transport jobs had little idea of what they were getting into. "It was often evident in the interviews [with London Transport recruits] that there had been an almost complete lack of information about employment opportunities and conditions" in London (Brooks, 1975, p. 40). Most of the Barbadian recruits Brooks interviewed said they joined London Transport because it provided the easiest way to get to Britain (Brooks, 1975, p. 42).

Banking: An Emerging New York Niche?
New niches may be created by processes similar to those that perpetuate continuing niches—that is, someone looked upon with favor by their employer will seek to share newly available job opportunities with co-ethnics. A new niche might be emerging in these Caribbean networks if the referring behavior of one woman continues. This woman decided that she did not want to go into nursing, as most of her relatives had, declaring that she "didn't have the stamina" to become a nurse and preferred the "glamour" of banking. She had obtained jobs for a few of her closest family members (including her husband), but none of them stayed in banking for any length of time. She is in the process of creating a niche, although possibly for a group of Caribbeans not from her island. She told me, "I like to hire the Guyanese. They're a very hardworking people. I've had five of them working for me for the last six years." If she continues to encourage other network members to follow in her footsteps and brings in other newcomers herself, this may indeed become a new New York niche.

Niche Characteristics
Niches can be distinguished by three variables:

Porousness: the ease or difficulty a network faces in getting its chosen members into jobs in the niche

Durability: the stability of the sector over time, indicating that generations of immigrants are able to find work there

Breadth: the ease with which someone who works at one status level can transfer useful job search information to someone who would work at a completely different status level

In New York, men's and women's niches differ on these three factors. These differences help to explain the gender differences in difficulty finding employment. The London niche for Caribbean teachers lacks all three characteristics, because the window for teacher recruitment (at least in the program these respondents used) was open for so short a time that only a few were admitted.

Male niches in New York proved to have neither a great deal of breadth nor porousness. Only two hard-to-get-into niches (tunnel and civil service work) were available to men, so few jobs in network-influenced sectors were open to them. Alternatively, medical service is a niche that exemplifies porousness and breadth. Female nurses, for example, found jobs for other nurses, but also for nurse's aides, and for at least one orderly, therapy aide, and X-ray technician. Caribbean women had the opportunity to target different medical service jobs for newcomers of all types, and conversely, to target different people for jobs requiring various skill or experience levels. Another reason for the success of women in the labor market is that female niches for this group are very durable—their niches have spanned several generations. As Maryanne explained, "In the 1920s, my mother's people were coming in as domestics. My mom came at the age of twelve, sent for by her own mother, who was a domestic." A third difference between male and female niches is that the breadth and durability of the women's niches meant they could more easily crossover from one female niche to another. There are many stories in which women entered as domestics until they could either find nurse's aide or nursing employment, or (if they had not completed their nursing training) study in the destination and later use their connections to other female niches to cross over. Men over the years have also worked to link their niches to one another. The older men in the sample had early in their careers worked in the sewer and water tunnels in jobs controlled by Local 147, but they managed to expand their niches and cross over into related civil service jobs in local government. The relative ease with which women have found employment may explain the strikingly high levels of labor force participation among West Indian women.[4] Twenty-two percent of Caribbean New Yorkers work in the service sector (Waters, 1999, p. 103)—where the women in this study were overwhelmingly concentrated.

Agencies

Randall: Yeah, I'd gotten that job through an agency on Fourteenth Street. They had an employment agency where you had to give the guy maybe $10 or $20 up front before you can get a job. That will guarantee you that you're going to get the job. A sweatshop job. I did discover after at least a year or two that if you go to the West Side on these agencies, you were going to a sweatshop, and if you go on the East Side, there they cater for the better type jobs and most of the time you don't have to put money out; it's the employer, the person who is seeking an employee, that paid for you, paid the agency the fee for finding clients.

Once networks are established in an industry or occupational space, word of mouth predominates in the process of filling slots. However, before networks are strongly operative in a job site and where niches are not yet well developed, the use of employment agencies fills in the gaps in the labor market where hubs operate but are still weak. Hubs, discharging their obligations to help spokes find work, served as go-betweens even in the use of agencies; some migrants did say that their hubs told them to which agency they should go in order to find work. While respondents didn't overwhelmingly say that hubs were involved in the job search process when agencies were used, care must be taken when interpreting that apparent lack of hub involvement, for when respondents did use the word *agency*, the meaning was not always clear. Sometimes they meant it to denote an employment agency in the standard sense of the word, as a broker between an employer and potential workers, where the applicants have to pay the agency in order to be offered a job; but sometimes they meant it to denote the agency that sends representatives to the Caribbean to formally recruit nurses or domestics. In the latter cases, certainly a hub was central to finding that job for the spoke. But agencies are also used when a hub is not in a monopoly labor market position vis-à-vis the spoke's own employment needs, and when the hub is insufficiently connected with other hubs or spokes who could facilitate job contacts for him or her.

Supporting the idea that men have difficulties getting jobs through their networks, in this sample it was the men who in overwhelming numbers spoke with me about their use of employment agencies. That is, only two females—one woman in New York and one in London—explained that they had found work through an agency. The New Yorker came to the United States in the 1950s. Sent for by her husband, she found domestic work, then became a nurse's aide, and then a dietary aide, all with the help of an agency her husband told her to call. (That her husband might not know where his wife, or any other woman, might find a job may not be so surprising. Notably, this woman later became a hub for her sisters, mother, and a female cousin. She, unlike her husband, knew about potential jobs for her female spokes, once she'd found her own way around the labor market.) The London woman says she got her job with London Transport through the "Department of Employment—I think in those days it was called the Labor Exchange. I didn't ever go to work where I knew somebody, you know, where somebody took me in. So it must have been through going to what these days they call *signing on* [*temping* in the United States]. And they tell you to take these [jobs], you know, where people were needed." Interestingly, both women used agencies many decades ago, when the networks studied here were relatively young; perhaps women's niches were not as powerful then as they are now. (And signs are that perhaps these Caribbean female niches may not be as powerful in the future, as employer tastes for ethnics from other countries begin to change hiring practices in nursing and domestic service.) Aside from these two women, the rest who reported securing jobs through employment agencies were men.

Contrast the situation of those who need agencies with that of a person who aspires to a career in an area of the labor market where the network has more influence and you will know why niches and agencies are extremes of monopoly influence in the labor market. For example, immigrant nurses in social networks can help others get jobs in the health services field, even if those seeking help do not have nursing degrees.

I wouldn't be surprised if 1199 [the National Health Care Workers' Union] in New York is 60 percent immigrants or children from immigrant parents. I don't know, maybe because there was a market for people in the health care business, but a lot of people I know from the islands gravitated towards the health care, maybe because it's easier to get a job there. I know a lot of nurses from the Caribbean, as a matter of fact, up to two or three years ago, they were recruiting nurses to come up and work up here in various hospitals. . . . They put them up and they have to work for the hospital for a certain amount of time and during that time they file for their papers. I think most of the people—especially from the Caribbean—go in [that field] because I think it's one of the places that they can [get jobs]. Granted most of the jobs that they get are low-paying, low-level jobs. Those who make it into the other part, when the come up here, they'll start out as a nurse's aide or housekeeper, but in the meantime they go to school.

A Last Word on Hub Workplace Referrals

Figures 3.4 and 3.5 (see page 91), which depict segments of two Caribbean networks, serve as reminders that hub-and-spoke networks are not just collections of unique hub-spoke dyads, because some spokes benefit from the help of more than one hub. We might speculate that different hubs specialize in different forms of social capital or take on different kinds of responsibility. Some hubs are more astute at making connections in the labor market or know more about the job search process, but perhaps many of these hubs do less co-resident sponsoring. Alternatively, some hubs might be more dedicated to sending for newcomers and helping them find their own housing while being less able to help them get on their feet in the labor market. Still others are the networks' Jacks- and Jills-of-all-trades; these hubs send for people, keep them co-resident, find them jobs, set them up in housing of their own, and then start the process all over again with another newcomer. Only if he or she is lucky enough to have a hub that knows both the labor and housing markets well, and the ins and outs of making oneself legal, will a newcomer need assistance from only one person.

Still, even those hubs who specialize in labor market contacts may face problems making job connections under certain circumstances. Helping a spoke find a job might be more of a problem for those hubs in cross-gender hub-spoke relationships—such as female hubs with male spokes, or male spokes with female hubs. Because the labor market is gendered (jobs for domestics and cab drivers, nurses and tunnel workers, are all gender-specific), a hub would likely have a difficult time placing in employment a spoke of the opposite sex. A mismatch between the skill level or gender of the spoke and the jobs a hub might know about may be one of the reasons a hub might have to enlist the help of another hub (that is, one with whom the spoke is not co-resident), or even the help of a well-connected spoke, in order to find his or her spoke a job.

As we have seen, finding a job for a spoke quite often means that the veteran immigrant brings the newcomer into his or her own place of work. It is not surprising that certain labor market positions, particularly supervisory ones (such as foreman, nurse administrator, and experienced domestic worker), may be preferable for hub householders who wish to bring in new workers. The foreman in the tunnel, the nurse in management or administration, or the domestic worker who is experienced or has been on her job a long while have put in the time and established enough trust to be able to recommend the applicant (unknown to the employer until the moment of introduction by the job market contact) on the basis of the hub's reputation. Earlier, Mac-Claine showed how this kind of thing works well in the tunnels as foremen are given free reign to choose whomever they want to work that day among those who are shaping up—working without benefit of union membership, that is, as a day laborer.

But while supervisors are obvious candidates for labor market hubs, the ability to find jobs for newcomers is not as narrowly mapped as one might think. That is, not all hubs have found jobs for persons who worked directly for them alone, or even in the same industries. That is, nurses do not find jobs only for nurses, and civil servants do not find only other civil service jobs. Recall the example from Chapter Three where Taran, a nurse, was shown to have found a job as a domestic for her friend Esmie by seeking out a doctor who needed a maid. Glennis also used her position as a nurse to help her friends, picking them up at the airport and getting them jobs as nurse's aides within days.

It is difficult to compare the labor market experiences of these workers with those of other migrants, for the published literature does not contain obvious examples with which to compare their work experience. Tilly (1998), Granovetter (1995), Waldinger and Lichter (2003), and Waters (1999) have all written books that reflect on the importance of social networks in securing jobs in the primary labor market for networks of immigrants. But each author has taken snapshots of the current state of clustering and dispersal of immigrants at particular job sites or in particular occupations. None of these authors has looked at the life course of the network, following individual immigrant employment trajectories over the migration process and aggregating them to illustrate characteristics of the network as it operates naturally over the entire breadth of the labor market, as I have here. So, my findings about the ways these networks operate and the findings of these authors are not directly comparable. Still, their findings reinforce much about the ways these Caribbean networks operate.

In his study, Tilly (1998, p. 154) found that networked persons hoard opportunities when they "acquire access to a resource [such as a set of jobs] that is valuable, renewable, subject to monopoly, supportive of network activities, and enhanced by the network's modus operandi," and "network members regularly hoard access to the resources, creating beliefs and practices that sustain their control [over the resource]." These beliefs and practices are the lessons employees in the niche use to school employers about the differences between immigrants who gain control over niches and other workers (such as those who may have held these jobs before the immigrants, or any other group that attempts to vie for similar positions). For example, these employees get employers to believe the immigrants have stronger work ethics, are more reliable and pliable, or more willing and cooperative. The creation of these ethnicized categories of workers facilitates exploitation of niches and the hoarding of opportunities in the niche, and creates barriers to entry for those considered to be outside the favored group (Tilly, 1998).

In the overwhelmingly West Indian–staffed food service work site where her participant observation took place, Waters (1999) learned that the official rule against hiring relatives was habitually broken, because managers believed that using network connections for hiring new workers allowed them more control over the workforce, partly because the person recommending the newcomer had a stake in the newcomer's own workplace performance. (And sanctions to the recommender did ensue: if the employee referred failed to perform, no additional recommendations would be accepted from the veteran employee.) Waldinger and Lichter (2003), who interviewed employers in service industries, found that once employers succumbed to the benefits of using network members to fill openings, they could not easily get out of such arrangements, and in some cases employers totally lost control of the hiring in that segment of the workforce. The workers Granovetter (1995) interviewed overwhelmingly found their jobs through personal contacts; job seekers preferred finding jobs in this way, and employers also preferred finding employees through networking.[5] In his study also, in the majority of cases, the *contact person* (such as a hub) initiated the job-seeking interaction between himself and the employer; it was not that the job seeker initiated his search by seeking out his contact (Granovetter, 1995, p. 33).

Just as I did, Waldinger and Lichter (2003) also found that immigrants need not be in key positions in order to make job referrals. Employers reported that they liked the idea of taking referrals because they enjoyed the measure of control that familiarity among coworkers ensured. But they also reported difficulties with taking too many referrals for relatives of employees, because that could encourage covering up for shoddy work, or collusion to gain power from management. Still, employers thought that hiring relatives connected in networks was not a bad idea, and that collusion could be avoided if an employer could place workers so that they didn't work directly with their relatives. But hubs with close ties can easily use formal recruitment channels to have their referrals hired into a hospital even without tipping the hat to management about their ties to one another. In fact, Waldinger and Lichter (2003) did find that employers reported they'd made attempts to hire outside of networks and found that in the end they'd hired connected kith and kin anyway. Those who made referrals actually *expected* that their friends and relatives would be hired, or at least considered, and the employer heard complaints from their veteran workers if the network referrals were not accepted. Workers not only had applicants lined up for work when job openings occurred, but they often also knew about openings well before bosses did, because they would know which current job holders were about to quit even before they gave notice. Thus, many times an employer had no time to advertise a position before he or she had all the applicants he or she could easily screen. Waldinger and Lichter (2003, pp. 124, 126) found that 93 percent of all firms surveyed used employee networks to hire new employees, and in all except department stores, managers said that networks were the most important recruitment method they used.

Moving Up: Trajectories in the Primary Market

Now that I have provided a general picture of what the distribution of network jobs looks like, I want to explain the sociological significance of this distribution in terms of its role in fostering the group's upward mobility. Three factors are relevant here. First, the job distribution of these network members shows that the jobs represent a great deal of economic variety. They not only encompass various skill levels, but *the job distribution crosses both niche and non-niche segments of the labor market.* Second, it is significant that *most jobs that network members secure for one another are in the primary (regular) labor market.* (Normally, job networking among immigrant groups is thought to take place in several other, alternative economic spaces that are either separate mini-economies or sectors in the main economy where the least desirable jobs are.) Third, immigrants take advantage of the variation in the kinds of jobs available to them by *following job trajectories* that propel them upward in earnings and status over the course of the immigrant's working life. Upward moves are accomplished through job shifts made possible by attaining credentials, skills, and education.

Employment Stability and Occupational Trajectories

When a social network manages to secure control over labor market niches in different sectors of the economy—not an easy task, and certainly one that could take network members decades to accomplish—migrants may be able to use niche and non-niche employment to hopscotch their way up the socioeconomic ladder. The pattern of moving up in status and pay by switching jobs, as MacClaine and others have done, is what I am calling a job or occupational trajectory. In my interview data I saw three noticeably different patterns of employment trajectories. (Keep in mind, however, that while I discuss these as theoretically distinct trajectories, in practice immigrants often combined trajectory patterns in their own work histories.)

While migrants reported adhering to a philosophy of doing whatever job they could as the opportunity came up, once they had entered into the labor market they often (but not always) tried changing their station, if it was possible and worthwhile to do. Thus, long-term job market success strategies for many involved creating mobility trajectories out of a succession of jobs. One kind of trajectory, then, was a deliberate upward movement accomplished by *leapfrogging between jobs of increasingly greater status* or with benefits that enhanced the migration experience. Much of the time this leapfrogging was made possible because immigrants jumped to jobs located in niches where their networks had strengths in numbers or social capital, although in a few cases this succession happened with movement between a string of odd jobs (especially for men). Note how one man's livelihood increased significantly with a jump between factory and tunnel work:

> I worked in an envelope factory. Everybody from Carriacou was working there. Whatever the boss say, we just do it. I worked there from 1970 to 1972. Then I got into construction [working in the water and sewer tunnels]. I knew some guys working there. I went to Seventy-ninth Street and I did one day's work. In one day I got one week's [worth of] wages [from the other job]. Then I shaped. I worked there twenty-three years.

A second kind of upward labor market trajectory was marked by *long-term employment stability.* Many black Caribbean immigrants—once they had found a suitable job—tended to stay in jobs for many years, whether or not they enjoyed the work. Many immigrants reported that they stayed in their current jobs for decades, and some kept the same jobs until they retired at advanced ages. Persons in stable trajectories of this kind used long tenure in positions along with increments in wages over the course of their working lives to sustain increasingly prosperous lives in the destination country. In addition to increased wages and job security, this kind of stability also earned employees their employers' trust—something that could prove quite useful when they wanted to secure employment for other co-ethnics in their network.

A third trajectory indicated a generally less stable job history but showed *reliance on educational achievement to make jumps in wage and status.* Howard's story is an illustration. He once worked at American Express for a year and a half, and while working there,

> [I completed a] six-month course in basic electronics or basic electro-mechanical—and towards the completion of that course the instructor showed me an ad in the papers for this company that was looking for technicians. I applied and that was it. Twenty-two years. In October it will be twenty-two years [at that workplace].
>
> VB: So, you're really happy with your job?
>
> Howard: I may not be happy with the company but [laughs]—no, no, no!

While Howard's life story also illustrates the long-term employment stability pattern (despite his unhappiness with the work), he also accomplished a leap in status and wages, made possible by his investment in education and training while working. Similarly, MacClaine's working history illustrates all three trajectory strategies.

There are two caveats to the success the job trajectory process represents that I wish to point out here. First, not all immigrants use—or can use—job trajectories. If one has little formal education and thinks of oneself as too old to obtain more, starting work as an unskilled domestic or spray painter (for example) and making a career of it may just be job trajectory enough—particularly if we keep in mind the roots in poor and rural underdeveloped economies that many of these people share. Second, the starting point for job trajectories does not necessarily depend on the skills one holds; rather, trajectory insertion normally begins wherever a given migrant can make it work. MacClaine is an example: he was a teacher before coming to the United States and first worked in New York under sweatshop conditions in a jeans factory. Alternatively, one might start working in an area of the job market, or in a particular job, where one has absolutely no experience, as many domestic workers in these networks had done—relying instead on the trust of an employer, who in turn was likely relying on a hub's recommendation. Often people come into the destination with skills but are unable to use them. One woman noted that her mother was a dressmaker in Trinidad but had to work as a domestic after migration to the United States. Too, former carpenters reported being unable to find work or working in other occupations upon migration. And London Transport workers are known to have held skilled jobs before migrating. So, many immigrant jobholders work their new jobs having no prior experience, but that does not mean the new jobs they do are unskilled; their work requires the use and development of job-specific skills that are often learned through on-the-job training (Waldinger and Lichter, 2003).

Importance of Access to Primary Labor Markets

As these immigrants network the labor market to secure employment for their co-ethnics, they achieve upward mobility, first via the establishment of job trajectories that allow movement in and out of labor market niches, but also because their niches are created in the primary labor market. Neither of these characteristics signifies normally referenced and readily acknowledged models for upward mobility for immigrants—that is, these networked immigrants' labor market strategies differ significantly from the enclave and entrepreneurial models of first-generation immigrant economic mobility.

One model widely believed to foster upward mobility in the immigrant community with the use of immigrant labor is that of the immigrant entrepreneur. Ethnic groups whose members have established ethnic-owned businesses are presumed to fare better than others. Moreover, because business owners tend to hire co-ethnics, improved economic outcomes are presumed to accrue more broadly to the whole as benefits of employment are spread to a larger segment of the co-ethnic community. Fewer members have to vie for less stable and less remunerative unskilled jobs in the larger economy. When co-ethnics hire their own, they counter employment-blocking prejudices in the primary economy. In fact, some scholars have even suggested that African Americans suffer depressed mobility precisely because, relative to other ethnic groups, they far more infrequently become entrepreneurs.

Scholarship on the ethnic enclave invites similar conclusions about the prospects for ethnoracial mobility. Prejudices presumed to initially greet a society's new ethnoracial groups cause the groups' economic and residential segregation, and promote a desire for self-segregation, which in turn encourages the establishment and growth of the ethnic enclave (or ethnic economy), understood to be a segregated slice of the economy made up of a wide variety of ethnically owned businesses where co-ethnics primarily provide goods and services to one another without having to resort to doing business in the larger multiethnic economy.[6] When these segregated mini-economies thrive, they presumably become the stepping stone to economic prosperity and mobility for the entire community.

While newer research by Waldinger (1994) and Waldinger and Lichter (2003) suggests otherwise, the prevailing sentiment had been that labor market niches like those described in this chapter occur primarily in immigrant enclaves. For example, Portes and Rumbaut (1990, pp. 85–6) write that

> employers as a whole may be indifferent toward a particular group, or they may have a positive or negative view of it. . . . *Positive typification*, as opposed to mere neutrality, has been far less common. Preferential hiring of immigrants as workers tends to occur only when employers are of the same nationality. Hence, when a segment of the local labor market is composed of ethnic firms, immigrants of the same origin often gravitate toward them in search of employment opportunities unavailable elsewhere. [Emphasis added.]

Generally, in regular network operations hubs are neither at the top of these primary labor market hiring structures nor are they the ultimate employer of record. Instead they are nurses and housekeepers, civil service and factory workers, bank employees and babysitters. To get their co-ethnics hired, these workers, as a group, have convinced their non-Caribbean origin employers to harbor enough "positive typification" toward West Indians to allow their network monopoly power sufficient to create labor market niches in sectors of the larger local economy. In the few cases where, in these networks, one black West Indian has worked for another, the employer-employee relationship has been a characteristic of the job's hiring structure within the niche (for example, Caribbean-origin nurse administrators, tunnel foremen, and school administrators have risen through the ranks), not an indicator of an enclave.

There are other extramarket economic models that successful immigrants are said to exemplify. For example, some economically segregated migrants work in the informal economy, which may or may not be an ethnic enclave. Informal economy activities are those in a secondary sector of the labor market, usually involving very unstable jobs, sometimes with poor working conditions and low wages that are often paid "off the books" or "under the table." Employment in this sector is of course not put forth as a mobility exemplar, unlike the other employment models mentioned in this chapter. But because the informal economy is known to be populated with concentrations of ethnic, racial, and foreign national groups, discussion of this sector is relevant to the idea of the niche. Again, the economic success of these network members is significant because it derives from the knitting together of primary labor market jobs in the community of immigrants.

I have indicated that three factors (job trajectories, primary labor market placements, and employment niches) are important in enabling upward mobility through the job market for networked immigrants, but we might consider adding to this a fourth factor: that the job search and placement process operate within a *self-perpetuating network*, that is, that new immigrants are continually brought into the jobs pipeline to renew the immigrant stream. Several reasons justify the importance that must be placed on this idea. If an employer has an opening and has to look outside of the network for a new hire, the reliability of a network's hubs is compromised and the employer has incurred new costs for completing a job search. Once the employer puts a new job-search infrastructure into place, he may be more likely to use it next time rather than let a position stay unfilled for some period for lack of a new referral from the network. Worse yet, employers may begin to *dissociate* an ethnic group from a set of jobs, which can cause a network to lose its monopolistic edge over other ethnically or nationally identified groups. When that happens, the entire niche is compromised. That niches vary in strength is evident from the niches in this sample; some (such as the tunnels, which are predominately Irish and West Indian to this day) are more stable than others, and some are more vibrant and have more breadth (for instance, hospital work still seems to be done primarily by the foreign born, including West Indians). For example, Caribbean nurses reported that they had their pick of jobs at the height of ethnic recruitment for this group. Perhaps even now, as the interview data suggest, some employers are still convinced. (Recall that Dawn was quoted in Chapter Three as saying her employer will hire anyone she recommends for the hospital where she works: "As long as they're your friends, Dawn. I know you won't bring me any riffraff.") But where tastes change and employers begin to think about alternative groups as having those ethnic qualities that are more desirable, an immigrant group begins to lose its hold on a given sector. An example appropriate here is given by Stiell and England (1999), who show that Jamaican domestics, once highly desirable in Toronto, are starting to be viewed with scorn and are being replaced in jobs and in favor by Filipinas, who now have the better reputation. Also, networks themselves age and wane—both because hubs age and get out of the business of making job referrals as they near retirement or think of returning home, and because new opportunities in other job sectors or even other countries make moving into a traditional niche sector less desirable for a given spoke. As a network loses its ability to fill jobs, it risks losing a stepping stone in an upward mobility strategy that some network members may rely on for labor market leapfrogging. When such an important factor as an economic niche is lost to a group that uses trajectories for upward mobility, the mobility of the entire group can be threatened. Thus, upward economic mobility requires continuing control over established niches, gaining control over new and vibrant niches, repeatedly renewing the network to continually supply co-ethnics for primary market jobs, and doing so in a manner that maintains employers' belief that it is worthwhile to hire workers from that network's particular ethnic group (and from no other).

The variation in the effectiveness of network strategies over time was a topic of discussion among the immigrants I interviewed. Many told me that jobs were easy to get when they first came to the States decades ago. Sonny, who lives now in Trinidad, told me, "I went to America. The longest I stayed there was five months. I first went in 1964 on holiday. I stayed three months—instead of fourteen days. Jobs were easy to get—I could get two or three!" Many domestics could easily find and switch jobs, and nurses told me they too faced plentiful job prospects. Even when her husband was offered a job in Maine, Joanetta and he decided that they wouldn't move out of New York, because moving to follow a job "sounded crazy" to them. She, a nurse administrator, told me, "There was a time in a nurse's career when she didn't have to [move around to follow a job offer]. If I wanted to work every day of 365 in a year, [I could]. I was in demand." Further, respondents were concerned that new immigration laws would make it very difficult to continue to send for people from the West Indies as they had done in the past. But they believed it is also more difficult to get jobs now because of changes in the economy.

Still, those newcomers who could not find jobs in their chosen field readily switched to other work, if they could.

I am working at the [omitted] Bank of New York. I started with them in November of 1994, the same year I came here, because of my banking experience. I think it's an easy thing for me to get into because I tried not to get back into banking [where I worked in St. Vincent]. I figured I had enough of it. I mean, all my years were in banking, so I wanted to try something else and I love secretarial work. I did a course with the North America Secretarial

School while I was back home, and I majored in secretarial science, and I felt, okay, this is my opportunity to get into that field, but then everywhere I applied this was like no response, or they didn't have any openings now or whatever. And then the bank called me, so I said "Okay, I'll take it."

Another man with teaching experience ended up teaching in New York and hating it. He switched jobs, but in the end chose to return to his island.

I taught in New York a short while. But there you don't feel as if you're making a difference, a contribution. They give you the worst classes as a new teacher. It's mostly babysitting. It was like a fraud for me to keep teaching there. I also worked some odd jobs. I was a security guard for a while. It was so boring. I was playing my clarinet to keep awake, but they made me stop. I worked for a cleaning agency—that was a little more exciting.

And as another returnee explained, "I went to Canada twice. First in 1984, in the winter. It's a better place to live than New York. . . . I had bad experiences trying to find a job—as a registered nurse—just plain discrimination."

Still, it may be significant that these two people, who were unhappy with the opportunities the labor market left open to them, both returned to the West Indies to live. Portes and Rumbaut (1990) suggest that many people come to the United States because their career aspirations back home cannot be sufficiently fulfilled. I would speculate instead that networked migrants who are unable to reach their aspirations back home are likely to be more skilled than the average migrant (unaffiliated border crossers, such as pioneers, or those who use coyotes, that is, aides who help migrants without proper papers cross borders), and may be more likely to return home if their career aspirations are again thwarted once they arrive in the United States.

Coping with Poor Working Conditions and Employment Discrimination

Even with access to advance information about working conditions, and even when occupational mobility and social mobility through income earned in the labor market have been secured, networked immigrants have suffered at the hands of employers, coworkers, and clients. Respondents told me about their experiences in holding down extremely low-paying jobs, having to do dangerous work, working under poor conditions, facing racial discrimination in pay and job opportunities and resentment from those they supervised, and dealing with employers who fought their efforts to organize into unions. They also told me about job instability, exploitation, sexual harassment, and boredom. Network members often struggled individually and as a group to counteract some of these conditions.

> I worked in a factory making brake pads. That was the most ridiculous place I ever worked in my life. It was cold, the snow blow, the factory was run down. I cry my nights and I used to from school go to this factory, and it's like two, three trains you got to take, so you had to eat on the run, and it was the most despicable place. I said, "Why did I leave [the West Indies]? I got it warm at home and comfortable." And you know, like, these guys were like slave drivers over you. You have a number of pieces of steel you got to cut. I got to keep it up, I got to keep it up. Use the machine or you still the line, and I didn't cut some of those physical things because my arm was this sore between the cold and the actual work.

Racism during the job search and on the job were factors that workers discussed. Respondents told me about racism on the job after being hired—instances where they were cheated out of job transfers and promotions, resented by their subordinates because they were black supervisors, cheated out of pay they deserved, and denied equal access to union membership. Job seekers were particularly vulnerable when facing a search outside of the network's sphere of influence.

> I don't care how much you want to work; the encouragement [sic] out there is sometimes very disheartening. Because you see a job in the papers, you go there and then they say the job was filled. You take the paper out six months later and the job is still posted. You go back there and they say—"Listen, I was here such and such a time," and they would turn around and say, "Well, you see, when we put the ad in we put it for nine months," or a year, or something. All these are the things that they will tell you, so, yeah, I discovered it was hard.

Ramdin (1999, p. 225) documented the habitual unfair treatment suffered by Caribbean women in England's health services field. "Black women were predominantly employed in the lower grades, serving doctors, 'professional' nurses, and of course patients. So discouraging were their promotion chances that few black nurses entered the NHS [National Health Service] as a vocation, and as a result they brought to light the real nature of nursing, thus undermining the hierarchical structure of the [British] Health Service, which relied so much on their 'wanting to be a part of it'. . . . Some agencies operated a dual pay scale: one for white nurses and a lower one for black nurses" (Ramdin, 1999, p. 225).

The point here is to counteract any unintended suggestion that getting jobs through the network is a ride down Easy Street for any newcomer. Network membership certainly makes jobs easier to obtain, gives employed network members people to whom they can turn when they have trouble on the job, and helps them move on to the next job when they have to leave their job. But it does not protect them from the negative aspects of being in a labor market that both pays less for and tends to exploit immigrant labor and looks down on members whose skin is black, labor force participants or not. If one is undocumented also, one often has little choice but to stay with whatever job one has until another employer will overlook the lack of legal status, which may exacerbate the job exploitation.

Still, network members manage to establish strategies to succeed in various ways. Here also the hub figure becomes central to many of the strategies networked immigrants must use to get and keep jobs. In the following example, one Long Island hub explained how he would coach his spokes on how to best interview in order to land the job.

> A lot of black kids don't interview well. We brought Janette to the house and interviewed her. I told her, "Don't worry about having no experience. You don't need the experience; it's how you carry yourself." After her interview, some people called me and told me that she was fantastic. We [my wife and I] did the same for Cousin Janice. I worked for [a pharmaceutical company] as a sales representative. I interviewed a lot of job candidates for the company. Whites rattle on and on in their interviews. With us, you have to pull the information out of you. My parents instilled in me that whatever you want to do, you can do it.

Network membership has similarly aided those who have migrated through formal recruitment, giving them more information about recruitment programs than recruited persons who migrate without network connections might have. For example, one woman explains that recruited nurses sent information about the process back home so that new recruits would know what they were getting into.

> Yeah, even though the hospitals were coming down to recruit, I never wanted to come up to America—I never took the opportunity because they were

coming down. Of course they would come and tell you one thing and you didn't know whether it was true or not. So I never took the opportunity from them until [my friend] started telling me about the opportunities and the opportunities. So then I worked with the hospital. Perhaps they thought it was because they were telling you how good it was, but not knowing my friend is the one who was reinforcing what they were saying. I came with an open mind, because she had explained to me what was going on and the accommodations were okay—it was a room with a bed and a chair and desk and things like that. But I didn't have to stay there all the time because I had Maryanne there in Brooklyn and I had Iris in New Jersey and my mother had some friends in Manhattan, so I just stayed [in the dorm] when I had to work.

Many told me stories about poor working conditions, not just in factories, but in the more lucrative niche jobs as well. MacClaine explained:

I remember my first day in the tunnels vividly. I was taken onto the site and there were lots of other men around. Often the foreman would call on men to come in on the job if they were shorthanded that day. I was given a job that day. We had to go down into the tunnel through an elevator that had no door, only a chain, and the men all packed into the elevator and went down. At the bottom it was an open chamber, and the lead men would drill holes with a drilling rig into the rock in the chamber walls. They would pack in powder, dynamite, and turn off the lights. They told us to cover our ears, and then there was this loud explosion. We had to wait for "smoking time"—for the smoke to clear—before turning on the lights again. To clear the dust they had to throw water around in the tunnel. Then the muck gang would come in and clear the muck, and they would start over again. My job that day was packing the powder and dynamite into the holes.

Jonita told me that she was hired only to clean, but—without a pay raise—she became housekeeper, cook, and dressmaker for the couple she worked for; after they saw her cook and sew for herself they discovered she was highly skilled at these things. It was when the employer-husband made moves to employ her also as his mistress that she decided to risk her chance at legal sponsorship by making moves to quit her job and find another. Glennis and others explained that formally recruited nurses also faced exploitation.[7]

Some in the network used schemes to get their loved ones out of dangerous jobs and into safer forms of employment. Maryanne explained that she helped two cousins to be formally recruited as domestics (getting the proper forms from Taran, who was familiar with the organization doing the recruiting). One cousin worked in the home of a Filipina doctor. The doctor, she says, treated her cousin "like a slave." The two cousins made up a plan that the domestic was to tell her employer that there was a family emergency in the Caribbean and that she had to fly home immediately. She left the home where she was working but instead went directly to Maryanne's home, where Maryanne lived with her mother. The spoke stayed there about a year and found other employment. Her connections stabilized her search for employment and maintained her safety and freedom from exploitation. Recruits who have no connections will have little choice but to go "blindly" into their new jobs, and little help getting out of bad situations.

Conclusion

Clearly the immigrant network is one of the most important institutions that help newcomers find jobs. The job search for the newcomer is facilitated by the hub householder, who uses his or her reputation to get the spoke in his or her charge a job. While the labor market position of the hub has some import, one cannot interpret a direct link between the job held by the recruiter and the job offered to the recruited. That is, nurses do not only find jobs for other nurses, and civil servants do not only find jobs for other civil servants—although I would speculate that most hub householders tell the spoke what one spoke said she was told, that is, to "get dressed Monday" and show up with the hub at the hub's own place of employment. Hubs also do other things to help spokes gain employment, including making contacts with other hub householders who can help the spoke find a job, providing fees for employment agencies that specialize in finding jobs for immigrants, and so on. In any event, in this scheme the newcomer's job search is facilitated by the hub, who uses her reputation to get the spoke in her charge a job. As noted, network members also incorporate both formal and less-than-formal labor recruitment strategies into their immigration assistance processes. Some nurses and domestics in these networks were recruited in formal programs. Recruited nurses passed on information about available opportunities and what to expect about the working conditions to women who were to be recruited after them. Domestics now seem to use conventional networking practices (word of mouth) to find jobs for one another, because now formal recruitment seems to be much less important to filling jobs in this industry.

Immigrants in networks use the labor market to create social mobility. In some cases they create job openings where none existed before. They match newcomers to jobs requiring varying skill levels, and do so repeatedly, even as the skill levels of jobholders change. They create opportunity ladders and job trajectories. They create niches, where large numbers of workers can be sure to find placements in different work sites over long periods. Controlling niches at different skill and remuneration levels means that immigrants can link higher and lower niche positions with non-niches ones, creating and making available several paths to upward mobility. These paths also reward those network members who are able to take advantage of the educational attainment for which so many of them strive. Networks also give support and sometimes a way out (that is, paths to new employment) to those who must tolerate extremely poor working conditions.

These immigrants resort neither to entrepreneurship nor to economic segregation in an enclave economy, nor to work in the informal sector. The migrants who have told their stories here are working within the primary economy. When these migrants work with co-ethnics, it is because these co-ethnics have managed to monopolize a segment of the primary economy to create a niche and gain the power to employ their compatriots, not because they work in an enclave or are entrepreneurs. Nor are these immigrants hiring newcomers directly, as immigrants in the enclave economy or in entrepreneurial positions might do. Instead, hubs are using employers in various schemes to ensure that their co-ethnics are hired. Here immigrants are using strong, not weak, ties. Such jobs tend to be found with the assistance of hubs, who are playing broker roles and who often hold positions of authority outside the workplace over the people for whom they are securing job placements. Where ethnicity is important, it is not because it is the marker of a semi-detached mini-economy; in the primary economy it is the job of the hubs and spokes, collectively, to convince the non-immigrant and often racially white employers that it is worth it to them to appoint co-ethnics to job openings. If they self-segregate, these networked workers do so *within the primary economy*, as they create *value for their ethnicity* in the primary labor market.

In this chapter we've also seen that niches are impermanent, and some that are important in one period may be less so in another. The dependence of upward trajectories on established employment streams is a blessing and a curse, because niches are only temporary minimonopolies in a labor market that moves along with changing economic conditions and changing tastes for immigrants. Because nurses were recruited from the Caribbean, that is, brought into a niche sector at a time of high demand for their labor, many of the women I interviewed had been able to make it into New York; similarly favorable conditions greeted those teachers who were recruited to London in these networks. But those opportunities are now closing—nurses now come to the United States from other countries (such as the Philippines) in greater numbers than before, and the London teachers reported that recruitment opportunities were closed off once their Caribbean immigrant group successfully entered the London school system. Moreover, hubs themselves age, losing their ability to keep up with the process of sending for others. As hubs age, so does the network—unless those hubs are replaced by others who may themselves create different labor market opportunities. In sum, networked immigrants navigate the labor market in ways that indicate time-specificity (in the impermanence and aging of niches, hubs, and networks).

The market and the ways that network members operate within it also demonstrate gender biases (in this case, toward ease of employment and upward mobility for women). While the breadth of men's occupations suggests that men have a harder time both securing jobs for male newcomers and helping them enter niches, both networked men and women have been able to create tiered niches (at least in New York) that have served as stepping stones to upward mobility. For example, women may immediately enter the lower status female niche as domestics or babysitters—regardless of their labor market experience, marital status, or education. From there, if mobility is possible or desirable, job incumbents may use either connections or educational advances to elevate their working position to that of nurse's aide, or nurse, or even (now) into banking. Men's niches are more temporally organized. Some have moved from tunnel work to civil service work, but the civil service niche became available only late in the life course of the networks I studied. Moreover, men who were not lucky enough to begin in the tunnels or in London Transport may have had a harder time finding work initially. Many men reported having to use agencies to find work, while others pieced together several lower level service and laborer jobs to make ends meet. Overall, it seems that men have had somewhat greater difficulties than women have in securing jobs, climbing job ladders, and therefore finding stable routes to upward mobility. Still, both men and women have taken advantage of opportunities to move outside of jobs with poor working conditions or poor pay.

When we think of immigrant mobility, we tend to think of assimilation—that is, a mobility reserved mainly for immigrant populations and racial outsiders, and one expected to take place across but not really within generations. Yet these migrants have been able to create better lives for themselves within their own lifetimes, because they have succeed in a twofold kind of mobility. First, networked immigrants have migrated across international borders that in the main serve to contain the Third World and protect the First World from intrusion; and second, immigrants have moved up the ladder of success, securing for their work pay that enables social and economic achievement on a scale that supports individual migrants, extended families, immigrant networks, and entire national economies. Upward mobility of the kind these network members demonstrate is inordinately remarkable because it occurs within the productive lifetime of a single individual, family, or network, and not just intergenerationally.[8]

In the end, regardless of how desirable labor market success may be, network members' quest for mobility is not over once job stability and income are secured. The next chapter examines and analyzes the ways that networked immigrants move upward in other segments of their adopted socioeconomic environments.

6

Deepening Network Footholds

THIS CHAPTER ADDRESSES NETWORK INFLUENCES on the life of the migrant after border crossing and employment have been achieved and co-residence has ended. Network connections are still operative and helpful as spokes secure independent housing, earn degrees and credentials, get even better jobs, and form careers and build wealth. Networks also serve as important sources of social support to migrants.[1] This chapter explains these socioeconomically integrative postmigration, post-jobseeking projects and analyzes their value in engendering and extending network members' upward mobility.

Spokes must leave the hub's nest and make room for the next person who will join the network, and do well enough to remain autonomous, if the network is to continue to be replenished. If the spoke never leaves the hub household, or returns to the co-resident state during periods of under- or unemployment, the network cannot successfully be perpetuated. Thus, spoke success is a key element of the hub-and-spoke network type. Also, a spoke's initial and continued success enhances a hub's reputation, which allows the network to be perpetuated, because the hub's reputation gives a hub the ability to select among potential migrants, which in turn encourages good performance on the part of the spoke, and trust on the part of employers, realtors, and other resource holders who have dominion over resources that largely lay outside of the network. The better one's spoke does over the spoke's lifetime, the more his or her hub is understood to be the initiator of that spoke's own successful journey up the mobility ladder, and (presumably) the more beholden the spoke is to the hub. The continuing relationship network that members have with each other are positive sum relationships, where both sides of the exchange are expected to benefit, from the first networked interaction to the last. The perpetuation of this tie between hub and spoke and the glue of the debt between them are what make the network's influence adhere for years and decades into the migrant's lifetime.

Even though network connections are maintained throughout the spokes' lives in the destination, the roles of hub and spoke become less important to spokes' membership in the community of co-ethnics. It becomes more important, then, to understand network relationships and resource exchanges longitudinally, which allows networks to be studied as a series of segments that guide the dynamics of integration. In this sense, it might be useful to understand the network as having a life course, one that waxes and wanes depending on its effectiveness in markets and in keeping connections active among its members.

Financing Dreams

Migration is commonly understood as an economic process for good reason—people move to earn money to support their families and increase their economic well-being. The interdependence of network relationships fosters the financing of this well-being in several ways.

Co-Residence as a Form of Saving

In Chapter Three I argued that co-residence is a key component of the black Caribbean migration process and the migrant culture of reciprocity. Spokes are brought into a destination country and are normally brought to stay at the home of the hub who sent for them. During co-residence the spoke is given bed and board, gifts of clothing (for many do not own the coats or boots necessary to survive northern winters), and other amenities and services (such as bus passes or help in learning to interview) to assist in their transition to employment. In the meantime, most spokes are not expected to pay rent—in fact, large monetary returns to the household are not accepted, although most hubs will expect the spoke to be mindful of their drain on household expenditures, particularly with regard to utility bills. Perhaps surprisingly, many of the people I interviewed reported that the costs of electricity and long-distance telephone service were the most scrutinized. (Certainly these utilities are inordinately expensive in the Caribbean, and were more expensive in the migration destinations in earlier years of the hubs' financially supportive activities than they are today.) Offers to assist with utility and grocery bills are welcome signs that spokes are ever mindful that they are the beneficiary of their hosts' hospitality. At the same time, the refusal of payments for these things and especially for rent indicates to the spoke that their monies earned are to be saved.

Co-residence is a practice that creates savings for the spoke. The targets for savings are several. Spokes are expected to send home remittances, particularly to finance the care of children fostered in the islands, but spokes are also expected to save so that they can soon enough be able to move out and care for themselves. In addition, spokes are expected to save money for things like security deposits and first and last month's rent on apartment leases, or even for down payments on homes they will own. While having a steady-enough income to pay rent or a mortgage is important, having the start-up funds for such big-ticket items is fundamental to residential independence. The thriftier a spoke is during co-residence, the sooner he or she can afford to make the move. The pressure is greater for married spokes and those intending to marry, or if a spoke is expected (by the hub or others) to assist in the migration of other spokes (such as sending for their own children).

Esusus

One way Caribbean immigrants save for big-ticket items is by participating in a rotating savings or credit association, or ROSCA (Besley, 1995). ROSCAs are by no means exclusive to Caribbean persons, nor are they solely organized by immigrants. In fact, this, like child fosterage, is a practice that many groups have adapted to their own particular cultural toolkit.

> Institutions of this form are found worldwide and travel under a number of different names: *Chit* funds in India, *Hui* in Taiwan, *Tontines* in Senegal and *Kye* in Korea are examples. Under typical rules of operation, a group of individuals gets together periodically and allocates a pot of funds to one group member, either by lot or bidding. The process continues, with past winners excluded, until each member has won the pot once. This type of institution serves to enhance household capital accumulation of indivisible items, since the pot of funds can be given to one member who can invest before he would have if he were left to accumulate on his own. Rotating savings and credit associations may also serve a risk-sharing function if individuals receive shocks to their health or incomes during the rotation cycle. . . . There is good evidence that such institutions make use of local information and enforcement

in their operations. Thus, a typical setting for a rotating savings association to be formed is a neighborhood or workplace. They do persist in developed countries to a degree. However, they tend to be confined to groups, such as recent immigrants, who are disadvantaged vis-à-vis formal credit markets. [Besley, 1995, pp. 120–21]

A few of the immigrants with whom I spoke reported that they were participants in such associations, which one person referred to as an *esusu,* or *susu.* Caribbean immigrants who participated explained that they used their savings to make down payments on the purchase of homes or to pay college tuition.

Remittances and Barrels

During these interviews about their migration history, respondents gave few details about sending cash remittances to the West Indies, although I presume that monetary remittances were sent by almost everyone who had both relatives back home (especially fostered children) and cash to spare. But a few migrants did discuss remittances of goods accomplished by "sending barrels" back home. Barrels are thick-walled cylindrical cardboard drums about two feet wide and three and a half or four feet tall, sealed at both ends with steel-edged rims. Each barrel is filled with new or used clothing, toys, books, and other goods and transported to the West Indies via parcel post. Migrants normally save goods over several months and decide to ship the barrel when the stash of saved goods is enough to fill it. As Nelson (2003) writes, "for many Caribbean immigrants and migrants to Canada, the United States, and the U.K., there is always an empty shipping barrel in our homes ready to be packed with food, clothing, and other staples to be sent to relatives back home. . . . Indeed, most Caribbean newspapers and magazines in Canada, the United States, and the U.K. feature prominent ads from shipping companies competing for this lucrative business."[2]

Most of the hubs who talked with me about shipping barrels discussed making shipments not just to relatives, but also as acts of charity to people other than direct family members, such as used clothing sent to churches for distribution, or supplies for school students. One hub collected used magazines to send to schools. Another hub, Valencia, regularly sent new goods for female traders to resell in informal sector markets and earn income—in particular, for a woman back home who stayed in Valencia's house in the Caribbean while Valencia was in New York. On the trip she was about to make to her home country, Valencia was planning to bring "a barrel and two grips" filled with "all kinds of things, . . . even pantyhoses" for her friend to sell back on the island and thereby earn her living.

Engendering Home Ownership and the Creation of Ethnic Space

Savings are made not just for savings' sake but to accomplish goals: providing shelter and food and supporting the education of fostered children, paying tuition for a migrant's own higher education, or making down payments on rental and mortgaged housing. When spokes are ready to make the move away from the initial co-resident arrangements, their savings are applied to establishing their new life in a new space.

It may be, however, that neither the new life nor the new space is wholly independent of their hub or other network members. That is, often a spoke moves from direct home sharing to renting from property-owning hubs who carve apartments out of the space in the owned home.

Often the spoke's new housing arrangement is, in itself, for both parties, a money-saving scheme, or to be more precise, a wealth-building opportunity. Clearly these subleasing arrangements benefit both spokes and hubs. Spokes who move from co-residence to rental arrangements gain greater personal and financial independence, and privacy. It is worth renting from someone with whom one is familiar, particularly if the spoke-renter has neither documentation to show he or she is in the country legally, nor long records of steady employment to show.

Hubs gain as well from this arrangement. They earn rental income that helps to pay the mortgage, but from tenants who will likely feel an obligation to protect the property. Some hub respondents entered into homeownership precisely in order to rent out space in this way—it allowed them to receive assistance paying their first mortgage. With these kinds of arrangements, some hubs managed to own multiple homes: for example, they would move from their first place of residence into a larger one better suited to their growing families but rent out the first home to newly independent spokes.

Spokes have entered home ownership in this way also. There are several instances in the data where hubs have found properties for their spokes in desirable areas, arranged for their financing by putting the spokes in touch with eager and sympathetic brokers, and in some cases, sold to their spokes the home in which the spoke was initially renting space. Spokes often use as a down payment esusu funds or loans from hubs, family, and friends.

Thus, even when co-residence ended for the respondents in this study, it was far from usual that the next step in independent living was a step that severed ties. It often brought about homeownership, and therefore a new form of wealth building, for network members (both hubs and spokes). An example from MacClaine's life might serve as an illustration of how these arrangements have been known to work. After MacClaine married and then ended the period of co-residence with his brother, he and his wife had a son and bought a house. They told me that the Brooklyn neighborhood they moved into was white at the time of their home purchase. In the new home, the little family lived on the first and basement floors, which were basically a one-bedroom apartment. The upper floors comprised a two-bedroom apartment, which they rented out to MacClaine's sister, who had soon afterward migrated with her husband and two sons. MacClaine says, "she was like a mother to me," and that their relationship remained close while both families shared a domicile. He said they all did a lot of "family things" together. Eventually MacClaine and his wife Belinda bought another house, and the sister and her family bought their own home as well. When they moved out, MacClaine and Belinda rented the downstairs apartment to Belinda's niece and her new husband; the niece's father was Harvey, Belinda's initial co-resident hub, who had also served as an employment hub for MacClaine by getting him a job in the tunnels. After the niece and her husband moved away, they rented the place to another West Indian friend. This new tenant was the man who was the employment hub who helped MacClaine get the civil service job he now has.

Black workers in London made similar arrangements to foster homeownership among newcomers and veteran immigrants. Ramdin (1999, p. 172) writes about a practice that he says began in the 1920s:

How, in these early days, did a black newcomer become a landlord? . . . Usually a number of people pooled their savings to raise the deposit to purchase a house. Once they had possession of the house, rooms were let to relations and friends, to new arrivals and 'refugees' from other lodgings. The accumulated rent was ploughed back into buying another house, and so on. In this way, a chain of ownership was formed, and fortuitously for the landlord concerned, black migrants tended to favour black landlords rather than white, though at times the rents (a "colour tax") charged were higher. [Ramdin, 1999, p. 172]

James and his wife, Heddy, told me that as hubs they combined periods of rent-free co-residence and renting out their home to others.

> James:I've done that for a lot of people already. It gives me pleasure to do that, you know. I don't want anything in return. I just like to, it's something I like to do.
>
> VB: Do you do things like finding apartments or housing?
>
> James: Same thing.
>
> Heddy: Believe that. The people in our apartments—we had three students living for years and—
>
> James: Yes. And I had people live with me for free because they're not working, you know.
>
> Heddy: And we gave them food and money so they could keep going to school—
>
> VB: Was this family?
>
> James: No, absolutely I don't know these people.
>
> Heddy: Well, one guy is from my country and I brought him.
>
> James: I didn't know these people before.
>
> Heddy: And he brought his other friend and asked me if he could stay there and then he brought his other friend and I said he could stay there and before you know it I got a whole shelter.
>
> James: Well, you see, I look at it this way: if it's not going to hurt me, why object?

Of course there is a downside to renting to or from co-ethnics. As Calvin explained, he rented out his home to people because he knew his co-ethnics would have difficulty finding good housing.

> It was very difficult for people to rent; most people don't want to rent [to people] with children, children could be destructive—not could be, they *are* destructive. I rented [out space to a couple] before, with two children, and they were doctors and they—[from the look of the property you would] think there was a war. People don't stop their kids. I found out that one—she likes graffiti. She likes to write all on the sheet[s].

Whether the spoke's next place of residence is for purchase or for rent, when hubs help spokes find housing after the co-resident period, the new domicile is often very close by to where the hub household is. When hubs help spokes become property owners themselves, the spokes are often encouraged to purchase homes near their co-ethnics; in this way, ethnic neighborhoods are created.

> When my brother came he stayed [lived] here with me and then he went back home and he come back again.[3] While he was here, that house [he points down the road to a nearby house] went up for sale right here—because people wonder, "How come your brother['s] living so close to you?" It just happen[ed] like that, you know, right here, and they called him and we convinced him to get the house rather than paying rent. It costs about the same thing to pay for—pay rent—you have to pay for a mortgage and you're renting and you don't own it. There's no equity—but if you put yourself out, even if you have to lie on the floor [and have no furniture because the money goes to pay the mortgage], there's a roof over your head.

Even Jonelle, the adolescent runaway spoke described in Chapter Four, ended up buying a home a short distance from the hub household from which she had fled years earlier. Still, she's happy; she acknowledges that her hub was finding homes for sale that were practically next door.

> Jonelle: It's in [my Queens neighborhood]. It's like fifteen, twenty minutes from Auntie [my hub]. I think that's a little close still, but I don't think she'll come over every minute. But it's sort of close—I understand that she went and see the place 'cause I told her where it was, so she drove over there and she said it looks okay. . . .

> VB: How did you pick that house? I mean, you didn't plan to be near your aunt but you ended up there, right?

> Jonelle: He [the realtor] showed me some addresses, and they were in [Auntie's Queens neighborhood], but I said un huh, [no] that's not it. He said to me [why?] and I said because my aunt lives there. Auntie used to have houses next to her for sale and she would tell me and I said, "Auntie, that's too close for comfort." But so we went to this real estate guy, somebody recommended him, because I wanted to go to Long Island or Queens.

Natalie and her husband were one of the couples that Carmella and Calvin helped to get into their neighborhood in Long Island.

> Natalie: I had another friend that worked with me that kept telling me about [a Long Island neighborhood]; we just wanted to come to the Island. First,

we wanted some place that was very integrated; we didn't want to be alone. Strange enough, when I started looking for a house I was looking in different areas on the Island. She said, "Come to [my Long Island neighborhood], you'll love it," She went as far as finding a real estate agent for me and she was looking around for houses and was very instrumental.

VB: Are you still close to her?

Natalie: Yeah, she was here [at my house] last week. And her husband is on the school board also.

When I interviewed Carmella and Calvin and asked whether they'd helped people beyond the period of co-residence, they said, "Oh goodness. Do you have enough paper? Where do we start?" before they explained how they nearly single-handedly made their neighborhood a black Long Island enclave.

Carmella: A lot of people moved here because of us. Even Natalie. I heard from on the job that she was looking for a place. I told her that our kids were doing well, why not move to [our town]? And also my sister—I got her out of Brooklyn.

Calvin: Do you know the real estate company Homefinders? There was a lot of racial steering done in the 1970s. Homefinders worked directly between the buyer and the seller, trying to keep the neighborhood white only. I got out here and got involved. I was elected as vice president for the Committee for a Better [our town]. I got involved in the politics of the village. I told a guy that I needed a house for my sister-in-law. [We got it.]

Carmella: We also helped friends—one from the Virgin Islands. Her husband's parents came and brought the family. We knew each other from church and from the Benevolent Society. They were in Rockaway. We took them around and show them houses. We are godparents to their children. We tell them where to move, yes, go there but not over there. We recommended the broker—[Company Name] Realtors—a Guyanese firm.

These Caribbean immigrants not only encouraged each other to become homeowners whenever possible, but also made great efforts to make home-ownership a reality where it otherwise (without network assistance) would be terribly burdensome and difficult. Veteran immigrants found and made recommendations about available homes for newly independent spokes in the areas where they already lived, and passed on the names of realtors and

mortgage brokers whom they knew would assist black foreigners to own property. They helped each other get around the racism now inherent in real estate
dealings, which perpetuates residential segregation by race. And they pooled
resources other than money to make working, schooling, and home ownership work out for the network subgroup they constituted. As James explains,

> Well, actually, it was a little rough at first, because whatever money I had saved
> was just enough to pay for my semester school fees when I got here, so I was
> lucky enough to get a job and, um, whatever I made I had to save, you know,
> for the next semester plus my books. And my brother was very lenient with
> me. I used to pay like $20 a week to stay with him and help out with food and
> stuff like that. It was very convenient. I never had any problems with that. I
> did that for about a year, and when he bought his first [house]—he has a two-
> family, two-apartment house. I rented one from him, but it was like a shell.
> We had to fix it, so he was going to medical school at the time; his wife was
> doing housekeeping work and I work in a factory [and go to college]. So the
> agreement was that I would fix both apartments in whatever way I could and
> deduct part of it every month from the rent. So I got, like, one person to come
> and do the repairs, whatever [was] necessary for just the bare minimum for us
> not to freeze, you know. I get the windows fixed and stuff like that and I went
> and I bought two stoves and two refrigerators, two hundred bucks, give one
> to him and one to myself. And I lived there for about one and a half years and
> continued to go to school.

But these plans or schemes to help one's fellow immigrant become a homeowner are just a part of the whole—they go together with plans to secure
educations, bring in family and friends for babysitting, and care for the elderly. It is just one other tool in the box of tools for co-ethnic mutual assistance—at least until the network ages to the point that immigrants are less
focused on helping co-ethnics, and what was primarily a first-generation network becomes a configuration of more isolated first- and second-generation
nuclear families.

> Yeah [my daughter] celebrated her fourth birthday here [in this house] and
> [my oldest daughter] celebrated her sixth. My mother brought them up
> and stayed with them [fostered them first in the Caribbean while we were
> here, and then she migrated and brought them with her and babysat them
> after she arrived]. It wasn't very traumatic for them [the kids adjusted well]
> because there was always—they knew my mother and father and they [my

parents] lived in the house [with us]. Just sort of, you don't move out; now everybody's moving out and building their own homes, but [the tradition is] you didn't move out. You built upstairs, or extended, so that you didn't move away. Now everybody's moving away and it's not an extended family any more because everybody is living separately. The parents are living and the children are scattered all about; it's not the same.

In England, the stories were somewhat different on two counts. First, there were fewer stories of families doubling up to enable housing purchases, although I did hear several, particularly among immigrants who came in the 1950s. The teachers' group did not double up in these ways, but of course they were provided with housing by the school districts that had recruited them.

> Audrey: The education director provided housing for my family. It was a culture shock in so many different ways. We moved into a children's home. Sixteen bedrooms. This was the first time I was living in shared quarters. It was good and bad. It was spacious—good for the children because there was lots of room, a big backyard. But we were living too close to people— shared kitchen, shared dining room. There were many children in the other families—the house had four families, thirteen children altogether. They were all Trinidadians, but I didn't know any of them before living there. I lived there two years.

I heard more often that respondents were living in council flats, apartments for which rents are government subsidized. Again, while my sample in London was small and skewed by the prevalence of recruited teachers, outside of this group the more recent immigrants did not rent from each other but lived in council housing. Thus, while many I interviewed in London were homeowners, the homeowners did not speak often of having the same kinds nor the same extent of network assistance in buying their homes as did those in the United States. I did hear of one incident of network assistance in which Pamela helped Audrey to buy a London home for herself and her two sons. Audrey had been repeatedly thwarted by white homeowners' racism; a home would be available until she showed up to look at it, and then suddenly it would be off the market. But in England at the time, homes could be bought sight unseen, and Pamela, the veteran immigrant, figured out a scheme to help Audrey get the home she wanted by posing as an agent but failing to report that she was an agent for Audrey. Thus the effort to keep Audrey out of that area failed, for they schemed to set up the home purchase through the agent, even though the buyer was really Audrey all along. Foner (1979) found that Londoners were actually more likely to live among whites or in white areas than were New York's West Indians—perhaps because (as she says) the latter live under far more segregated conditions.

What is significant about Carmella and Calvin—and what they have in common with a few other hubs—is that they were the first black persons to move into what was at the time fully white neighborhoods. Three hubs (or hub-spouse couples) reported being the first blacks in their neighborhoods.[4] This characteristic has a great deal of sociological significance when we consider it as the initiator of a pattern of home ownership that fosters the creation of ethnic space in these large metropolitan centers in global cities. Black Caribbean immigrants (as do other ethnics) encourage others to follow them to residential spaces once they get a foothold in an attractive neighborhood. Their efforts to help others resettle in the same area help establish a small Caribbean enclave of hubs and spokes.

Hubs' own accounts of their helping behavior, along with findings from Crowder (1999) and Charles (2003) together suggest the following pattern in the creation of black neighborhoods of homeownership. Work by Charles (2003) shows that most African American persons are disinterested in becoming the first blacks to move into an area and instead register their preference to move into an area where black persons already reside in some number (although they do prefer their neighborhoods to be integrated and not all black). (See also Massey and Denton, 1993.) By contrast, the Caribbean persons I spoke with did not wholly indicate an unwillingness to be the first to move into white neighborhoods. Instead, these hubs seemed willing to move into (and perhaps preferred) predominately white neighborhoods, which are well known to have the socioeconomic features of a high quality of life—increased safety and freedom from crime, better schools, superior housing at lower relative cost, and other amenities. The willingness of some hubs to be the first blacks to live among whites is not surprising given that they think somewhat differently than African Americans about American racism. (Chapter Seven explains how these migrants uniquely distance themselves psychologically from Western-style racism when they encounter it.) When Caribbean homeowners encourage other migrants to move near them—either by recommending to their co-ethnics realtors who show potential movers homes adjacent to those who provided referrals, or because the hubs point out adjacent homes to newcomers themselves—they create a small newly Caribbean outpost in these formerly black-absent areas. It is possible that such an enclave sufficiently integrates the area so that African Americans are more likely to move in. As this occurs there may be a point when the unfortunate phenomenon of white flight begins. Unless curbed, white flight transforms the once-white neighborhood to fully black. At this stage, the neighborhood composition is that described in Crowder's (1999) Global Positioning System mappings: he found black (predominantly African American) neighborhoods to have a Caribbean concentration, or nucleus, somewhere inside.[5]

Securing Education

As noted several times before, black Caribbean migrants repeatedly reported to me their interest in securing educations for themselves and their fellow network members, including children brought over for the express purpose of educating them. As Ashton explained, "Schooling made me great. If you don't have education, shame on you! I was a bright scholar. I never failed an exam. When I reached seventh standard, they put me to teach. I'll tell you why: We studied while others played."

Many migrants I spoke with worked and went to school at the same time—whether they came to work or be educated, they spoke and lived their lives as if employment and education always went together. They took advantage of opportunities to gain education whenever possible, and often had the support of employers to accomplish their educational achievements.

> Um, I did, um, two years at Cornell. I had to go back to school again 'cause they, in banking, you really have to keep up because it changes, so they're very good 'cause they pay for everything. So I did a two-year program at Cornell University. They have an off campus in the city, so I just finished that in [19]92 or [19]93, and it was refreshing to go back to school, go back to the library, do research; it was really interesting.

English-speaking Caribbean transplants also use education to help themselves switch jobs—going to nursing school or earning college degrees while working in lower-end jobs, and changing to fields to where they could earn higher pay and greater prestige. Education and credentialing became a key component in making immigrants' workforce trajectories successful vehicles for upward mobility. MacClaine's labor force experience, described in the preceding chapter, is an example. He said he wanted to go to school for two reasons. First, education was very important to him. Noting that "education was a privilege, not a right, in the West Indies," he explained that he was very fortunate in that he got to go to high school there. "School is provided for all children up to standard form six, which is up to ages twelve or thirteen. One could only go to school [meaning high school] if someone paid the school fees, or if they got a scholarship." Second, he wanted steady work, which meant he had to leave New York City's tunnels. He explained that sometimes the sons of the tunnel workers would talk about going to school, but their fathers would bring them onto the job site, and once they saw their first check they would "forget all about school" because the money was good. MacClaine continued going to school and working full shifts, finally using education to leapfrog out of this job and into another, safer and more stable position. Randall explains how his labor force experience also pushed him to use education to make a move up the job ladder. At the point in his interview from where I take this quote, Randall was explaining how employment agencies would not send him to jobs for which he wasn't eligible, that is, those that required greater skill levels than he had. Lamenting this, he sought education because he wanted to make himself eligible for better jobs.

> I think there's where the motivation to go back to school came by, in conquering that kind of experience. I figured the only way to a better life or decent job was through education, and up to there, to me, it holds more true than any time, that I didn't have the experience to know. As I said, I had no other skills, but I decided I'm going to try to get a skill, that if I can do it well, and do it on my own, probably I can go into business on my own. So as I said, with the computer age changing, and the electronic [age], I went to Brooklyn Community College, which today is known as Brooklyn Technical College, and I enter[ed] an associates program in electrical engineering technology. [Here, Randall described his job trajectory at length and stated how, ten years later, as a father and experienced worker,] I start[ed] to put my learning and experience into play. . . . If you want to do something, and you really want it badly, then you are going to do it. When people say they can't, I don't believe in people saying "I can't do it." You can't do it because you don't want to do it.

James has a perspective similar to Randall's on two points—that education is the key to the West Indian immigrant's success, and that all one needs is determination to get it.

> Even though you have to do it here, you got to survive on your own. The key is to get here; when you get here the second step is to use your intelligence

and not to forget why you came here. So in the event that you have to return, you will return with what you came for, which is basically an education that most people come to this country [for]. Life in the Caribbean is beautiful; furthering your education is a problem.

Education is an important theme in the immigration histories of black transplants from the Caribbean, coming up again and again as those who were interviewed spoke about education as one of the more important things anyone could secure in life. This sentiment about the importance of education was consistent in the transcripts, whether or not the speakers themselves had obtained educational credentials.

Supporting Compatriots Through Ethnic Organizations

When I was doing this fieldwork, there was much discussion among immigration scholars about the impact of ethnic associations on immigrant communities, especially in the area of mutual assistance. Even though at the time I suspected no direct relationship between membership in networks and in ethnic associations, I did make some inquiries about it.[6]

Ethnic associations among these respondents tended to be island or country specific, while the immigrant networks tended to be interethnic (that is, cross-island or pan-Caribbean) efforts. Maryanne told me about the Trinidad Nurses' Association and the Trinidad and Tobago Nurses' Guild. Members of the latter group meet monthly at each other's homes and annually hold a luncheon ("it was in June") and a tea party ("which was just last week—in November"). They also give scholarships and "send machines home," such as EKG monitors and such. They also provide information and assistance to "people who aren't here right, which they don't call illegals but undocumented immigrants." For these people, the organization arranges health care and dental care, child welfare, and prenatal and maternal care. Maryanne explained that her nurse friends, like Taran, are all members, and that Maryanne went to their tea last year. She explained that "Barbados, Jamaica, St. Vincent, Haiti, and even Dominica" all have their own nurses' associations.

I argued (in Chapter Three) that hubs are more likely than spokes to keep ties back home and to provide assistance to persons back home through these ties. But spokes also want to help loved ones and make charitable contributions. The interview data suggest that spokes may be more likely to offer charitable assistance to those back home via their participation in ethnic associations (rather than by becoming hubs). By assisting others through vol-

unteering or donating money or goods through ethnic associations, immigrants don't have to take on as much responsibility as if they tried to organize
these remittance assistance or community support activities on their own.

I can't remember how I connected [with the Claudia Jones Organisation]. I
knew that Claudia Jones was an organization that was being set up; in fact,
I didn't know who Claudia Jones was—I had to be told who she was.[7] . . .
There were a group of people, but [Aurora, one of the organization's founders]
was spearheading, kind of. It was motivated by the feeling that kids who were
born here of African-Caribbean origins, especially Vincentian kids who didn't
have a clue who they were, and actually in order to be assertive and competent
in this society you had to know who you were, where you came from and
you know who you were. So she was involved at the time with organizing
the kids and getting money for taking kids back home [to the Caribbean]
for the holidays, right? So she would take kids home, good kids home, you
know, so that they [could] get to know the Caribbean and could learn what
the Caribbean was like. . . . People here just didn't feel they could afford to
take their large families back home regularly, you know. . . . Their perception
was the black kids were having problems in school and so on because they
had poor self-esteem and lacked a sense of identity. So one of the ways of
addressing it was for the black community to try and do something about it.
And [Aurora] was very much involved in all that. Well, that's how I saw her
at the time, whether she was involved with other things [I don't know, but]
that's how I got connected to her, when she was fundraising to take those kids
abroad. And then I think it developed into supplementary school [the Saturday
School] after that. And it developed into Claudia Jones [Organisation] in a
dynamic sort of range of activities like supporting the elderly and developing
groups around various issues dealing with the Caribbean and the Caribbean
community. So I got involved in that way, you know, like the Supplementary
School and stuff like that, and what else? Oh yea, she was setting up courses
linked, I think, to the University of London, London University. But I was
never sort of like a very active person in that, because I had too many other
things that occupied my time. I supported them when I could, but I wasn't a
full active member of it.

The Claudia Jones Organisation (CJO), established in 1982, is a community
organization originally started by Caribbean women in London. (It had formerly been the Hackney Black Women's Support Group.) Now, "member-

ship is open to any individual family whose origin is African Caribbean," but only women are full members, while others of African Caribbean descent or birth have associate membership. The CJO has many objectives, including advancing education, promoting knowledge of "positive aspect[s] of Caribbean culture and history," providing recreation and leisure activities, and offering support to Caribbean women and their families.[8] Their several charitable projects include Education (where they have Supplementary School, Easter Schemes, Summer School, and career advice and training), the Elderly Project (including Twice Weekly Drop-In, crafts classes, home visits, and other support), Health (including support groups for lupus, fibroids, and hysterectomy; information on other ailments endemic to the black community; and counseling and support), and Cultural Welfare (which sponsors the Friday Night Women's Group, an annual event to celebrate emancipation of black slaves in the Caribbean, and other events and activities). As a pan-Caribbean community organization, it is one of the larger groups among transplanted black Caribbean Londoners.

As I said earlier, there are many such organizations—some are island specific, some are centered around professional associations, some are devoted to bettering the lives of children, but all are involved in supporting segments of the ethnic community.

Carmella: My husband and I were in another group [the British Virgin Islands Hospital Fund] to get medical equipment for the hospital. We'd have dinner dances, parties, raising funds. We equipped the hospital nursery [in] 1971–72. The organization was set up to rebuild the hospital. We donated washing machines too.

Calvin: There, kids all grew up together. There was the British Virgin Island Benevolent Society. We attended one of those dances, and saw each other— I was a member of the Junior Society too. It's almost defunct now. That organization was set up to supplement members in illness, unemployment, etcetera. It was set up in the 1940s where there was no such thing as unemployment insurance. They'd also give scholarships, give donations for books. And Christmas: people not well off would get some money. People now in the Virgin Islands are affluent, so the need [for these organizations] is not there. These organizations are now crumbling.

Just as networks and labor market niches age, ethnic associations age also. Sometimes the disintegration of the organization's effectiveness is presumed to be because the need for charity overwhelms migrants' resources, available time, and commitment.

Hilma: The last time I was down there [back in my country] I visited the school. As a matter of fact they had me there as a speaker, and I told them a little bit of my accomplishments, things like that. I send [them] magazines, and help them a little bit.

VB: How did your relationship with the school begin?

Hilma: Well, on visits. I usually try to go home once a year. I love Union Island. The place is like, so peaceful. I just started when I, about five years ago. We had a club formed. I got involved in getting materials and going there and seeing how school was taught. It told me one thing: there's a lot of opportunities here. And there's none over there! I mean, there's nowhere to go. It's just so depressing, so depressing. So I just said, "Look, I have to do something." So I just got involved with it. I keep in touch with one teacher and just send everything to him, and that's about it.

VB: Can you tell me more about the club [you mentioned you're in]?

Hilma: It's a club over here [in New York]—my husband used to belong to it, but it's no longer in existence. Um, we all got together; we used to have parties and we help the school in Union Island, but you know, people move, you know, and there was a lot of—how should I say? What should I say? There was a lot of problems because ideas that, maybe I didn't agree with, um, with this person and nothing could have—nothing came off the ground. They knew more about Union than I did, so, um, what they did with all the money, they just focus[ed] it and [sent] it to, um, the hospital. I don't know if you remember, um, Union never had a hospital before, so they put all that money into the hospital. . . . Everyone from Union Island really belonged to the club, but because they couldn't see eye to eye, the club just—people thought they wanted to support [the school], but when time came for, you know, doing the actual work, no one had time, no one did anything. Even now, to send—it's hard to send magazines because it takes a lot. You have to be a driving force in order to get things done.

Another respondent confirmed the failing of this particular club but explained that the people involved still maintained a semiformally organized group, but they focus more now on their own mutual support and recreation.

I used to be part of the [Union Island Association]. On my part the reason why I'm no longer a member of any such organization is twofold. Number one, it is very difficult for people from Union Island to have a continuous organization that will last forever, because we are very independent. It's a small place but we are extremely independent of each other, as you notice. You know people come here from St. Vincent or Trinidad, you will find there is another organization [for them]. This island is too small even to think about organizations. We do have organizations; we do get together to do things, but we all have our own ideas as to how it should run and we tend to go our separate ways after a while. We do have, however, a sport club; that's about seven or eight years old now, a little over eight years. They're called the Professors, but the only thing that keeps this club together, this organization together, is the sport playing cards, a game they call All Fours, a sport you know. It's played four people to a table, just like Bridge, and we all love the game, so because we all love the game, I believe the club has lasted so long. I'm a cofounder. We enjoy the game; we pay no dues, raise no funds, do absolutely nothing, ha ha ha, but play cards. If we have to buy uniforms, each one will pay for his own uniform. Once in a while we get [Charmaine's husband, the physician,] to sponsor us by paying for the uniform or giving a trip to Boston or something like that, that's about it. This is really a Trinidad and Tobago sport, but you have people from Union Island, people from Grenada, St. Vincent, Guyana, Venezuela who all participate in this competition. It takes place twice a year, in the spring and in the fall. Since 1987 we've been champions three times, and champion of champions twice.

Being a member of these kinds of organizations seems for these immigrants to be a normal part of life. Some people reported that they began such activities at young ages, rising to the top of such groups like the Girl Guides (a.k.a. Girl Scouts) and participating in drama and sports clubs. While noting that many (but not all) respondents reported participating in groups that could properly be called ethnic associations (even if they operated as such on a very local level), they also described significant levels of activity and leadership in many forms of social organization, including (for New Yorkers) neighborhood councils, town meetings, church groups, the Masons, the NAACP, the Urban League, their PTAs (parent-teacher associations), and Big Brother and Boy Scouts programs.

Well, I started up, like, a Big Brother [program] with a lot of kids in the neighborhood. Like you see, in my family, my father is the Simon Legree type—[children] you're not seen or heard—so I found my escape out of the house with doing things with kids because my father was very strict.

So I started off like a big brother to a couple of boys in the neighborhood, then I was in the Boy Scouts, then I was in the drum and bugle corps; and in addition to that I had a newspaper route. So I basically was out of the house most evenings; I just came home for dinner and did my homework. Oh yes, I was into the neighborhood—as a matter of fact, I ended up running for a local election in the area when I was eighteen. I didn't win the first time, but the second time [I did].

Londoners reported involvement in church groups, youth clubs, school holiday programs for children, Community Police Liaison meetings, (the Redbridge) Women's Group, and the Afro-Caribbean Society (a university-based organization). Respondents on both sides of the Atlantic, then, reported extensive involvement in churches, other (non- or pan-ethnic) professional associations, and social clubs, along with strictly "ethnic" associations.

Some specific ethnic organizations cited by New Yorkers include the Port of Spain Nurses' Guild, Tobago's Women's Federation, and for Londoners, the St. Vincent and the Grenadines Association and, of course, the Claudia Jones Organisation. The Trinidad and Tobago (TT) Alliance is an umbrella group for TT ethnic organizations operative in New York. The Trinidad and Tobago Nurses Organization of the USA provides material and other assistance to hospitals in that country, and also meets in a large conference every four years, sometimes with similar organizations in other countries. The St. Vincent and the Grenadines Ex-Teachers Association comprises former teachers in New York who provide material and programmatic assistance to schools in that country, and to second-generation Vincentians in New York in ways similar to the London-based Claudia Jones Organisation—that is, they take Caribbean children to dances and cultural events and to Harlem's Schomburg Library to instill pride in the youth. I was told they also provided assistance in the form of remittances to the indigent and televisions to schools, gave money "here and there" for emergency needs, and were raising money to bring to New York two persons who were in need of advanced medical assistance. One group, which Elaine called only the Benevolent Association, is "one of the oldest groups here; it's like eighty some years, seventy-five to eight years old. We pay a death benefit of $500 if you die and [if] you're sick up to ten weeks, you get a little stipend. We link it into scholarships for two young persons, and [we're] paying for it so they can get some education, because you see high schools down there's not free like up here."

Migrants have also been involved in soccer and Carnival clubs and in pageants. (I learned long after some interviews were over that some respondents were involved in sports clubs and in bands with which they rehearsed all year in order to play Mas [dance in the street with a calypso band] with them at Carnival, but they did not often mention these activities in response to direct questions about organizations in which they participated.) In some cases, respondents explained that the social support and material assistance aspects of organizational participation were often combined, as when a Carnival group sponsored one's soccer club, and together the groups would have parties that were also fundraisers. The parties help keep group cohesion, because as one man in New York reported, "it's not that easy to keep people interested in a cause, you know." But as several respondents reported, these less formal ethnic organizations have also provided social and material support for both group members in the destination and those fondly thought-of kin and friends who remain in the country of origin.

> You know why we formed that group? For the same reason, some of the objectives of the first group that we formed is that since we—we usually have little parties and stuff like that but then we decided to form this nurses group so that we can get together. So that if this one is ill, we can take care of that person; those are some of the objectives. But now I think that some of our objectives are changed because of the political environment and stuff like that. But it's really so that we should take care of one another, and also that we can help take care of the people of Trinidad and Tobago with medical supplies and stuff like that.

When the network is no longer central in a spoke's life, or when there has been a falling out among network members, social support can be found in the larger association, where one may maintain contact with brethren and sistren with whom one shares a worldview. Mandy—like Erksine, a London transplant—seemed to concur when she spoke about the same organization:

> That's an organization set up for Vincentians to socialize with each other. They do things like have cultural evenings and social events—dances—help people if they're in need—send medical supplies to the hospitals [in St. Vincent and the Grenadines], that sort of thing. And we have a yearly event, especially since St. Vincent became independent [in 1979]—where they celebrate independence with a dance. That is very well attended by Vincentians. They're very loyal.

'Cause sometimes they moan about the music or [that] it's not well organized, but they still come back the next year, because they don't see it as something they go to just to have a dance. It's the socializing aspect of it that I think are important to a lot of them. . . . because you know, you meet Vincentians that you have not seen for a long time. "Oh my God, I haven't seen you for all these years!" you know. And Vincentians who live outside of London were coming to London for this event, you know, because they know they're going to meet up with people that they have not seen for years. And you're talking about between one thousand and two thousand people, and the majority of them are Vincentians—and to have that following, and the organization has been going for about twenty-five years. It's quite an achievement to still have such a following after all these years.

One of the London teachers also mentioned that she joined a group set up by another London teacher and her spouse—a "diversity group" that came together for social purposes.[9] Erksine reflected on a formal ethnic organization of persons from St. Vincent and the Grenadines in London that blossomed perhaps twenty years or so after her arrival in the 1950s when, she says, people's own informal ways of supporting each other and socializing began to fail because people were "branching off and going to different places to live." Perhaps these formal and informal ethnic associations become more important to immigrants as their own migration networks age and wane, or as they move on to better housing and job opportunities that take them to greater geographical distances from one another.

Staying Strong with Religion and Faith

In some accounts, people spoke of religion as a catalyst that opened opportunities to migrate or brought about needed jobs, and as a spiritual talisman for keeping family members safe or allowing them to overlook racism and personal slights. As noted in Chapter One and elsewhere, Jocelyn believed that God had brought her the news of opportunities to teach in London, and she felt she should arbitrate to choose only the religiously faithful to partake of the good fortune. Apparently most of those in her group subscribed to similar thinking; many of those I spoke with were similarly devoted to religious practice and thinking, and openly spoke about it. New Yorkers were just as open about their religiosity. Many persons on both sides of the Atlantic answered my questions about their involvement in ethnic and voluntary associations by reporting on their church activities instead.[10] Opportunities for success (postmigration survival and upward mobility) were generally attributed to the influence of a higher power. In all the cases I encountered, this was described as God, or Jesus Christ. (These migrants were predominantly Christian but mainly of Protestant faith. No one identified him- or herself as specifically Catholic, but no one was asked directly about his or her faith or religious practice. Some volunteered information about their adherence to the Anglican, Methodist, or Pentecostal church, but most were not so specific.) In the following excerpt, which exemplifies the belief some migrants hold that a higher power distributes benefits to them (via the network), Taran explains that after some difficulties at work she had decided to resign her job as a nurse administrator and hospital supervisor. At the time she was paying for the schooling of three kids (one in boarding school, one in college, the other in medical school), and she quit the job without having another in hand.

> I asked, "God, guide me in what to do." I resigned even without being interviewed for another job—I never cried—it was a release[, a relief,] when it happened. I met a friend at a party who worked for an agency. I was worried about how to adjust from the operating room to bedside nursing. I sent my resume in. They said, "You are the lady I want." I began the night they called me. When I got the paycheck I was so surprised! With three kids in school to pay for! [It was a lot of pay!] I stayed two years. [My oldest] was now out of [medical] school, and [the second] got out of college the same year I quit. God did it, I was only the vehicle. Another example of that, let me tell you about [my youngest's] boarding school fees. I couldn't pay one year, and after talking with the administrators [they let me] pay their school fees in installments—because of God. In the midst of this all, I never gave up my church. I came in with God, and I'm leaving with him. I keep my trouble to myself. I stay up nights to pray and study, I have faith, and one that doesn't crumble under stress.

Apparently, although she hinted that the agency-employed friend was the one who helped her find the new job (that is, she could have explained her job market luck as a network phenomenon), she instead attributed her good fortune to God. To be specific, it is divine intervention or guidance to which she attributed the serendipity at meeting her friend at the party, the availability of the job at the time, the quick hiring, the lucrative paycheck, and the fortuitous timing of tuition due dates and her children's graduations. Similarly, she invoked God in describing some of her hub activities in giving back to her island community.

> People see a symbol in me when I go [back to visit]. Each Christmas I send toys to my church there. Usually I take them [rather than just ship them back]; I feed the elderly and homebound, and give money. I take down turkey and hams. I go on Thursday and come back on Sunday. I don't let people know it's me doing it. My blind brother—he died two years ago—was one who came out one Christmas and said to me, "Sister, is that you?!" I said, "Nevermind, just eat. The Lord has provided for us." After that, some started to realize it was me doing the work. . . . I grew up in the church. It's good to look at your background, look back and help others who are there. A woman once told me, "This is a Richardson trait," religion, and helping people.

While I do not have the data to support religiosity as a distinctly network-oriented phenomenon, per se, devotion to religious practice and belief and credence to the idea of a divine entity at work in one's life were certainly central to many black Caribbean immigrants' life histories and migration experiences.

Conclusion

As co-residence ends, spokes move on to more independent relationships with hubs, but the ties between them are not severed and they remain interdependent in their social and economic arrangements. For example, spokes begin their new lives in co-resident arrangements with migration veterans who provide sheltered environments and offer the support spokes need to adapt quickly to the destination economy and culture. Later, the not-so-newcomers move on to lives of greater social and economic independence from their hubs, but they remain connected to other migrants in important ways. In some cases, network members' connections help the formerly co-resident move onto rental properties, some of which are owned by other network members. If an immigrant is well-enough connected or in a relatively resource-strong network, he or she might find assistance all the way to the stage of home ownership—assistance that includes targeting appropriate neighborhoods, that is, neighborhoods that will be welcoming to West Indian newcomers. The signs of such welcoming might be finding mortgage brokers who will lend and realtors who will show homes—even if the neighbors might not hold their arms open as wide.

While these arrangements benefit the individuals in a given network, they benefit the collective as well. By uniting the interests of homeowners, renters, and co-resident newcomers who can hardly afford rent, network members create a system of greater cross-class unity than might otherwise be evident. That is, rather than creating divisions between homeowners and renters or between people with assets and people without them, the network unifies their common plight, allowing hubs to pay their own mortgages by renting out space to spokes who need greater independence but also decent homes at affordable rates. Network members also join together in rotating credit and savings associations to help each other secure down payments for their new homes, and they make referrals for each other to mortgage brokers and realtors they know will be helpful. So, just as people use niche and non-niche connections within labor markets to encourage upward labor market mobility among those with low- and high-status jobs, network members arrange assistance at various levels of access to housing (that is, between homeowners and renters) to help people at all levels achieve upward mobility in housing markets.

Network members also assist others in securing educational advancements. They make arrangements that will help one another get into colleges and universities; they also (as the data in Chapter Four show) help to arrange for young persons to migrate in ways that give them access to precollege educations that they might not otherwise be able to obtain.

Network members also shore up one another with social support. Through membership in formal ethnic associations and informal social organizations, involvement in soccer and church clubs, and participation in outings, immigrant co-ethnics get together both to arrange charitable outreach to their destination and home communities and to enjoy themselves. In support of family and friends back home, network members in highly economically developed destination cities use their networks to coordinate efforts to send remittances of cash and goods to family members and friends as well as to indigents and institutions (such as schools and churches). Sometimes this support is in the form of social remittances, but it is not always clear that these are as beneficial to home society dwellers as are economic remittances (Levitt, 2001).[11] Network social support initiatives are also directed toward the new community of co-ethnics, as with tutoring or health information programs, or through parties, which enable them to keep in touch and emotionally support one another. Finally, immigrants also look to religiosity and activism (as members of churches and ethnic organizations, and outside of this in their daily lives) for the moral fortitude to continue their socioeconomic struggles in the new destination.

7   "We Don't Have That Back Home"

AS IMMIGRANTS STRUGGLE with establishing their foothold and bringing chosen others along with them as they attempt to climb the ladder of ethnic success, they encounter the gatekeepers not only to the borders and labor and housing markets of the destination country, but also to status positions in racial stratification systems. Migrants' entry into the hierarchical racial system, the last space left to be examined in this study of network adaptation, is the subject of this chapter.

While back in the Caribbean, these migrants knew they were "black" but they were neither forced to acknowledge nor contend with its more racist repercussions on a daily basis. Soon after arriving in their new city, however, black immigrants confront a new racial regime that they describe as very different from what they knew back home. The following excerpt from Erksine's experience explains how the confrontation with racism in postwar London affected her.

We found a way, everybody that come from the island, to get together. And it's like everybody, even though we had one room, we'll say, "Come over." And we have a nice time, drinking, eating, and talking, so it was always we as a group would entertain each other. And that is how we survived, because it was a very, very depressing, terrible experience then because there was a lot of prejudice about. And although it was in the [19]50s we came here, there was still [unclear] and they were just getting back London into shape. So there was a lot of depressing scenes about and there were few people who were nice. . . . The prejudice that some of these people think—that if they allowed us to live in [rent] their house, then we were going to do something to them and they were going to be [in danger] in some way. And if they do [rent to us], some of their English friends would never speak to them. And it was widespread as something they didn't hide. Or they would close the door in front of your face. And another: in a mocking way I used to feel they talk to you, call you "girl" and "dear." They couldn't believe we had brains and we can learn and we know, we can hear, we can see, we can understand. I think the majority of them thought when—they had to talk in such a way because we didn't have a brain, we didn't have no knowledge or understanding about anything whatsoever. . . . And one night I cried and I cried and I cried, "I wanna go home." Because of the harshness to which I live and it wasn't a better way than the way I left home anyway. I mean I had a good life back home [compared] to where I come and start in England. And then I decided, "Right, it's going to be five years, no more than five years I'll stay in England." And that decision sort of hardened me up a bit and then I started fighting back. Fighting back at the cold winter and fighting back at those hypocrites who will call you "girlie" and mock you. It was a really snobby sort of, although they're trying to say they're nice, but to me "Who the hell you calling 'girlie'?" you know, sort of things—and it was often done. And you know it in yourself they don't love you. Why are you calling me "love"? So, you know, you just try to normally ignore them as much as possible and get on with your life.

To be clear, Erksine—now in her sixties—has lived in London since she was a teenager, which means she managed to cope with the stresses racism imposed on her well enough that she could construct for herself a new life in England that extended far beyond the five-year limit she had imposed upon herself. She described her dismay over the extent of racism she faced after arrival. She reported that being in an immigrant network helped her to cope with the experience, for her immersion in a community of people from back home provided a social buffer from the world of antiblack racial encounters. She also reported that she made a decision to limit her time in England, and therefore her exposure to racism, and concluded by saying that she managed to ignore racism and "get on with her life." Ultimately, we might interpret these two decisions—to stick close to her compatriots and to limit her exposure to the risk of racism—as having enabled her to declare that she would ignore racism to the extent that she wouldn't let it hinder her quest for upward mobility. In this her experience is similar to those of other black Caribbean immigrants in London and New York. Others too described an ideal type (in the Weberian sense) of cognitive transition; they too reported being surprised and discouraged initially, but they soon began to avoid racist encounters and learned to ignore them altogether.

Time and experience in the Western world seem to lead to common understandings about Western systems of race, expressed as three basic ideas in the immigrants' interviews: first, that the American and British societies are racist; second, "We do not have such racism back home"; and third, "We can ignore the racism that exists" in the new "home." Some hold this third belief despite having been directly affected by racist behavior. The published literature on race and black immigrants offers some explanations for these sentiments. My data suggest that it is incorrect to assume, as some (such as Sowell, 1978) contend, that the successful black immigrant need not contend with racism in American society. Rather, I show that many "successful" West Indian immigrants express knowledge of racial problems in their destinations, and that some describe themselves as direct targets of racist behavior. I argue that the migration experience itself (that is, having a society of foreign origin as a social referent) and the immigrant's participation in a social network mediate the effects of racism and racial stratification on these immigrants. In this chapter I rely heavily on respondents' own words to show the progressive adaptation to racism that is evident in their migration histories.

Comparing Racial Structures

For analytical purposes, I define *racial stratification* as a social system that classifies people according to a hierarchy of specific phenotypic categories, or *races*. (Both the American and British racial systems are largely dichotomous in that whites occupy the top rungs of the racial hierarchy and blacks the bottom rungs.) I define *racism* as the process that maintains this hierarchy. Some key mechanisms of this process include racial stereotyping and discrimination in housing, labor, and other markets. Racial categories, the racial hierarchy that comprises them, and the political, social, and economic systems that support racial stratification together make up what I call a *racial structure*. Racial structures vary across time (history) and space (geography). People who are born and raised in a given racial structure become socialized into that structure. Immigrants, however, must adapt to the new racial structures to which they are exposed when they relocate to the destination country. For example, in their home countries these people were Barbadians or Trinidadians or Vincentians; their West Indianness was understood and expressed as a national identity. While upon migration their national identities remain, these people become *West Indian* in the United States and *Black Caribbean* in Britain. These ethnic labels originate and become uniquely salient in the destination, where they connote a particular set of identities that indicate concordant slots in the destination's racial hierarchy.

Social science literature suggests that differential coping with racism may be a matter of culture (especially when focused on the micro level of small-group interactions, such as communities of co-ethnics). The first of a more contemporary cohort of debaters on this issue is Thomas Sowell (1978), who has suggested that West Indians come to the United States and find greater economic success than the native-born African Americans with whom they share a phenotype and racial label, and that differential economic outcomes are evidence against the salience of race and racism in the mobility of blacks of either ethnicity. By implication, then, culture explains both the difference in economic outcomes between African Americans and black West Indians and the persistence of African American economic immobility. Other thinkers have taken this last idea and run with it; work on the persistent socio-economic dysfunction of the underclass is exemplary. William Julius Wilson (1980) may be the best known contemporary commenter on the subject because of his writings on the ways that changing economic structure created the underclass whose status is perpetuated by their inappropriate culture and their inability to adapt to economic change. (In two texts, Wilson [1980, 1987] argues that U.S. racial policy is not a root cause of the underclass's problems and that race-based public policy programs are not the solution. Many social scientists disagree, including Steinberg [1989] and Massey and Denton [1993].) An inability to adapt in culturally appropriate ways is also evident in Alejandro Portes's (1995a) critique of the idea of immigrant assimilationism, which brought him to the idea of segmented assimilationism—that some young people may assimilate into society in ways that bring about upward mobility, while others face downward assimilation instead. Thus many social scientists have tended to rely on cultural explanations for differential social outcomes for people of different races.

But structures such as political and economic systems can be much more powerful influences than one's culture. For example, living under rigid racial systems (like apartheid or Jim Crow) can be expected to influence one's perspectives on available mobility opportunities more strongly than would other race-related social factors. Along with offering an ideal typical adaptation to racism in the case of the Caribbean immigrant, this chapter is a testimony to how structural forces (immigrant networks and their structures, having foreign-born status, and population composition) influence one's interpretation of the possibilities for economic and social success for oneself and for one's community. What is often misread as cultural differences among racial subgroups may instead be evidence of differences in adaptations to racial structures, which in turn may be caused by a group's position in socioeconomic structures. West Indians arrive with conceptions of race and racism different from those found in Europe and North America. But it is too simplistic to read the West Indian responses to racism as resulting from their having a different culture. Rather than seeing culture as the independent variable that explains dependent economic outcomes, what is interpreted as West Indian culture actually depends on two structural factors: first, the social structures of the network and the economic niches in which they are able to operate; and second, the immigrant experience itself, which provides one with the ability perpetually to claim outsider status (in the sense that one may live within a new racial regime but be not of it).

By implication, then, those who are not immigrants (who have no country of origin with which to compare the system in which they currently live) and who do not benefit from immigrant network membership (that is, they do not have a similarly like-minded community of outsiders with whom to relate) will not have the experiences that might similarly insulate them from the racism that accompanies social life in the West. Nonimmigrants of color (a group that includes both native-born African Americans and native-born second-generation offspring of West Indian immigrants) have a different experience than immigrants of color—not because they downwardly assimilate to a less than optimistic view of modern urban life (as is suggested by Portes, 1995a, and Portes and Rumbaut, 2001) or have a stubbornly pessimistic and mistaken view of their life chances that prevents them from taking steps that would allow them the best advantage with new economic opportunities (as is suggested by the underclass idea promoted by Wilson). Instead, it is because access both to immigrant network resources and to their foreign-born perspective create a cognitive transition that allows them to distance themselves from the experience of race and racism. That transition creates a psychological and social distance from racism that is difficult to achieve among phenotypically black persons who are neither foreign born (that is, who are immersed in these racial regimes from birth) nor members of immigrant networks (that is, who do not have social groups and resources that support the maintenance of distance from those racial regimes) (Bashi Bobb and Clarke, 2001).

Foreign-born status is important because immigrants' responses to new racial structures are in part shaped by their premigration experiences in their countries of origin. Immigrants characterize the racial systems of the West Indies as different from those in the Northern cities (mainly London and New York) to which Caribbean people move (Gopaul-McNicol, 1993; Sutton and Makiesky, 1975; Bryce-Laporte, 1972). Next I briefly recount the perceptions that West Indians hold about race and racism in the West Indies, describe the ways they come to understand racism and its corresponding racial hierarchy, and discuss how they cope with these realities.[1]

Immigrants' Interpretations of Racism in New York and London

Immigrants interviewed for this study spontaneously discussed their adaptive racial processes while recounting to me their individual migration stories. These migrants were asked merely to tell the story of their migration history, basically answering the questions, *Would you explain to me the circumstances that brought you here, and tell me about your experience finding work and housing after arriving? Who (if anyone) helped you to come here, and how did they help you?* and *Who did you help to come here, and how?* New Yorkers almost always brought up the idea of race spontaneously when they explained what their experiences in the new destination were like. Black immigrants in London did not discuss their experiences with race with the same degree of spontaneity—with them I more often had to ask the race question directly.[2] I did not take this to mean that race had less of an impact on their lives. For example, the Londoners I interviewed were very activist about their encounters with racism. Many in the network I studied there participated in antiracist community organization of black Caribbean ethnics, and some (recall the teachers who migrated as a group) saw their lives as the texts that society would read to understand the black Caribbean experience and felt that for that reason they should become racial models.

Even with their "reticence" to discuss race (for perhaps this characteristic is only a figment, attributable to the open-ended nature of the interview), many of the immigrants interviewed in London did echo the New Yorkers in their understandings and experiences of racism as an obstructing force in a black person's life, as well as the ability to ignore British-style racism (the way New Yorkers said they could ignore U.S.-style racism). Foner (1998) found that the Jamaicans she interviewed in New York were not as shocked by racism as those she interviewed in London, but I found the opposite among these black immigrants from the Eastern Caribbean islands. In fact, I surmised that these British residents felt the idea of racism to be somewhat less remarkable, which is not to say they thought it was unimportant. Perhaps it was the fact that immigrants to New York were perceived as more successful that contributed to the immigrants' sense of shock—they may have presumed that racism could or should not be a factor if one could emigrate and achieve so much. Perhaps also the responses of the immigrants to Britain were colored by their longer-term residence in the Western world, because they are part of an earlier migration stream. (In this sample, the Caribbean respondents in Britain had been there longer than the New York immigrants had been in the United States.) Thus, perhaps for those in Britain the shock of their adaptation experience was farther away in memory and therefore less controversial or worth talking about when asked specifically about their migration stories, than the racializing experiences in their more recent lives. In any case, because I found that the New Yorkers were more shocked and more forthcoming about discussing race, their words on the subject may, in this chapter, overwhelm the words of the Londoners with the same Eastern Caribbean origins.

There were some basic similarities between the accounts of transplanted Caribbean persons in these two cities. When Londoners and New Yorkers recounted experiences of racism, they described discriminatory encounters in the schools, at the workplace, and when searching for housing.

Racism in the Public and Postsecondary School Systems

When asked directly about their experience with racism in the United States, a New York couple described several encounters and their activist responses. The following report of their encounter with their local school system is representative.

> Carmella: How about [our daughter's] experience in getting admission to college? She was straight A, class president.

Calvin: Our friend [name withheld], now vice principal at the junior high school, said years back that if she continues at the rate she's going we should not waste our time, just go straight to the Ivy League. When it came time to apply to schools, her counselor didn't even mention this. Even before that—

Carmella: She was the first black Student of the Month with the chamber of commerce. With all the others, they got their picture in the paper, and then again in the lobby of the school. We saw nothing. [Our daughter] kept asking them and asking them. Finally I said I would take care of it, don't ask them anymore. I called the school and asked who was responsible for the publicity. All they had was a clipping of her in the guidance office. They said that a teacher was responsible but that the secretary was ill. I said, "For two months?" I asked for the principal but was connected to the assistant principal. I told him the story and said that it was a good thing to have the other students see, especially the black ones. She could be a role model. I said, "Get it done or I will get the papers on you all myself." She gave the guidance counselor a list of the schools she was interested in. He said to her, "You know, these are expensive schools. Why not try Rutgers, Hofstra, or community college?" So I said I'd do my homework. I did research and passed this [research] on to others. It's racism, but I don't want to believe it. Even though my husband is on the school board! I had to fight. I worked part-time to be with my kids. I wanted to help them succeed and to watch out for them. I looked after them because otherwise they would have been shafted. I ordered cassettes, *How to Get into the College of Your Choice*, to help in the last year. I gave the cassettes to the guidance department of the school. [My daughter] got into MIT in engineering. When it happened, the counselor shouted, "We did it!" And I said, "Excuse me? We?"

Londoners also recounted similar incidents of discrimination in the schools. One London mother reported:

I can remember, this chappie came to me and said he was an Anglo-Indian and he had married my friend, who was white, and he said to me, "Are you going to join this, em, society that they just started for the parents of mixed-race children?" I thought to myself, "Why do I need to join this society? I don't see the relevance of it." And then when my [mixed-race] child—my first child was born—when she got to three years and seven months and started school, and within two weeks of starting school I realized that in those two weeks of starting school, somehow it was conveyed to my child that being black wasn't something very nice to be. I felt then I needed to do something. I needed to give her a sense of identity.

Racism in the Workplace

While niche sectors of the labor market may have provided relatively easy access to jobs for these Caribbean migrants, such co-ethnic concentrations did not create working environments that were free of racism and discrimination. Recall MacClaine's report in Chapter Five on the freedom that foremen had from supervision, which meant they could deny men work; creating obstacles to union membership was just part of the story. He implied, as did other tunnel workers in their interviews, that black men were denied opportunities to work continuously, especially so they would not be eligible to join the union and qualify for the union book. Others who worked outside of niche sectors also reported difficulties finding work and said that racial discrimination against them was the cause. Jobs advertised in newspapers were reported as filled once the black immigrant applicant showed up at the job site, and these jobseekers reported that they would see the same ads in the paper soon afterward, and even in the long term. When confronted with the discrepancy, interviewees said, employers responded with the less than plausible excuse that they were forced to pay for long-running ads in city papers, so the ads ran far longer than their search for potential employees.

Housing Discrimination

The following excerpt is from a London resident whose experience was echoed by others. When she went to look at a home she knew was for sale,

> they withdrew it off the market. That's the type of thing they would do if you come around and view it. If it's a black person, then they might suddenly draw it off the market, but they won't say to you it's because you're a black person or whatever, 'cause English people don't work that way. You know, it's not so outward, you know, it's more subtle. So you would see [it for sale, then not], and then you might see it reappear on the market again. This is what happened to their house. And it reappeared on the market and when they went to view it again it came off the market again. So you get the hint, you know, there's no way they're selling you this house. Unless, I suppose, if you wanted to be devious, you could send somebody else to view it [and then finish the deal through solicitors]. Maybe people do go to that lengths—I don't know.

Tales of housing discrimination included experiences that occurred after the home in question was purchased. A New York immigrant explains:

> We were the first blacks to move into this area many years ago, and the day of the closing, close to the night, they attempted to destroy this house. And when my aunt heard, she said, "I'm buying and having them deliver [to the house] a bed. You can take everything else up and sleep there," and that's how we handled it. [We slept there, even without furniture.] They weren't coming after that. And nobody did. They [had] attempted to destroy it with water. They flooded the whole house, and throw a can of black paint through the picture window. Therefore, it destroyed the walls of the dining room and the rugs in the dining room and sitting room.

Subjective Understandings of Origin-Destination Differences in Racial Structures

These brief examples of racist experiences in schooling, in the workplace, and in housing are indicative of others that respondents discussed. I give these few simply to provide a sense of the kinds of encounters that immigrants described when they explained that they did face racism in their new destination cities. As the interviews continued, respondents contextualized their thinking about racism, explaining their interpretations of these encounters and the reasoning that shaped their reactions. One thing they brought up in the interviews was their sense that the racial structures in the Western world were different from the systems they were familiar with back home.

We Don't Have That Back Home

The West Indians in my sample explained that they were shocked or surprised by the racism they encountered in Europe and North America, many explaining that "we don't have that back home." As one New York respondent told me,

> Racism is not really a priority there [in the West Indies], you know. You don't look at a black and white situation. You more look at an economic situation, you know? It doesn't matter, really, whether you're black or white or whatever it is. If you don't have the money you don't have the position in society that I'm talking about. If you have the money you have the position. But when I came here I realized that not only is there economics you have to deal with, you [also] have to deal with the color of your skin, so that was kind of a shock to me.

A married couple, interviewed together, explained:

Carmella: A lot of West Indians criticize Americans. I understand why they do what they do. I criticized them too.

Calvin: It really hit me when Emmet Till got killed. I mean, we were the same age! It could have been me. In 1964 I was in the Navy. I was sent to Texas; then Greenville, Mississippi; then Alabama. So I remember writing my parents and saying that I hadn't seen poverty like that, ever. There were people living with newspapers to the windows and cardboard to the doors. It brings you back to reality.

Another respondent, still living in Tobago, questioned whether it is race that one is seeing or just the economic inequality that accompanies class differences.

Racism? In Tobago? I don't know. What is racism? They talk about it, talk about it, talk about it. We have it, but is it really classism? Let's say you have two men, one black and one white, and they both went to school. But what if one have more money?

According to these respondents, although the racial hierarchy in the West Indies is, as a system, coincident with the distribution of access to resources, it does not in itself hinder access to socioeconomic opportunities. (They feel instead that the lack of access to education is a greater barrier—which helps explain their commitment to securing education for themselves and their children in the new destination.) These immigrants described race in the West Indies as more like a class system; other researchers have published similar findings (Gopaul-McNicol, 1993; Foner, 1985; Dominguez, 1975). But we know that class, race, and color are also intertwined in the United States (Keith and Herring, 1991). The way these immigrants speak about their lives back home is different from how they speak about the race-class stratification system in the United States. Reid (1970 [1939]) and Ho (1991) describe how class and race are interconnected in the Caribbean. According to Ho (1991, p. 151), the West Indian system is "a three-tiered, color-class hierarchy in which social class distinctions often dwarfed racial considerations." What Young (1993, p. 35) writes about race in Jamaica seems to apply to the English-speaking Eastern Caribbean islands:

The reason racism is so often difficult for many West Indians to articulate is that "color and class interweave to such an extent that it is nearly impossible, and in any case impractical, to separate each from the other" (Phillips,

1976, p. 27). This claim can be further empirically supported if one looks at the social structure. Kerr (1952), Hendriques (1953), Miller (1967), and De Albuquerque (1979) all contend that the lighter-skinned people, including the Chinese, tend to belong to the upper social class, while people of darker skin color tend to belong to the lower class. There is a very small middle class, made up of mulattos or blacks, while the large lower class is predominantly black with a few mulattos (Phillips, 1976). The fact that whites, who number less than 5 percent of the population, completely dominate the upper class while the blacks dominate the lower and middle classes seems to confirm that ethnic differences are reinforced by socioeconomic differences.[3]

The words of one respondent living and interviewed in Barbados, reinforce these ideas:

> Race is the silent killer. There's a lot of race problems in Barbados, but it doesn't come out like in the States. Here we also have a class problem. Some whites mix with colored—I consider myself colored. I was invited to join an exclusive white cricket club—they asked me to join. I mix with them, but I don't like them much. There are a few wealthy blacks, but whites hold most of the wealth. Then there are a few whites who are police or in the fire service. Whites own the businesses. They are not intellectually superior, but they manage somehow to maneuver their kids into the top positions.

Another woman explained:

> At first you figure out that there is racial stratification, [but] you come in and the whole intent is survival and once you figure out how to survive, our orientation is—[that] education is the neutralizer. We are oriented that it doesn't matter how poor you are, as long as you are educated you are going to break that barrier, and so for us that's a paramount thing. Most immigrants you run into, even if they are taking one class, the first thing that they would tell is that they are going to school. If you meet an older person who you know from your country, the first thing they would ask you [is], "Boy? Girl? Are you going to school? What are you taking?" The whole orientation is that education is the key, because again we come from a society where, yeah, there is some racial difference, but yet you're from a majority. The concept of being a minority is foreign to me. . . . When you get to faith in the job market [in New York], I think that's the time when you really realize that there is something beyond education; it's something beyond effort. And you say, well—no matter how

much experience you have and how much you show that you've been able to defy all the odds—it's still not parity, and then I think that is the turning point for the immigrant, to where you become aware now of the other societal problems that exist in your new country that is going to impact your ability to succeed. I made all this effort and all of a sudden I'm not going to succeed because I don't have an opportunity; I'm not going to be given the opportunity.

Immigrants' comments on racial structures reflect their experience of the reality they live, and they explained that their experiences in their home country differ considerably from their experiences with race in the destination. The respondents offered their perceptions of the history and demography of the nations where they have lived, but also their reflections on their justifications for ignoring racism.

They explained that they have different reactions to racism than the reactions African Americans are presumed to have because, to their minds, the experience of living in different social structures has profound effects on one's perceptions. They cited as examples of important social structures such things as differences in population composition (the relative size of dominant and minority populations), historical forms of race relations (slavery, colonialism, and Jim Crow), and class. These immigrants believe that their exposure to particular configurations of these elements led them to expect that racism would not be an obstacle that would block their way on the path to upward mobility. Their reflections emphasized structural elements that influence one's thinking, and such thinking stands in stark contrast to the cultural elements normally emphasized by writers on immigrant adaptation and immigrant identity construction. These structural differences explain why black immigrants can say with conviction, "We don't have that back home."

As an example of a structural factor that might affect perceptions, we might consider the ways population composition may shape one's understanding of the connection between race and class, especially as manifested in everyday practices of racial discrimination. All things being equal, in societies where there are more whites than blacks the influence of racial discrimination may be easier to see than the influence of class, whereas in black-majority societies the influence of class may seem greater than that of race. Of course not all things are held constant across populations of like racial compositions; certain political and economic configurations (such as systems of apartheid or Jim Crow) will have a marked influence on the psychological impact of racism on the population's subgroups. However, population composition may indeed have some effect, independent of politics and economics. As some immigrants argued, being socialized in the black-majority islands of the Lesser Antilles may help to shape one's racial thinking about oneself.

> [Our] whole orientation is that [education] is the key [to social mobility]. We come from a society where there is some racial difference but—the concept of being a minority is foreign to me. I realize, yes, black people are minorities [here] but I don't see myself as a minority because I didn't grow up being a minority. You realize that [because] you are a black immigrant you never had a minority attitude. To think like a minority you have to be trained to think that you are a minority. Regardless of what other black people in this country tell you, you weren't socialized that way, so it really never impact[s] you. [It's only later,] when you realize that your color is an issue, and compounded with your color is your accent—and all of a sudden you start realizing, not only have I made enormous sacrifices and have achieved despite those odds, but I'm even lower now than I ever was because not only am I out of money, I'm out of money in a foreign country, educated now to know differently and expect more, and only to experience so much less.

Another respondent explained, "It becomes very demoralizing and demotivating; then you really start to empathize with the black experience in this country."

Carmella and Calvin, living in New York, had similar sentiments:

> Carmella: A lot of West Indians criticize [African] Americans. I understand why they do what they do. I criticized them too. I was ignorant of what they went through here in slavery. I thought, Why didn't they just poison them, or whatever? But it was so intense and lasted so long. [My husband and I] fought all the time [about this]. Because I didn't understand.

> Calvin: She didn't understand what American blacks went through. Slavery here was crueler.

A population's racial composition has both historical and contemporary influence on social relations. This same woman spoke about the historical significance of a black majority population:

> I mean, slavery is slavery. I'm not minimizing the mental impact and the physical debilitation on a racial population, but I'm saying when you have

slave masters who are the minority—even though we came from a level of servitude—there was a level of respect, and that respect was based on fear. It's a different level of fear when you're a majority and there's one white man than when you're a minority and there are many white people. I'm not saying there weren't beatings and all that kind of things, but not to that extent in the Caribbean. All you had to have was one beating, beat that slave, and they would poison three or four of your animals. And that white man would get up that morning and see three or four of his animals dead and he knew that he try that shit one more time and he was going to be dead. Because those people cooked for him. They fed his children and, believe you me, the message was loud and clear that you can't beat and kill everybody. You did certain things that instill a certain level of fear, but everybody knew their boundaries. Well, this didn't happen in this country because you had a minority, and what we know as slavery is not your experience of slavery, so the black experience here is not the black experience there.

The effect of the racial composition of these islands is not just a historical artifact. If one has fewer encounters with whites and sees blacks in all levels of socioeconomic strata, it is plausible that one may perceive an absence of racism. A returnee once again living in the West Indies explained:

From the top of your head it's easy to say we don't have racism in the West Indies. Here the majority of people are colored. Everyone you meet in the street is black. Whites own businesses. But they know that they depend on blacks to buy from them. Once in a while you may come up against a brick wall. But generally you may not see yourself with a problem. I would agree— we really don't have a race problem.

That the West Indies islands have white minority and black majority populations may have several effects. There are at least four reasons why the minority-majority composition of the West Indies population may encourage a vocabulary of class to predominate in descriptions of social stratification in the West Indies. First, in the West Indies racial stratification is not highly visible. Successful blacks are visible in everyday life given that there are black people who hold some powerful political and economic positions. That is, most whites are "rich," but not all blacks are poor. This is so because, in the absence of a system of apartheid, there are too few whites to occupy all seats of power. Blacks, by their sheer numbers, occupy many different levels in the class system.

Second, the vocabulary of racial enmity has necessarily been muffled by the social limits deemed pragmatic by whites, who are the minority population. The limited number of whites constrains the way they can behave toward blacks, even if they hold racist beliefs. Vehement racial ideologies, such as the ones that have historically occupied prominent social space in the United States and South Africa, would not be as pragmatic for white minority populations such at those in the West Indies. Instead, a colonial ideology predominates (deemphasizing race and emphasizing a hierarchy of culture—with the values of the motherland on top and the natives on the bottom).

Third, the range of classifications by color in West Indian racial systems differ from the black-white dichotomy of the European and American systems, where the former is mostly described as having a third or middle category, *mulatto* or *colored*. Few whom I interviewed elaborated on color classification schemes in the West Indies. But a respondent in Barbados told me,

> It used to be that you had to be white to work in banks and on Broad Street years ago. Then it was [that you had to be light skinned]. But now it doesn't matter. In all honesty we can't say there isn't any problem at all. Whites still do their best to keep down blacks, but they can't do much.

The colored or mulatto class had access to better schooling, jobs, and housing than the white elite structure made available to the darker-skinned classes. Mulattos were deliberately treated differently from the darker-skinned blacks, making them a buffer race and reducing the ability of coloreds to achieve levels of mobility equal neither to mulattos nor to whites.

Fourth, the socioeconomic structure of opportunities in Third World former colonies ensures limited access to upward mobility, regardless of race or color. For example, under the British-style educational system of some West Indian islands, entrance into secondary schooling is by examination, and the number of slots is limited. Thus only a few of the most talented will have a chance for higher educational opportunities. In another example, one can also note that Third World economies such as these can hardly employ all those who need jobs, which is one important reason that out-migration has been an important safety valve for the West Indies throughout its history.

In a less-developed economy that works in the favor of very few, nearly everyone is in the same poor socioeconomic boat; this, and the fact that blacks are in the majority, helps to obscure the ways in which race constrains social mobility and maintains socioeconomic stratification. In the West Indies, the countries' underdeveloped economies, which ensure that there is little room at the top to begin with, and the small number of whites resident on the islands mean that society is hardly structured in a way that would lead the average black person to see himself as socially or economically held back purely because of his race. That is, the economies are small, the economic opportunities are few, and while nearly all whites reap the benefits of being near the top of the socioracial hierarchy, there are not enough of them to warrant being seen as hoarding for themselves most of the economic opportunities. (This, however, does not mean that racism does not exist there—a point to which I return later.)

The composition of a racialized society's population greatly defines the separate social spaces that racial groups occupy. The situation is quite different for native-born blacks in the United States, who must break into a white-occupied social space in labor and housing markets in order to achieve social mobility.[4] For them, social structures are racially segmented, recreating racial differentiation in social and economic arenas that keep white-occupied social space intact (Waldinger, 1996; Cose, 1995; Massey and Denton, 1993; Sullivan, 1989). West Indians in U.S.-based networks, however, may not need to penetrate white social space, per se, to achieve their first steps toward social mobility. This is because the social network brings new migrants into both new and established economic niches in housing and labor markets. When one is an immigrant to a country where one's assimilation is made to a minority social space, being part of a social network can have an important mitigating influence on social mobility and one's cognizance of the debilitating effects of racial stratification.

In this area, we see one way in which New Yorkers differ from Londoners. In the United States as well as in Britain, black immigrants are racially incorporated into a structure that positions blacks at the hierarchical bottom. However, ethnicity plays an important role as well, for immigrant ethnicities are commonly identified with particular races. In the United States, that bottom racial category, black, contains native-born African Americans as well as Caribbean-born (West Indian) and African-born (African) immigrants. People in the United States have been taught to differentiate between African Americans and West Indians, following a folkloric idea that West Indians can be expected to succeed educationally and economically relative to the African American. In Britain, blacks are Caribbean-born so-called Black British and African-born immigrants. (In both destinations, Africans are small in number relative to Caribbean-born persons.) There is no other ethnic group in the black category from which Caribbean-born persons may distinguish them-selves or their group. Thus the racial hierarchy has a demographic compo-nent: social mobility from the bottom of the hierarchy results when a group is able to distinguish itself ethnically from other groups in that bottom position. Caribbean persons in the New York area, and in the United States in general for that matter, have the opportunity to use their networks in ways that make them distinguishable from other black persons, whereas those in Britain have fewer such opportunities, and these differential opportunity structures exist as a function of history and population composition.

These structural differences also explain, however, why the second genera-tion will be far more aware than the first of racial difference, the hierarchy of racial categories, and how their particular racial category fits into the racial structure. The assimilation pattern of members of the second generation sug-gests that they will be far more exposed and sensitive to the more painful as-pects of racial differentiation (Bashi Bobb and Clarke, 2001). In a way, members of the immigrant generation are right to believe that they will not be stopped by racism—for as long as they remain tied to their networks and reliant upon them for jobs and housing, they will also remain reliant upon an ethnic com-munity with an orientation toward a homeland that exists outside the relations to which they are daily subjected. Their offspring, however, do not have the psychological benefit of that faraway reference, for their home is precisely the place where such racial differentiation and racist treatment is commonplace.

What I am suggesting here is that the social structures of race are often misread as cultural differences in adaptation among groups of different gen-erations and different national origins. Just as the presumption that black children of immigrants assimilate downward to a wrongheaded thinking that limits their efforts in unfortunate and seemingly preventable ways relies heavily on constructions of culture and (mis)adaptation to it, to read the West Indian immigrant's ability to ignore or adapt to racism as resulting only from their having a different culture is also problematic.

Just as I am suggesting that culture is conflated with structure in explana-tions of one's ability to adapt to a new society (including its racializing ele-ments), many also conflate race and ethnicity. Race is a process of ascribing racial labels to persons on the basis of characteristics of their phenotype in order to treat them according to the status position in the racial hierarchy that their racial label connotes. Ethnicity, however, is not the same thing.[5]

Upon arrival in the United States and Britain, these Caribbean immigrants are seen as phenotypically black and are therefore racially assigned to the black category. The black racial category is the one that (arguably) anchors the bottom of the racial hierarchy in North America, Europe, and the Western world in general (Mills, 1999). In Europe, "the connotations of blackness have been so powerful . . . that the term 'black,' as a standard template of the biologically or culturally inferior, has been universally mobilized in European society in a cross-referential way to racialize almost all other minorities, designated as 'black,' from Jews and Gypsies, to the Irish and Chechens" (MacMaster, 2001, p. 3). Relief from racial animus requires convincing those who police the color line that one does not belong on the disadvantaged side of that line. In some cases, ethnicity may help if one's own ethnicity allows differentiation from a similarly racialized group with which the race police are familiar. To be specific, in the United States, the group that is at best seen as unable to make it and at worst long-hated for their inferior and outsider status are African Americans, persons with black phenotypes presumed to have descended from slaves brought from West African shores to the Americas. Their origins in the United States, then, are presumed to rest in the southern portion of the country and in the institution of black slavery. In Britain the group that fits this description is the Black British, who some believe comprise the immigrant black Caribbeans, who are believed to have come to England only after the 1940s.[6] The British subscribe to the idea that their race problems arrived only when the black population was "imported." (The history of black enslavement in the British world seems to be unrelated to the British mainland; rather, it appears to be a problem centered on the former British colonies from which most black Caribbean persons residing in Britain come.) Black Caribbean persons in Britain, then, have no historically or numerically significant native-born group of black persons from which they might ethnically distinguish themselves. Thus they hold the position at society's racial bottom.

When does establishing a differentiating ethnicity work? When one's group gains a consciousness of the hierarchical nature of ethnoracial categories and then makes efforts to construct and maintain a significant social distance from the hierarchy's bottom, which is associated with the lowest-caste status. The task of ethnic differentiation may be easier for black persons from the Caribbean in New York than for those in London. Black immigrants to New York can play themselves off against African Americans, with whom they share a racial classification but differ in their ethnic positioning. If they convince employers and realtors that they are "different," and show this by their accents, different ways of relating to whites, and different work ethic (which may simply result from the pressure to conform to the standards and pressures of being in the immigrant network and the standards set by the veteran immigrants who recommend a newcomer for a job)—then a mythology about West Indian ethnic superiority may be easier to perpetuate. Immigrants to London would be somewhat less successful at this. Structurally speaking, they occupy both the bottom rung of the racial hierarchy and the bottom position ethnically—there is no other socially significant black ethnic group from whom black Caribbeans in England may distinguish themselves. As stated, the British believe that their "black problem" is caused precisely by the immigrants who continue to arrive from these former colonies and not by racism itself.

Ideal-Typical Black Caribbean Immigrant Response to Western Racial Systems

Racial systems vary by country and historical period; that is, racial categories and the hierarchies they comprise are neither constant nor transferable across sites and settings (Bashi, 1998). Thus it is no surprise that when West Indians arrive in the United States and are exposed to racism here, they soon begin to understand that this is not the same hierarchical system to which they are accustomed in their countries of origin. As exemplified by Erksine's comment quoted at the start of this chapter, the responses of phenotypically black Caribbean immigrants to Western-style racism follows a progression. This set of responses is ideal-typical in the sense that not all respondents reported going through each stage I name in the following sections; but consistently and collectively immigrants reported that their thinking about their new situation changed over time, as did their actions in response to racial affronts. Of course the first step is the realization that one is in a different racial structure, for one understands that one is racially categorized in a different way and therefore has a new corresponding set of racisms with which to contend. This realization triggers a set of adaptational responses that include ignoring and avoiding racializing encounters.

Realization

Many respondents did not expect to encounter the Western-style racism that faced them upon arrival, and thus were surprised by their first encounters with it. Some (but not all) had knowledge about racism in the Western world prior to migration. Of those who knew to some degree what to expect, some were afraid. As Natalie explained,

> Oh, [New York] was different. You know, a big city. It was kind of scary coming at that age [fourteen]. You heard so much good and a lot of negative things about New York. The negative was the one that I was scared about. Like the racial problems here, that sort of scared me. I learned about them back home, by watching TV, reading the newspaper. At that age my impression was that you wouldn't know how to speak to people of other races. You were kind of afraid to approach them 'cause you didn't know what they thought about you and stuff like that. I was afraid, not that something would happen but that I would be rejected. It wasn't until my twenties that I experienced blatant racism though.

Joan Anne and her husband also arrived with knowledge of racial strife in the United States, but they came to New York many years before Natalie, when the nation was in a state of upheaval about the racial state of affairs. For some time after their arrival they refused to travel outside New York, believing that their anger at the extent of the antiblack racism they found in U.S. society would draw them into activism in the civil rights movement. Joan Anne explained, "We did not grow up in an atmosphere where you were subjected to that kind of behavior. So putting us in up here, my husband was afraid that we would react under pressure. You know how folks were reacting in the West Indies—because we are not going to stand for it." Anita, who returned to Union Island after living in New York for a few years, expressed a similar view:

> Racism? We never knew what the word was. White people were here on the island. They see us and we see them. They hire us, but here you just do business. In New York you see differently. You say to yourself, "Why are these people behaving like that? We did them nothing." We are shocked that they don't accept us. They are our destruction. West Indians are shocked because they are fool-hearted.

Although some respondents reported that they knew about racial problems in the United States prior to migrating, almost all were shocked and surprised to experience racism firsthand once they arrived. Many newcomers didn't know racist behavior when they first saw it.

> James: Oh man, you know, you may realize my personality is a jovial one, so maybe they used to give me a racist remark and maybe I used to just overlook

it and say it's stupid. But when you just come to the United States and because you're not accustomed to racism you, you're not sensitive to it. Yet after [some time] you become sensitive to racism. I mean I start knowing what is a racist remark, but when I just came, I didn't know. I thought they were just making a joke or something.

The sense of surprise and shock at the realization of learning that one is in a racial regime that negatively frames the black position at the bottom of the racial hierarchy is not unique to those I selected for my study. Other researchers have uncovered similar sentiments from West Indians in the United States and England (see Gopaul-McNicol, 1993, Chapter Five; Young, 1993, p. 107; Foner, 1985, Chapter Two, especially p. 45). This sense of surprise does not comes from the immigrants' lack of awareness about the existence of racism. (Many received reports about racism while still in their nations of origin, from sojourners who preceded them to the West, or from media accounts.) A more likely interpretation of their shock is that these immigrants simply failed to see themselves as potential targets of racism. Indeed, some realized only in retrospect that some of their negative experiences were the result of racism.

America was what I expected it to be, because I read a lot about America before I came. I would say, though, that I didn't encounter—I mean I'm talking about the negative aspect of the race relations. But now when I look back, especially when you are looking for jobs you realized that there was a lot of subtle type of discrimination. It wasn't that flagrant because you go in an agency and they have all these signs telling you they don't discriminate against race, color, but as far as getting the job is concerned. . . .

This quote suggests that the respondent is not sure whether it is one's race or one's color against which employers might be discriminating. Two other respondents, one living in Brooklyn and the other in Trinidad, expressed concern that the likelihood that this kind of confusion can occur may induce black people to make accusations of racism for which they have no proof. Other interviewees downplayed racism's impact, describing it as just another one of the components of a more generalized culture shock (which among other things included surprise at the ability to speak informally to bosses and that younger people did not always "respect their elders"). Some discussed being victims of discrimination from both whites and African Americans—

the former a group that demonstrated racial prejudice while the latter seemed to dislike West Indians because they were foreigners. As this respondent suggests, all such forms of discrimination are to be ignored.

In Union Island, there's no great population of white people, but the tourists came there and we treated them like people. I lived in St. Vincent, where there is a good enclave of so-called white people and we worked together but we didn't see black and white, we saw people. We worked together, socialized together—so, when coming to America, and they were calling you "black," [saying] "West Indians come from a tree," "You're a monkey," "Why don't you go back where you came from?"—and you're trying to serve them! You work in the hospital and they would spit on you and tell you don't touch them and tell you to take your black so and so away from them—that was dramatic to me because I never had experience of people spit on me. I mean, my first [response] was to hit back. Someone spit on me and call me black! And then my cousin say, "If you want a job you can't do it." You got to swallow your teeth and take it. Even after graduating from school with a B.S. degree and you go in a white place—even black Americans discriminated against us, saying to us on the job that those of us from the Caribbean think we're superior. They resented us. So it was strife not only against the white people, but also the black people from America calling us black monkeys coming by the banana boat. But after a while you learn to rise above it, like water off the duck's back.

On the other hand, most immigrants talked only of white racism, maltreatment that clearly came in response to what they perceived as one's blackness. Ellie, a young immigrant now fourteen years old, was quite sure she knew that being black was the problem.

The only thing I knew back home was the—Indians, the Indians was a superior race; they always said, like, Indians will make a fine life and the blacks wouldn't—but that racism back there was, like, smaller, you didn't really understand it. When I came up here I had to start learning what racism was. Because when you go to the stores and stuff like that, people follow you around, you go on the bus and people hold their pocketbooks. So, I want to know why, you know, why when I come to America people do this? What is so different? They don't discriminate because you're West Indian. They are discriminating against you because you're black. Period.

Immigrants begin to see that they are targets of racist behavior after experiencing racist episodes repeatedly. These can be personal encounters, which often happen at school, or at work.

> Heddy: I took anything racial, especially then [when I first arrived], at face value. The older woman I was tutoring in math was pleasant. But my friend was telling me, "Oh, you're so stupid. She's racist! What in the hell make you think these white people are your friends? She's just using you!" Well, that was my first time [experiencing racism], and I just couldn't understand. I said, "You don't even know her. How could you just look at a person and hate them?" She said, "Oh, I don't hate them, they hate me." Ha, ha, ha—and now, in retrospect, I see exactly what she was saying.

A young black man reported:

> I worked on commission, but [my boss] would always hold on to the money till the very last. He would get paid, but he wouldn't pay me. And we had many arguments about getting paid. So that's one of the first things I began to realize, you know, how whites treat blacks.

Many finally simply conceded the inevitability of racism. It was not uncommon for immigrants to conclude that racism was just a part of life in the United States, and one must just accept it.

> It's a hurt you learn to deal with. Eventually you just go on and do the best you can knowing that racism—you know it was here before I came, it's going to be here probably after I'm gone. But I did my best to take a stand on it, you know, for a very long time. Even now, you know, I'm still aware that it exists—there's no way, you know, you can deny it once you go out into the business world. Even working in the school system.

James reported that it was his mistake to respond to racism directed at him—even as he paradoxically explained that such racism didn't really bother him:

> I had several [racist] experiences in Arkansas when I was working as a night manager. I had people call me nigger and boy, [saying] "You can't even count, what took you so long to give me my change?" you know, and they'll hold up two bills, U.S. currency bills, and say, "Do you know this is a $20 and do you know this is a $5, eh boy?" and stuff like that—I made a mistake and lost my cool once. This man told me, "You people don't know how to count. Why do they have

people like you behind the counter anyway?" and I told him, "So that I can take [steal] your money! Do you want your change or not?" Ha, ha, ha. Even more so when I went into people's homes, and I wouldn't be allowed to go in certain areas in the house, you know, when I used to work with this construction guy. They wouldn't allow me in, or if they are going to give me water, they will give it to me in some disposable cup or something. But it never bothered me, because I knew what I came here for.

Thus, among the immigrants in these networks there are mainly two ways of rationalizing the reality of racism in the United States.[7] Most of those I interviewed explained that they cope with racism by deciding to "overlook" or "ignore it." On the other hand, although many feel they can safely ignore racist acts, some devise strategies of avoidance. In the extreme case of avoidance, the immigrant decides to leave the destination country and return home. I discuss both of these responses in turn.

Ignoring It

One widespread response to white racism by West Indian immigrants was simply to overlook or ignore it. Some respondents even stated that racist acts do not bother them. James recounted his experience at a party in Arkansas:

> The highlight of the music was playing Dixie on the piano. "I wish I was in the Land of Dixie." Can you imagine this? And I joined them singing, yes I did. [His wife, Heddy, present at the end of this interview, suggested to us that her husband didn't know what this meant.] Of course I knew what it was. [Heddy said, laughing, "Those white people thought you were crazy."] No, if you're the only black person in the crowd and they're singing. . . . What do you want me to do? Do you want me to show them I'm offended by it? I wasn't. It doesn't make any difference to me whether they're singing "I wish I was in the Land of Dixie," or whatever, because I don't really care as long as you don't hurt me physically.

Immigrants may believe they can ignore racist acts, especially in the period immediately following their arrival. As stated, they often reported that they did not see race as a unique social system (that is, separate from class) back home. This might lead them to fail to expect race in the United States to be a separate system. Even as they begin to see racism in the United States and identify it as such, they understandably may not attribute it to a racial *system*.

Instead, they may see racist behavior as an individual attribute, emanating from the racist's own ignorance about black West Indians. Thus, a nurse related that

> I did private duty nursing for the rich Jewish people, and one woman said, "Oh, you speak such good English. Where did you learn to speak such good English?" I was mean and I said, "Oh, while I was swinging from tree to tree, the missionaries left books and I would read." And she thought I was serious. She told people on her job that her mother's nurse was whatever—so the doctor came the next day and said, "Miss, did you tell Miss Whatever Her Name Was that you were swinging from tree to tree?" I said yes. [He said,] "She is not very bright and she has been telling people you said this. Well, will you please correct her and tell her that it's not so?" I eventually spoke with her and told her that we had schools and vacations and shops and everything we do here, but on a smaller scale. That was one of the things that—and pulling your hair to see if it was real. But now everybody goes to Jamaica and St. Thomas and travels around, so I guess they're more educated. They had a lot of money, but they weren't intelligent people at all.

Some respondents said explicitly that racism does not bother them. "After all," they concluded, "I am here to accomplish something"—that is, do better socioeconomically than they did back home, get an education, get enough money to send remittances or to send for someone less fortunate. They refused to let racism stand in their way, particularly because they saw their position in the new city as superior to the one they had back home. "I didn't know about racism back home. Here I was the only black guy in fourteen white guys on the [water tunnel construction] gang. I had goals I'm trying to achieve and I never let it bother me. There's a saying, 'As long as your paycheck is right.'" And a young immigrant explained, "New York is definitely a racist state. No two ways about it. I've had incidents pointed out to me that individuals are definitely being racist. You'd rather not overlook it, but you have to ignore those situations."

Others rationalized the inevitability of racism further, saying that, yes, there is racism, but life is too good in New York to think of leaving. One respondent, Natalie, described her feelings of anger at being called nigger as she walked on a street near her home. I asked her if she felt differently about New York following this experience. She replied, "No, because I guess New York was a place where everybody wanted to come to, so stuff like that you tend to overlook it, internalize it, you try to avoid situations where this happens."

After recounting his experiences with racism, James said,

I knew I came to get an education but I knew in my mind that if I have an opportunity to live here, I'll live here. And yeah, I was better living here irregardless of whether I have legal status or not. You will have to come and pick me up and put me in a plane because I ain't moving. I'm not going anywhere. Life is sweet. [Laughs] Especially in New York City.

Two of my New York informants—one who lived in England for quite some time—did talk about differences between British- and American-style racism. Both agreed that British style racism was more overt, but one preferred the more direct racism of the British over the subtle racism of Americans, because British racism is so obvious that "you know where you stand."[8] Others felt differently. One woman suggested that because of the poor economic conditions that people suffered there, life in Guyana was harder than in Britain, so as long as she has the economic means to make herself a good life in Britain, racism is not a problem.

[I took in my sister's kids after she died and, with the expanding family, needed money to get on my feet.] I went to the bank, Barclay's. I got a loan under those circumstances, having been out of the country [and back in Guyana] for seven and a half years, from Barclay's, with which I could get the basic things like beds, and a cooker, fridge. So I'm saying that considering what I had just gone through in Guyana, for a couple of days trying to—coming here, doing a temping job, just having come back, having nothing, getting a loan—I had no trouble getting jobs. Even if I saw racism, and I could be very introverted, I've got neighbors, and I know my neighbors' first names, and I have them in mind as people who would check on me. I haven't got time for—even if it's out there, as long as it doesn't stop me from getting me what I want—even if there was racism applied to it, it wouldn't stop me if I didn't want it to.

Even the fourteen-year-old Ellie, quoted earlier, noted that she learned to ignore the racism she was exposed to. (Note that she was born in America, sent to England, and then lived in the Caribbean until she was fourteen.)

It's very hard on a West Indian because you have to remember your roots, but you have to also learn the culture. Because if you want to live in society, you can't pretend you're back home, because back home is different from America. You have to adjust to both worlds, you have to understand their culture and you have to remember your culture. So, to me growing [up] back home will make you a stronger person because you never experience racism there. And to come and learn racism, you understand it but from your mentality. You know, you don't go out and react, from how your parents bring you up. Like most of us go to church. Your Christian upbringing when you come up here, you still remember those beliefs, those advice. So when you see racism and stuff like that you remember what they taught you back home, and you don't react against it.

Avoidance

Usually when people spoke of the inevitability of U.S. racism, their words implied that they cannot simply ignore racism but instead must avoid situations where they might be exposed to it. As a nurse administrator from Jamaica explained,

> Everyone here experiences prejudice, especially [where I work,] in the hospital, where you see all kinds of people. I used to do private duty nursing, where patients abuse you. It hasn't happened to me, but I've seen them spit in your face. Prejudice is overt in the South, but more covert in the North. Here [in New York], it's more hypocritical. They won't tell you to your face. It doesn't bother me, because I don't invite them to my house. And I know who I am.

James, who found himself singing "Dixie" with his hosts, said,

> And another time I was invited to a wedding but I didn't go to this one. Everything was going to be Southern style with the Confederate flag draped along the aisle and the groom was going to be dressed in Confederate uniform and everything was going to be Southern style where they have this racist attitude. I didn't tell anyone, but I was invited though. I had to work—that was my excuse.

Medford, who returned to Trinidad after living in New York, said:

> As an individual you could develop your own protective systems. My personal thing is I can make the world better for me, by changing my attitudes and what I do. It will not change the system, but I could get an area in the system where I could operate. For instance, you go to Bank A and get that sort of behavior. Then try Banks B, C, D, E, until you get a bank that treats you how you want to be treated. Now it has not changed the fact that Bank A is racist. But I would no longer be dealing with that racist bank. And that is basically

how I see most things. I cannot offer a wholesale idea for the entire system, but individuals, I feel, because we have a choice, can choose to be in a place where we are comfortable.

Other immigrants noted similar sentiments: "There was some racism in New York, but I didn't take it on. In Brooklyn College I was there for a purpose." Some immigrants were more resolute about avoiding their exposure to white people altogether. One woman explained that she didn't want whites for neighbors because she did not like their behavior and felt that they did not control their children. Another woman spoke of avoiding doing business with whites:

I knew all these things [about racism in the United States] before I came here. I would hardly spend my money in a neighborhood that is white. Why do that when I can spend my money down on Thirteenth Avenue? They don't come up in Flatbush or on Church Avenue where I live to come and spend their money. I can't separate myself from them totally, but there are some things I don't do at all. And that's because I came here well informed.

Another man took avoidance of U.S. racism to its extreme, being so vigilant about "remaining completely divorced from the American psyche and system" that he chose never to live in the United States.

I go to North America once a year. It's the land of many opportunities. [But] the value of life doesn't seem to be focused in the right direction. First you have to deal with the problem of race. It's difficult to understand and accept. You can have immigration from all over the world: China, the Caribbean, Mexico— these people arrive in North America. And you have Native Indians. Yet when you visit you get the distinct feeling from the majority of white folks that it's the inalienable right of one particular race to have first choice. The Native American as well as all nonwhites are treated or regarded as not altogether equal. I think that's what's basically wrong with America. Arising out of that you have discriminating practices and racism in all levels of government and in society. This necessarily leads to strife. Unless America deals with this it will self-destruct. America is the land of many great opportunities. But unless you can enjoy a certain quality of life, I consider that life in the Caribbean for a professional person is much better. When I compare North America to St. Vincent, that's the reason I didn't want to go.

What I speak of here is not culture per se, as in a "culture of poverty," a limiting mind-set that overtakes a subgroup of a population that lives continually under a constrained set of unfortunate and debilitating circumstances. These circumstances somehow become a way of life both qualitatively different from mainstream middle-class society and heritable, so that it afflicts subsequent generations.[9] That is, I am not arguing that these black immigrants live out an oppositional "culture of hope" (Steinberg, 2001) where they read racism's effects as ineffectual or irrelevant to their lives. Moreover, even if one is to read their sentiments as optimism, these feelings certainly do not transfer to their second-generation offspring, who are far from likely to inherit their parents' perspectives, because they have a different experience of participation in their Western-style racial regimes. In other work I have argued that children of immigrants *cannot* share their parents' perspectives on this because the former live in a completely different cognitive racial world than the latter (Bashi Bobb and Clarke, 2001).

Upon arrival, West Indians may not be immediately aware of the extent of antiblack racism in the United States and Britain, nor of its direct applicability to them. Even those immigrants with prior knowledge of Western-style racism may be shocked and surprised when they first encounter racist attitudes and behaviors directed toward them. However, their ideal-typical response, evident in an ability to distance themselves from racism, emerges from a set of experiences and ways of seeing, from perceptions about the ways class and race conjoin, not from a culture. Immigrants from the West Indies do not arrive thinking like a minority person; they do not necessarily expect racist behavior from whites, even though some come to accept racism as an inevitable and fundamental fact of life for those who walk the streets of New York and London in black skin. As a result, some attempt to ignore racism, or say it does not bother them.[10] They try to detach themselves from racist acts that directly target them or in which they are indirectly involved, either through rationalization or avoidance. Immigrants in New York are there because they seek a better material existence. Many stay in New York and try to avoid either contact with whites or situations where racist acts are likely. Some even decide that this struggle is not worth it and instead choose to leave New York altogether. No matter what the response, they all come to realize that racism is a central feature deeply rooted in the very fabric of American life and social structure.

How Networks Influence Immigrant
Thinking on Race and Racism

Immigrant social networks are made up of international movers who are linked to other migrants from the same points of origin and also to friends and family members who remain in the country of origin. As a group, network members assist others in their network by providing information, financial and material aid, and other resources valuable in achieving international migration and resettlement. By assisting newcomers, immigrant network members foster subsequent migration, because the information that veteran immigrants provide through their networks can be used to lower the risks to migration for individuals and families still residing in the country of origin. Some also see the importance of networks in defining a space for political and socioeconomic action (transnationalism), for exercising political and economic power in a social space that remains separate from both the sending and receiving societies involved. Networks, then, link sending and receiving countries, contributing to the self-sustaining nature of international movement. Thus the social network has emerged as the concept that can best explain both the context in which the decision to migrate occurs and how international movement is operationalized through the immigration and resettlement processes. The existence of immigrant networks among groups of foreign origin have been well documented (Thomas and Znaniecki, 1996; Hagan, 1994; Mahler, 1995; Massey, Alarcón, Durand, and González, 1987; MacDonald and MacDonald, 1964). Research (beyond that presented here) exists to support the idea that networks separate and isolate immigrant and native groups in the labor and housing markets (Kasinitz and Rosenberg, 1996; Waldinger, 1995; Massey and Denton, 1984). It is well known too that native-born blacks used networks of friends and family to learn of job and housing opportunities that encouraged migration to the northern United States in the first half of the twentieth century (Marks, 1983). Furthermore, contemporary networks among African American communities have also been documented to provide social support, but mainly among people who share both the same race and the same class positions (Stack, 1974; Cross, 1990). Native-born people of all colors have social networks, as do all immigrant groups, including foreign-born blacks. The individual who functions outside of a social network is the rare exception. Although having within-group support tends to isolate network members from the larger society, this social isolation is not always a negative. Network membership shapes the worldview of its members, and one's racial worldview is no exception. In the case of racially marginalized persons, social isolation operates to shield network members (both individually and as a group) from immediate exposure to and consciousness of the ways race and racism function against them in the United States.

Newcomers to the United States who arrive with the help of a network are not pushed into the larger society but instead have waiting for them upon their arrival a ready-made community of immigrants. These networked immigrants work together and live near one another, most often in primarily West Indian neighborhoods and in workplaces where West Indians predominate. This is because networks allow the creation and maintenance of economic niches of co-ethnics in the labor and housing markets. This immigrant network is the primary means by which newcomers find jobs and housing. Networks also connect people to consanguine and fictive kin back home. As an insular community consisting of immigrants from the same point of origin, a network gives its members material and emotional support and separates them from the larger society in many ways. Because this support and separation coexist with network membership and participation, being in an immigrant social network (at least initially) insulates black immigrants emotionally and psychologically from American racism.

Racism and Network Insiders

Even as socially isolated as they are, Western Indians are not unaffected by racism living and working within immigrant social networks. In fact, my respondents reported having had several racist encounters, and some reported episodes that are far from innocuous. As noted earlier, however, these West Indian immigrants are able to detach themselves from U.S.-style racism by overlooking racist acts, ignoring racist behavior, or avoiding situations where racist episodes might be likely. I contend that it is membership and participation in the social network that largely enables this detachment.

The implications of membership in an immigrant network for racial attitudes and responses to racism are at least three. The first effect is psychological; the immigrant experience in general and membership in the social network in particular allow black immigrants to insulate themselves, emotionally and psychologically, from U.S.-style racism. As an example, recall Erksine's quote from the beginning of the chapter, where she explained that getting together with people from back home helps immigrants to feel better about their condition as new to a place that is not entirely welcoming to them. The second effect is influenced by economics: network membership helps one to achieve what is perceived as success (compared with American-born blacks and persons left back home), especially with regard to securing the related achievements of home ownership and occupational mobility (see Chapters Four, Five, and Six). The third effect is a little more complicated to explain and therefore will be addressed more fully in the next chapter. Suffice it to say for now that this third benefit emerges from an interaction between the psychological insulation offered by the network (the first effect) and the advantages realized in housing and labor markets (the second effect). It is an understanding of the group as a set of "ethnic heroes." When this benefit accrues, the success of the ethnic group is converted into a Horatio Alger story of bootstrap mobility that is externally imposed on the group (see Steinberg, 1991) but perpetuated by the group's own success-seeking activities, including pressuring one another to conform to norms. Other scholars have suggested that these "heroes" can actually create themselves, or have in particular times and spaces where a group's members have had some agency over their employment and public image. In these cases, these subgroups transformed the public disdain that once plagued them into images of increased ethnic status (see Brodkin, 1998; Ignatiev, 1995). When this third psychosocial benefit is realized, the group as an ethnic whole is able to successfully project itself as an ethnic success.

Until a black immigrant realizes the pervasive nature of race in the life of a black person in the Western world, he or she is largely unaware of the effect that being black there has on one's life chances; that is, he or she may know this in a historical sense, but not as a weight that persons of color contend with daily and in almost every interpersonal or interinstitutional encounter. This ignorance about the burden of racism is a shield against the discouragement one might feel if one knew without a doubt that having black skin should adversely affect one's attempts at social mobility. In many ways, a new immigrant who arrives with the aid of a social network can be protected from this realization because network membership can be a kind of prism through which the effects of racism can be distorted.

Immigration is selective—especially in the case of network migration. Selectivity implies that only those with the means and motivation to migrate do so, and in this case the means include having a hub householder willing to help. Selectivity also means that it is the best and brightest who arrive and participate in the housing and labor markets here in the United States. They usually come to urban centers, and specifically to jobs and industries that center and depend on immigrant labor (Sassen, 1988). They are not randomly distributed throughout the labor and housing markets (Kasinitz and Rosenberg, 1996; Waldinger, 1995; Massey and Denton, 1993; Piore, 1979). It follows then that if one arrives with the help of a network, one will automatically be connected to other immigrants who themselves have gained success and created relative safe spaces for themselves. So, networked migrants do not face open market competition in every market encounter. Concurrently, immigrants who are network members will be somewhat isolated from society at large and more immersed in an immigrant socioeconomic subsystem of employment niches, residential clusters, social cliques, ethnic associations, and cultural enclaves. This is true for all who migrate with the help of a network, regardless of race.

Whether immigrants find work through a labor recruiter or through their connections with a social network, they are likely ultimately to work in a place where there are other immigrants like them. There they will encounter other co-ethnics during most of their work day. Even if problems with racism exist, and even if these encounters become intolerable enough for the worker to seek out a job change, West Indian immigrants who are members of networks that have marked off labor market niches can (because of their access to network knowledge of jobs) more easily change to a new job in the same industry, leaving behind that particular racist whom they may believe has a personal problem working with blacks. The idea of systematic racial discrimination may evolve in a new immigrant only slowly, after prolonged job searches outside of niches or without network assistance, or after repeated exposure to racist behavior within the co-ethnic job niche.

Housing is the other socioeconomic area in which West Indian immigrants are isolated. Newcomers voluntarily find and may desire housing where other immigrants live. Black immigrants in search of housing, then, do not harshly or even consciously confront the involuntary nature of racial segregation in housing markets. In addition, racially segregated housing means that black people (immigrants included) are less likely to live around whites, so even if they face racist behavior at work, they may leave it behind when they go home. Those willing to be the first in white neighborhoods move there precisely because they desire the amenities of those neighborhood more than they desire freedom from racism.

When immigrants follow one another in a hub-and-spoke system, they find jobs and housing with help from other network members. The very nature of network membership allows one to avoid much contact with people outside the network, and one need not be aware of the effects of race in the United States in order to get one's first job and a place to live. One may even change jobs and homes a few times before having much exposure to the larger society in New York. So it is not just the emotional support from network members or an inherent group culture that allows the West Indian immigrant to feel he or she can ignore racism. Black immigrant social networking gives members social support and access to housing and job niches that allow them to cope with and adapt to the racial stratification they face when they arrive.

Networks create two social processes that may enable West Indian immigrants to ignore racism for some time, to feel it does not apply to them, or otherwise to detach from U.S. racism. One process is social isolation: West Indians live and work among other immigrants and may not be as exposed to racism (at least in the initial period after arrival) as the average person in New York City with a black phenotype. Another process is that of social mobility, which provides, first, a labor market "floor" through which even undocumented immigrants may use their network to find jobs, and second, a measure of upward mobility, at least to the bounds to which their network labor market extends. Problems arise for immigrants when they seek mobility beyond the purview of their network. Racism is certainly a factor in immigrants' lives well before they reach this point, as the testimonies of the early part of this book suggest. However, once they desire mobility outside of their network's grasp, they will lose the protection and insulation that the network offered in earlier stages of the settlement process.

Reaching Beyond the Network: Increased Exposure to Racism

Although newcomers who arrive with assistance from social networks are somewhat protected from fully conscious knowledge about or exposure to racism, this protection may not last for very long. Eventually they realize that racism is systematic and that they are not exempt. This realization may occur, as noted, through unavoidable and repeated exposure to it within network niches. It also occurs when the immigrant steps outside the purview of network influence. This situation is most obvious when an immigrant is ready to attempt even greater upward mobility in housing and labor markets.

Heddy, who earned her Ph.D. here and built an extremely successful professional career, told me,

> So you come [and get an education] and you make that sacrifice and you work and you do well and you expect that the next thing that is going to happen is that you're going to show up and you're going to get a job, a good job, and you realize, hey, there is no job, and that is the shocker. Then you realize. Now you start dealing with social problems—I think that's the time when you really realize that there is something beyond education, it's something beyond effort—and no matter how much experience you have and how much you show that you've been able to defy all the odds, you know, and still succeed, there is still not parity. And then I think that is the turning point for the immigrant, to where you become aware now of the other societal problems that exist in your new country that will impact your ability to succeed. And all of a sudden you say, "What was that effort for?" you know? Because I made all of this effort, and all of a sudden I'm not going to succeed because I don't have an opportunity. I'm not going to be given the opportunity.

West Indians who reach the limits of their network's ability to assist their upward rise in the labor market will find themselves facing the racial discrimination that pervades the U.S. labor market in general. The idea that West Indians face labor market discrimination just as African Americans do belies the popular idea that blacks' cultural values cause some groups to strive and succeed where others fail (Sowell, 1978; Glazer and Moynihan, 1970) because it shows that race does indeed affect social mobility. Independent of one's culture, immigrant status is reason enough to strive for economic success. Most newcomers are unaware of the ways black skin affects socioeconomic outcomes in more developed economies. It is that very attempt at upward mobility that forces the black immigrant to confront the barriers that the U.S. racial system brings to him and native-born blacks and not to the immigrant or native-born person who has white skin.

Employer willingness to recruit and preferentially hire immigrants (Waldinger, 1995) and differential immigrant network access to job niches (Hagan, 1994) suggest that job searches for West Indians—especially within niches—are easier than for African Americans. According to Bonacich (1972, p. 475), this special treatment is enough to create antagonism between the two groups of blacks—which may be one explanation for why West

Indians feel the pressure of job competition from African Americans they encounter:

> The central hypothesis [of the theory of ethnic antagonism] is that ethnic antagonism first germinates in a labor market split along ethnic lines. To be split, a labor market must contain at least two groups of workers whose price of labor differs for the same work. The concept *price of labor* refers to labor's total cost to the employer, including not only wages but also the costs of recruitment, transportation, room and board, education, and health care (if the employer must bear these), and the costs of labor unrest.

Whether or not one endorses the split labor market hypothesis, it is true that both immigrant status and network regulation of immigrant job performance lower the price of West Indian labor to the employer relative to the price for American-born blacks. First, networks lower the cost of recruitment to employers, through which hub householders and others find jobs for newcomers. Second, networks incorporate the means for selecting potential immigrants on their willingness and commitment to work hard, and it can also sanction poor workers. This labor control further lowers the costs of labor for employers. Thus network members may get a leg up from their association with other immigrants and the niches to which they are attached. The labor market floor for African Americans may be lower than the floor on which West Indian immigrants stand.

Reid (1970 [1939]), in his classic and seminal study of black immigrants, suggests that West Indians are "relieved" to live among other blacks, but he gives no evidence to support this statement. Perhaps at first they do not mind living among other black homeowners, or in a predominantly West Indian neighborhood. Nevertheless, it does not follow that the immigrant will long be pleased with that outcome once they begin to realize that racism and its concomitant relative deprivation are systematic. These immigrants come from predominantly black populations; living among other blacks is not something they automatically think of in negative terms. But it is to be expected that when a family is successful enough, it will desire larger, better housing in better school districts. These moves will likely encourage black immigrants to move outside of the neighborhoods where they began their climb up the U.S. social ladder. And when they begin to search for better housing, and in particularly those amenities (larger and better housing in better school districts) that correlate with neighborhoods with large numbers of more affluent whites, they are certain to confront the racism that pervades U.S. housing markets (Massey and Denton, 1993, 1984).

Being an Outsider

If one is not a member of the immigrant social network, then of course none of the benefits of network membership accrue. Two groups considered briefly in this section are not members of the West Indian immigrant social network and have different experiences with the U.S. racial system as a result. They are the second-generation children of immigrants (second-generation West Indians), and African Americans (specifically, native-born blacks who are not of West Indian parentage).

Disadvantaged American blacks, by lacking membership in these immigrant networks—with their well-established labor and housing market niches—lack the opportunity to advance by using immigrant networks to bring them better housing and jobs. They also are unable to avail themselves of the psychological insulation that comes with the ability to think, for example, that being a black immigrant is different from being a native-born black (African American), whose group is at the bottom of the racial hierarchy. Thus, for African Americans the combined effect of lack of socioeconomic access and lack of a foreign referent may be that they feel little sense of their agency to change their own socioeconomic situations (Cose, 1995; Massey and Denton, 1993). African Americans do not have open access to these networks, even if they are interested in securing the jobs these immigrants might hold (Kasinitz and Rosenberg, 1996; Waldinger, 1995). While their own African American networks may provide psychological and economic support (Stack, 1974) that may counteract antiblack stereotypes (such as blacks are bad, lazy, and so on), networks available to the average African American may have few of the relevant success stories, especially when compared to the stories of the average immigrant network member.

Too, members of the second generation of Caribbean immigrants lack their parents' vision of an alternative society, which allows the first generation to deny the messages that the racial hierarchy sends about the characteristics of people with a black phenotype. The second generation—by definition a subgroup of the native-born black population—grows up within Western racial systems, under the psychological influence of what it means to be black in America, England, or Canada. Thus, the source of their parents' psychological insulation (having a foreign referent, which includes the experience of living under and believing in a foreign racial regime where class is seen as the more important factor) is not a referent for the native-born child. Indeed, the parents alternative vision and their ability to ignore racism can be experienced as denial of the second generation's reality. Certainly, the second generation's potential employers don't see members of the second generation as different from any other black people. Second-generation persons do not have accents, the one cultural marker that employers and others can readily use to recognize the difference between West Indians and African Americans. Thus the children of immigrants have neither the psychological shelter nor the vision of their immigrant parents' network (as an opening for career advancement) that the network provided for their parents. The experience of the second generation is very different from that of the immigrant.

Oh yes, if you were born here, you're born with—you're socialized to be a minority. My children are minorities; I will never be a minority. Because, again, they look at things based on the society they live in. When I came to this country I have already been socialized—I came with what were the realities for me in my country—so it takes me time to understand and figure that out, [and then] it's too late. I've already invested too much to even convince myself that they are met. Once you have made an investment, you buy into a strategy, and it's a helluva thing to convince yourself that you're wrong. So I have to ditch this strategy, and that's not easy to do. So, for us as immigrants who came with that socialization and that strategy, [you] invested too much when you came not knowing the social structure, and you went full speed ahead on one track—and you're too far down the pipeline now to abandon it. And it may be easier in the world of investment to ditch [a strategy] because it's other people's money, ha ha ha, so let them belly up to the loss and write it off for taxes. But when it's your life, you don't ditch it. You ride it out and you hope by riding out you get some type of satisfaction, or you could maneuver the process, and somehow it may not be utopia but something will evolve. [But for your kids, it's different.] I mean, you tell them what you know to be your reality and they look at you and say you are a lunatic and they go on and do whatever the hell they want to do. You're either beating the hell out of them or you get so frustrated and say maybe they're right and just leave them be. This is their country. What do I know?

Second-generation blacks, even as children, will see very different kinds of social barriers than do their parents, who have as a reference point the remembrance of a different life back home. Immigrant parents also have an immigrant ethic (which encourages them to strive for their targeted goals, despite whatever obstacles they might face), other network members (who buoy them with financial and emotional resources in times of trouble), and the many models of success that veteran immigrants in these networks represent. Because the second generation—the immigrants' native-born children—has a different reference group, these network benefits are not necessarily resources for them.

Even if second-generation immigrants are still able to get housing and some jobs through their parents' network, two forces play against the likelihood of the network working for them in ways similar to how it worked for their parents. The first force is a sense of mobility that would suggest that the children of immigrants should take jobs outside the purview of the network. For the most part, only those children in the network who are willing to work in the areas of the labor market where the network's strengths lay (in the networks I studied, these were water and subway tunnel construction, domestic work, nursing, and civil service) can benefit from network job contacts. Thus the information about immigrant niches in the primary labor market may not be as useful to members of the upwardly mobile second generation, who attempt to move upward or away from where their parents stand. However, a network's information about available jobs may be more useful to the second generation in an ethnic enclave economy than to the second-generation members looking to rise in the primary labor market. Second, parents may not want their children following in their footsteps. For example, a mother who bought her house and sent for her children through her career as a domestic may not see it as a positive thing if her daughter, too, works as a domestic.

Finally, children are not similarly protected from racism, because they have to traverse social space their parents (at least immediately) do not have to cross. The children of immigrants—and immigrant children, for that matter—come into contact with the white world daily (with white teachers, school officials, store owners, police officers, and so on) and do not in their waking hours spend most of their time with co-ethnics. Also, they may not get support for their alternative worldviews from their immigrant parents. For even if these parents become cognizant of their children's different reality, to admit that difference is possibly to concede that racism might defeat their children. That is, to recognize the effect of racism on life chances—as the immigrant adult may not do—is to agree that the adult immigrant's worldview may represent a losing strategy.

Even though young immigrants benefit from network membership more than the second generation does, they may also experience the network differently than their older network counterparts do. For example, the youngest immigrants move directly into school, not work; therefore their social experience is very much like that of the second generation. Ellie was quoted earlier speaking about her experience being followed in stores. Here she explains why she and Amsie, her immigrant grandmother—who has openly said that racism doesn't bother her—have very different responses to racism:

> I'm fourteen and I came [to New York] in 1990. With my grandmother's case it's different, because when she came she went straight to work. So she don't have to go to school, she don't really have to go to the stores and stuff like that, like the younger folks have to.

The experience of the immigrant who relocates as an adult is different from that of the young immigrant. While these immigrants may (at times) give primacy to their ethnic identity to create social distance from their negative experiences of black racialization, their children have no such option. Children of West Indian immigrants do not so much choose between membership in an ethnic group (West Indian) and a race (black) as they try to navigate a system that recognizes blackness on sight and recognizes ethnicity for black native-born people rarely, if at all. For the native-born black children of immigrants, no choice exists between ethnicity and race (Bashi, 1998). Ethnic recognition comes only for those children who choose to claim an ethnicity by struggling against being defined as black by those who equate black race with black phenotype, that is, a racial system that includes white adults such as teachers, school officials, store managers, and others with authority, as well as the young white peers they encounter in school.[11]

Conclusion

Importantly, despite achieving what is perceived as success relative to American-born blacks, West Indians who emigrate to the United States and the United Kingdom believe they have entered racist societies. Thus, racism affects them, certainly at least to the extent that they are able to identify and name it when they see it, and more important, to the extent to which it affects them directly. Some immigrants sooner or later realize that one's difficulty comes not just from the struggle one should expect in moving to a new country and beginning at the bottom of the job ladder, but also from being black.

Even if West Indians do succeed socioeconomically, their social mobility does not exempt them from racist animosity, any more than it does for native-born middle-class blacks (Cose, 1995).

In sum, West Indian immigrants do not immediately understand either the Western racial structures they confront or the ways that others' racist behavior will apply to them, though they are not ignorant of the existence of Western racist ideology. They do, however, show signs of an ideal type of immigrant adaptation to racism, which has been presented here as if it progressed along a timeline coincident with the length of stay in the destination and exposure to racist behaviors by whites. Initially, West Indians may not be aware that racist behavior by whites is intentionally directed toward them, but for many there is a period of realization. How might we explain this sense of realization, even among immigrants who claim to have been made aware of Western-style racism before their arrival? Many transplants to New York may have thought that racism was something that happened only to American blacks (or to so-called African Americans, which they are not), and as foreigners they may have expected that they would be exempt from such treatment. Respondents in London would not have thought this way. In Britain there is no group comparable to African Americans, no African British, so to speak. In fact, blacks in Britain are considered to be imports. Thus there is no readily identifiable native-born black British group from which Caribbean-born black persons might see themselves as culturally and ethnically separate. Perhaps those respondents who were well aware of the practices of Western antiblack racism thought that racism was something one might encounter rarely, as was the case when they lived in the West Indies. Transplants to London and New York may not have understood racism to be as pervasive an influence as it was until they themselves experienced it on a daily basis, but they only gradually recognized racial affronts as systematic.

Clearly it takes some time before many West Indians realize that negative acts or encounters they experience are racist. Once they recognize racism and realize that antiblack racism does apply to them, they ignore racist acts directed toward them or act themselves to avoid settings and encounters where they expect racism to impose upon them. Some choose to respond to this realization by ignoring the racist behaviors of others or by avoiding contact with whites altogether. But the West Indians I interviewed nearly all developed a consciousness about the U.S. racial structure and racism by whites toward blacks, even if in the end they believed they could ignore or avoid it.

The experience of growing up in a black-majority society in their countries of origin and enjoying membership in an immigrant social network allows black immigrants to insulate themselves emotionally and psychologically from Western-style racism for some time. After moving overseas, an immigrant has the opportunity to see the stratification system at work, as his or her daily interaction with whites brings the understanding that racism is part of daily experience when one is of black phenotype and encounters whites who demonstrate discriminatory practices. Even while this awareness emerges, however, immigrants, by their participation in the immigrant social network, are to some degree insulated from the full effects of racism in the United States. Networks act as a shield in three ways. One, they may limit immigrants' interaction with whites who may behave in a racist manner. That is, although they are in the primary and secondary labor markets and not in ethnic enclaves, immigrants work and live alongside other immigrants because their social space is within job and housing niches. Two, these niches bring to the West Indian immigrant population a degree of socioeconomic success relative to their native-born black counterparts, and thus socioeconomic separation from them. Three, the labor market success that members experience along with access to labor and housing market niches belies the racist stereotypes about the inability of black people to succeed in America. On three levels, then, this separation allows insulation (which has both psychological and physical counterparts) from racist enmity.

There is an important corollary here: people who are not full members of these social networks will not have the ability to take complete advantage of this insulation. I maintain that, generally speaking, the second generation is in this category, as are native-born African Americans. Neither group has the marker of difference—an accent—that may make whites treat them better. They have neither an idyllic vision of life back home to sustain them, nor the escape hatch of becoming a returnee when they become fed up.

Being an immigrant striving to find work and earn a living better than one could earn back home gives the newcomer one outlook and set of experiences; having black skin in the United States gives another. All immigrants go through the first struggle. For West Indians, movement to the United States brings the unique problem of being rendered invisible (Bryce-Laporte, 1972), because for most Americans foreign-born blacks are indistinguishable from the African American population. It is the foreign referent (an orientation in a socially and politically structured society toward inhibiting "thinking like a minority") coupled with the socioeconomic isolation that network member-ship in the destination country brings that allows West Indians to discount the effect of racism on their lives—at least in the periods nearer to arrival and integration into the immigrant network. To the degree that West Indians may separate themselves ethnically (a project with which an accent helps greatly) or socioeconomically (which is aided by the immigrant social network, par-ticularly its labor market and housing niche creation properties), they may be able to articulate the ability to disregard racist animosity. As James explained, he sees racism but cannot understand it and he is not willing to take it on.

> You know, you have blacks on one side and whites on one side and unless you're a foreign black they look at you like you're diseased or something, you know? Where black folks are afraid to walk on the same side of the streets as the white folks. It was just gross. A country so advanced to be so stupid, you know? I could never see the reason for it and I really never accepted it.

8 Networks as Ethnic Projects

THE CHAPTERS IN THIS BOOK have engaged different aspects of the ways membership in immigrant social networks has shaped the process and experience of international migration for black Caribbean migrants. Their marginalization as Third World and their racialization as black have placed them near the bottom strata of several interlinked hierarchical systems, but they have increased their socioeconomic status via their network activities: questing for legitimacy in the legal system that governs border crossing and immigration processes; seeking jobs and being incorporated into primary labor markets; deepening social and economic footholds by saving money, accumulating wealth, and moving into home ownership wherever possible; socially supporting one another; and jointly adapting to new racial hierarchies. These practices in turn enable other achievements that extend the lifespan and socioeconomic reach of the network: the enhancement of hubs' reputations in workplaces, destination neighborhoods, and island communities; assurance of spokes' socioeconomic success as workers and homeowners; and maintenance and perpetuation of the network itself as newcomers are asked to join veterans who migrated before them. Thus the group's socioeconomic integration is managed.

Society's dominant members use ethnoracial logic to measure the group's socioeconomic status and create a reputation that Steinberg (1989) called an *ethnic myth*. Such myths are self-reinforcing, as gatekeepers decide to share with or withhold resources from those groups they see as meritorious or undeserving, respectively. Ideally, network incorporation assures economic and social well-being for the migrants and those they support back home. Migrant groups hope that their struggles bring about ethnoracial uplift, elevating their social and economic position above the lowly place where the ethnoracial hierarchies of the destination countries of the Western world regularly place newcomers.[1] This struggle for uplift is what I label the *ethnic project*.

This chapter highlights a number of factors that come to bear on why immigrant networks of the hub-and-spoke variety have brought mainly success to black Caribbeans' socioeconomic endeavors. To show this, a review of the characteristics of this network is required. First, I link network members' joint accomplishments to network structure and function. Afterward, I summarize the ways network accomplishments aggregate to socioeconomic mobility and ethnoracial uplift. Last, I speculate on why not all ethnic projects succeed.

Network Achievements

Geographic Mobility

Network members use legal and illegal means to get co-ethnics across national borders and into destination countries—even in those situations where government policies are explicitly against the migration of the class of people of which the network is a part. In so doing, networks move people from positions of oppression and deprivation to places of relative freedom and prosperity. Their geographic mobility is a major first step in a global strategy for social and economic mobility. In the case examined in this book, black migrants connected by networks—or more specifically, potential migrants connected to hubs who have the desire, means, and know-how to assist in their relocation—enter into Western nations where it has been explicitly determined that black migration is less than desirable. Their migration occurs despite the existence of a near blockade against them, because they have specialized knowledge of the legalities of migration at the time of new migrant selection.

To make border-crossing happen, network members (specifically, hubs) develop network-specific immigration schemes—strategies to help their co-ethnics get into the country with or (if need be) without documentation and help them gain proper legal documents. So successful are these strategies that networks continue to have a reputation for flouting immigration laws intended to stem inflows.

Mobility in Labor Markets

Hubs are spokes' key resource in finding a job, often but not always using their workplace reputations to find jobs for co-ethnics in the same worksite. Hubs' power to select newcomers is important here because a hub's ability to make job referrals can be seriously compromised if new jobholders do not perform sufficiently to support the referral-maker's reputation.[2] Employed newcomers tend to enhance hubs' workplace reputations; compliant workplace conduct reflects a tacit agreement with the group's culture of reciprocity.

Newcomers' lives stabilize as they became "legal" with their employers' assistance. Employers are brought to newcomers for this purpose either through the employers' own formal labor-recruitment program or via the network members' informal recruitment of employers who had access to legalization. Such networking pleases employers to the degree that many rely heavily on networks to fill vacancies. Employed network members increase their hold on destinations by creating job trajectories that propel them even higher in socioeconomic status or by using their resources in the labor market to help secure legal status for other compatriots or to create niches that will allow easier access to jobs for new network entrants.

The more tightly hubs can control migration selection, exercise postmigration control over migrants in ways that positively affect their workplace performance, and move toward monopoly power over segments of the labor market, the greater are the chances of creating a labor market niche and developing it into a regenerating employment resource for newcomers. Niches can be useful because they allow co-ethnics to sufficiently control access to job openings so that immigrants can continually find placements. Among these Caribbean migrants, women have access to more niches than men do, and their niches are broader, more porous, and more stable (that is, they are open to people of more varied education levels and skill sets, are easier to get into, and have been available to these networks for decades).

Niches are not the only important thing in securing labor market success, but they are crucial because they allow for relative ease of employment in primary markets. Some Caribbean niches are clusters in the primary labor market. While primary labor market employment brings the disadvantage of migrants having to convince employers who are not co-ethnics that they are worth the risk of employment, it also brings an advantage to these immigrants by giving them access to greater opportunity and an ability to move upward rather than be marginalized from the larger economy (as employment outside the primary market would mean).

But network members also need access to jobs outside of niches, especially those newcomers and others who do not have the education or credentials required to immediately enter niche positions. Migrants use their abilities to find jobs both within and outside of niche positions in order to create job trajectories; attainment of education and credentials, and long tenure in the same job, enable increases in labor market status and earn wage increases and promotions. Trajectories bring not only socioeconomic mobility but also rescue from dangerous jobs and threatening employers.

Mobility in Housing

Spokes live rent-free initially and are encouraged to save to get on their feet (to ready themselves for financial and residential independence even while sending remittances back home). Once savings are sufficient, many spokes move on to rental housing that is owned by co-ethnics who themselves could use assistance with mortgage payments. The latter convert single-family housing into apartments to achieve their goals of property ownership. Propertied migrants encourage newcomers to own property themselves, and in some cases transfer the ownership of early-owned properties to newcomers when they move on to develop other properties. Veteran migrant homeowners also encourage newcomers to move into the neighborhoods where they themselves live, in the end creating new classes of co-ethnic wealth-holders. Networked immigrants create housing when they buy homes (or restored "shells," that is, exteriors that are largely gutted of their interiors) and convert them into multifamily housing. In this way, renting space from co-ethnic homeowners provides good rental housing options for newcomers with fewer resources who might face anti-immigrant or antiblack prejudices in the open housing market.

Although the first step in saving and wealth creation is rooted in co-resident living arrangements, network members encourage renters to buy homes instead of continuing to rent, organize communal saving (in esusus) to secure large sums for down payments, recommend specific homes and neighborhoods to those seeking to purchase housing, and refer potential homeowners to agreeable realtors and mortgage brokers. In Chapter Six I speculated that these processes have sometimes created housing opportunities within formerly white-only spaces in suburban environments. Where the neighborhood racial "tipping point" is reached, white flight occurs to the extent that the neighborhood becomes black; in some places where African Americans are seen to predominate, Caribbean transplants have created a contiguous core space.

This housing-acquisition system encourages group coherence because it unifies interests where a class divide between the propertied and propertyless would normally exist. These cross-class alliances mutually benefit all who seek footholds in the housing market; homeowners and their renters, people with propertied assets and people without, all converge in the interest of acquiring and preserving property, sometimes even transferring it from the haves to the have-nots. (Their connections to one another are reminiscent of the ways that long-tenured co-ethnics with workplace authority are connected with the unskilled in jobs to make a web of jobs that benefit the group as a whole.)

Social Support

While the culture of reciprocity for this group is one that supports the idea of self-sufficiency, mutual social support seems to be widespread. There really is no contradiction. The idea is to help someone until they can help themselves; someone else either helped you or will help you in the future. Migrants keep in touch and provide each other with social and emotional support—long after the border-crossing moment has passed—in ethnic and voluntary associations, churches and other religious gatherings, and informal social settings. Migrants make charitable donations to institutions such as churches and schools. While these activities are in the main organized by hubs, spokes are also involved to the extent that they are members of ethnic organizations engaged in charity work. Both hubs and spokes organize remittances for those who remain in countries of origin—even though spokes generally tend to keep fewer ties back home. In addition, a few social-support activities (such as rotating savings groups or joining together in co-resident living spaces) provide mutual financial assistance to network members as well. Through their formal and informal groupings—organizational meetings, annual fundraiser, parties, and *Mas*-playing—migrants have provided one another with social support that has shored them up emotionally from the burdens of life overseas.

Ethnoracial Solidarity Against Racism

Network coherence and group socioeconomic success allow psychological distancing from negative racialization. Racial adaptation causes immigrants to resolve to distance themselves from the black stereotype and other negative aspects of the way blackness plays out in these "advanced" societies. Cognitive recognition of one's own racial degradation in the racial adaptation process creates among network members an even greater resolve to work for the betterment of those left behind, and for the second generation (Plaza, 1998; Bashi Bobb and Clarke, 2001). Many see their ability to help others as the marker of their own progress. As Plaza (1998, pp. 258–59) writes, "The most common avenues through which these men projected their accomplishments were their children's success, their involvement with Caribbean-based organizations, and their ability to continue to help out family and kin remaining behind in the Caribbean." Moreover, what Plaza found among Caribbean transplants to Canada I also found—that is, that one's work ethic and educational achievements matter most, and that immigrants reference home (in particular, the ability to move back there and escape Western-style racism)—as a mechanism for coping with racism.

Unfortunately, while the immigrant generation has specialized knowledge of both racism and the rare experience of intragenerational upward mobility, they don't seem to be aware of how unique their experiences are. They don't fully realize the extent of what they have accomplished, and they make the mistake of believing that anyone can do what they've done. This means, for example, that they don't understand what their children face. The second generation does not experience a similar racial adaptation trajectory because they were born and have been raised as "black" in a society that does not recognize their ethnicity in the ways it does for their parents; they neither have the same ideas of success nor accept the bottom of the job ladder as a useful first step onto a mobility ladder (Bashi Bobb and Clarke, 2001). In the end, black immigrants' spectacular mobility is insufficient to combat the oppressive power of race for themselves and their second-generation offspring.

Factors in Ethnic Network Success

Chapters on the hub-and-spoke structure; processes enabling border crossing, successful labor market integration, post-co-residence adaptation, and housing market mobility; and the psychology of network participation have provided several detailed examples of how these processes work together to encourage upward mobility, and we have noted that other immigrant groups can be determined as behaving in similar fashion. Over time, for some groups, networking actions lead to an ideology of self-determination and success that is *ethnicized*, or presumed to emerge from the culture of the immigrant group. But reading these same activities in a more structural way, we can tally specific actions that denote the experience of successful immigrant social networks: *migration selection, opportunity hoarding, mutual assistance,* and *ethnic differ-*

entiation. I explain how each contributes to an ethnicized ideology of upward mobility. Where attempts at surmounting structural obstacles and ethnicized ideology meet, ethnic projects are under way.

Migration Selection and Reciprocity

In the inter- and transnational networks examined in this book, veteran migrants who control the network's social capital (that is, the hubs) hoard and use judiciously their knowledge of the ways to get someone across the border into the new destination and help them resettle into new employment. At first the new migrants they sponsor and assist (that is, the spokes) are supported in a co-resident relationship where they are given many of the supports they need to begin stable lives. During the co-resident period, newcomers must live up to house rules that often chafe them by proscribing their social lives, monitoring their discretionary spending of earned income, and so on. For example, while it may be the case that hubs do not always take money for rent, they would not condone spokes spending their earnings on fancy clothes or cars. The culture of reciprocity presumes that as the hub does the favor of providing free rent and board, the spoke should return the favor by saving sufficiently to hasten the end of the co-resident period. This pressure is surely a pressure to succeed: to find a job, earn as much money as possible, do well enough to keep the job, enhance the hub's reputation at the workplace (if hub and spoke work at the same site) or as a referent, and if applicable, get the employer to sponsor the spoke in his or her quest for legalization; to earn a reputation sufficient enough to find subsequent employment; to save enough to secure subsequent housing; and to move on and make a place for the next co-resident immigrant. Obligations are more personal too and include a constrained social life (often involving scrutiny about with whom one can socialize or become romantically involved), policing of discretionary spending and requiring the immigrant to focus on saving his or her earnings, monitoring one's commitment to religiosity, and so on. Thus the hub-spoke relationship has built-in mechanisms for soliciting good performances from a migrant, both as a newcomer and later, when he or she is living more independently.

The obligations that spokes have are not limited to the co-resident period and may even extend beyond debts to the hub who assists most during co-residence. A glance at the network maps in Chapter Three show that many newcomers have been aided by several network members. As the number of individuals who help increases, so do the reciprocal expectations among network members. Veteran migrants help relative newcomers and settlers with young families buy homes in good neighborhoods. If the area is predominately white, the need for mutual assistance and support from co-ethnics will likely become crucial. Veteran homeowners—who may be the first to move into new neighborhoods—literally find homes for potential new homeowners, help get their children into the right schools, help them get better jobs than the jobs with which they began their migration experiences, and introduce them to mortgage brokers and realtors they know will assist them to move into white neighborhoods with the amenities that middle-class seekers of a better life will value. Another reciprocal obligation applies, because exemplary citizenship as a renter or homeowner in a wider community of co-ethnics will be expected. Even as a spoke becomes economically independent and lives with his or her own family, the spoke must live up to the expectation of being a good neighbor, in order to keep the realtor in the frame of mind of being willing to sell to the next black Caribbean family. Spokes must pay their mortgage in order to keep their home, an action which also secures the referee's reputation with the brokerage company. Continued obligations prevail in the labor market, because migrants must be seen as good workers in order to move sequentially or laterally across the labor market niches over which various hubs in the network have connections.

I am arguing neither that newcomers would perform poorly without the aid of the veterans in the network, nor that it is only the pressure of the culture of reciprocity that makes someone work hard. But the structure of the network's processes does ensure that newcomers face the pressure to comply with all manner of performance expectation. While these controls are first imposed during co-residence, they never clearly end.

This is where the importance of migrant selection becomes most evident. Hubs pick and choose among those with whom they are connected—relatives and friends alike—and make their own decisions about who they wish to send for, even though Western immigration laws clearly specify which overseas persons residents can apply to bring in. Both labor and housing market behavior and social activities are circumscribed by the selection process. Some groups are said to succeed precisely because of migrant selection; that is, the best in the pool of potential migrants are able to migrate, where *best* means most motivated and resource rich.

The hub, then, is a powerful individual, for he or she is one person who has considerable influence in migrant selection, at least among migrants with network connections. As hubs help their chosen ones, they gain greater expertise and are thereby able to wield even greater power over subsequent selection. Further, their network influence increases because they hoard this information, sharing it only with those they choose to assist. Spokes who get jobs through their connections with hubs are likely to experience both gratitude and performance anxiety to some degree. These feelings may be magnified if the spoke is in a co-resident relationship with the hub. In these kinds of networks, a spoke's livelihood (shelter, income, and social support) is secured because of the hub's direct intervention, as are the gains that benefit those in the spoke's circle of loved ones (through fosterage and remittances, for example). Even in times of disappointment—the realization of how cold it is in northern latitudes, how dirty major urban centers are, what First World racism, poverty, homelessness, and urban blight look like (for there is little of that on the islands, where, in particular, homelessness is unheard of)—the co-resident experience is one that in many cases allows a spoke to project a brighter future, for a trajectory of future gains may be predicted from the current position.

Migrant selection exerts a great deal of influence on the hub's life as well. If a hub has chosen his or her spokes wisely, he or she benefits by enhanced reputation in the employer's eyes, which allows the hub to develop increasingly monopolistic power over available vacancies. (Note that this reputation accrues whether or not the spoke works in the same place as the hub does.) Moreover, the hub's reputation back home is also enhanced: he or she is increasingly known as the go-to guy or gal, who can find a person a job and get them installed in it with seemingly little difficulty. Spoke success marks the hub as being the person who really knows how to help one to make it in the destination. A spoke's employer becomes more reliant on the hub when subsequent vacancies occur, but sometimes does not even wait for a vacancy before hiring help nominated or referred by the hub who has a proven record of making strong referrals. Others back home note the success of their overseas relatives and seek out the hubs who are known to make things happen. Because hubs seem more likely than spokes to keep ties back home, and because they demonstrate similarly selfless and altruistic behavior when they return, they fuel this kind of thinking about them.

Thus, *bounded solidarity* and *enforceable trust* become core elements of the hub-and-spoke network's culture of reciprocity, wherein a cycle of reputation and success is built, among both the group of potential and veteran migrants still transnationally linking their nation of birth to their adopted nations, and the employers, realtors, bankers, and others in their communities who benefit from migrant network members' transactions with one another and with them.[3]

Selection as Precursor to Ethnic Differentiation
and Reputation Management

Perhaps this is a good time to bring up again Pamela's story, first revealed at the beginning of the first chapter, but this time to focus on her sister, Jocelyn, who took it upon herself to select applicants for positions available in a London school district seeking to recruit teachers (from Australia and Canada but not from the Caribbean). Jocelyn decided at the time that a commitment to "living a Christian life" was the appropriate criterion to solicit applicants for this opportunity. With this choice, she created for herself a community of like-minded people who she (correctly) believed would uphold her image of what black Caribbean persons could be if they decided, as she had, that they should be model representatives of their ethnic group overseas. Similarly, Dawn's New York City hospital-based employer knew she'd never recommend any "riffraff," and that anyone Dawn recommended would be one of her co-ethnics.

These hiring practices support the meaningfulness of ethnicity in the job market, whereby the right person for the job is defined not only (if at all) by his or her skill and experience, but also by his or her fit with the job, a characteristic that may be measured by the job applicant's receipt of a recommendation from a current employee who is a co-ethnic. Still, employers can envision incurring lots of problems if they fill jobs by hiring friends and relatives of current employees, because "at bottom, *employers want workers whose first loyalty is to the organization, not to each other*" (Waldinger and Lichter, 2003, p. 14, emphasis in original).

But organizational loyalty is a natural by-product of one's inclusion in the network acculturation process of a hub-and-spoke network. The hub's power in selecting a spoke creates a situation that in behavioral terms equates a spoke's loyalty to the hub with the spoke's loyalty to the organization. The cycle is self-reinforcing. On the job, for instance, the hub puts his or her own reputation to the test by recommending the spoke for employment. At stake is the employer's willingness to take future recommendations from the hub, and perhaps the hub's own ability to recruit and train new employees. Also, the spoke wants to perform well on the job and in the eyes of the hub. What's at stake, literally and figuratively, is the spoke's place in the network (as well as the spoke's opportunity to have a place to work and, in a co-resident network, a place to stay). In addition, the employer wants to keep his search costs low when there are places to be filled, to keep turnover low, and to be able to rely on the recommendations of his better employees. What's at stake is the employer's ability to rely on his employees to keep performance at high levels and the workplace environment running smoothly. The reputations of all concerned hinge on the performance of newcomers who are described in ethnic terms because the network operates in ways that promote performance characteristics believed to be widespread across the ethnic group. While employers and other gatekeepers may be prone to generalizing good performance across ethnic groups, perhaps some groups themselves encourage this behavior (through the actions of hubs such as Dawn and Joycelyn, who manage their group's image with the referrals they make to gatekeeping outsiders).

Opportunity Hoarding

Hub's migration-selecting activities are possible only when they control relatively scarce opportunities that can be judiciously doled out to chosen newcomers. Network cultures of reciprocity can be sustained only when there are sufficient rewards for compliance. If no one needs a hub—that is, if migrants can find other ways of getting into a destination country or can find jobs without help—the compliance and obligation structure must break down.[4] Said another way, ethnic success relies on newcomer compliance, which in turn depends on restricted or hoarded opportunities.

Roger Waldinger and Michael Lichter (2003) go to great lengths to explain how employers in certain workplaces lose control over hiring practices, necessarily ceding control to immigrant networks. Often immigrant hubs will know about job openings even before the employer does, and they are able to find replacements the moment they hear that someone is about to leave their position. It is often easier for the employer to allow the recommendation network to fill open positions than to ignore recommendations and instill a whole new hiring process, particularly if hiring co-ethnics is a practice that has previously produced outstanding results for the employer. To secure their ability to make future referrals and protect their reputations, hubs make sure to set up mechanisms that allow newcomers to quickly learn to be comfortable in the job environment and catch up on the best ways to perform the required tasks. Waldinger and Lichter found that crucial performance-enhancing on-the-job training occurs among co-ethnics. Once the newcomer performs well, the solidity of the hub's reputation increases, and it becomes more so with the satisfactory performance of each new hire. The repetition of this cycle of network hoarding and hiring is what creates a hub's workplace reputation for making recommendations.

Employers and the larger society don't think in terms of Dawns and Joycelyns, or hubs, but of the ethnic group as a whole. Employers and realtors allow hubs to pass opportunities on to their chosen others (that is, to hoard) because they expect these opportunities to be passed on to people who they know will perform well. Writ large, well-managed migration selection and opportunity hoarding create an *ethnicized* group reputation. Instead of thinking that Harvey finds great tunnel workers, the lore becomes, "West Indians make great tunnel workers." Instead of "Taran always knows the best domestics and nurses aides," employers believe that "West Indians are great domestics" or that they "work well in hospital settings." Indeed, positive experience with a categorical type is precisely what encourages authority figures to open up the possibilities for opportunity hoarding (Tilly, 1998, pp. 91–95).

Ethnic Differentiation

Successes in border crossing, employment, housing, saving, wealth building, educational and credential attainment, and pensions become uniquely *ethnic* successes in the minds of group members just as they do for outsiders and onlookers. The evidence for ethnicity lies in ethnically segregated workplaces and neighborhoods, and in accomplished ethnic voluntary and savings associations. Socioeconomic gatekeepers (employers, mortgage brokers, realtors, landlords, and so on) learn to see network successes as ethnic when they reap benefits by opening the gates to referents' co-ethnics and compatriots. Gatekeepers thus become inclined to extend benefits to others who are similarly group-identified, that is, recommended by persons from the same homeland or region, with whom they have transacted before. An example comes from Tilly's (1998) chapter "How to Hoard Opportunities," which tells about immigrant job hoarders from Roccasecca, Italy, who created their ethnic differences in the earliest part of the twentieth century by, first, controlling access to landscape gardening jobs in Mamaroneck, New York, then controlling entire economic niches, and finally excluding non-Italians (especially black Americans) from similar kinds of access.

When forcibly segregated from opportunities by the host society's dominants, networked persons learn to think of themselves as *compadres* or co-ethnics. Facing the realities of exclusion, network-connected immigrants do not assimilate as much as learn to fend for themselves in ways they hope will bring prosperity within the socioeconomic bounds they manage to hoard for their own group. When immigrants work collectively to improve their life chances and to succeed, they may (but do not always) read their collective success as an ethnic one. Similarly, where societal and economic forces converge to hinder immigrants, these influences are interpreted by network members as ethnicity-based rallying points. (For example, note that members of the Claudia Jones Organisation responded to negatively prejudicial treatment in the London school and medical treatment systems by creating supplemental Saturday Schools to boost the educational outcomes of Caribbean children, and by launching initiatives to boost Caribbean women's health outcomes.) It is precisely where tensions between mobility's successes and segregation's setbacks occur that opportunities for ethnic solidarity and identity emerge.

Foner (1979, 1998) notes that the context of migration is important in shaping ethnic understandings of success. According to Foner, black Londoners live less segregated lives than black New Yorkers and therefore face the brunt of racist animosity more directly. Black New Yorkers, by contrast, feel the weight of racist animosity less than Londoners do because as an ethnic group they are more invisible among the black population as a whole. Foner also notes that when New York transplants spoke to her about race and their lives in New York, they mainly described the differences between themselves and African Americans. West Indians in New York were concerned with differentiating themselves; they may have wanted to attribute their success relative to African Americans' socioeconomic performance to ethnic (that is, cultural) differences. By doing so, they may have intended to distance themselves from those African Americans who would remain at the bottom of the racial ladder. Many other groups have also used ethnic differentiation to foster group solidarity and sell their positive group image to gatekeeping others. Most notably, the Irish, Jews, and Chinese have carried out projects of ethnic uplift (Ignatiev, 1995; Brodkin, 1998; Cornell and Hartmann, 1998). That is to say, neither the process of uplift nor the process of hub-and-spoke network formation is unique to black immigrants from the Caribbean.

Generalizing Hubs and Spokes

Clearly I am arguing that the structure of an immigrant network affects its function. Hubs are veteran immigrants who control the network's social capital; spokes are those on whom social capital is spent to help them integrate into the new destination. Both migrant types adhere to a culture of reciprocity that establishes a set of rules that makes the migration process run smoothly. Hub-and-spoke networks have the potential to accrue societal and economic successes for their members, but network members' control over immigration selectivity coupled with their ability to hoard opportunity are key factors in generating success. Hubs (who are characteristically different from the spokes they assist) position themselves to create and maintain networks, police behavior of their spokes, and sell their ethnic group to gatekeepers because they are genuinely altruistic toward spokes, but they also wish to enhance their own reputations with gatekeepers in the destination and with co-ethnics back home. To a far greater extent than spokes, hubs keep or renew ties back home, make sacrifices for the network, buy into the network's culture of reciprocity, help other migrants get jobs (likely because of their own position in the labor market niche in question), and drive the migration selection process. Selectivity is one of the key driving forces in the struggle for upward mobility. Hubs select among many potential migrants who desire to move, choosing those who they believe will perform best under the circumstances the network has arranged for itself, including those who will be beholden to the hub and to employers, those who will "act right" in neighborhoods where they move, and so on. In sum, it is not that hubs choose only the best and brightest for migration but that they choose those potential migrants who are most likely to be reputation enhancers. (This can be true regardless of whether the latter is the hub's motivation; for example, hubs may believe that those who would perform best in the destination country are also the most deserving of assistance.)

Perhaps not all networks have a hub-and-spoke structure, but surely many do. Those groups that have hubs but whose hubs may not as easily control selectivity are likely to be less economically and socially successful and less likely to accrue the network benefits outlined earlier. Examples are cases in which potential newcomers have many alternatives to waiting for help from hubs; these migrants more easily come on their own, diluting the possibilities for organizing monopoly power in labor and housing markets, which in turn prevents the marketing of the group's ethnic cache to society's social and economic gatekeepers. (This may be the case, for example, for Mexicans and other Central Americans, who in large numbers can walk across borders to the United States with the help of so-called coyotes and in defiance of help-withholding hubs.) By contrast, those networks that are organized more tightly into hub-and-spoke configurations may be better able to achieve apparent or real social mobility for their members because they have more control over how migrants are inserted into markets and perceived positively as ethnic "ones of a kind"—that is, as unique and desirable employees, neighbors, and citizens.

Evidence Supporting the Existence of Hubs and Spokes Among Other Groups

I have sufficiently shown that black Caribbean migrants manifest a hub-and-spoke type of network. But how widespread are these practices? Do all West Indians come to the United States or England in this way? Do other immigrant groups network like this? Many times, after giving talks on the research material presented in this book, I have been asked questions like these, but I must leave these questions for other researchers to answer, for several reasons.

First, the method I used prevents my generalizing beyond those who used hub-and-spoke networks; that is, my snowball sampling scheme was predicated on an ethnographic definition of helping behavior. I talked, via a snowball sample, only to hubs or spokes who exchanged help in the ways they told me about, and I spoke neither with any other kind of immigrant nor to immigrants who came to the United States by other methods. (This is not to say there were no other immigrants linked to these networked immigrants, but they were not identified by my respondents because these immigrants either failed to help others, moved across borders without help, or for other reasons were not network members—for example, perhaps they were ostracized). The idea was not to conduct a representative-sample survey of West Indians, but only to map two immigrant networks. Indeed, I could not complete this task. I started the mappings with what I thought were two distinctly disconnected peoples (from two different islands), but their networks were broad, pervasive, and transnational enough that, once their connections were followed around the globe (from North America to the Eastern Caribbean and Leeward Islands to England), the two networks actually merged into one. That everyone in the sample was connected to everyone else leads me to suspect that most West Indians use hub-and-spoke-type networks, although I have little empirical and no statistical evidence to back up that claim.

The second reason I cannot definitively answer questions about the generalizability of this model is that my research is, to my knowledge, the first of its kind in attempting to understand in so broad a manner the structure and function of immigrant networks. As I explained in the introductory chapter, while migration scholars have written about immigrant social networks for quite some time, they have not unpacked the "black box" that networks represent. Interested in proving that networks perpetuate migration, Massey (see 1986, 1990a, 1990b as examples) spent many years working to estimate the probabilities of immigrating to the United States given network connections, and to do so he studied only pairs of persons—individuals who knew other individuals who could provide migration assistance. In a very large body of work he successfully demonstrated that probabilities of migrating increased with knowledge of some person who had migrated before.[5] While describing and highlighting cases of networks that contradicted the prevailing idea that networks are normatively sources of social and economic capital readily shared in positive information-and-resource transactions, Mahler (1995) and Menjívar (2000) studied their respective networks in a way that would explain the downside of being in a network. However, neither scholar looked in detail at the structure and function of those networks themselves. Ho (1991), Vickerman (1999), and Waters (1999) each specifically studied groups of West Indians, but their goals too were different from mine, and the resulting research does not lend itself to findings about those networks' structures. Because my research was designed to study the properties and processes of entire networks (and on that count differs significantly from other immigration research published to date), I can only infer from secondary research sources not intended to study immigrant network structures whether the hub-and-spoke model applies to other groups. Using this very limited set of scholarship, I offer a qualified but strong affirmative to the question about the general prevalence of the hub-and-spoke network form.

Anecdotal and statistical evidence do exist to support the idea that other immigrant groups have hublike figures who perform specific altruistic acts to help establish co-ethnic newcomers in destination countries. Take, for instance, the following example of a Salvadoran veteran "hub" (Mahler, 1995, p. 53):

> On Long Island, a perfect example of this phenomenon can be seen in the network that interconnects the town of Concepción de Oriente in eastern

El Salvador and Western Long Island. By all accounts, it was begun by Don Miguel Yanes. Don Miguel was the head of sanitation and public health in the small rural town of Concepción de Oriente in La Unión Department of El Salvador. In 1971 a high-school friend from the city of San Miguel helped Don Miguel get a visa to the United States through government contacts. The two went to live on Long Island, where Don Miguel's friend had relatives. Don Miguel then found a job quickly at a plastics factory in the Westbury, Long Island, neighborhood called New Cassell. (After two decades he still works at the same job.) Eight years later, just as the civil war in El Salvador was escalating, he returned to Concepción de Oriente with a green card, which he had obtained by marrying a Puerto Rican woman. He told his family and friends—a group comprising nearly the entire population of the town—about his good fortune and the opportunities for work in Westbury. Shortly after he returned to Westbury, *Concepcióneros* started streaming in, most staying a few days or months at Don Miguel's home while they looked for housing and jobs nearby. When I went to interview the "godfather," as he is called, Don Miguel told me that so many, perhaps as many as a thousand, of his townspeople have come to the United States that he no longer even knows them all.

As I do, Mahler also speculates that such networks are begun by pioneers who bring home tales of their successes, but she further argues that pioneers likely suffer inordinately in the destination country and are "anxious to recoup [their] social status upon returning home... [Then,] smitten with the idea of migrating themselves, [spokes] leave [home], using the guidance of the pioneer and often staying with him or her in the host country" (Mahler, 1995, p. 53). Later in the book, Mahler gives another example:

They told me stories in which they figured as naive newcomers who fell easy prey to older migrants with greater expertise. Typically, this fall from innocence occurred during a time of particular vulnerability: the pursuit of the first job. . . . Jaime's example is a good case in point. A baseball jacket manufacturer from Lima, Peru, he arrived on Long Island in 1988 to a royal welcome. His sponsor, a Peruvian immigrant from his Lima barrio, took him in, gave him food, and provided a room for him. The next day, however, the tides turned. Jaime was put to work in his sponsor's construction business laboring fourteen hours per day, six days per week. For his efforts, he was paid $250 but docked $50 each week for the lunches that the sponsor's wife packed for him daily. In addition, he had to pay the sponsor back $200 per month in rent. Jaime remembers these first six months bitterly: "I had to separate me from myself. If I hadn't I would have cried. I had to leave behind my personality—like taking my clothes off and putting new ones on." Jaime says that he was willing to work hard, but not to be exploited, not to lose his dignity. In one short week he descended from boss to laborer, from man to mouse. As soon as he found another opportunity, he left his sponsor and now exclaims proudly, *"Yo bailo con mi proprio pañuelo"* (I'm dancing to my own tune now). Determined never to be so humiliated again, particularly at the hands of a compatriot, Jaime in three short years has found a steady union job working in a nursing home and serves as a manager for an office-cleaning firm at night. He even employs some of his own relatives now. He recently bought a house in Gold Coast and has sublet it to many fellow Peruvians, turning a profit by charging them more in rent than he pays for the mortgage. [p. 102]

Other researchers have reported similar findings, where hub equivalents in other networks act as bridgeheads and gatekeepers who are often unwilling to help friends and family back home fulfill their wishes to emigrate (Böcker, 1994; Thomas and Znaniecki, 1996).[6]

Jacqueline Hagan's (1994) book explains the transmission of information about how to become legal from the more knowledgeable to those less so. Although many of the Mayan immigrants to Texas in her sample were ineligible for the amnesty offered under the Immigration Reform and Control Act, "more than half the study sample applied successfully and were granted temporary [legal] status" (p. 120), having been helped by hublike legal experts in their network or by relying on employers who could legalize them.

Most migrants in the community filed during the last months of the application period and sought assistance from neighborhood, Spanish-speaking notarios with whom they were more culturally familiar. . . . [N]otaries benefitted from the fact that the notary public serves as the functional equivalent to legal counsel in much of Latin America, including Guatemala. Notaries were willing to compile, organize, and notarize papers for about a hundred and fifty dollars. In most cases, names of notaries were obtained from others who had used their services. Thus, a legalization network developed among applicants in the community. They shared information about access to services and about their experiences with different attorneys, notaries, and INS officials. In the final analysis, four or five notaries did the bulk of the paperwork for the entire community. The only exception to this pattern was a select group of immigrants who had established contacts with U.S. residents (employers, close friends) who were willing to assist them. [Hagan, 1994, p. 122]

Likewise, Hagan discovered that Mayans used different kinds of co-residence over the migration experience, demonstrated gender differences in job networking effectiveness (in her case, women had a much harder time with employment than men), used jobs to make themselves legal (here too men found more success), and created employment monopolies, which in turn encouraged long-term loyalties to jobs—even low-paying ones—so that the group could maintain control of the niche. Two examples from her text help illustrate these points. Regarding co-residence, Hagan (1994, p. 56) writes, "Unlike many other arriving migrants who may have no social resources in Houston, the newcomer Mayan moves directly into a sponsoring household in the community, which provides room, board and, usually, access to employers." And hinting at the existence of hub-controlled employment concentrations, she recounts an immigrant telling her that it is the worker who does the hiring and not the manager (p. 62): "It is difficult for them [the managers] to do it [that is, hire a nonimmigrant worker for a maintenance job] because we [the immigrant maintenance workers] do not let it happen. We know when a worker is going to ask to move up [to another department], and we ourselves are already deciding who to bring in [as a replacement]."

Another example of a hub-and-spoke type of network is evident in Tilly's (1998, p. 166) account of Macedonian migration:

When I lived in Toronto during the 1960s, my next-door neighbors were Macedonians. A steady stream of visitors from Macedonia came through their house. One day my neighbor explained, in roughly these terms: "We have short-order restaurants [the day of "fast food" had not yet arrived], and when we need someone to work in one of them, we send back home for a young man. He cleans up and starts cooking as he learns English, then graduates to running the counter. When he's saved up some money and gotten pretty good in English, we try to set him up in his own restaurant. Then he hires newcomers." At that point, as my neighbor didn't say, the new restaurant owner owed plenty of money to his relatives and had to rely on them for help in recruiting his work force; these ties reforged the migration chain. In that way, retail trades often become semi-monopolies of one national group or another—Indian newsstands or Korean groceries in New York, Macedonian short-order restaurants or Italian barbershops in Toronto. [Bracketed text in original.]

Although Tilly uses the term *migration chain*, he obviously did not mean that these migrants came exclusively in dyads—one employee per store owner. While some "chaining" might have taken place, it is more likely that a hub-and-spoke arrangement prevailed. Hubs would set up selected newcomers in their own shops; storeowners in turn were pressured into hiring a number of immigrants chosen by the initial sponsor, to whom he or she owed money.

Gordon (1983) found that not an overwhelming number of the Jamaicans she studied (19 percent of migrants arriving pre-1940 and 34 percent of post-1960 arrivals) reported they had come specifically to join family. Instead, greater numbers (55 percent of pre-1940 and 41 percent of post-1960 arrivals) reported coming "under the auspices" of relatives who "sponsored" them, and even more (71 percent of pre-1940 and 69 percent of post-1960 arrivals) said they lived with relatives upon arrival. These migrants didn't specifically use family reunification, but they did join relatives and manifest a co-resident pattern. Also, reflecting the possible influence of network members on the choice of subsequent homes after the co-residence period ended, 83 percent of migrants who arrived before 1940 and 79 percent who arrived after 1960 reported they have relatives and friends in the neighborhood in which they live. One notable difference between these Jamaicans and the Eastern Caribbean migrants is that few of the Jamaicans (only 5 percent pre-1940 and 11 percent post-1960) said they "involved friends and relatives in their search for employment" (Gordon, 1983, p. 40).

A reading of Fjellman and Gladwin's (1985) work can also support a model of extended and transnational networks over any model that surmises a bi-national chain of dyadic links. These authors, using the case of Haitian migrants, track a process they call the migration of "family fragments," which involves dispersing persons to places all over the world. (Specifically, they mention Miami, Montreal, New York and other northern U.S. metropolitan areas, and the Bahamas as network destinations.) These networked migrants, too, use both legal and illegal means of arriving and stretch their arrivals over long periods (some networked migrants are recent arrivals while others are not). They also report that many spokes wait their turn to be sent for: there are "still others, in Haiti or, perhaps, the Bahamas, who are in line to move when appropriate resources and sponsorship can be arranged" (Fjellman and Gladwin, 1985, p. 305). The authors go on to present co-resident hub-centered migration histories, further illustrating the "sequential and 'multinational family' nature of Haitian migration" (p. 307). Interestingly, these families' experiences mirror those of black Eastern Caribbean immigrants. These Haitians also use transnational networks, move among international sites as opportunity becomes available, remain co-resident in order to achieve the goal of homeownership, foster their children back home, use various legal and illegal means for reuniting their group, and often have women migrate and settle first and then send for the men.[7]

Although Jasso and Rosenzweig (1990) did not study networks per se, they provide evidence that supports the existence of spokes (that is, immigrants who don't help others and are more host-country than home-country oriented). Studying no particular foreign-born ethnic or racial group but a representative sample of all immigrants, they explain that few naturalized citizens make use of family reunification visa entitlements. They write, "Part of the reason for these low rates is that many of the naturalized citizens are themselves brought in by U.S. citizen relatives" (p. 210). These naturalized citizens were sent for, but they tend not to send for other family members in return. We can speculate that because their citizen relatives brought them in, these relatives have already brought in everyone the naturalized citizen might send for and that consequently there are few remaining relatives to bring. But the authors also present data that suggest otherwise, that is, that plenty of relatives remain back home, ready to migrate if they have the chance.[8] Altogether, then, these passages suggest that some who are brought in just don't bother to help others; that is, spokes exist in immigrant communities generally. Jasso and Rosenzweig (1990, p. 210) also present evidence of co-residential patterns; they show that the "household structure for the U.S. foreign-born is strikingly more 'extended' than that of the native-born," and that the households of the foreign born became increasingly co-resident between 1960 and 1980 (but that co-residence among the native born decreased over the same period). Further, they explain that "the trends in sibling co-residence mirror hemisphere-specific changes in U.S. immigration law: in particular, the foreign-born from the Western Hemisphere exhibited an almost twofold increase in sibling co-residence between 1970 and 1980, the period when the sibling sponsorship entitlement was extended to the Western Hemisphere" (p. 210). These facts support two contentions: first, that co-residence is an important part of the hub-sponsored immigration experience; and second, that members of immigrant social networks respond quickly to changes in immigration law by using whatever opportunities they can to get their chosen relatives and friends into the country.

To conclude this section, I rebut three speculations that these authors make where they interpret data to support the idea of the migration chain, and I argue instead that a hub-and-spoke interpretation can easily be made from the same data.

While Jasso and Rosenzweig's quantitative analysis is based on the immigration laws current at that time, in their text they rightly do not presume that everyone follows the law as written. For example, they clearly suggest that using migration chains is another way to get around the limitations imposed by family reunification restrictions. Their focus on migration dyads in a chain is evident when they note that sending for one's aunt would not be allowed, but one could send for her by first sending for one's own parent and then having the parent send for the sibling. While this is true, a hub can simply get the aunt a babysitting job or work as a domestic. Avoiding restrictions altogether instead of chaining through them means that the aunt would arrive much faster and that her legalizing paperwork could come through far more quickly.

In another passage, the authors speculate on the reason for a decreasing number of children's applications, noting that while the demand for immigration of siblings of citizens had increased enormously (nearly tripling between 1980 and 1989 to 1.5 million applications), the number of applications for children had remained steady. The authors' presumption is that "potential immigrants tend to have fewer children than their compatriots or delay childbearing" (Jasso and Rosenzweig, 1990, p. 198). Rather than interpreting a decline in applications as a decline in childbearing, one may instead see it as signaling increased use of fosterage.

Finally, the authors note that the family members being sent for are most likely to be adult siblings of immigrants, who are far from the main category of immigrant family members allowable under family reunification. These kinds of immigrants make sense under a hub-and-spoke interpretation: they are age and ethnic peers who can more easily be recommended for jobs in the same occupational sectors.

Conclusion: Mobile Networks as Ethnic Projects

In this chapter I have argued both that hub-and-spoke networks may be fairly widespread in immigrant communities and that the hub-and-spoke structure of network migration is one that is particularly well-suited for launching upward mobility projects. The reason this structure is primed for mobility is that it enables a particularly stringent form of migrant selection that encourages a kind of policing of network members' behavior, pushing newcomers to the network to conform to certain standards on the job and in their neighborhoods, lest they threaten their and their sponsor's standing in the network community. Moreover, these conformist achievement behaviors create a reputation for the individuals who altogether become identified with the co-ethnic group. Insiders reinforce this group-identified reputation, necessarily advertising these beliefs through a kind of ethnic self-promotion to gatekeepers (employers, realtors, mortgage companies, and others); outsiders identify networking behaviors with an ethnic group (perhaps both creating and spreading stereotypical "knowledge" of said group); and gatekeepers open or keep open opportunities to the co-ethnics in the immigrant network, perhaps at first because they too benefit from their transactions with network members, but perhaps also because they come to believe the ethnic stereotype. There may be many immigrant groups who are unable to make their own networks operate in ways that bring about equal levels of socioeconomic success or racial uplift. Those who do find success and uplift perhaps have better control over how their network members are inserted into markets and therefore are perceived as ethnic "ones of a kind," unique and desirable as employees, neighbors, and citizens (and hub-and-spoke configurations may be more likely to achieve this). In cases where the culture of reciprocity promotes a "pay it forward" kind of altruism, along with long-term obligations to the group by those who receive such assistance, social mobility might be especially likely.

Networked immigrants may actively cultivate ethnicized images in order to ensure that future benefits accrue to network members, and perhaps to the ethnic group as a whole. When ethnicity is propagandized by group members, I have called the campaign an "ethnic project." (The term *ethnic project* expands on Omi and Winant's [1994] notion of the *racial project*, wherein groups use race as a mechanism to further their political and economic ends.) The project is designed to create ethnic value. Especially for groups who are inserted near a society's hierarchal bottom (as all immigrant groups seem to be on their initial entry), ethnic projects are crucial because they dictate an ethnic and racial group's ability to rewrite the role originally given to them in the script of global and local social, economic, and racial stratification.

Ethnic projects, however, can be hindered by the competing interests of gatekeepers, who control access to jobs, education, housing, and destination countries themselves (via their control of immigration policy). Gatekeepers express their tastes for immigrants, and at various times some groups are more desired than others. Their tastes are contested by network members who, in their own struggles to survive, work around them or even attempt to change them. (Where networks can gain monopoly power in neighborhoods or job sites, they can convince employers to hire their members. Where networks gain enough experience in making someone legal or getting them legally into the country in the first place, they are able to organize migration around the rules for securing documentation for the compatriots they most wish to send for.)

Migrants from the Eastern Caribbean are well aware that their racialization as black and their status as Third World has been used against them to keep them out of Western nations and to keep them away from opportunities for advancement that are afforded to mainly Northern and Western European others. True, immigrants may not always specifically use a language of antiracist struggle to describe their migration efforts. But when one considers the repeated efforts of legislators and law enforcers to keep them out of these more developed countries and beyond the resources available to more desired groups, one might be more apt to see the immigrant network's success at getting people across geographic and socially stratified borders as a successful effort against racism in immigration law, and as a strike against the enormous social and economic inequality between the First and Third Worlds. The power of membership in social networks reverberates through the life chances of those in the group in important ways. As a whole, then, network members' actions organize the group in a struggle for uplift and mobility in a context of global inequality. When successful, they secure educations, incomes, assets, lifestyles, and recognition for the ethnic value of their people that they might otherwise not obtain.

Reference Matter

Notes

Chapter One

1. I have changed the names of all respondents interviewed for this project to pseudonyms, a purposeful act meant to protect their anonymity.

2. *The Western world* and *the West* refer to those nations with origins in Western Europe or that adhere to European culture. As a former British colony, the United States can claim to have its roots in the West. Using the term *West* to describe Europe and the United States is not uncommon when invoking or referring to a colonial or imperialist power with European origins. The term *North*, which also is sometimes used to describe these nations, tends to invoke the idea of an economic development or technological divide between these nations and those of the less developed world, albeit with no clear reference to colonialism and imperialism as having created that divide. In the chapters that follow I use both *the West* and *the North* to indicate collectively the North American and Western European destinations to which Caribbean migrants move.

3. Persons may be said to have weak ties if they have connections to others with whom they invest little time or emotional intensity or with whom they share little intimacy. Groups with more weak ties than strong ties among their members, then, are presumed to be less isolated than those with only strong ties, and they are also less bound by a comprehensive social cohesion. Groups with only strong ties are more isolated from outsiders than groups that have both strong and weak ties. Evidence has shown that because they have links to outsiders, those with weak ties more easily secure jobs within local labor markets and have better job search information than others (Montgomery, 1994; Granovetter, 1973, 1995).

While we tend to think of the most useful labor market ties as weak ones, the most useful migration ties are presumed to be close. Perhaps this is because migration laws in the United States give primacy to "family reunification," in which migration sponsorship depends on the existence of a very close relative at the destination who is willing to help. Alternatively, perhaps it's that intimacy is implied in the transfer of help with housing, job placement, and acculturation, the kind of assistance new migrants need.

The networks studied here, however, raise questions about the conditions under which weak and strong ties are operative. First, having a close tie is insufficient to get help crossing national borders. (Distant relatives and friendly nonrelatives are often the ones who help others immigrate. In this case, a weak tie, Pamela's uncle, was the link that activated the migration of seven families.) Second, where weak ties facilitated border crossing, ties were *transnationally* and not just locally important. Third, some spokes had both close and weak ties in their networks, getting assistance from more than one individual. (See Chapters Three and Four for more information, and Figures 3.2 through 3.5 for visual examples.) I found that the strongest hub-spoke ties were those among migrants who had been postmigration co-residents.

4. European migrants dominated world flows in the three periods before the mid-1960s: during the mercantile period—roughly from 1500 to 1800—when Europeans moved for the purposes of colonization and settlement; from 1800 to 1925, during the period of industrial growth in the Americas and Oceania; and even between 1925 and 1960, when migration slowed to a trickle (Massey et al., 1998).

5. Portes and Bach (1985, pp. 3–7) suggest that preceding research has elevated the importance of pull factors over push factors in labor migrations, while push factors (like inhospitable political conditions) are more important in refugee migrations.

6. For some Caribbean islands, remittances were found to make up substantial proportions of household and even national income. In Tortola, cash from overseas made up 45 percent of household income, and for some rural households in Montserrat, remittances were found to make up 70 and 100 percent of household income. In some years, cash from remittances exceeded returns from chief exports in Nevis, Carriacou, and Monserrat (Bascom, 1991).

7. There is a countervailing point of view in John Higham's *Strangers in the Land: Patterns of American Nativism, 1860-1925*, a history of immigration that posits that the United States was welcoming of and profited from immigration in times of labor shortage and prosperity and hostile to immigration in periods of labor glut and depression.

8. A wide gulf separates formal network analysts (in the main distinguished by the methodology they employ to map network patterns) and migration theorists (a group different from the former in prioritizing the search for empirical clues to the operation of network processes in various migration-related settings) (Gurak and Caces, 1992). Texts on network analysis, such as Scott's *Social Network Analysis* (1991) and Wellman and Berkowitz's *Social Structures* (1988; see also Wellman, 1988) are well-

known and early examples of the former. In 1978, Wellman founded the International Network for Social Network Analysis, an interdisciplinary organization of scholars interested in these methods. The group publishes its own bulletin, *Connections*, and journal, *Social Networks*. "Social network analysis is focused on uncovering the *patterning* of people's interactions" (Freeman, 2004, p. 602). Themselves members of an interdisciplinary group, migration scholars are less interested in the patterns and more interested in how network membership affects migration-related processes, such as achieving documented or undocumented border crossings, complying with changes in immigration legislation, finding jobs, or sending remittances. Massey and colleagues' *Return to Atzlán* (Massey, Alarcón, Durand, and González, 1987) and Hagan's *Deciding to Be Legal* (1994) are examples of this kind of scholarship. Theoretical, empirical, and methodological differences between the research produced by social network analysts and that of migration scholars who study immigrant social networks remain, and such differences have evolved to the degree that the two areas of scholarship rarely engage one another.

9. "[The] frequent utilization of immigration research [by economic sociologists who write on social capital] is not surprising, because foreign-born communities represent one of the clearest examples of the bearing contextual factors can have on individual economic action. With skills learned in the home country devalued in the receiving labor market and with a generally poor command of the receiving country's language, immigrants' economic destinies depend heavily on the structures in which they become incorporated and, in particular, on the character of their own communities. Few instances of economic action can be found that are more embedded" (Portes and Sensenbrenner, 1993, p. 1322).

10. Immigrants are commonly mislabeled "legal" or "illegal," but they are more properly identified as having proper documentation that specifies their legal status, or are instead undocumented. I use the terms *legal* and *illegal* in quotation marks when I want to mark awareness that these are misnomers, however commonly used they are.

11. Scholars who have researched and written about negative social capital include Menjívar (2000) and Portes (1998); but see also Portes and Rumbaut (2001) as well as Mahler (1995), Hamilton and Chinchilla (1996), and Faist (2000).

12. Studies of the influence of network membership on attainment of employment show that networks are quite important in determining who gets jobs and who is effectively barred from them. In the 1990s, much was made of the problem of "spatial mismatch"—it was thought that the poor's geographic concentration in inner cities meant they were spatially isolated from less-skilled jobs in the suburbs to which they were best suited; but studies of networks have shown that even where the poor and jobs are in close physical proximity, those most in need will remain isolated from jobs if they cannot penetrate the networks that control access to employment (Kasinitz and Rosenberg, 1996).

13. The interviews were modeled after the open-question/open-response method developed by Robert Weiss (1994). This method neither uses an instrument nor follows a strict list of questions, which would amount to an orally administered survey. Instead, Weiss suggests that the interviewer follow a *substantive frame* that guides a conversational-style discussion. The interviewer uses the frame to be sure all the topics of interest are covered in the time the respondent and interviewer share.

14. Because I started my interviews with two unrelated persons who came from different islands and did not know each other, I assumed that I was studying two separate immigrant networks. However, as the interview part of the research came to a close, it became clear to me that the two networks I studied were not really separate at all, for had I continued interviewing by following the snowball that the sampling method had created, the networks would have overlapped significantly. For one, the women in the "separate" networks worked in the same sectors in the economy, and one of the nurses in one network knew of a nurse in the other. Also, it became clear that women in London in one network made friends with people in the other network through the Claudia Jones women's community organization, and these friends were relatives of the New York immigrants in my "other" network. So, by the time I did interviews in London, it was clear that my "two" networks were really one transnational network of immigrants. This transnationalism, moreover, was more complex than is normally understood in the migration literature, for it spanned not just one place of origin and one destination, but several origin and destination sites as well. (Each group also had relatives and friends in cities in Canada, but I did not do interviews in that country.)

15. Of these, two respondents were from the Virgin Islands, two were from Grenada, and three were from Barbados.

16. Thomas-Hope (1986, p. 424), citing R. A. Pastor, 1985.

17. Europeans are widely believed to have been the first world travelers, although the embrace of this notion is surrounded by considerable dispute. What is not disputed is that Europeans were the first to develop racial categories to define the people they encountered (Smedley, 1993; Jordan, 1968).

Still, there is evidence that the people labeled black were at least similarly migratory, if not more so than the European. Research indicates that phenotypically black persons very early on traveled the lands we know now as Asia and Europe and reached the Americas well before Columbus's arrival (Van Sertima, 1976). To this day there are few nations that are able to report that they have no black persons among their native born. Unfortunately, this record of global travel is far from lauded in our current era of racialized readings of world history and modernization. Many of us still learn only one reading of the historical record, that is, that the root of modernism and economic prosperity of the West comes solely from European ambition at the root of European travel. Quite another reading argues that rather than purely entrepreneurial (read nonracialized and economically justified) processes, European actions undertaken by migrants were in large part both racializing and exploitative, and these actions signify the origins of global inequality (Bonilla-Silva, 2003; Winant, 2002; Smedley, 1993).

The point is that racial differentiation has always occurred in nations populated or colonized by Europeans. Even the Irish, Jews, and others now considered by most Americans to be white were once seen as racially nonwhite (Ignatiev, 1995; Brodkin, 1998; Steinberg, 1989).

Chapter Two

1. "World-system theory and its close ally dependency theory have many flaws. Their economic history sometimes has been wrong. The naked political bias and revolutionary polemic evident in some of their writings show how easy it is to fall into blind dogmatism. The attack against capitalism has not been accompanied by a convincing explanation of what might replace it. There are major empirical and theoretical gaps. But this cannot deprive them of their importance and real virtues. Studying individual societies in isolation from each other is both misleading and dangerous. It hides the powerful transnational forces that have been a major part of all social and economic transformations since the fifteenth century. It yields incomplete, and often wrong, conclusions about the nature of social problems. Sociology has tended to fall into this kind of trap. World-system theory can thus be seen as a necessary remedy. Whether or not one agrees with all of its conclusions, it is abundantly clear that a world-wide perspective has become a minimal requirement for the intelligent study of social change" (Chirot and Hall, 1982, p. 102).

2. But the race game is rigged. Because the categories are themselves hierarchical, simply naming the groups and looking at their outcomes is more of a sorting exercise than a study in analytical rigor. It is tautological to label groups hierarchically but to expect those hierarchical labels to explain something other than the outcomes of the hierarchical systems of which they are a part (Bashi, 1998).

3. Latin American examples of transnationalism include the organizing work that Mexican labor leaders did in the United States to encourage Mexican laborers to return to Mexico and continue labor organizing among workers there; reciprocally, Mexican, Salvadoran, and Guatemalan organizing tactics were used to organize workers in California in successful campaigns to increase union membership, wages, and benefits (Hamilton and Chinchilla, 1996, pp. 205, 214). Similarly, Caribbean women create transnational families, shuttling adults and children across network households in ways that both care for and culturally transform them (Ho, 1993). Transnationalism's cultural effects are probably most evident when networks operate to perpetuate and transform the web of migrant, destination, and origin communities' cultures. Migrants screen soccer talent and transport players from one country to another, maintaining vibrancy in a transnational soccer culture (Massey, Alarcón,

Durand, and González, 1987). Migration is also said to alter gender relations both at home and among those residing in the United States (Zamudio, 1999; Hagan 1998).

4. Although it perpetuates a historical inaccuracy, the terms *West Indian* and *Caribbean* are used nearly interchangeably here. It should be noted, however, that *West Indian* is the term commonly used in the United States to refer to phenotypically black persons from the Caribbean, while the term *Black Caribbean* is more often used in the United Kingdom to refer to the same group.

5. Murray, 1991, p. 28, citing Major, 1870.

6. With regard to the demand for labor for mining in Hispaniola, Williams (1984, p. 33) writes, "At the beginning there were enough Indians to satisfy the demand. But it was in the colonial's interest to obtain as much as he could from his labourers in the shortest possible time. . . . The results are to be seen in the best estimates that have been prepared of the trend of population in Hispaniola. These place the population in 1492 at between 200,000 and 300,000. By 1508 the number was reduced to 60,000; in 1510, it was 46,000; in 1512, 20,000; in 1514, 14,000. In 1548 Oviedo doubted whether five hundred Indians of pure stock remained. In 1570 only two villages survived of those about whom Columbus had assured his Sovereigns, less than eighty years before, that 'there is no better nor gentler people in the world.'" The Spanish example was followed throughout the region by that of Spain's colonial successors.

7. The triangular trade was the main engine of the eighteenth-century world economy. Blacks were transported to the Caribbean and traded as enslaved chattel. Slaves and the materials they produced (such as sugar and molasses) were sent to the North American mainland; cotton as well as tobacco, lumber, and sugar produced in the United States went from there and the Caribbean to England. Manufactured goods from England were sent to the Americas; rum, guns, ammunition, and cloth were exported from North America to West Africa. Because on a world map these trade routes make a triangle, the pattern was named the triangular trade.

8. "In 1828, as a result of agitation in the West Indies and in England, all civil and military distinctions between free British subjects of any colour were abolished by Order in Council in all the Crown colonies. Jamaica legislated in the same sense in 1830, Barbados in 1831"(Parry, Sherlock, and Maingot, 1987, p. 164). Conniff (1987, p. 16) says, by contrast, that emancipation came to the British West Indies in 1838, noting that this act freed more than one-half million black persons. While the specific dates of the various orders may be unclear, it is clear that while "all of the Caribbean islands had slavery in 1790, . . . none of them did in 1900" (Stinchcombe, 1995, p. 13). As freedom of movement came to these islands, blacks in Jamaica and the Windward Islands took up farming and moved to cities, while those in the Eastern Caribbean migrated instead (Conniff, 1985, p. 17).

9. The National Industrial Conference Board reported West Indian immigration (gross figures, not including Cubans) as fluctuating between nine hundred and fifteen

hundred persons annually from 1908 through 1922. (See National Industrial Conference Board, 1923, Appendix Table A, 123–30.) It wasn't until 1944 that annual entrants reached more than two thousand, and the number of black migrants from the Caribbean to the United States rose quite significantly and consistently after that date. (See Figures 2.1 and 2.2.)

10. One example: "On the twenty-first [of March, 1911] a party of two hundred blacks arrived at the border station at Emerson, Manitoba, opposite Pembina in North Dakota, and requested admission to press on to Amber Valley, to which relatives had preceded them. The Canadian officials subjected them to the most rigorous examination possible and found, contrary to expectations, that they could not stop a single member of the groups. Not one had less than $300 (or $100 more than the law required), all were in excellent health, and all had documentary proof of good moral standing. They seemed to presage a wave of healthy, moral, and prosperous black men. The Secretary of the Edmonton Board of Trade, aware of those already passing through the city, now demanded that all Negroes be barred from entry, and a member of the government of Alberta (who refused to give his name) suggested through the press that the Dominion should apply a head tax on Negroes at once" (Winks, 1971, p. 308).

11. "In 1952, the Minister of Citizenship and Immigration was asked in the House of Commons to explain the blatantly racist ruse of using climate to restrict non-white immigration. He said, 'In light of experience it would be unrealistic to say that immigrants who have spent the greater part of their life in tropical or semi-tropical countries become readily adapted to the Canadian mode of life which, to no small extent, is determined by climatic conditions. It is a matter of record that natives of such countries are more apt to break down in health than immigrants from countries where the climate is more akin to that of Canada.' The minister was asked to produce the record to which he referred. He had no record. . . . In 1953, [the use of climate to exclude blacks] was dropped from the immigration act" (Boyko, 1995, p. 167).

12. *Western Mail and South Wales Echo*, July 8, 1935, quoted from pp. 83–84 in Ramdin, 1999.

13. Avery, 1995, quoting from Satzewich, 1991, pp. 126–27.

14. Jaffee, 1961, writes, "Senate Report 1515 contains a mountain of 'facts,' the core of which, once the façade of scholarship is stripped away, consists of prejudice and fear. Typical is the treatment of 'race.' Although they admitted its weakness, the authors followed Blumenbach's outdated classification (formulated in 1775) and listed five 'races'—Caucasian, Mongolian, Ethiopian, American Indian, and Malayan or the white, yellow, black, red, and brown. The white race is further subdivided into the Teutonic, Latin, Slavic, and 'other' (Celtic, Iranic, and Semitic) groups. Subclassification within the white race, it develops, is related to 'type' as revealed by skin pigmentation" (pp. 104–5). "The formula seems to be light = Teutonic; dark = Latin; mixed = Celtic, Iranic, Semitic, and others. The extraordinary complexity of classification by

skin pigmentation is not mentioned in the report, nor is the difficult task of formulating a racial typology through measurements of head form, body, blood type, skeletal structure, etc. mentioned" (f. 19, p. 105). "The relationship between this information and American immigration policy in the mid-twentieth century is at first quite obscure. But it becomes clearer as the 'facts' unfold indicating that the report's authors assume a relationship between degree of assimilability and pigmentation categories within the white race" (p. 105).

15. "Another consideration that argued against new restrictive legislation [in the post World War I period] was that experience had shown during the Depression years that immigration could be effectively restricted with the already available laws. Western Hemisphere immigrants, although quota-free, were fully subject to the same [racial] criteria of admissibility and exclusion as other immigrants and could be excluded for any one of many reasons on the judgment of the immigration inspector. It can be assumed, therefore, that such powers were used as they were thought needful to restrict the number of Western Hemisphere immigrants as was done for European immigrants. Furthermore, the same powers could very well be used selectively as between different countries of Western Hemisphere origin; for example, the public charge provision could be applied with different force to immigrants from Canada and Mexico" (Hutchinson 1981, p. 488).

16. Other newspapers were split in their opinions—some were in favor, some were not—but many also seemed indifferent or were silent on the issue (Jaffe, 1961, Chapter Seven).

17. "A special note should be made of the status of 'dependent areas' (colonies) of other countries. Under the 1965 Act, all colonies were permitted 200 visas to be counted against the country ceiling of 20,000 and the hemisphere ceiling of the mother country. The intent and impact of this continuation of previous policy was to check the volume from colonies in the Caribbean and high demand places such as Hong Kong" (Keely, 1979, p. 58).

18. "For the most part few Canadians specifically cited race as their reason for wishing to block West Indian immigrants, but the arguments of the 1950s and 1960s echoed those of the 1920s" (Winks, 1971, p. 443).

19. Here, Jakubowski quotes from Hawkins, 1989. (See Jakubowski, 1997, p. 11.)

20. Avery, 1995, quoting a "memo from assistant deputy minister to deputy minister, 13 January 1965, 195" (see note 34, p. 319), referenced in Satzewich, 1991, p. 175.

21. Three developments may have prompted the racially significant changes to U.S. immigration law in 1965. First, in the 1960s, independence came to many new Caribbean nations. Jamaica—and Trinidad and Tobago, the two largest British West Indian island colonies—gained independence in August 1962. Barbados won its independence in November 1966. Antigua, Barbuda, St. Kitts-Nevis-Anguilla, Dominica, Grenada, St. Lucia, St. Vincent, and the Grenadines each entered into a "free and vol-

untary association with Britain as an Associated State" in 1967, a condition that could be terminated at any time by either country (Parry, Sherlock, and Maingot, 1991). Even after independence, black immigration from the Caribbean was hardly encouraged, and may have been prevented in practice if not by letter of the law.

22. Quoted in Paul, 1997, p. 182, who also quotes from *Parliamentary Debates* (Commons), 5th ser. [1981], v. 997, c. 935.

23. *Ibid.*, c. 997.

24. The data on the United States used in Figures 2.1 and 2.2 were compiled from Davie, 1936; U. S. Bureau of Immigration, 1906, 1925, 1926, 1931, 1932; U.S. Bureau of Foreign and Domestic Commerce, 1936, 1939; U.S. Bureau of the Census, 1943, 1949, 1960, 1991, 1992, 1994; and U.S. Immigration and Naturalization Service, 1945, 1950, 1952, 1989, 1993, 1999. The data on Great Britain were compiled from Board of Trade, 1907, 1915, 1928, 1939, 1940; Central Statistical Office, 1952, 1956, 1965, 1975, 1989; and National Statistics, 2001. The data on Canada were compiled from Statistics Canada, 1965, 1983, and no date.

Note that the published statistics of Canada (in the *Historical Statistics* and through CANSIM II, the Canadian government's online statistical service) report a data series of Caribbean immigration only for the years 1956 through 1976. Estimates of the number of West Indians who immigrated to Canada published through other sources over this and later periods vary. Avery, 1995, finds that in 1961 there were 12,000 West Indians in Canada, increasing to 68,000 over the following decade, and by 1981 there were 211,000, "with the largest number coming from Jamaica (77,950), Trinidad (38,465), Haiti (26,755), and Guyana (37,975)" (Avery, 1995, p. 215). Again, Henry (1987, p. 215) estimates that by 1982 there were about 320,000 West Indians in Canada.

Chapter Three

1. Two exceptions come to mind. In one case, the spoke entered a third country and years later transferred from there to the chosen destination—the United States. In another, the spoke (a female) chose to enter a formal recruitment program rather than suffer co-residence with an undesirable hub (her strict uncle).

2. My intent here is not to paint the immigrant networks of black Caribbeans as perfect arrangements of the purest form of benevolence. I am purposely failing to emphasize instances where respondents discussed alcoholism, domestic violence, divorce, depression, and other family-centered difficulties—problems that many very successful families of all ethnicities suffer. But in this chapter I also did not stress my discussions with respondents about lifestyle changes within their migration stories, such as talk about how life in the Caribbean differs from Western life, or about how religious faith, in particular, the Christian religion, centered the lives of certain individuals and gave them resolve to keep struggling when adversity struck. My goal here

was to emphasize the aspects of immigrant network membership that promote mobility and increase stores of social capital.

3. Other immigrant groups have demonstrated a hub-and-spoke pattern similar to that identified among these black Caribbean immigrants. Evidence of the applicability of this pattern to other groups is presented in the conclusion to this book.

4. Some define altruism as effort or a gift made on another's behalf, with no gain earned in return for that effort or gift. It would not be my contention that if a person gained from his action, that gain erased any possibility of altruistic motivation.

5. If, instead of succeeding, a pioneer fails, he has two choices. He can live in that failed space, either returning home after a short time or staying in the destination and keeping the failure a secret. If the failure is to be a secret but the migrant's orientation is to the home country, then he must lie about his failure and report false successes; but by doing so the migrant will soon be pressured to help others migrate. In this way, the relative deprivation of those left behind is exacerbated by myths about the good life in the golden global city told both by the migrant and those back home who hear the tall tales (Mahler, 1995).

Chapter Four

1. Thomas-Hope (1986, pp. 427–28) argues that we unnecessarily make sharp distinctions between *migration* and *circulation*—for many Caribbean migrants who go back and forth stay in the destination for very long periods: "While a total of twenty or thirty years spent overseas is not uncommon, a Barbadian study has shown that the average period was thirteen years."

2. None of the men interviewed in New York told me that they were formally recruited, although some men in the London networks had been (mainly by London Transport, the organization that runs London's mass transit system). Although many respondents (men and women) did know and say that their mothers were recruited, none said that their fathers or other men in the previous generation were recruited. This is unexpected given that these men performed work that Marshall (1987) has indicated was traditionally contract work. Adult male interviewees in both the United States and the United Kingdom did tell me that their fathers participated in the interisland migration by working for oil companies, doing farm work in the United States, or working on the Panama Canal. However, they did not (or could not) tell me how their fathers got these jobs. This may be an indication that social networks have historically operated in these kinds of recruitment circles, just as nurses in these networks used their own recruiters to help obtain jobs for their friends.

3. Briggs (1984, p. 154) writes, "For obvious reasons, other illegal immigrants from the Caribbean—for instance, English-speaking blacks from the British West Indies and French-Creole-speaking blacks from Haiti—do not use Puerto Rico as their port

of entry." While the absence of Spanish-speaking ability or Puerto Rican accents may be a deterrent in the general sense, at least one respondent used Puerto Rico as the port of entry for himself and his children. This person spoke with a heavy English-speaking Caribbean accent, had dark nutmeg-colored skin, and was hardly phenotypically Latino in the way that North Americans may expect the typical Hispanic to appear.

4. Henke, 2001. He also writes, "Separation stress must not be underestimated. Bernice Frazer of the Department of Child and Adolescent Psychiatry at Kings County Hospital in New York City points out, 'Ninety-five percent of the children we see have migrated from the West Indies. They are from homes where one or both parents are absent' (quoted in Pragg, 1990). The children resent the separation and are unwilling to subordinate themselves to the guidance of parents who left them. The psychological costs of migration have not yet been explored and are often unacknowledged or misdiagnosed" (Holger, 2001, pp. 116–17). The main complaint among my respondents who were fostered was the difficulty in adjusting to the dangers of Western life, about which they knew very little. They were accustomed, instead, to the freedom of island life, where the entire village knew and cared for the welfare of the child, who was largely free to roam during the day once age-related chores had been completed. Often these caretakers were cherished grandparents, who had different rules than parents. In cases where the children migrated later and rejoined their parents in the West, the children had to limit friendships and movement and live under the continued scrutiny of parents with whom they were no longer familiar.

5. In the Mexican case she studied, Hondagneu-Sotelo defined *family stage migration* as migration "with husbands preceding the migration of their wives and children" (Hondagneu-Sotelo, 1994a, p. 39).

6. Iona tells the story of the rivalry between her grandmothers this way: she explains that as she was being sponsored by her maternal great aunt, her paternal grandmother sent Iona's father away to England. He wanted to marry Erksine (the mother of his child), so his mother "insisted that my father went abroad. It was all for good reason, so that he could earn money, so that he could support me and all this. But she had a real plan on her agenda, which was to keep my mother and father apart." Although Iona's father made his own mother promise to hand over his remittances to Erksine, "she didn't. So, my [maternal grandmother] was thinking that he went away and he wasn't supporting me, and all along he had been. She thought he was a scoundrel, that he was so good and supportive until he went and suddenly he changed to be, you know, an uncaring monster. . . . So, she [then] forced my mother into this marriage [with another man]." This second man was a violent abuser, and Iona's family members—the great aunts who cared for her, and her uncle and aunt who at that time had already migrated to England—all conspired to help Erksine get to London. Ostensibly to protect her, they arranged another marriage for her after her arrival, but this time, while it took some effort, Erksine had become clever enough to manage

to avoid the marriage altogether. As a footnote to the story, Erksine did have other children in England. When it was discovered that the childminder she'd hired rained abuse and neglect upon her younger children in London, these youngsters were sent back home to be fostered by the older generation of adults who remained there. Her sister-in-law also sent her oldest son back home from England.

7. The London interviews were conducted after I had completed the interviews in the West Indies; while I may have spoken to the relatives of Londoners who remained back home, I did not do so as a result of snowball sampling from the London sample. However, after I began interviews in London, I learned that my New York and London networks were actually connected—by friendship and blood—and that the networks had several members in common. Thus, some of those interviewed in the Caribbean were likely potential members of the London networks as well.

Chapter 5

1. Where two or more respondents indicated that they had held jobs in a given sector, I highlighted that sector by use of bold type. Most sectors had far more than two respondents—and only in the London Transport sector did I have as few as two respondents (one male, one female). I have nevertheless highlighted London Transport as a niche because historical evidence clearly shows that this is a very large employment niche for Caribbean migrants to London. (See Brooks, 1975, for example.) I just happened to have very few respondents in my sample who worked in that sector. All the teachers I spoke with, save one, had been brought to London under Jocelyn's personal hub recruitment scheme (described in Chapter One).

2. From "The Sandhog Project," at http://sandhogproject.com/sandhogs.

3. Consider the following quote from the Wikipedia entry on "Conscription in the United States," available online at http://en.wikipedia.org/wiki/The_Draft#The_draft_and_immigration (accessed March 29, 2006):

Selective Service (and the draft) in the United States is not limited to citizens. Permanent residents in the United States (holders of green cards) who are males of appropriate age, are required to enlist in Selective Service. Refusal to do so is grounds for denial of a future citizenship application. In addition, immigrants who seek to naturalize as citizens must, as part of the Oath of Citizenship, swear to the following:

that I will bear arms on behalf of the United States when required by the law; that I will perform noncombatant service in the armed forces of the United States when required by the law; that I will perform work of national importance under civilian direction when required by the law; [19]

Noncitizens who serve in the United States military enjoy several naturalization benefits which are unavailable to non-citizens who do not, such as a waiver of application fees. [20] Non-citizens who are killed in combat while serving in the U.S. Armed Forces may be posthumously naturalized, which may be beneficial to surviving family members.

4. Waters (1999, p. 98) explains that "the literature on the socioeconomic performance of West Indians does agree that they do considerably better than native blacks in labor force participation. . . . [but this propensity to work shows itself] most strikingly among the West Indian women. . . . Indeed, the high labor force participation of foreign-born black women is remarkable—they are more likely to be in the labor force than any other major demographic group in New York. In 1990 foreign-born West Indian men had labor force participation rates 12.3% higher than native-born African Americans (89.1% vs. 76.8%). Among women the foreign-born exceeded the native-born by 13.8% (83.0% vs. 69.2%). Philip Kasinitz [1992] reports that while in 1980 West Indians were less likely to have households headed by single females than was the case for African Americans, even among the more deprived households in this category households headed by West Indian females did better than the poor households headed by native-born females. The West Indians are less likely to be on welfare and more likely to be employed. This high labor force participation rate is all the more remarkable as recent West Indian immigrants were overrepresented in the very lowest education categories."

5. Granovetter's sample included only males (99 percent of whom were white) in professional, technical, and managerial jobs who lived and worked in a Boston suburb.

6. Light and Gold (2000, p. 4) write, "An ethnic economy consists of coethnic self-employed and employers and their coethnic employees."

7. Glennis's story may be worth repeating here to make the point. She had an uncle who was on the Medical Board in Jamaica. He had already brought up her two sisters to New York. She did not want to arrive through sponsorship with him because he was too controlling and bossy, treating the sisters as if he was their father. So she did it on her own, going first to Montreal and then moving to New York to stay with the sisters. She moved to Montreal at age nineteen, applying to nursing school with her "batchmate" (friend in the same cohort) and studying obstetrics there. The recruiting lawyer on whom she relied and the hospital administration were together exploiting nurses who were hired there, paying them very little—$162 per month when the going rate was supposed to be about $300—and withholding papers (licensing) from the newer recruits. Glennis caught on fast and quit within two months, after accomplishing two things: finding another position with a different hospital and paying off the lawyer. She paid off the second half of the lawyer's fee right away because she didn't want to be obligated to him.

8. The achievement of significant upward economic and social mobility by one person in that person's lifetime is so rare that, according to Wilkerson (2005a, 2005b), no regularly published national statistics describe it.

Chapter 6

1. Despite general acknowledgment that immigrant network members benefit socially and psychologically from network support, the research in this area is limited. For example, a search conducted December 2004 using the academic search engine EBSCOHOST turned up thirty-two articles published since 1984 in which the authors identified their work with the keywords *networks* and *social support*. Of these, only one was about immigrant networks.

2. Quoted from Nelson, 2003, footnote 12, p. 542. In this passage, she refers to Lewis, 1997.

3. Usually this kind of back-and-forth travel is done to obtain papers certifying one's migration as legal. As is explained in Chapter Four, there is an extremely long wait to enter the United States with one's legal paperwork in place. As an alternative to waiting for the paperwork, many Caribbean migrants enter the country legally but overstay their visas. There is some time between initial arrival, the period of undocumented stay, and finally, formal approval to enter as a legal resident with the right to stay. Once the approval for legal residence is given, the migrant who has overstayed a visa to the United States must return to his homeland, making it look as if he had been there all along. He then uses his new and legal paperwork to reenter the United States.

4. It is unclear whether other hubs had this experience because the interviewing was ethnographically done. That is, people were asked only to talk about their life experience as migrants in a new country—it was not an oral survey in which everyone was asked the same question. The ethnographic method of interviewing differs from surveys in that the same questions are not asked of each respondent. The former trumps the latter in its ability to obtain a richer story that results in the text of an oral history, one full of experiences—and interpretations of those experiences—that are of importance to the storyteller, not the chronicler of the story. The latter is more easily controlled by the chronicler because the issues of importance are decided upon in advance and translated into questions posed to each respondent. One drawback of the ethnographic method is that one cannot say things like "X percent of the respondents agree that . . ." or "Y percent of the sample had this characteristic"; their collective answers cannot be enumerated because not everyone is asked the same question.

5. Crowder found this phenomenon in a few U.S. cities. The extent to which it happens outside of these areas (that is, in other U.S. cities or in London or Toronto, where black English-speaking Caribbean immigrants are also found in large number) is unknown.

6. See note 4. I do not know the extent to which memberships in ethnic organizations are important for the group as a whole. However, some people did discuss ethnic organizations in their telling of their postmigration experiences, and what I did hear about their participation in ethnic organizations showed that they were important in helping migrants adjust to their new society.

7. Claudia Jones was a Trinidad-born feminist, activist, communist, journalist, and community organizer, and according to one source has been described as the "mother of the Notting Hill carnival." Born in Port of Spain in 1915, she moved with her sisters to Harlem eight years later. She became involved in the Young Communist League and in their efforts to defend the Scottsboro Boys, and in 1948 she joined the Communist Party USA. She later became editor of Negro Affairs for the party's paper, *Daily Worker*, and was elected to the party's National Committee. She lived and worked in the United States, all the while being repeatedly arrested and detained for these activities under Senator Joseph McCarthy's hunt for persons conducting "un-American" activities. She was convicted of advocating the overthrow of the government and was deported in 1955. After her deportation, Trinidad refused her entry and she moved to London, where she continued organizing for social justice among Caribbean peoples at home and abroad, and for victims of McCarthyism. She founded the *West Indian Gazette*, Britain's first black community newspaper, and in 1959, the famed Notting Hill carnival. She died in 1964 and was laid to rest next to Karl Marx. (See the BBC and BBC Radio Web sites http://www.bbc.co.uk/history/historic_figures/jones_claudia.shtml and http://www.bbc.co.uk/radio4/womanshour/timeline/claudia_jones.shtml; also 5X5 Media's "Black History Pages," http://purpleplanetmedia.com/bhp/pages/cjones.shtml, all accessed March 13, 2005. FBI files about Claudia Jones, unclassified under the Freedom of Information Act, can be found at http://foia.fbi.gov/foiaindex/jones_claudia.htm, also accessed March 13, 2005.)

8. The quote in this sentence is from a flyer entitled "Welcome to Claudia Jones Organisation."

9. Remembering that one goal of the London group was to impress upon Britons that they were upstanding citizens, branching out to socialize among nonblack, non-Caribbean-born people may be one way to further this goal.

10. They were not suggesting that they went to predominantly West Indian-attended or monoethnic churches. I have attended services with three different respondents and each was a member of a congregation that was completely mixed in sex, race, ethnicity, and age. Instead, they were explaining that the church was the center of their community activity.

11. "Social remittances are the ideas, behaviors, identities, and social capital that flow from host- to sending-country communities (Levitt, 1999). They are like the social and cultural resources that migrants bring with them to the countries that receive them. The role these resources play in promoting immigrant entrepreneurship, community development, and political integration is widely acknowledged. What is less understood is how these same ideas and practices are transformed in the host country and transmitted back to sending communities such that new cultural products emerge and challenge the lives of those who stay behind. . . . . Ordinary people, at the local level, are . . . cultural creators and carriers. Migrants send or bring back the

values and practices they have been exposed to and add these social remittances to the repertoire, both expanding and transforming it. Later migrants bring this enhanced tool kit with them, thereby stimulating ongoing iterative rounds of local-level global culture creation" (Levitt, 2001, pp. 54–55).

Chapter Seven

1. There are similarities and differences in the conception of race among the various West Indian Islands. Racial composition in the Caribbean varies by island, and these differences have some impact on responses to race both in the country of origin and in the United States. But I focus only on the similarities of racial systems in the West Indies, saving a discussion of interisland differences for another context.

2. The race question was posed only to respondents after I had spent quite some time in the field. I was using a grounded-theory approach that allows the respondent to decide what is important to analyze, and it took several interviews before it was clear to me that racial adaptation was as important to them as other mobility-related topics, such as jobs and housing. After that realization I asked respondents directly about how race had made an impact on their migration experiences—but only if the respondent had not brought up the issue by the interview's end. Using this approach, I found that many of the Londoners had to be directly asked about their experiences with racism or their adaption to a racial regime different than the one with which they had grown up. And even when asked, the Londoners were less forthcoming, and less verbose, than the New Yorkers in answering the questions.

3. See References for complete bibliographic information on sources cited in this passage.

4. Massey and Denton (1993) suggest that white-occupied social space is becoming less and less visible to those who live in predominately black and poor urban ghettos, while the social space occupied by blacks is harder for whites to see and understand. Residential segregation ensures that blacks and whites live very different lives of affluence and poverty, affecting both the culture and socioeconomic factors that impact the quality of life for both groups.

5. Races are constructed by the dominant culture, made into categories that have social, political, and economic significance for the persons within them, and assigned to persons according to phenotype (among other things). Ethnicity is a separate social space: ethnic groups are self-identified, and members of ethnic groups are said to be so because of their culture and ancestry. Where ethnicity and race are related, it is in the sense that certain ethnicities are associated with particular racial groups. For example, when Americans conjure up an image of a German, a particular phenotype is called to mind. Persons of black phenotype born in Germany are not immediately thought of as German. I have heard such persons described in the United States as

Afro-Germans. Other national groups are similarly thought to indicate prevailing phenotypes. It is in this way that ethnicity and race can be said to be related. (See Bashi and McDaniel, 1997.) Ethnicity is also related to racial assignment in the sense that ethnic identities can emerge from and be shaped by the racial classification assigned to a given ethnic group (Brodkin, 1998).

6. The settlement of the black community of Britain is believed to have begun with the 1948 arrival of the ship *Empire Windrush*, described in Chapter Two. Thus the so-called Black British are said to comprise the black transplants of former British colonies in the Caribbean and Africa and their descendants. What adds to the confusion about who the Black British are is that some also use the term to include nationals of former British colonies in Asia and their descendants. (For an example from the British Broadcasting Corporation, see http://news.bbc.co.uk/1/hi/uk/112688.stm, a Web page presenting historical information that relies both on presumptions about blackness among those from the Indian subcontinent and on the historical importance of the *Windrush*.) The Black British are assumed, then, to be a relatively recent immigrant group that, along with their British-born descendants, have brought with them Britain's "race problem." To be sure, half of the British population believes that Britain is a racist society, while 44 percent believe that immigration has damaged Britain over the last fifty years (BBC, 2004; see also Paul, 1997. For evidence that points to a contrary understanding of the black presence in Britain, see http://www.blackpresence.co.uk).

7. These responses are not mutually exclusive. That is, someone may ignore direct verbal or other types of racist attack when they experience them and try to avoid them otherwise.

8. This contradicts Foner's (1985) suggestion that West Indian immigrants can tolerate racism in New York more easily than in London, since the native-born African American population in the United States acts as a social buffer between the West Indian immigrant and the white population. By contrast, in Britain, where West Indian immigrants are the first resident minority population, immigrants are directly targeted for racist acts and their presence is seen as the root of many social ills.

9. "According to [Oscar] Lewis [who coined the term in a 1959 study of poor families in rural Mexico], the poor, by virtue of their exclusion from the mainstream of the societies in which they live, develop a way of life all their own, one that is qualitatively different from that of the middle-class societies in which they live. Like all cultures, the culture of poverty is a 'design for living' that is adapted to the existential circumstances of the poor. The pressure of coping with everyday survival leads to a present-time orientation; the lack of opportunity, to low aspirations; exclusion from the political process, to feelings of powerlessness and fatalism; disparagement of the poor on the part of the society at large, to feelings of inferiority; the inability of men to provide adequately for their families, to mother-centered households; unrelenting

poverty, to passivity and a sense of resignation. Thus, for Lewis the culture of poverty comes into existence as a reaction and adaptation to conditions of poverty. [But h]ere Lewis makes a theoretical leap. Once a culture of poverty is formed, he argues, it assumes a "life of its own" and is passed on from parents to children through ordinary channels of cultural transmission" (Steinberg 1989, p. 107).

10. Respondents did express sentiments that can be read as sympathetic with African Americans. Statements along these lines indicated they believed that living under racism like this from birth would cause one to become discouraged. Other comments suggested they understood that the African American experience was different, and worse, than their own. Their feelings about African Americans and what they see as the African American experience, however, are not directly addressed in this book.

11. Thus, when Mary Waters (1996) tallies the number of young West Indians who call themselves black and those who call themselves West Indian, she misunderstands that, for young black immigrants and especially for the native-born black children of immigrants, no choice exists between ethnicity and race (Bashi, 1998b). When deciding "Who is black?" (Davis, 1991), most Americans don't ask about ancestry; when one looks black, one is black, according to the rule of hypodescent that guides most Americans' thinking about race in a system for which the dividing line between black and white is most salient. Likely markers of difference (such as accents) that might give pause to one who rushes to apply the one-drop rule (defining as black anyone with any drop of "black blood" or black ancestry, no matter how far back in one's heritage, and equating blackness with being African American) are absent from the native-born children of black Caribbean immigrants. Thus, while the children themselves may claim a foreign ethnicity, claims from persons with no obvious foreign markers are likely to be ignored. This ability to ignore ethnic difference certainly affects the outlooks that youths of the second generation have on their prospects in the Americas, and these differences are evident between the first and second generations (Bashi Bobb and Clarke, 2001).

Chapter Eight

1. The overwhelmingly British Protestant colonial settlers dominated with their politics and culture, expecting all immigrants to North America to adapt. Outsiders were considered inferior (at least initially); see Steinberg, 1989, and Waters, 1990.

2. I do not have the data to report on the ways that all the gatekeepers who interact with these Caribbean networks read their ethnicity, and research on gatekeeper attitudes is not plentiful, with the exception of information on the labor market. Waldinger and Lichter, 2003, suggest that bosses report preferences for workers they believe are suitable for subordination; it is a matter of "who is the best underling? A group's perceived capacity for subordination may well preclude its fitness as a source

of colleagues, neighbors, friends, and spouses—but be no issue when deciding which groups of workers get added to the payroll" (p. 144). They argue also that reliance upon networks is not the same as having prejudices against persons not so connected. White employers in the low-skilled labor market, though, do hire those they believe are different from themselves, and have shown that they "were reluctant to take on those workers who were least removed from their own status," that is, those racialized as white or those with whom they shared class standing (Waldinger and Lichter, 2003, p. 156). In fact, being an immigrant, for those employers, was a plus; immigrant "otherness" was a positive signal for employers. (But feeling positively about them as workers did not translate into feeling positively about them as people, and employers had clear and elaborate ideas about the existence of a hierarchy of races when considering their workforce. They were not able to distinguish among ethnicities with the group called Hispanics, which they seemed to treat as a racialized cluster of nationalities. Moreover, stereotypical racial ideas were held even when employers personally knew people of other racial groups who did not fit them. But even a positive valuation of an ethnoracial group as workers did not translate into feeling positively about them as *people*. And in the current period, African Americans (arguably at the bottom of the racial hierarchy) are disliked both as workers and as people.

In the site Waters (1999) studied there was an official rule against hiring relatives, but that rule was habitually broken and reliance on kin networks was so prevalent that the company had not in nine years put an ad in the paper to advertise vacancies. Recommendations were routinely accepted under well-known circumstances. "Each worker is allowed to recommend someone for a position. If the new person does not work out, then that person cannot recommend any more friends or relatives. If the new person works out well, then not only can the original person recommend another prospect, but the new hire can also" (Waters, 1999, p. 106). Managers looked for flexibility (a willingness to do anything), no complaints (about wages or dead-end jobs), and loyalty (for jobs that should not demand it, according to Waters, and this was even more important than job experience). These employers reported clear preferences for immigrants over Americans. White employers use culture to explain the behavior of both black immigrant and black American groups: *ghetto blacks* are characterized by the desire for more money, laziness, and preferences for welfare, but they are all the employers claim to see when looking at black Americans; West Indians are perceived to work harder, get into less trouble, and be less materialistic.

3. See Portes and Sensenbrenner (1993). Waldinger and Lichter (2003, pp. 101–2) suggest that these authors were the first to develop these ideas.

4. Because hub-and-spoke networks are surmised to restrict access to the destination, they likely operate differently from immigrant networks with less restrictive access. In Mexican migration (as in other Central American streams where migrants can literally walk across borders to desirable destinations), many potential newcomers

can pay for the services of a *coyote*, who can help them get across the border. Moreover, seasonal jobs are not controlled by hubs as much as they are controlled by growers. When one has options for border crossing and employment, there is little need to wait for one's family to assist with a move, little need to listen to family members' advice. Sarah Mahler's (1995) work about Salvadorans and Peruvians in Long Island is telling: many potential migrants failed to heed veterans' warnings about their difficult lives in New York; they came anyway, only to find themselves in postmigration lives marked by harsh living conditions and co-ethnics who took advantage of them.

5. This was true even when the person with migration knowledge was the potential migrant himself. That is, if the Mexican resident in question had been to the United States on a previous trip and therefore had information that would help in subsequent trips, the probability of his taking future trips increased.

6. Mahler's account of the Salvadoran culture of reciprocity, however, differs in that Salvadorans' migration experiences were marred by co-ethnic exploitation, which seems to have spread along network ties.

7. The Haitians argued that it was advantageous for women to migrate first and make decisions about the timing and manner in which the migration of subsequent network members would take place, because women qualify for service-sector jobs (such as positions as domestics), which are more likely to escape INS scrutiny, and they are as able as men to transfer residency if they have it already (Fjellman and Gladwin, 1985, p. 307).

8. The authors indicate that the number of family reunification applications has never approached the limit for family entries because visas were capped at the national quota levels; thus the need for family visas has far exceeded the number allowed (Jasso and Rosenzweig, 1990, p. 189).

References

Almaguer, Tomás. 1994. *Racial Fault Lines: The Historical Origins of White Supremacy in California*. Berkeley and Los Angeles: University of California Press.

Amin, Samir. 1977. *Imperialism and Unequal Development*. New York: Monthly Review.

———. 1973. *Neo-Colonialism in West Africa*. New York: Monthly Review.

Appiah, Kwame A. 1989. "The Conservation of 'Race.'" *Black American Literature Forum*. 23(1, Spring):37–60.

Arango, Joaquín. 2000. "Explaining Migration: A Critical View." *International Social Science Journal*. 52(165, September):283–96.

Avery, Donald H. 1995. *Reluctant Host: Canada's Response to Immigrant Workers, 1896–1994*. Toronto: McClelland and Stewart.

Basch, Linda. 1987. "The Vincentians and Grenadians: The Role of Voluntary Associations in Immigrant Adaptation to New York City." *New Immigrants in New York*, Nancy Foner, editor. Pp. 159–93. New York: Columbia University Press.

Basch, Linda, Nina Glick Schiller, and Cristina Szanton Blanc. 1994. *Nations Unbound: Transnational Projects, Postcolonial Predicaments, and Deterritorialized Nation States*. New York: Gordon and Breach.

Bascom, Wilbert O. 1991. "Remittance Inflows and Economic Development in Selected Anglophone Caribbean Countries." *Migration, Remittances, and Small Business Development: Mexico and Caribbean Basin Countries*, Sergio Díaz-Briquets and Sidney Weintraub, editors. Pp. 71–99. Boulder, CO: Westview Press.

Bashi, Vilna. 2004. "Globalized Anti-Blackness: Transnationalizing Western Immigration Law, Policy, and Practice." *Ethnic and Racial Studies*. 27(4, July):584–606.

———. 1998. "Racial Categories Matter Because Racial Hierarchies Matter: A Commentary." *Ethnic and Racial Studies*. 21(5 Sept.):959–68.

Bashi, Vilna, and Antonio McDaniel. 1997. "A Theory of Immigration and Racial Stratification." *Journal of Black Studies*. 27(5):668–82.

Bashi, Vilna, Antonio McDaniel, and Eliya Zulu. 1995. "Child Fosterage in the African Diaspora: A Theory for Cross-National Comparison." *Meetings of the Population Association of America, Panel on Fertility and Fosterage in Africa and the Diaspora*. April 6–8, 1995, San Francisco, CA.

Bashi Bobb, Vilna. 2001. "Neither Ignorance Nor Bliss: Race, Racism, and the West Indian Immigrant Experience." *Migration, Transnationalism, and Race in a Changing New York*, Hector R. Cordero-Guzman, Ramon Grosfoguel, and Robert Smith, editors. Pp. 212–38. Philadelphia: Temple University Press.

Bashi Bobb, Vilna, and Averil Clarke. 2001. *Experiencing Success: Structuring the Perception of Opportunities for West Indians*, Nancy Foner, editor. Berkeley: University of California Press.

Besley, Timothy. 1995. "Nonmarket Insitutions for Credit and Risk-Sharing in Low Income Countries." *Journal of Economic Perspectives*. 9(3, Summer):115–27.

Betancur, John J. 1996. "The Settlement Experience of Latinos in Chicago: Segregation, Speculation, and the Ecology Model." *Social Forces*. 74(4):1299–324.

Board of Trade. 1940. *Statistical Abstract for the United Kingdom*. No. 83. London: His Majesty's Stationery Office.

———. 1939. *Statistical Abstract for the United Kingdom*. No. 82. London: His Majesty's Stationery Office.

———. 1928. *Statistical Abstract for the United Kingdom*. No. 71. London: His Majesty's Stationery Office.

———. 1915. *Statistical Abstract for the United Kingdom*. No. 62. London: His Majesty's Stationery Office.

———. 1907. *Statistical Abstract for the United Kingdom*. No. 54. London: His Majesty's Stationery Office.

Böcker, Anita. 1994. "Chain Migration over Legally Closed Borders: Settled Immigrants as Bridgeheads and Gatekeepers." *The Netherlands' Journal of Social Sciences*. 20(December 2):87–106.

Bonacich, Edna. 1972. "A Theory of Ethnic Antagonism: The Split Labor Market." *American Sociological Review*. 37:547–59.

Bonilla-Silva, Eduardo. 2003. *Racism Without Racists: Color-Blind Racism and the Persistence of Racial Inequality in the United States*. Lanham, MD: Rowman & Littlefield.

———. 2000. "'This Is a White Country': The Racial Ideology of the Western Nations of the World-System." *Sociological Inquiry*. 70(2, Spring):188–214.

Borjas, George J. 1990. *Friends or Strangers: The Impact of Immigration on the U.S. Economy*. New York: Basic Books.

Boyd, Monica. 1989. "Family and Personal Networks in International Migration: Recent Developments and New Agendas." *International Migration Review*. 23(3, Fall):638–70.

Boyko, John. 1995. *Last Steps to Freedom: The Evolution of Canadian Racism*. Winnipeg, Manitoba: Watson & Dwyer.

Briggs, Vernon M., Jr. 1984. *Immigration Policy and the American Labor Force*. Baltimore and London: Johns Hopkins University Press.

British Broadcasting Corporation. 2002, November 21. "Is Britain a Racist Country?" Available at http://news.bbc.co.uk/1/hi/in_depth/uk/2002/race/1998159.stm. Accessed October 12, 2004.

Brodkin, Karen. 1998. *How Jews Became White Folks: And What That Says About Race in America*. New Brunswick, NJ: Rutgers University Press.

Brooks, Dennis. 1975. *Race and Labour in London Transport*. London and New York: Oxford University Press.

Brown, J. S., et al. 1963. "Kentucky Mountain Migration and the Stem Family: An American Variation on a Theme by LePlay." *Rural Sociology*, 28:48–69.

Bryce-LaPorte, Roy S. 1972. "Black Immigrants: The Experience of Invisibility and Inequality." *Journal of Black Studies*. 3(September):29–56.

Buff, Rachel. 2001. *Immigration and the Political Economy of Home: West Indian Brooklyn and American Indian Minneapolis, 1945–1992*. Berkeley: University of California Press.

Calavita, Kitty. 1994. "U.S. Immigration and Policy Responses: The Limits of Legislation." *Controlling Immigration: A Global Perspective*, Wayne A. Cornelius, Philip L. Martin, and James F. Hollifield, editors. Pp. 55–82. Palo Alto, CA: Stanford University Press.

———. 1984. *U.S. Immigration Law and the Control of Labor: 1820–1924*. London: Academic Press.

California Newsreel. 2003. "The House We Live In," episode 3 of *Race: The Power of an Illusion*, Larry Adelman, executive producer and series creator. http://www.pbs.org/race/000_About/002_04–about-03.htm.

Carnegie, Charles V. 1987. "A Social Psychology of Caribbean Migrations: Strategic Flexibility in the West Indies." *The Caribbean Exodus*, Barry B. Levine, editor. Pp. 32–43. New York: Praeger.

Castles, Stephen. 2000. "International Migration at the Beginning of the Twenty-First Century: Global Trends and Issues." *International Social Science Journal*. 52(165, September):269–81.

Castles, Stephen, and Mark J. Miller. 1993. *The Age of Migration: International Population Movements in the Modern World*. Second edition. New York: Guilford Press.

Central Statistical Office. 1989. *Statistical Abstract for the United Kingdom*. No. 125. London: Her Majesty's Stationery Office.

———. 1975. *Statistical Abstract for the United Kingdom*. No. 112. London: Her Majesty's Stationery Office.

———. 1965. *Statistical Abstract for the United Kingdom*. No. 102. London: Her Majesty's Stationery Office.

———. 1956. *Statistical Abstract for the United Kingdom*. No. 93. London: Her Majesty's Stationery Office.

———. 1952. *Statistical Abstract for the United Kingdom*. No. 89. London: Her Majesty's Stationery Office.

Charles, Camille Z. 2003. "The Dynamics of Racial Residential Segregation." *Annual Review of Sociology*. 29:167–207.

Chase-Dunn, Christopher, and Peter Grimes. 1995. "World-Systems Analysis." *Annual Review of Sociology*. 21:387–417.

Chirot, Daniel, and Thomas D. Hall. 1982. "World-System Theory." *Annual Review of Sociology*. 8:81–106.

Clifford, Elizabeth J. 1997. "Racing the Nation: Immigration Policy, Race, and National Identity in Canada and the United States, 1905–1925." Dissertation. Northwestern University, Evanston, IL.

Colen, Shellee. 1989. "'Just a Little Respect': West Indian Domestic Workers in New York City." *Muchachas No More: Household Workers in Latin America and the Caribbean*, Elsa M. Chaney and Mary G. Castro, editors. Pp. 171–94. Philadelphia: Temple University Press.

Commission for the Study of International Migration and Cooperative Economic Development. 1991. "Immigration and Economic Development." *The Unsettled Relationship: Labor Migration and Economic Development*, D. G. Papademetriou and P. L. Martin, editors. Pp. 221–41. Westport, CT: Greenwood Press.

Conniff, Michael L. 1985. *Black Labor on a White Canal: Panama, 1904–1981*. Pittsburgh, PA: University of Pittsburgh Press.

Cornell, Stephen, and Douglas Hartmann. 1998. *Ethnicity and Race: Making Identities in a Changing World*. Thousand Oaks, CA: Pine Forge Press.

Cose, Ellis. 1995. *The Rage of a Privileged Class*. New York: HarperCollins.

Cross, William E., Jr. 1990. "Race and Ethnicity: Effects on Social Networks." *Extending Families: The Social Networks of Parents and Their Children*, Moncrieff Cochran, Mary Larner, David Riley, Lars Gunnarsson, and Charles R. Henderson, editors. Pp. 67–85. Cambridge, MA: Cambridge University Press.

Crowder, Kyle D. 1999. "Residential Segregation of West Indians in the New York/New Jersey Metropolitan Area: The Roles of Race and Ethnicity." *International Migration Review*. 33(1, Spring):79–113.

Davie, Maurice R. 1936. *World Immigration: With Special Reference to the United States*. New York: Macmillan.

Davis, F. J. 1991. "Who Is Black? One Nation's Definition." *Other Places, Other Definitions*. Pp. 81–122. University Park: Pennsylvania State University Press.

De Albuquerque, Klaus. 1979. "The Future of the Rastafarian Movement." *Caribbean Review*, 8(4):22–25, 44–46.

Dean, Dennis. 1993. "The Conservative Government and the 1961 Commonwealth Immigration Act: The Inside Story." *Race and Class*. 35, 2:57–74.

DeWind, Josh, and Philip Kasinitz. 1997. "Everything Old Is New Again? Processes and Theories of Immigrant Incorporation." *International Migration Review.* 31(4, Winter):1097–111.

Djajić, Slobodan. 1999. "Dynamics of Immigration Control." *Journal of Population Economics.* 12(1):45–61.

Donato, Katharine M., Jorge Durand, and Douglas S. Massey. 1992. "Stemming the Tide? Assessing the Deterrent Effects of the Immigration Reform and Control Act." *Demography.* 29(2, May):139–57.

Espinosa, Kristin. 1997. "Helping Hands: Social Capital and the Undocumented Migration of Mexican Men to the United States." Dissertation. University of Chicago, Department of Sociology.

Evans, Peter. 1979. *Dependent Development: The Alliance of Multinational State and Local Capital in Brazil.* Princeton, NJ: Princeton University Press.

Faist, Thomas. 2000. *The Volume and Dynamics of International Migration and Transnational Social Spaces.* Oxford and New York: Oxford University Press.

Fan, Stephen S.-W. 1997. "Immigration Law and the Promise of Critical Race Theory: Opening the Academy to the Voices of Aliens and Immigrants." *Columbia Law Review.* 97:1202–40.

Fjellman, Stephen M., and Hugh Gladwin. 1985. "Haitian Family Patterns of Migration to South Florida." *Human Organization.* 44(4):301–12.

Fogel, Walter. 1978. *Mexican Illegal Alien Workers in the United States.* Los Angeles: Institute of Industrial Relations, University of California at Los Angeles.

Foner, Nancy. 1998. "West Indian Identity in the Diaspora: Comparative and Historical Perspectives." *Latin American Perspectives.* 25(3, May):173–88.

———. 1985. "Race and Color: Jamaican Migrants in London and New York City." *International Migration Review.* 19(4, Winter):708–27.

———. 1979. "West Indians in New York City and London: A Comparative Analysis." *International Migration Review.* 13(2, Summer):284–97.

Frank, Andre G. 1967. *Capitalism and Underdevelopment in Latin America.* New York: Monthly Review Press.

Freeman, Lin Clarke. 2004. *The Development of Social Network Analysis: A Study in the Sociology of Science.* Vancouver, BC, Canada: Empirical Press.

Garis, Roy L. 1927. *Immigration Restriction: A Study of the Opposition to and Regulation of Immigration into the United States.* New York: Macmillan.

Garrison, Vivian, and Carol I. Weiss. 1979. "Dominican Family Networks and United States Immigration Policy: A Case Study." *International Migration Review.* 13(2, Summer):264–83.

Gilbertson, Greta, and Douglas T. Gurak. 1992. "Household Transitions in the Migrations of Dominicans and Colombians to New York." *International Migration Review.* 26(1, Spring):22–45.

Glasser, Ira, executive director, ACLU. 1996. "Scapegoating Immigrants—Again." Available at http://www.aclu.org/library/vision17.html. Accessed July 25, 2002.

Glazer, Nathan, and Daniel P. Moynihan. 1970. *Beyond the Melting Pot: The Negroes, Puerto Ricans, Jews, Italians, and Irish of New York City.* Second edition. Cambridge, MA: MIT Press.

Glenn, Evelyn N. 2002. *Unequal Freedom: How Race and Gender Shaped American Citizenship and Labor.* Cambridge, MA, and London: Harvard University Press.

Glick, Jennifer E. 1999. "Economic Support from and to Extended Kin: A Comparison of Mexican Americans and Mexican Immigrants." *International Migration Review.* 33(3):745–65.

Glick-Schiller, Nina, Linda Basch, and Christina Blanc-Szanton. 1992. "Transnationalism: A New Analytic Framework for Understanding Migration." *Towards a Transnational Perspective on Migration; Annals of the New York Academy of Sciences,* vol. 645. Pp. 2–24. New York: New York Academy of Sciences.

Gopaul-McNicol, Sharon-Ann. 1993. *Working with West Indian Families.* New York: Guilford Press.

Gordon, Monica H. 1983. "The Selection of Migrant Categories from the Caribbean to the United States: The Jamaican Experience." Occasional Paper no. 37. New York: New York University, Center for Latin American and Caribbean Studies.

Gould, Stephen J. 1994. "The Geometer of Race." *Discover Magazine.* 15(11):65–69.

Granovetter, Mark. 1995. *Getting a Job: A Study of Contacts and Careers.* Second edition. Chicago: University of Chicago Press.

———. 1973. "The Strength of Weak Ties." *American Journal of Sociology.* 78(6):1360–1380.

Grosfoguel, Ramon. 1997. "Migration and Geopolitics in the Greater Antilles." *International Migration Review.* 20(1, Winter):115–45.

Gurak, Douglas T., and Fe Caces. 1992. "Migration Networks and the Shaping of Migration Systems." *International Migration Systems: A Global Approach,* Mary M. Kritz, Lin L. Lim, and Hania Zlotnik, editors. Pp. 150–176. Oxford: Clarendon Press.

Hagan, Jacquelíne M. 1998. "Social Networks, Gender, and Immigrant Incorporation: Resources and Constraints." *American Sociological Review.* 63(1, February):55–67.

———. 1994. *Deciding to Be Legal: A Maya Community in Houston.* Philadelphia: Temple University Press.

Hall, Stuart. 1996. *Race, the Floating Signifier.* Produced by Sut Jhally, directed by Sut Jhally. Northhampton, MA: Media Education Foundation. 63 minutes, 1 videocassette.

Hamilton, Nora, and Norma S. Chinchilla. 1996. "Global Economic Restructuring and International Migration: Some Observations Based on the Mexican and Central American Experience." *International Migration.* 34(2):195–232.

Hart, Richard. 1998. *From Occupation to Independence: A Short History of the People of the English-Speaking Caribbean Region.* Barbados: Canoe Press.

Hawkins, Freda. 1989. *Critical Years in Immigration: Canada and Australia Compared.* Montreal: McGill-Queen's University Press.

Hendriques, Fernando. 1953. *Family and Color in Jamaica.* London: Eyre & Spottiswoode.

Henke, Holger. 2001. *The West Indian Americans.* New Americans Series, Ronald H. Bayor, series editor. Westport, CT, and London: Greenwood Press.

Henry, Frances. 1987. "Caribbean Migration to Canada: Prejudice and Opportunity." *The Caribbean Exodus,* Barry B. Levine, editor. Pp. 214–22. New York: Praeger.

Higham, John. 1955. *Strangers in the Land: Patterns of American Nativism, 1860–1925.* Rutgers, NJ: Rutgers University Press.

Hintzen, Percy C. 2001. *West Indian in the West: Self-Representations in an Immigrant Community.* New York: New York University Press.

Ho, Christine. 1993. "The Internationalization of Kinship and the Feminization of Caribbean Migration: The Case of Afro-Trinidadian Immigrants in Los Angeles." *Human Organization.* 52(1):32–40.

———. 1991. *Salt-Water Trinnies: Afro-Trinidadian Immigrant Networks and Non-Assimilation in Los Angeles.* New York: AMS Press.

Hondagneu-Sotelo, Pierrette. 2001. *Domestica: Immigrant Workers Cleaning and Caring in the Shadows of Affluence.* Berkeley: University of California Press.

———. 1994a. *Gendered Transitions: Mexican Experiences of Immigration.* Berkeley and Los Angeles: University of California Press.

———. 1994b. "Regulating the Unregulated? Domestic Workers' Social Networks." *Social Problems.* 41(1, February):50–64.

Hutchinson, E. P. 1981. *Legislative History of American Immigration Policy, 1798–1965.* Philadelphia: University of Pennsylvania Press.

Idea Works, Inc., and Board of Curators at the University of Missouri. 1995. "A Historical Look at U.S. Immigration Policy." Available at http://www.missouri.edu/socbrent/immigr.htm. Accessed July 25, 2002.

Ignatiev, Noel. 1995. *How the Irish Became White.* New York and London: Routledge.

Jaffe, Erwin A. 1961. "Passage of the McCarran-Walter Act: The Reiteration of American Immigration Policy." New Brunswick, NJ: State University of New Jersey.

Jakubowski, Lisa Marie. 1997. *Immigration and the Legalization of Racism.* Black Point, Nova Scotia: Fernwood Publishing.

Jasso, Guillermina, and Mark R. Rosenzweig. 1990. *The New Chosen People: Immigrants in the United States.* New York: Russell Sage Foundation.

———. 1989. "Sponsors, Sponsorship Rates and the Immigration Multiplier." *International Migration Review.* 23(4):856–88.

Jaynes, Gerald D. 2000. "Introduction: Immigration and the American Dream." *Immigration and Race: New Challenges for American Democracy,* Gerald D. Jaynes, editor. Pp. 1–43. New Haven, CT, and London: Yale University Press.

Jordan, Winthrop. 1968. *White over Black: American Attitudes Toward the Negro, 1550–1812*. Chapel Hill: University of North Carolina Press.

Kalmijn, Matthijs. 1996. "The Socioeconomic Assimilation of Caribbean American Blacks." *Social Forces*. 74(3, March):911–30.

Kasinitz, Philip. 1992. *Caribbean New York: Black Immigrants and the Politics of Race*. Ithaca, NY, and London: Cornell University Press.

Kasinitz, Philip, and Jan Rosenberg. 1996. "Missing the Connection: Social Isolation and Employment on the Brooklyn Waterfront." *Social Problems*. 43(2, May):180–196.

Keely, Charles B. 1979. "The United States of America." *The Politics of Migration Policies: The First World in the 1970s*, edited by Daniel Kubat et al. Pp. 60–84. New York: Center for Migration Studies.

Keith, Verna M., and Cedric Herring. 1991. "Skin Tone and Stratification in the Black Community." *American Journal of Sociology*. 97(3):760–779.

Kelly, Maria Patricia Fernández. 1995. "Social and Cultural Capital in the Urban Ghetto: Implications for the Economic Sociology of Immigration." *The Economic Sociology of Immigration: Essays on Networks, Ethnicity, and Entrepreneurship*, Alejandro Portes, editor. New York: Russell Sage Foundation.

Kerr, M. 1952. *Personality and Conflict in Jamaica*. Liverpool, UK: University Press.

Kibria, Nazli. 1994. "Household Structure and Family Ideologies: The Dynamics of Immigrant Economic Adaptation Among Vietnamese Refugees." *Social Problems*. 41(1, February):81–96.

King, James C. 1981. *The Biology of Race*. Berkeley: University of California Press.

Kirschenman, Joleen, and Kathryn M. Neckerman. 1991. "We'd Love to Hire Them, But . . .": The Meaning of Race for Employers." *The Urban Underclass*, Christopher Jencks and Paul E. Peterson, editors. Pp. 203–32. Washington, DC: Brookings Institution.

Knight, Franklin W., and Colin A. Palmer. 1989. "The Caribbean: A Regional Overview." *The Modern Caribbean*, Franklin W. Knight and Colin A. Palmer, editors. Chapel Hill: University of North Carolina Press.

Koser, Khalid. 1997. "Social Networks and the Asylum Cycle: The Case of Iranians in the Netherlands." *International Migration Review*. 31(3):591–612.

Kritz, Mary M., Lin L. Lim, and Hania Zlotnik, editors. 1992. *International Migration Systems: A Global Approach*. Oxford: Clarendon Press.

Kuo, Wen H., and Yung-Mei Tsai. 1986. "Social Networking, Hardiness and Immigrants' Mental Health." *Journal of Social Health and Social Behavior*. 27(2, June):133–49.

Lee, Erika. 2002. "The Chinese Exclusion Example: Race, Immigration, and American Gatekeeping, 1882–1924." *Journal of American Ethnic History*, 21(3):36–63.

Levitt, Peggy. 2001. *The Transnational Villagers*. Berkeley and Los Angeles: University of California Press.

———. 1999. "Social Remittances: A Local-Level, Migration-Driven Form of Cultural Diffusion." *International Migration Review*. 32(124):926–49.

Lewis, Hope. 1997. *"Lionheart Gals Facing the Dragon: The Human Rights of Inter/National Black Women in the United States."* 76 *Or.L.Rev.* 567, 570.

Light, Ivan, and Steven J. Gold. 2000. *Ethnic Economies.* San Diego, CA: Academic Press.

Lipsitz, George. 1998. *The Possessive Investment in Whiteness: How White People Profit from Identity Politics.* Philadelphia: Temple University Press.

Lofland, John, and Lyn H. Lofland. 1995. *Analyzing Social Settings: A Guide to Qualitative Observation and Analysis.* Belmont, CA: Wadsworth.

López, Ian F. H. 1996. *White by Law: The Legal Construction of Race.* New York and London: New York University Press.

MacDonald, J., and L. MacDonald. 1964. "Chain migration, ethnic neighborhood formation and social networks." *Milbank Memorial Fund Quarterly,* 17(1):82–97.

MacMaster, Neil. 2001. *Racism in Europe: 1870–2000.* New York: Palgrave Macmillan.

Mahler, Sarah J. 1995. *American Dreaming: Immigrant Life on the Margins.* Princeton, NJ: Princeton University Press.

Major, R. H., editor. 1870. *Selected Letters of Columbus.* London: Hakluyt Society.

Marks, Carole. 1983. "Lines of Communication, Recruitment Mechanisms, and the Great Migration of 1916–1918." *Social Problems.* 31(1):73–83.

Marshall, Dawn. 1987. "A History of West Indian Migrations: Overseas Opportunities and 'Safety-Valve' Policies." *The Caribbean Exodus,* Barry B. Levine, editor. Pp. 15–31. New York: Praeger.

Marx, Anthony W. 1998. *Making Race and Nation: A Comparison of the United States, South Africa, and Brazil.* Cambridge, UK: Cambridge University Press.

Massey, Douglas S. 1998. "March of Folly: U.S. Immigration Policy After NAFTA." *The American Prospect.* 37(March/April):22–33.

———. 1995. "The New Immigration and Ethnicity in the United States." *Population and Development Review.* 21(3, September):631–52.

———. 1990a. "The Social and Economic Origins of Immigration." *Annals of the American Academy of Political and Social Science.* 510(July):60–72.

———. 1990b. "Social Structure, Household Strategies, and the Cumulative Causation of Migration." *Population Index.* 56(1, Spring):3–26.

———. 1988. "Economic Development and International Migration in Comparative Perspective." *Population and Development Review.* 14(3, September):383–413.

———. 1986. "The Settlement Process Among Mexican Migrants to the United States." *American Sociological Review.* 51(5, October):670–684.

Massey, Douglas S., Rafael Alarcón, Jorge Durand, and Humberto González. 1987. *Return to Aztlán: The Social Process of International Migration from Western Mexico.* Berkeley: University of California Press.

Massey, Douglas S., Joaquin Arango, Graeme Hugo, Ali Kouaouci, Adela Pellegrino, and J. E. Taylor. 1998. *Worlds in Motion: Understanding International Migration at the End of the Millennium.* Oxford, UK: Clarendon Press.

Massey, Douglas S., Joaquín Arango, Graeme Hugo, Ali Kouaouci, Adela Pellegrino, and J. E. Taylor. 1993. "Theories of International Migration: A Review and Appraisal." *Population and Development Review.* 19(3, September):431–66.

Massey, Douglas S., and Nancy A. Denton. 1993. *American Apartheid: Segregation and the Making of the Underclass.* Cambridge, MA, and London: Harvard University Press.

———. 1984. "Racial Identity Among Caribbean Hispanics: The Effect of Double Minority Status on Residential Segregation." *American Sociological Review.* 54(5, October):790–808.

Massey, Douglas S., and Kristin E. Espinosa. 1997. "What's Driving Mexico-U.S. Migration? A Theoretical, Empirical, and Policy Analysis." *American Journal of Sociology.* 102(4, January).

McMichael, Philip. 2000. *Development and Social Change: A Global Perspective.* Second edition. Thousand Oaks, CA: Pine Forge Press.

Menjívar, Cecilia. 2000. *Fragmented Ties: Salvadoran Immigrant Networks in America.* Berkeley and Los Angeles: University of California Press.

———. 1997. "Immigrant Kinship Networks and the Impact of the Receiving Context: Salvadorans in San Francisco in the Early 1990s." *Social Problems.* 44(1):104–123.

Miles, Robert. 1993. *Racism After "Race Relations."* London: Routledge.

———. 1989. *Racism.* London and New York: Routledge.

Miller, E. L. 1967. "A Study of Body Image, Its Relationship to Self-Concept, Anxiety and Certain Social and Physical Variables in a Selected Group of Jamaican Adolescents." Unpublished master's thesis, University of the West Indies, Kingston, Jamaica.

Mills, Charles W. 1999. *The Racial Contract.* Ithaca, NY: Cornell University Press.

Montgomery, James D. 1994. "Weak Ties, Employment, and Inequality: An Equilibrium Analysis." *American Journal of Sociology.* 99(5, March):1212–36.

Moss, Philip, and Chris Tilly. 2001. *Stories Employers Tell: Race, Skill, and Hiring in America.* New York: Russell Sage Foundation.

Munck, Ronaldo. 1988. *The New International Labour Studies: An Introduction.* London: Zed Books.

Murray, John A., editor. 1991. *The Islands and the Sea: Five Centuries of Nature Writing from the Caribbean.* New York: Oxford.

National Industrial Conference Board. 1923. *The Immigration Problem in the United States,* Research Report no. 58. New York: National Industrial Conference Board.

National Statistics. 2001. *Annual Abstract of Statistics.* No. 137. London: His Majesty's Stationery Office.

Neckerman, Kathryn M., and Joleen Kirschenman. 1991. "Hiring Strategies, Racial Bias, and Inner-City Workers." *Social Problems.* 38(4, November):433–47.

Nelson, Camille A. 2003. "Carriers of Globalization: Loss of Home and Self Within the African Diaspora." *Florida Law Review,* 55:539–581.

Omi, Michael, and Howard Winant. 1994 [1989]. *Racial Formation in the United States:*

From the 1960s to the 1990s. Second edition. New York and London: Routledge.

Palloni, Alberto, Douglas S. Massey, Miguel Ceballos, Kristin Espinosa, and Michael Spittel. 2001. "Social Capital and International Migration: A Test Using Information on Family Networks." *American Journal of Sociology*. 106(5, March):1262–98.

Parry, J. H., Philip Sherlock, and Anthony Maingot. 1987. *A Short History of the West Indies*. Fourth edition. New York: St. Martin's Press.

Pastor, Robert A. 1985. "Introduction: The Policy Challenge." *Migration and Development in the Caribbean: The Unexplored Connection*, R. A. Pastor, editor. Pp. 1–39 Boulder, CO: Westview Press.

Paul, Kathleen. 1997. *Whitewashing Britain: Race and Citizenship in the Postwar Era*. Ithaca, NY, and London: Cornell University Press.

Phillips, A. S. 1976. *Adolescence in Jamaica*. Kingston: Jamaica Publishing House.

Piore, Michael J. 1979. *Birds of Passage: Migrant Labor in Industrial Societies*. Cambridge, UK: Cambridge University Press.

Plaza, Dwaine. 1998. "Strategies and Strategizing: The Struggle for Upward Mobility Among University-Educated Black Caribbean-Born Men in Canada." *Caribbean Migration: Globalised Identities*, Mary Chamberlain, editor. Pp. 248–63. London: Routledge.

Portes, Alejandro. 1998. "Social Capital: Its Origins and Applications in Modern Sociology." *Annual Review of Sociology*. 24:1–24.

———. 1995a. "Children of Immigrants: Segmented Assimilation and Its Determinants." *The Economic Sociology of Immigration*, Alejandro Portes, editor. Pp. 248–80. New York: Russell Sage Foundation.

———. 1995b. "Economic Sociology and the Sociology of Immigration: A Conceptual Overview." *The Economic Sociology of Immigration*, Alejandro Portes, editor. Pp. 1–41. New York: Russell Sage Foundation.

Portes, Alejandro, and Robert L. Bach. 1985. *Latin Journey: Cuban and Mexican Immigrants in the Unites States*. Berkeley: University of California Press.

Portes, Alejandro, and Ruben G. Rumbaut. 2001. *Legacies: The Story of the Immigrant Second Generation*. Berkeley and Los Angeles: University of California Press.

———. 1990. *Immigrant America: A Portrait*. Berkeley: University of California Press.

Portes, Alejandro, and Julia Sensenbrenner. 1993. "Embeddedness and Immigration: Notes on the Social Determinants of Economic Action." *American Journal of Sociology*. 98(May 6):1320–1350.

Pragg, Sam. 1999. "Children Hardest Hit in Migration Wave." Internet Newsgroup reg. carib. Posted by InterPress Third World News Agency, January 2, 1999.

Ramdin, Ron. 1999. *Reimagining Britain: Five Hundred Years of Black and Asian History*. London and Sterling, VA: Pluto Press.

Reid, Ira D. A. 1970 [1939]. *The Negro Immigrant: His Background Characteristics and Social Adjustment, 1899–1939*. New York: AMS Press.

Salyer, Lucy E. 1995. *Laws Harsh as Tigers: Chinese Immigrants and the Shaping of Modern Immigration Law.* Chapel Hill and London: University of North Carolina Press.

———. 1988. *The Mobility of Labor and Capital: A Study in International Investment and Labor Flow.* Cambridge, UK, and New York: Cambridge University Press.

Satzewich, Vic. 1991. *Racism and the Incorporation of Foreign Labour: Farm Labour Migration to Canada Since 1945.* London: Routledge.

Scott, John. 1991. *Social Network Analysis: A Handbook.* London and Newbury Park, CA: Sage.

Scott-Joynt, Jeremy. 2004. "The Remittance Lifeline." BBC News Online, February 18. http://news.bbc.co.uk/go/pr/fr/-/2/hi/business/3516390.stm. Accessed February 1, 2006.

Simmons, Alan B., and Jean P. Guengant. 1992. "Caribbean Exodus and the World System." *International Migration Systems: A Global Approach,* Mary M. Kritz, Lin L. Lim, and Hania Zlotnik, editors. Pp. 96–114. Oxford: Clarendon Press.

Sloan, Irving J. 1987. *Law of Immigration and Entry to the United States of America.* Fourth edition. London: Oceana Publications.

Smedley, Audrey. 1993. *Race in North America: Origin and Evolution of a Worldview.* Boulder, CO: Westview Press.

Smith, Geri. 2005. "Channeling the Remittance Flood." Latin Beat, *BusinessWeek Online,* December 28, 2005. Available at http://www.businessweek.com/bwdaily/dnflash/dec2005/nf20051228_4272.htm?campaign. Accessed February 1, 2006.

Smith, Robert. 1993. *Los Ausentes Siempre Presentes: The Imagining, Making and Politics of a Transnational Community Between New York City and Ticuani, Puebla.* New York: Institute of Latin American and Iberian Studies, Columbia University.

Solomos, John. 1993. *Race and Racism in Britain.* Second edition. New York: St. Martin's Press.

Solomos, John, and Les Back. 1996. "Racism and Society." *Races, Racism and Popular Culture.* Pp. 156–201. New York: St. Martin's Press.

Sowell, Thomas. 1978. "Three Black Histories." *Essays and Data on American Ethnic Groups,* Thomas Sowell, editor. Pp. 7–64. Washington, DC: Urban Institute.

Stack, Carol B. 1974. *All Our Kin: Strategies for Survival in a Black Community.* New York: Harper Torchbooks.

Stark, Oded. 1991. *The Migration of Labor.* Cambridge, MA, and Oxford, UK: Blackwell.

Statistics Canada. 1983. *Historical Statistics of Canada.* Ottawa: Statistics Canada and Social Science Federation of Canada.

Statistics Canada. 1965. *Historical Statistics of Canada.* Cambridge: University Press; Toronto: MacMillan.

Statistics Canada. No date. Census *Nation* tables. Accessed July 2001 at CANSIM, http://www.statcan.ca/english/ads/cansimII/index.htm.

Steinberg, Stephen. 1991. "Occupational Apartheid." *Nation.* 253(20, December 9):744–47.

―――. 1989. *The Ethnic Myth: Race, Ethnicity, and Class in America.* Boston: Beacon Press.

Stiell, Bernadette, and Kim England. 1999. "Jamaican Domestics, Filipina Housekeepers and English Nannies: Representations of Toronto's Foreign Domestic Workers." *Gender, Migration and Domestic Service,* Janet Momsen, editor. Pp. 44–62. London and New York: Routledge.

Stinchcombe, Arthur L. 1995. *Sugar Island Slavery in the Age of Enlightenment: The Political Economy of the Caribbean World.* Princeton, NJ: Princeton University Press.

Sullivan, Mercer L. 1989. *"Getting Paid": Youth Crime and Work in the Inner City.* Ithaca, NY, and London: Cornell University Press.

Sutton, Constance, and Susan Makiesky. 1975. "Migration and West Indian Racial and Ethnic Consciousness." *Migration and Development: Implications for Ethnic Identity and Political Conflict,* Helen I. Safa and B. M. DuToit, editors. Pp. 113–44. The Hague, Netherlands: Mouton.

Thomas-Hope, Elizabeth M. 1986. "Caribbean Diaspora, the Inheritance of Slavery: Migration from the Commonwealth Caribbean." *The Caribbean in Europe: Aspects of the West Indian Experience in Britain, France and the Netherlands,* Colin Brock, editor. Pp. 15–35. London: Frank Cass.

Thomas, William I., and Florian Znaniecki. 1996. *The Polish Peasant in Europe and America: A Classic Work in Immigration History,* Eli Zaretsky, editor. Urbana and Chicago: University of Illinois Press.

Tienda, Marta. 1980. "Familism and Structural Assimilation of Mexican Immigrants in the United States." *International Migration Review.* 14 (3, Autumn), pp. 383–408.

Tilly, Charles. 1998. *Durable Inequality.* Berkeley and Los Angeles: University of California Press.

Tilly, Charles, and C. H. Brown. 1967. "On Uprooting, Kinship, and the Auspices of Migration." *International Journal of Comparative Sociology.* 8(2, September):139–64.

Todaro, Michael P. 1976. *Internal Migration in Developing Countries: A Review of Theory, Evidence, Methodology and Research Priorities.* Geneva, Switzerland: International Labour Office.

―――. 1969. "A Model of Labor Migration and Urban Unemployment in Less Developed Countries." *American Economic Review.* 59(March):138–48.

United Nations. No date. "Growth in United Nations Membership, 1945–2003." Available at http://www.un.org/Overview/growth.htm#60. Accessed March 17, 2004.

U.S. Bureau of the Census. 1994. *Statistical Abstract of the United States: 1994.* 114th Edition. Washington, DC: U.S. Government Printing Office.

―――. 1992. *Statistical Abstract of the United States: 1992.* 112th Edition. Washington, DC: U.S. Government Printing Office.

―――. 1991. *Statistical Abstract of the United States: 1991.* 111th Edition. Washington, DC: U.S. Government Printing Office.

———. 1943. *Statistical Abstract of the United States: 1942.* Washington, DC: U.S. Government Printing Office.

———. 1960. *Historical Statistics of the United States: Colonial Times to 1957. A Statistical Abstract Supplement.* Washington, DC: U.S. Government Printing Office.

———. 1949. *Historical Statistics of the United States, 1789-1945: A Supplement to the Statistical Abstract of the United States.* Washington, DC: U.S. Government Printing Office.

———. 1943. *Statistical Abstract of the United States: 1942.* Washington, DC: U.S. Government Printing Office.

U.S. Bureau of Foreign and Domestic Commerce. 1936. *Statistical Abstract of the United States: 1936.* Washington, DC: U.S. Government Printing Office.

U. S. Bureau of Immigration. 1932. *Annual Report of the Commissioner General of Immigration to the Secretary of Labor. Fiscal Year ended June 30, 1932.* Washington, DC: U.S. Government Printing Office.

———. 1931. *Annual Report of the Commissioner General of Immigration to the Secretary of Labor. Fiscal Year ended June 30, 1931.* Washington, DC: U.S. Government Printing Office.

———. 1927. *Annual Report of the Commissioner General of Immigration to the Secretary of Labor. Fiscal Year ended June 30, 1927.* Washington, DC: U.S. Government Printing Office.

———. 1926. *Annual Report of the Commissioner General of Immigration to the Secretary of Labor. Fiscal Year ended June 30, 1926.* Washington, DC: Government Printing Office.

———. 1925. *Annual Report of the Commissioner General of Immigration to the Secretary of Labor. Fiscal Year ended June 30, 1925.* Washington, DC: U.S. Government Printing Office.

———. 1906. *Annual Report of the Commissioner General of Immirataion to the Secretary of Comerce and Labor For the Fiscal Year Ended June 30, 1906.* Document no. 68. Washington, DC: U.S. Government Printing Office.

U.S. Department of Housing and Urban Development. 2004, October 1. "Common Questions About Migrant/Farmworkers." Available at http://www.hud.gov/local/fl/ working/farmworker/commonquestions.cfm. Accessed December 30, 2004.

U.S. Immigration and Naturalization Service. 1999. *Statistical Yearbook of the Immigration and Naturalization Service, 1998.* Washington, DC: U.S. Government Printing Office.

———. 1993. *Statistical Yearbook of the Immigration and Naturalization Service, 1992.* Washington, DC: U.S. Government Printing Office.

———. 1989. *Statistical Yearbook of the Immigration and Naturalization Service, 1988.* Washington, DC: U.S. Government Printing Office.

———. 1952. *Annual Report of the Immigration and Naturalization Service. For the Fiscal Year ending June 30, 1952.* Philadelphia: U.S. Department of Justice.

———. 1950. *Annual Report of the Immigration and Naturalization Service. For the Fiscal Year ending June 30, 1950.* Philadelphia: U.S. Department of Justice.

———. 1945. *Annual Report of the Immigration and Naturalization Service. For the Fiscal Year ending June 30, 1945.* Philadelphia: U.S. Department of Justice.

van Sertima, Ivan. 1976. *They Came Before Columbus: The African Presence in Early America.* New York: Random House.

Vickerman, Milton. 1999. *Crosscurrents: West Indian Immigrants and Race.* New York: Oxford University Press.

Vogler, Michael, and Ralph Rotte. 2000. "The Effects of Development on Migration: Theoretical Issues and New Empirical Evidence." *Journal of Population Economics.* 13:485–508.

Waldinger, Roger. 1996. *Still the Promised City? African Americans and New Immigrants in Postindustrial New York.* Cambridge, MA, and London: Harvard University Press.

———. 1995. "The 'Other Side' of Embeddedness: A Case-Study of the Interplay of Economy and Ethnicity." *Ethnic and Racial Studies.* 18(3):555–80.

———. 1994. "The Making of an Immigrant Niche." *International Migration Review.* 28(1, Spring):3–30.

———. 1987. "Changing Ladders and Musical Chairs: Ethnicity and Opportunity in Post-Industrial New York." *Politics and Society.* 15(4):369–401.

Waldinger, Roger, and Michael I. Lichter. 2003. *How the Other Half Works: Immigration and the Social Organization of Labor.* Berkeley: University of California Press.

Wallerstein, Immanuel. 1974. *The Modern World System.* New York: Academic Press.

Wang, Peter H. 1975. *Legislating Normalcy: The Immigration Act of 1924.* San Francisco: R and E Research Associates.

Warren, Robert. 1990. "Annual Estimates of Nonimmigrant Overstays in the United States: 1985 to 1988." *Undocumented Migration to the United States: IRCA and the Experience of the 1980s,* Frank D. Bean, Barry Edmonston, and Jeffrey S. Passel, editors. Pp. 77–110. Santa Monica, CA, and Washington, DC: Rand Corporation and Urban Institute.

Waters, Mary C. 1999. *Black Identities: West Indian Immigrant Dreams and American Realities.* New York: Russell Sage Foundation.

———. 1996. "Optional Ethnicites: For Whites Only?" in *Origins and Destinies: Immigration, Race, and Ethnicity in America,* Silvia Pedraza and Ruben Rumbaut, editors. Belmont, CA: Wadsworth.

———. 1990. *Ethnic Options: Choosing Identities in America.* Berkeley: University of California Press.

Weiss, Robert S. 1994. *Learning from Strangers: The Art and Method of Qualitative Interview Studies.* New York: Free Press.

Wellman, Barry. 1988. "Structural Analysis: From Method and Metaphor to Theory and Substance." *Social Structures: A Network Approach*, Barry Wellman and S. D. Berkowitz, editors. Pp. 19–61. Cambridge, UK, and New York: Cambridge University Press.

Wellman, Barry, and S. D. Berkowitz. 1988. "Introduction: Studying Social Structures." *Social Structures: A Network Approach*, Barry Wellman and S. D. Berkowitz, editors. Cambridge, UK, and New York: Cambridge University Press.

Wilkerson, Isabel. 2005a, June 12. "Angela Whitiker's Climb." *New York Times*, Section 1 (National Desk) (3), p. 1.

———. 2005b, June 12. "A Success Story That's Hard to Duplicate." *New York Times*, 1 (1), p. 24.

Wilkinson, Michael. 2000. "The Globalization of Pentecostalism: The Role of Asian Immigrant Pentecostals in Canada." *Asian Journal Of Pentecostal Studies*. 3(2): 219–226.

Williams, Eric. 1984. *From Columbus to Castro: The History of the Caribbean*. New York: Vintage Books.

Williams, Patricia J. 1997. *Seeing a Color-Blind Future: The Paradox of Race*. New York: Noonday Press.

Wilson, William J. 1987. *The Truly Disadvantaged: The Inner City, the Underclass, and Public Policy*. Chicago: University of Chicago Press.

———. 1980. *The Declining Significance of Race: Blacks and Changing American Institutions*. Chicago: University of Chicago Press.

Winant, Howard. 2002. *The World Is a Ghetto: Race and Democracy Since World War II*. New York: Basic Books.

Winks, Robin W. 1971. *The Blacks in Canada: A History*. New Haven, CT, and London: Yale University Press.

Young, Virginia H. 1993. *Becoming West Indian: Culture, Self, and Nation in St. Vincent*. Washington, DC, and London: Smithsonian Institution Press.

Zamudio, Patricia. 1999. "Huejuquillense Immigrants in Chicago: Culture, Gender, and Community in the Shaping of Consciousness." Dissertation. Northwestern University, Department of Sociology.

Zlotnik, Hania. 1999. "Trends of International Migration Since 1965: What Existing Data Reveal." *International Migration*. 37(1):21–61.

Index